A PEOPLE PASSING RUDE

A PEOPLE PASSING RUDE: BRITISH RESPONSES TO RUSSIAN CULTURE

Edited by
Anthony Cross

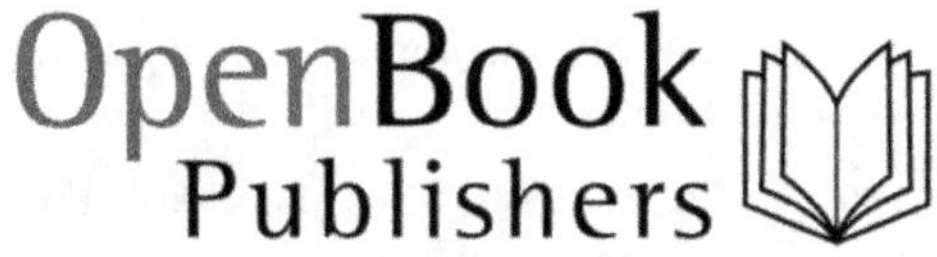

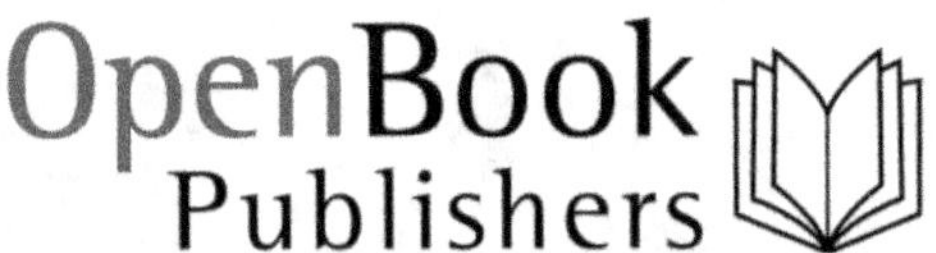

Open Book Publishers CIC Ltd.,
40 Devonshire Road, Cambridge, CB1 2BL, United Kingdom
http://www.openbookpublishers.com

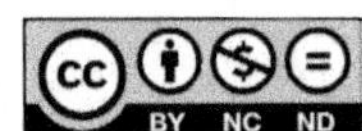

As with all Open Book Publishers titles, digital material and resources associated with this volume are available from our website at:

http://www.openbookpublishers.com/product/160

ISBN Hardback: 978-1-909254-11-4
ISBN Paperback: 978-1-909254-10-7
ISBN Digital (PDF): 978-1-909254-12-1
ISBN Digital ebook (epub version): 978-1-909254-13-8
ISBN Digital ebook (mobi version): 978-1-909254-14-5

Cover image: *Russians Teaching Boney to Dance*, a caricature by George Cruikshank published on 18 May 1813 and adapted from an original 1812 caricature by Ivan Terebenev. An early example of a British response to Russian art! By kind permission of the Anne S.K. Brown Military Collection, Brown University Library.

All paper used by Open Book Publishers is SFI (Sustainable Forestry Initiative), and PEFC (Programme for the Endorsement of Forest Certification Schemes) Certified.

Printed in the United Kingdom and United States by
Lightning Source for Open Book Publishers

Contents

Illustrations

Contributors

Tamsin Alexander holds a BMus from King's College London and MPhil from the University of Cambridge. She is currently in the second year of her PhD on an Arts and Humanities Research Council (AHRC)-funded place at Selwyn College. Her research, under the supervision of Dr Marina Frolova-Walker, is on the reception of Russian opera across Europe in the 19th century, considering contrasting reactions to the repertoire in Britain, Germany, France and the Czech lands.

Tatiana Bogrdanova is Associate Professor in the Department of Germanic Philology at the Kalmyk State University in Elista, Republic of Kalmykia. She received her PhD from the Lomonosov Moscow State University. Her main research interests are in English and Translation Studies and she has published a number of articles in Russian scholarly journals.

Philip Ross Bullock is University Lecturer in Russian at the University of Oxford, and Tutor and Fellow at Wadham College, Oxford. He is the author of *The Feminine in the Prose of Andrey Platonov* (2005), *Rosa Newmarch and Russian Music in Late Nineteenth and Early Twentieth-Century England* (2009), and *The Correspondence of Jean Sibelius and Rosa Newmarch, 1906-1939* (2011). He has a particular interest in the reception of Russian culture in Britain, and is currently co-editing *Russia in Britain: From Melodrama to Modernism* with Rebecca Beasley.

Verity Clarkson read Modern History at St Hilda's College, Oxford before completing an MA in History of Design and Decorative Arts at the University of Brighton. She recently completed a PhD thesis on 'The Organisation and Reception of Eastern Bloc Exhibitions on the British Cold War "Home Front" *c.*1956-1979', funded by an AHRC Collaborative Doctoral Award (University of Brighton and the Victoria and Albert

Museum). She currently teaches part time at Brighton and also works in collections research at the Crafts Council.

Peter Cochran did his PhD, an edition of Byron's *The Vision of Judgement*, at Glasgow, under the supervision of Drummond Bone. He is responsible for the editions of Byron's works and correspondence on the website of the International Byron Society, for the Byron entry in CBEL3, and the entries for John Cam Hobhouse and E.J. Trelawny in the NDNB. He has lectured on Byron all over the world, and written and edited several books, including *Byron and Bob, Byron and Hobby-O, Byron's Romantic Politics,* and *'Romanticism'—and Byron*, together with numerous articles on the poet.

Anthony Cross is Professor Emeritus of Slavonic Studies at the University of Cambridge and a Fellow of the British Academy. His main research interests are Anglo-Russian cultural relations and 18th century Russia. He is currently completing an annotated bibliography of English-language first-hand accounts of Russia, 1613-1917.

Julian Graffy is Professor of Russian Literature and Cinema at University College London. He is the author of *Gogol's The Overcoat* (2000), *Bed and Sofa: The Film Companion* (2001); *Chapaev: The Film Companion* (2010); and several articles about Russian literature and film. He is currently engaged in a study of the representation of the foreigner over a hundred years of Russian film.

Louise Hardiman is a doctoral student in the Department of History of Art, University of Cambridge. Her research concerns the exchange of ideas between the Russian and British 'arts and crafts' revival movements of the late 19th and early 20th centuries, and her thesis, supervised by Dr Rosalind P. Blakesley, is provisionally entitled 'Netta Peacock and British Engagement with the Russian Decorative Arts, 1890-1917'.

Michael Hughes is Professor of Russian and International History at the University of Liverpool. He has published two books on Anglo-Russian relations in the early 20th century, as well as further books on British foreign policy, and is currently completing a biography of Stephen Graham.

Svetlana Klimova is a Lecturer in Russian Stylistics at the Linguistic University of Nizhnii Novgorod (Russia). Her doctoral dissertation was devoted to Russian Byronism at the beginning of the 20th century. The results of her research are published in the book *Dva avtora, dve kul'tury, dve epokhi* (*Bairon v vospriiatii Bunina*) (2011). She is currently working on the project 'Russia and Russians in British Culture at the Beginning of the Twentieth Century'.

Claire Knight is a PhD candidate in the Department of Slavonic Studies at the University of Cambridge, where she is completing her dissertation on postwar Stalin-era popular cinema. She is also interested in British media perceptions of the Soviet Union during the wartime Anglo-Soviet Alliance. Her chapter in this volume arises from her work as an assistant at the Churchill Archives Centre, Churchill College.

Nicola Kozicharow is a PhD candidate at the University of Cambridge supervised by Dr Rosalind P. Blakesley, and her dissertation title is 'Dmitrii Stelletskii and Filipp Maliavin in Emigration: Dreaming of Russia and Resisting Change'. Her research engages with Russian émigré artists in France between the wars. She received her MPhil in History of Art from Cambridge University (2011), M.A. in History of Art from University College London (2007), and B.A. in History of Art and Slavic Studies from Brown University (2006).

Muireann Maguire is Fellow in Russian Literature and Culture at Wadham College, Oxford. Her book *Stalin's Ghosts: Gothic Themes in Early Soviet Literature* is forthcoming. Her collection of Russian 20th century ghost stories in translation, *Red Spectres*, will be published in 2012. Her current research examines the cultural mythology of the scientist in Russia in the 19th and early 20th centuries.

Richard Marks is Honorary Professor of the History of Art at the University of Cambridge and Emeritus Professor of the History of Art at the University of York. His research interests are in devotional imagery of the 'long' middle ages in Western Europe, Byzantium and Russia, on which he has published extensively.

Emma Minns is Associate Director of Postgraduate Research Studies at the University of Reading. She has a long-standing interest in the reception of Russian arts and crafts in Great Britain at the turn of the 19th century and the visual representation of Russian writers. She has been investigating the development of pictorial statistics in Soviet Russia as part of the

AHRC-funded 'Isotype Revisited Project' (Department of Typography & Graphic Communication, University of Reading).

Rachel Polonsky is an Affiliated Lecturer in the Faculty of Modern and Mediaeval Languages at the University of Cambridge, and Fellow of Murray Edwards College. She is the author of *English Literature and the Russian Aesthetic Renaissance* (1998) and *Molotov's Magic Lantern* (2010).

Scott Ruby, who holds a PhD from the Courtauld Institute of Art, London, is Associate Curator of Russian and Eastern European Art at Hillwood Estate Museum, and Gardens in Washington, DC. Recent publications include 'The Power of Porcelain: the Gardner Order Services for the Empress of Russia' for *Ars Ceramica* (forthcoming), 'A Toast to Vodka and Russia' in *The Art of Drinking* (2007) and *Masterpieces of Early Christian Art and Icons* (2005).

Alexandra Smith is Reader in Russian Studies at the University of Edinburgh and the author of *The Song of the Mockingbird: Pushkin in the Works of Marina Tsvetaeva* (1994) and *Montaging Pushkin: Pushkin and Visions of Modernity in Russian Twentieth-Century Poetry* (2006), as well as numerous articles on Russian literature and culture. Currently she is working on several publications related to the project 'Reconfiguring the Canon of Russian Twentieth-Century Poetry, 1991-2008' funded by the AHRC.

Marilyn Schwinn Smith is a Five College Associate, affiliated with Five Colleges, Inc. in Amherst, MA. She received her PhD from the University of Massachusetts, Amherst with a thesis on Marina Tsvetaeva's Civil War *poema, Perekop*. She has published on Tsvetaeva, Virginia Woolf, Vsevolod Garshin, Jane Harrison and Aleksei Remizov. She is currently writing on John Cournos as an American writer in Europe.

Olga M. Ushakova, who received her PhD at the Lomonosov Moscow State University, is a professor in the Department for Foreign Literature at the Tiumen State University, West Siberia. She is the author of a monograph *T.S. Eliot and European Cultural Tradition* (2005) and other articles on T.S. Eliot, modernism, and Anglo-Russian literary relations. She is currently working on a study of T.S. Eliot and Russian Culture.

1. By Way of Introduction: British Perception, Reception and Recognition of Russian Culture

Anthony Cross

Over 450 years have elapsed since the English navigator Richard Chancellor arrived by chance in the White Sea and made his way to the Moscow of Ivan the Terrible. It was a 'discovery' that eventually would lead to the establishment of commercial, political and cultural relations between Great Britain and Russia that provide a fascinating history of political estrangement and reconciliation and cultural rejection and acceptance.

Much has been written both about English influences on Russian life and culture—that were much in evidence from the time of Peter the Great and were particularly apparent in the reign of Alexander I—and about the reverse process that was slower to manifest itself but gained momentum after the Crimean War, leading to the 'Russian Fever' that over the years 1890-1930 developed, peaked and ebbed away, to be replaced by the challenge of the Soviet Union. There is always much more to be researched and written.

The present collection offers a wide chronological perspective on British responses to Russian culture from the 18th century to the present day, encompassing major areas of cultural life from literature and theatre to art, music and cinema. The overall theme allowed contributors to fill lacunae in the existing literature or re-visit subjects already seemingly explored. Not unexpectedly the weight of the volume is on literary topics, but there are

The essays in this collection, now revised, expanded and annotated, were first presented as contributions to the Fifth Colloquium in Russian Studies held at Fitzwilliam College, Cambridge, 31 August-2 September 2011.

important contributions in the field of art, and not least of exhibitions that brought the work of Russian artists, collectively or individually, before the British public, and of music. While contributions to British awareness of the political and scientific culture of Russia are absent from this volume, the significance of the Russian church is testified in a study of British perceptions of icons and in the contribution devoted to 'Holy Russia', as perceived and propagandized by a leading English author of the beginning of the 20th century.

Of course Russian culture is infinitely greater than the sum of the particular parts here presented and there is no pretension to offer a comprehensive treatment of the subject. Nonetheless these contributions add significantly to the store of material on the basis of which, one hopes, one day will be written an authoritative and definitive history of British reception and perception of Russian culture.

The contributions to his volume are presented in roughly chronological order to afford the reader some awareness of growing British exposure to various aspects of Russian culture, although some essays concentrate on a single episode or event strictly located in time, while the time span of others is over decades or even centuries. In this introduction I have attempted to provide in some detail a survey of the 'early' period of Anglo-Russian intercourse, up the end of the reign of Alexander I (1825), and then to offer a context in which to site the bulk of the studies in the collection that belong to the 19th and early 20th centuries. My emphasis is on British awareness of Russian literary, artistic and musical culture projected, however succinctly, against important historical and political events.

More than three centuries were to pass before Russian culture, broadly understood, achieved wide recognition in Britain, both for its distinctive nature and for the significant contribution and enrichment that it was seen to bring to western literary and artistic endeavours. Along the long road that led from the 16th century to the last decades of the 19th there were many individuals who in works of history and travels and in articles in journals attempted to acquaint the reading public with notable aspects of Russian culture. There were also events, mainly political and military, that focused public attention on Russia and heightened interest in its people and their customs, traditions and history. Traditional stereotypes and hardened prejudices, particularly with regard to nations, are, however, hard to eradicate and negative British perceptions of Russia were no exception.

Among the earliest and most influential Elizabethan accounts of Russia were those collected and published by Richard Hakluyt in two editions at the end of the 16th century, but two other publications, appearing before Hakluyt but then included by him in emasculated form, were influential in establishing a largely negative perception of Russia that extended way beyond intense cold and ubiquitous bears to religious obscurantism, tyrannical rule, and almost wilful ignorance. The poet George Turbervile, secretary to Sir Thomas Randolph during his embassy to Muscovy in 1568, penned poetic epistles to London friends with damning pictures of 'a people passing rude to vices vile inclin'd' that were published for the first time in 1587,[1] some four years before the appearance of the scholarly Giles Fletcher's much more widely known and influential *Of the Russe Commonwealth,* a country he had observed at close quarters as Elizabeth's ambassador in 1588-9. If he could pronounce that the Russian clergy, 'being ignorant and godless themselves, are very wary to keep the people likewise in their ignorance and blindness',[2] few would doubt the rightness of his judgment, even in a period when English society was much taken with things Muscovite, as the plays and poems of Shakespeare and his fellows eloquently illustrate.[3] The views he elaborated were embraced and emphasized in a 17th-century England that saw relations with Muscovy at a low ebb, particularly following the execution of Charles I: in 1682 John Milton in his *Brief History of Muscovia,* a compilation based on 16th-century accounts, echoed Fletcher in suggesting that the Russians 'have no learning, nor will suffer it to be among them' and Samuel Collins with the authority and expertise of several years as physician to Tsar Aleksei Mikhailovich opined that they were 'wholly devoted to their own Ignorance ' and 'looked upon Learning as a Monster, and feared it no less than a ship of Wildfire'.[4]

1 Lloyd E. Berry and Robert O. Crummey (eds.), *Rude & Barbarous Kingdom: Russia in the Accounts of Sixteenth-Century English Voyagers* (Madison, Milwaukee and London, 1968), p. 75.

2 *Ibid.*, p. 228.

3 There is an abundant literature on this fascinating period of Anglo-Russian relations. See, e.g. M.P. Alekseev, 'Shekspir i russkoe gosudarstvo XVI-XVII vv.', in M.P. Alekseev (ed.), *Shekspir i russkaia kul'tura* (Moscow-Leningrad, 1965), pp. 784-805. A recent addition is Daryl W. Palmer, *Writing Russia in the Age of Shakespeare* (Aldershot, 2004).

4 John Milton, *A Brief History of Muscovia: and of other less-known Countries lying eastward of Russia as far as Cathay* (London, 1682), p. 21; [Samuel Collins], *The Present State of Russia in a Letter to a Friend at London* (London, 1671), p. 2.

At the end of the century, as England anticipated with excitement the visit of Petr Mikhailov, aka Peter the Great (however camouflaged and officially underplayed), Jodocus Crull, author of *The Antient and Present State of Muscovy*, contrasted the prevailing view of a country, where 'the Discouragement of Learning and Sciences, their Knowledge, even of the Priests themselves, not reaching beyond Reading and Writing their own Language', with his as yet unsubstantiated hopes in 'a most Genuine and Active Prince', who would learn from his travels and bring to his people the fruits of wise laws and just rule.[5] Peter, the bringer of enlightenment to his 'frozen' country, the earnest disciple of all that was best in Europe, mostly to be found, of course, in England, was to be the dominant image down the 18th century, summed up succinctly, if far from uniquely, in the lines that James Thomson added to his 1744 revised edition of 'Winter' from *The Seasons*:

Immortal Peter! First of Monarchs! He
His stubborn Country tam'd, her Rocks, her Fens,
Her Floods, her Seas, her ill-submitting Sons;
And while the fierce *Barbarian* he subdu'd,
To more exalted soul he rais'd the *Man*.

Indeed, Thomson suggests, the Russia as perceived by Turbervile, Fletcher, Milton, Collins and Crull was a thing of the past:

Sloth flies the Land, and *Ignorance*, and *Vice*,
Of old Dishonour proud: it glows around,
Taught by the Royal Hand that rous'd the whole.
One scene of Arts, of Arms, of rising Trade:
For what his Wisdom plann'd, and Power enforc'd,
More potent still, his great *Example* shew'd.[6]

Others, both during Peter's lifetime and during succeeding reigns, were not so sure, although the tide of opinion down the century, bolstered by panegyrical poems, plays, biographies and histories, flowed decidedly towards Petrolatry.[7] The people as opposed to the potentate were the problem, although increasingly, and particularly during the reign of Catherine the

---

5 J[odocus] C[rull], *The Antient and Present State of Muscovy, containing a Geographical, Historical and Political Account of all those Nations and Territories under the Jurisdiction of the Present Czar*, I (London, 1698), p. 171; II, p. iv.

6 James Thomson, *The Seasons and the Castle of Indolence* (London, 1849), p. 196.

7 For the fortunes of Peter in Britain during the 18th century, see my *Peter the Great through British Eyes: Perceptions and Representations of the Tsar since 1698* (Cambridge, 2000), pp. 40-102.

Great, British diplomats, residents and travellers made valiant attempts to detect the spread of enlightenment and the achievements of native talent in literature and the arts.[8]

Under Catherine there was a veritable cultural explosion and something of its import was conveyed to the British public by a trio of authors, resident in or visiting Russia during the last decades of the century.

The first into print was the Rev. William Coxe, a Cambridge don, who visited Russia in 1778 as the travelling tutor of a young English milord on the northern version of the Grand Tour in 1778. The two weighty tomes of his *Travels in Poland, Russia, Sweden, and Denmark* appeared in 1784, when he again visited Russia in the same capacity and gathered material which he incorporated in subsequent editions. In all, six editions, endlessly augmented and revised, appeared by 1803. Coxe devoted the whole of chapter eight of volume II (some thirty-seven pages) to 'a review of the lives and works of a few of the most eminent writers, who have contributed to polish and refine the language, and to diffuse a taste for science among their countrymen'.[9] He takes issue with the followers of Montesquieu who attributed the slowness of Russian cultural development to 'the effects of climate, or to an innate want of genius' and looks for the true cause in 'the government, religion, and particularly [...] the vassalage of the peasants, which tend to check the diffusion of the arts and sciences'.[10] He concentrates attention on the achievements of Lomonosov and Sumarokov and out of 'the numerous band of poets' which followed them mentions only Kheraskov as the author of 'the first epic poem in the Russian tongue'.[11] Testimony to the fact that what Coxe wrote about Russian literature was destined to have wider dissemination was the insertion in the second edition of the *New and General Biographical Dictionary* (1784) of nine entries on Russian writers, all based on his work.

Coxe knew no Russian but was acquainted with many German scholars in Russian service and their work, which he used with acknowledgement. Russian was certainly one of the languages of Matthew Guthrie, one of a plethora of Scottish doctors practicing at or near the Russian court, who arrived in St Petersburg in 1769 and from 1778 occupied the post of chief

8 See my 'British Awareness of Russian Culture (1698-1801)', *Canadian Slavic Studies*, XIII (1979), pp. 212-35.

9 *Travels in Poland, Russia, Sweden, and Denmark*, II (London, 1784), p. 184.

10 *Ibid.*, p. 181.

11 *Ibid.*, p. 209.

physician to the Noble Land Cadet Corps until his death in 1807. He was an indefatigable 'communicator' to British societies and British journals on all manner of subjects from gemmology and botany to literature and folk culture. Under the pseudonym of 'Arcticus' he contributed numerous articles to the Edinburgh journal *The Bee* in the early 1790s, including much on Russian folklore. Sadly, his English-language *magnum opus,* 'Noctes Rossicae, or Russian Evening Recreations', divided into ten 'dissertations' covering dance, song, musical instruments, games, rites, and early Russian history, remained in manuscript: only a preliminary French version appeared in St Petersburg in 1795 and was better known to a Russian public than to British readers.[12]

A greater impact was made by the series of works on Russian history published after his return to England by the Rev. William Tooke, the long-serving chaplain to the British community firstly in Cronstadt and then in St Petersburg between 1771 and 1792. Tooke saw himself as a 'compiler' and translator rather than as an original author, using the best authorities, Russian and German, to acquaint his fellow countrymen with Russia's past and present history.[13] Of particular interest in the present context is his translation of Heinrich Storch's *Picture of Petersburg* (1801), which included a long chapter on Russian literature, which Tooke had earlier included without acknowledgement in the third edition of his popular *Life of Catharine II* (1798).[14] Storch/Tooke provided British readers with the most extensive survey of the arts and sciences during Catherine's reign, naming almost everyone of importance in Russian literature since the death of Lomonosov. Tooke also took the opportunity of publishing the first English verse translations of Russian poems, in this case, by Sumarokov and Derzhavin.

It was thus during the dark years of Paul's reign (1796-1801) that the literary and artistic attainments of Catherine's reign received their widest acknowledgement in Britain. The literary efforts of the empress herself, particularly for the theatre, also received notice, at times ironic, at times fawning, although Guthrie, who had published both in *The Bee* and as a separate booklet *Ivan Czarowitz, or the Rose without Prickles that Stings not,* his version of Catherine's tale *Skazka o tsareviche Ivane,* failed to find

12 See my 'Arcticus and *The Bee* (1790-4): An Episode in Anglo-Russian Cultural Relations', *Oxford Slavonic Studies,* NS II (1969), pp. 62-76; K.A. Papmehl, 'Matthew Guthrie: The Forgotten Student of 18th Century Russia', *Canadian Slavonic Papers,* XI (1969), pp. 172-81.

13 See my 'The Reverend William Tooke's Contribution to English Knowledge of Russia at the End of the Eighteenth Century', *Canadian Slavic Studies,* III (1969), pp. 106-15.

14 *Life of Catharine II, Empress of Russia,* III (3rd edn, London, 1799), pp. 394-439.

a publisher for his translation of her 'Shakespearean' opera *Nachal'noe upravlenie Olega (The Beginning of Oleg's Rule)*.[15] It was, however, the foremost prose writer of the day, Nikolai Karamzin, who was the first to receive the accolade in Britain of translated volumes (1803) of his tales and travels, albeit via German and in hardly flattering versions, that were not always welcomingly reviewed.[16]

Karamzin brought, as it were, Russian literature into the 19th century, although his considerable achievements in Alexander's reign, first as the editor of *The Messenger of Europe* (*Vestnik Evropy)* and then as the great historian of pre-Petrine Russia, were never truly appreciated in Britain. His history was never translated into English (as it had been into French and German), although it was to be endlessly used by British writers attempting their own accounts of early Russian history. There was, however, a translation of his influential essay from *The Messenger of Europe,* 'O knizhnoi torgovle i liubvi ko chteniiu v Rossii' ('On the Book Trade and the Love of Reading in Russia', 1802), that appeared in the first volume of a new journal entitled *The Literary Panorama* in 1807. The translator was a member of the Russian embassy in London, A.G. Evstav'ev, who not only made many contributions to the journal but also had published in London in 1806 his version of Sumarokov's tragedy *Dmitrii Samozvanets,* the first play by a Russian author to appear in English.[17]

The early flurry of translations and articles in the first years of the century was not sustained. It is a sad fact that the rising Russophilia in England—that weathered the temporary setback of Alexander I's rapprochement with Napoleon at Tilsit and, following Napoleon's defeat and the occupation of Paris, reached fever pitch with the arrival of the tsar and his entourage in London in 1814—did not extend to an interest in Russian culture, other than the fashion craze for everything Cossack. However, it might be argued that it was in the context of this pro-Russian feeling that such a positive

---

15 See my 'A Royal Blue-Stocking: Catherine the Great's Early Reputation in England as an Authoress', in R. Auty *et al.* (eds.), *Gorski Vijenats: A Garland of Essays Offered to Professor Elizabeth Mary Hill* (Cambridge, 1970), pp. 85-99.

16 See my 'Karamzin in English', *Canadian Slavic Studies,* III (1969), pp. 716-27. Translations of three of his tales, by a different hand, had already appeared in the *German Museum* in 1800-1.

17 See my 'Russkoe posol'stvo v Londone i znakomstvo anglichan s russkoi literaturoi v nachale XIX veka', in A.S. Bushmin *et al.* (eds.), *Sravnitel'noe izuchenie literatury (Sbornik statei k 80-letiiu akademika M.P. Alekseeva)* (Leningrad, 1976), pp. 99-107. On Sumarokov's fortunes in England from the middle of the 18th century, see my 'Angliiskie otzyvy ob A.P. Sumarokove', *XVIII vek,* XIX (1995), pp. 60-9.

reception was given to the publication of the first volume of John Bowring's *Rossiiskaia antologiia: Specimens of the Russian Poets* in 1821. It was warmly reviewed in at least a dozen periodicals and a decade after its appearance the *Edinburgh Review* accurately caught the reasons for its appeal:

> There had grown up, almost with the suddenness of an exhalation, a poetical literature betraying no marks of its barbaric origin; possessing, in fact, the very qualities found associated with a long-established literature [...] that but for some occasional traits of nationality which give it a certain distinctive and original character, we had great difficulty in believing that any thing so trim and so polished could have been imported from the rough shores of the Don and the Volga.[18]

The first volume was soon reprinted and a second volume appeared the following year and was also reissued; individual poems thereafter were often reproduced in almanacs and journals and one poem, his version of Derzhavin's 'Bog' ('God'), was issued in London as late as 1861 as a broadsheet. Bowring presented twenty-three poets for the first time, and in some cases the only time, in English dress. Not neglecting the older generation from Catherine's reign, such as Lomonosov, Kheraskov and Petrov (but no Sumarokov), he included poets whose work straddled the reigns such as Derzhavin, Bogdanovich, Dmitriev, and Karamzin, and younger poets associated very much with Alexander's reign, such as Batiushkov, Davydov, Viazemskii and Zhukovskii.[19] Bowring, who knew little Russian despite his assurances to the contrary, relied on prose translations supplied by a Petersburg friend, who also provided the informative notices on the poets, and turned them into poetic paraphrases which the British critics and public accepted at face value, but there is no doubting the historical importance of the anthologies on the long road to British awareness of Russian literature.

It was in the wake of the success of Bowring's work that Russian literature became an object of greater, but still modest, interest, witnessed in the title of *The Magazine of Foreign Literature; Comprehending an Analysis of Celebrated Modern Publications of France, Germany, Italy, Spain, Portugal, Russia, and America, with copious extracts, translated into English* (1823) and in its substantial, if ultimately condescending, reviews of two Russian plays, Fonvizin's *Nedorosl'* (as *The Spoiled Boy*) and Krylov's *Modnaia lavka* (as

---

18 *Edinburgh Review*, LIII (January 1831), pp. 323-4.

19 See my 'Early English Specimens of the Russian Poets', *Canadian Slavic Studies*, IX (1975), pp. 449-62.

The Milliner's Shop).[20] In the same year came the anonymously published *Letters, Literary and Political, on Poland* with direct reference to Bowring's example. Its author, Krystyn Lach Szyrma, who was visiting Scotland as travelling tutor to two Polish aristocrats, added to his letters on Polish literature a general survey of Russian literature with special reference to such as Lomonosov, Derzhavin, Karamzin and Zhukovskii.[21] Some thirty years later, as we shall see, Szyrma was to play a more notorious role in the dissemination of Russian literature in Britain.

There was understandably no mention of Pushkin in Bowring's anthology, but it was precisely in 1821 that his name appeared for the first time in the British press in connection with the publication of *Ruslan i Liudmila*.[22] It was Bowring, however, who in an article in the *Westminster Review* in 1824, adapted from a Russian original, may be said to have initiated British interest in the great Russian poet.[23] It was an interest that was infinitely deepened throughout the 1830s by a remarkable and unsung critic, William Henry Leeds, whose considerable contribution to acquainting the British public not only with the work of Pushkin but with the contemporary Russian literary—and artistic—scene is the subject of my chapter in this collection and will not be further elaborated here.

The three decades of the reign of Nicholas I, ending with the Crimean War, were dominated in terms of periodical criticism by Leeds—albeit anonymously but most tellingly in his major reviews for the *Foreign Quarterly Review* throughout the 1830s—and Thomas Budge Shaw. Shaw, unlike Leeds, knew Russia from first-hand experience as a family tutor and later adjunct professor of English literature at the Tsarskoe Selo Lyceum from 1840 until his death in 1862 and, unlike Leeds, signed both his articles and the major translations he made.[24] It was in 1843 that Shaw published his translation of Bestuzhev-Marlinskii's Caucasian tale *Ammalat Bek* in *Blackwood's Edinburgh Magazine*. Shaw wrote a long introduction to the tale, notable initially for a crushing demolition of Bowring's poetic

---

20 *Magazine of Foreign Literature* (London, 1823), pp. 267-74, 395-401. See also the informed and well-written 'Literary Intelligence' from Russia, pp. 61, 191, 320.

21 *Letters, Literary and Political, on Poland, Comprising Observations on Russia and Other Sclavonian Nations and Tribes* (Edinburgh and London, 1823), pp. 73-81.

22 *New Monthly Magazine and Literary Journal*, III (1821), p. 382.

23 *Westminster Review*, I (1824), p. 98.

24 On Shaw, see L.M. Arinshtein, 'Tomas Shou—angliiskii perevodchik Pushkina', in A.S. Bushmin *et al.* (eds.), *Sravnitel'noe izuchenie literatury* (Leningrad, 1976), pp. 117-24; Patrick Waddington, 'Shaw, Thomas Budge', *Oxford Dictionary of National Biography*, L (Oxford, 2004), pp. 127-8.

paraphrases, but offered essentially as 'a brief sketch of the history of Russian literature', or rather, of Russian prose from its origins to the contemporary work of Zagoskin, Lazhechnikov and Gogol.[25] It is evident that Shaw was, not surprisingly, unaware of Leeds's anonymous articles from this period, but it is equally clear that they were making common cause. Shaw emphasized that he translated from the original Russian and he followed Bestuzhev's tale the following year (1844) with *The Heretic*, his translation of Lazhechnikov's *Basurman*. Other important first translations of stories by Gogol and Pushkin were to be published in journals in 1847-8 and it is as a translator and biographer of Pushkin that Shaw is above all known. In 1845 *Blackwood's* published over three consecutive numbers his essentially biographical memoir of the poet, interspersed with verse translations of some twenty-three lyric poems that brought him admirers in both Russia and Britain.[26] Shaw's foray into British journals to promote Russian literature was, sadly, short-lived; after 1848 he devoted himself to writing about and teaching English literature in Russia.

The name of Pushkin in the context of frequently sweeping and frequently contradictory verdicts on the state of Russian literature began to appear in British travel accounts of Russia published during Nicholas's reign. Many were delivered with the self-confidence that only a stay in St Petersburg, a brief visit to Moscow, and a few conversations in French in society salons and homes could bring. The well-named Thomas Raikes, who was in St Petersburg in 1829-30, had no hesitation in asserting that 'to talk of Russian literature is to talk of that which does not exist and never has existed', even though he was to meet Pushkin, describe him as 'the Byron of Russia, the celebrated, at the same time, the *only* poet in this country', but then condescendingly offer his verdict that 'it will be no great injustice to suppose that his compositions may be overrated by his readers'.[27] Visiting the capital a year after Raikes but publishing his book six years earlier, the naval officer Charles Frankland also believed that 'their literature is still in the cradle', but was more attentive to Pushkin with whom he spoke on some three occasions, mainly on political and social matters.[28] The most positive reaction to Pushkin and his work, but based on conversations not

---

25 *Blackwood's Edinburgh Magazine*, LIII (March 1843), pp. 281-8.

26 *Ibid.*, LVII (1845), pp. 657-78; LVIII (1845), pp. 28-43, 140-56.

27 Thomas Raikes, *A Visit to St Petersburg, in the Winter of 1829-30* (London, 1838), pp. 192, 84-7.

28 Charles Colville Frankland, *Narrative of a visit to the courts of Russia and Sweden, in the years 1830 and 1831*, II (London, 1832), pp. 74, 227, 232, 235-46, 249-50, 269-70.

with the poet but with mutual friends, came from another naval officer, Frederick Chamier, who had been in Petersburg in 1827-8 and published anonymously his 'Anecdotes of Russia' in a London journal in 1830.[29]

When Raikes eventually published his book in 1838, he was able to record in a footnote the death of Pushkin, as did the Scottish traveler Robert Bremner, who had left St Petersburg just weeks before the fateful duel.[30] Bremner believed that despite the censorship—and if there is one red thread through all travel accounts then it is the pernicious role of the censorship on the import of foreign books and on the contents of Russian journals and books—'Russian literature is advancing with great rapidity' and he enumerated the attainments of various authors from the age of Catherine to Pushkin. His garbled notes from what would seem to have been a German source, to judge by the transliteration of names, ends with a listing of 'Shukoffskij and Batzuschkoff', 'Prince Wiasemskij and Wostokoff', 'Gribogedoff' and 'Schazykoff' that would leave the reader as befuddled as Bremner obviously was.[31] Indeed, they are reminiscent of the lines in *Don Juan,* where Byron (whose own perception of Russia is the subject of Peter Cochran's opening article in this collection) ironizes over the 'Thousands of this new and polished nation / Whose names lack nothing but pronunciation'. Similar listings and ugly transliterations were also found at this time in a totally unexpected and extensive 'Notice on the Language and Literature of Russia' that Admiral Adolphus Slade, whose Russian venture began and ended with Odessa, included as an appendix to his travel journal.[32]

Bremner and Slade had possibly used the same German source, Friedrich Otto's *Lehrbuch der russischen Literatur* (1837), which was translated into English by the Oxford don George Cox and published in 1839 as *The History of Russian Literature, with a Lexicon of Authors,* an event which promised far

29 *New Monthly Magazine,* XXIX (1830), pp. 73-81.

30 A detailed description of the duel and death of Pushkin, 'one of the greatest men that had ever adorned the literature of Russia', also appeared in the first edition of Murray's 'Russia', the indispensable travellers' vademecum. See *A Handbook for Travellers in Denmark, Norway, Sweden, and Russia, Being a Guide to the Principal Routes in those Countries, with a Minute Description of Copenhagen, Stockholm, St. Petersburg, and Moscow* (London, 1839), pp. 161-3. The overall editor for the volume was T.D. Whatley, but the 'footnote' on Russian literature was written by A.H. Layard, who had visited Russia the previous year.

31 Robert Bremner, *Excursions in the Interior of Russia; Including Sketches of the Character and Policy of the Emperor Nicholas, Scenes in St. Petersburgh, &c. &c.,* I (London, 1839), pp. 278-83.

32 Adolphus Slade, *Travels in Germany and Russia: Including a Steam Voyage by the Danube and the Euxine from Vienna to Constantinople, in 1838-39* (London, 1840), pp. 505-12.

more than it gave to English readers. In his introduction Cox stressed the need for an English audience to become acquainted with Russia's march towards civilization, but what he chose to translate hardly helped his cause.

There was also over the same period some, if limited, attention given to the state of the arts other than literature. Richard Marks in the opening pages of his chapter charts the lack of appreciation of the icon among British visitors and writers over some two centuries, but it was not merely the icon but the work of 18th- and 19th-century Russian painters, sculptors and architects that was neglected. It was inevitably the treasures of western art accumulated in the Hermitage and in other palaces that were the magnet for visitors to the Russian capital and if their attention was directed to the famous 1812 gallery it was to admire the work of the English artist, George Dawe. Similarly, the buildings they admired the most were designed by western architects, notably Quarenghi, Cameron, Rossi and Montferrand. Nevertheless, at the beginning of Nicholas's reign, British readers were presented with a virtually comprehensive account of the state of the arts in the Russian capital by Dr A.B. Granville, physician to the Vorontsov family in 1827, whose two weighty volumes went through three editions between 1828 and 1835. Granville paid much attention to the various institutions, including the Public Library, which gave rise to a long disquisition on modern Russian literature, the theatres and a naming of actors, actresses, ballet dancers, and dramatists, as well as musicians, including 'the great Russian composer' Bortnianskii, the Academy of Sciences and its great collections, the Academy of Arts, where he meets Vorob'ev, the topographical artist and lauds the talents of Orlovskii.[33]

Bremner was another to devote many pages to the state of the fine arts, opining that 'several native artists of great promise have lately appeared, and those best acquainted with the nation believe that the Russians will yet rise high as painters'.[34] Elizabeth Rigby, who was to marry a future President of the Royal Academy, Charles Eastlake, a few years after her visit to St Petersburg in 1839, believed that 'with regard to the literature of Russia, it is neither sufficient in volume nor nationality to warrant an opinion', but was more tolerant of Russian progress in music and painting.

---

33 Augustus Bozzi Granville, *St Petersburgh: a journal of travels to and from that capital; through Flanders, the Rhenish Provinces, Prussia, Russia, Poland, Silesia, Saxony, the Federated States of Germany, and France*, II (London, 1828), pp. 100-33 (Academy of Sciences); pp. 138-44 (Academy of Arts); pp. 237-50 (Public Library); pp. 376-93 (Theatres).

34 Bremner, I, p. 276.

She was present at a performance of Mikhail Glinka's *Life for the Tsar* (*Zhizn' za tsaria*) and found the music 'strikingly national, and one trio in particular appeared to combine every peculiar beauty of Russian melody and pathos, and will doubtless acquire a European celebrity'. She went to the Academy of Arts to see Karl Briullov's best-known work, 'The Last Day of Pompeii', first publicly exhibited in 1834, and produced a detailed description of the painting and appreciation of 'this first Russian painter of any eminence'; she returned later to visit the artist and the sculptor Baron Klodt in their studios.[35]

It was not, however, these scattered pages on Russian art that furthered British awareness: exhibitions on British soil were to be the key. In June 1851 Russia took part in the Great Exhibition at the Crystal Palace and its display of applied arts in particular aroused great enthusiasm and it was to the Russian exhibits that Queen Victoria first made her way on her official visit, as Scott Ruby recounts in his contribution to this collection. There were, however, no Russian paintings but a glittering display of malachite objects, vases, plates, jewellery and silver.

The outbreak of the Crimean War in 1854 stimulated a steep rise in interest in Russia that fortunately went beyond jingoistic poetry and declamatory rhetoric and saw the publication not only of a number of historical and geographical accounts, with particular and expected emphasis on the generally unknown region of the Crimea and southern Russia, but also of works that portrayed with some understanding the life 'in the interior' of the country. Anonymous 'ladies', after the fashion of the time, but in fact English governesses formerly in the employ of Russian aristocratic and gentry families, Rebecca McCoy and Charlotte Bourne, produced particularly informative accounts of their long sojourns in Russia that proved popular with the British public. The literary interest in Miss McCoy's book is above all her detailed description of a visit to see Gogol's *Revizor* (*The Government Inspector*), a play she considers 'truly national' and 'the best I ever witnessed on the Russian stage'.[36] Miss Bourne, spending her winters in Moscow with the Dolgorukii family, actually saw Gogol, 'a very little man, with a nose that *seems to listen*', on one occasion, and elsewhere she discusses his controversial *Vybrannye mesta iz perepiski s*

35 [Elizabeth Rigby], *Letters from the shores of the Baltic* (2nd edn, London, 1842), I, pp. 54-60; II, pp. 270-4.

36 [Rebecca McCoy], *The Englishwoman in Russia: Impressions of the Society and Manners of the Russians at Home* (London, 1855), pp. 89-95.

druz'iami (*Selected Passages from a Correspondence with Friends*, 1847), but her account is full of literary references as well as containing her metric translations of three stanzas from Pushkin's *Evgenii Onegin*—the first to appear in English.[37]

Gogol was at least named in these accounts but that was not the case with a version of his great novel *Mertvye dushi* (*Dead Souls*) that was published in England precisely at this period and formed with 'translations' of two other masterpieces of Russian literature a trio of travesties and hoaxes. Hiding under the umbrella of interest in life in Russia there appeared in quick succession: *Sketches of life in the Caucasus, by a Russe, Many Years Resident amongst the Various Mountain Tribes* (London, 1853); *Home Life in Russia, by a Russian Noble; Revised by the Author of 'Revelations of Siberia'* (London, 1854); *Russian Life in the Interior, or, The Experiences of a Sportsman. Edited by James D. Meiklejohn* (Edinburgh, 1855). Only in the last case was the original author acknowledged, 'Ivan Tourghenieff of Moscow', although its editor, a young Edinburgh University graduate, had further embroidered on the already distorting French version by Ernest Charrière, *Mémoires d'un seigneur russe* (1854). It is interesting that it was precisely this version which introduced Turgenev to the British public and 'inspired' other earlier and later English translations in the periodical press (including Dickens's *Household Words*) rather than the subsequent French version (1858) by Hipploythe Delaveau, authorized by the Russian author but not prompting a further English variant. This was not the case with *Sketches of Life in the Caucasus*, for within a year the 'Russe, Many Years Resident amongst the Various Mountain Tribes' was revealed to be Mikhail Lermontov, author of *A Hero of Our Own Times: from the Russian; now first translated into English* (London, 1854), and followed in the same year by an incomplete *A Hero of Our Days*. The interest of the first version, however, lies in the still unestablished identity of the 'Russe' (or Englishman, masquerading as such) who appropriated Lermontov's novel as his own true story and prefaced it with an essay on Russian literature that was as informed and detailed as any of similar surveys appearing in England in the preceding decades and included laudatory pages on the work of such as Pushkin and Gogol and in a nice touch praised 'the

37 [Charlotte Bourne], *Russian Chit Chat; Or, Sketches of a Residence in Russia* (London and Coventry, 1856), pp. 95-6, 105, 107, 239. (On Bourne, see my 'Early Miss Emmies: British Nannies, Governesses and Companions in Pre-Emancipation Russia', *New Zealand Slavonic Journal*, 1 (1981), pp. 1-20).

fiery genius of Lermontoff'.[38] The lines on Gogol, praised for his 'faculty of analysis and a creative power, rarely found united in the same individual', were unprecedented in English criticism, but he was never to find real favour with English readers and was within months the victim of an outrageous act of plagiarism. *Home Life in Russia* like *Sketches of Life in the Caucasus* was presented as the work of a Russian but revised by the author of 'Revelations of Siberia'. Carl Lefevre, writing specifically about the reception of Gogol at this period, called it with mounting fury 'a malicious forgery', 'a forgery and purposeful distortion' and 'an arrogant and vicious forgery'.[39] Its 'editor' was none other than Krystyn Lach Szyrma, who thirty years earlier had published the anonymous *Letters, Literary and Political, on Poland* with its informative essay on Russian literature but who had just cause for his present hostility to Russia. He deliberately (ab)used and plagiarized *Dead Souls* to create a book that purported to 'throw light upon the domestic life of our 'ancient allies' and present foes', suggesting that its 'Russian nobleman' author 'must not be regarded as an enemy to his Fatherland: he acts under a salutary impression that the *exposé* can do no harm, and may possibly effect some good'.[40] Lach Szyrma's piracy was soon pointed out in a review in the *Athenaeum*,[41] but Gogol's cause did not prosper. Other authors were to prove more accessible to the British public.

It was a representative of the older generation, the fabulist Ivan Krylov, who was to become the first widely known Russian author in the final decades of the 19th century.[42] Versions of Krylov's engaging fables with their blend of humour and sound common sense had appeared in

38 *Sketches of Life in the Caucasus, by a Russe, Many Years Resident amongst the Various Mountain Tribes* (London, 1854), pp. 1-34. For a discussion of this work and other early English versions of Lermontov, see Chin Wen, 'From Glaring Cheat to Daring Feat: Two Episodes in the Reception of M.Yu. Lermontov in Victorian England', *New Zealand Slavonic Journal*, 2 (1980), pp. 1-16. Wen is over censorious in her discussion of the essay, pp. 3-5.

39 Carl Lefevre, 'Gogol and Anglo-Russian Literary Relations during the Crimean War', *American Slavic and East European Review*, VIII (1949), pp. 106, 110, 112.

40 *Home Life in Russia*, by a Russian Noble; Revised by the Author of 'Revelations of Siberia', I (London, 1854), pp. i-iv. Lach Szyrma (1790-1866) after his time in Edinburgh returned to Poland to become professor of moral philosophy at Warsaw University from 1824 to 1831. In 1831 he became a colonel during the Polish revolution of 1831 and was minister of home affairs in the revolutionary government in 1832 before seeking refuge in England, where he became a naturalized citizen in 1846.

41 *Athenaeum* (2 December 1854), pp. 1154-5.

42 See my 'The English and Krylov', *Oxford Slavonic Papers*, NS XVI (1983), pp. 91-140. A recent Russian study which relies heavily on my work is N.V. Kritskaia, *Angliiskii vertel dlia russkikh gusei: basni I.A. Krylova v kontekste angliiskoi kul'tury XIX-XX vv.* (Tomsk, 2009).

Bowring's anthology and in two long articles by W.H. Leeds, but it was only in the 1860s that Krylov achieved wide popularity through the efforts of H. Sutherland Edwards, devoting a long chapter to 'Kriloff and the Russian Fabulists' in his book entitled *The Russians at Home* in 1861,[43] and of W.R.S. Ralston in particular. In early 1869 Ralston (1828-89) published his *Krilov and His Fables* that enjoyed a remarkable success, going into four editions by 1883. Ralston's versions were, however, in prose and thus encouraged an Englishman teaching English in St Petersburg, John Henry Harrison, to offer *Kriloff's Original Fables* in verse in 1883.

Ralston was a major figure in encouraging the surge in British interest in all aspects of Russian culture, but particularly literature, during the reigns of Alexander II and Alexander III.[44] A librarian at the British Museum and a serious self-taught Russian scholar, Ralston's interests in Russian folklore led to the publication of *The Songs of the Russian People* (1872) and *Russian Folk-Tales* (1873) and this aspect of his output is examined by Tatiana Bogrdanova in her contribution to this collection. Over some twenty-five years until his death in 1889, he worked tirelessly as a propagandist of Russian culture,[45] but it was as the translator and champion of Ivan Turgenev that he is probably best remembered. His translation of Turgenev's *Dvorianskoe gnezdo* as *Liza* (1869), which the Russian greatly admired and which was frequently re-issued into the mid-20th century, was a landmark in Britain's virtual love-affair with the novelist that dominated the late 19th century.

Two years after Ralston's *Liza* there appeared *On the Eve,* a translation of Turgenev's *Nakanune* by Charles Turner (1832-1903), who taught English at the University of St Petersburg and in whom Ralston saw a rival, if a very inferior one. Ralston was to write to a Russian friend in 1882 that 'his [Turner's] translations used to be abominable, his *Nakanune* version was simply infamous. But he has recently married in St Petersburg, and I suspect that his wife does his translations for him'.[46] Ralston was responding to

---

43 H. Sutherland Edwards, *The Russians at Home: Unpolitical Sketches* (London, 1861), pp. 245-79. The work re-appeared as *The Russians at Home and Abroad: Sketches, Unpolitical and Political, of Russian Life under Alexander II,* I (London, 1879), pp. 115-62.

44 See M.P. Alekseev and Iu.D. Levin, *Vil'iam Rol'ston—propagandist russkoi literatury i fol'klora* (St Petersburg, 1994).

45 See Patrick Waddington, 'A Bibliography of the Writings of W.R.S. Ralston (1828-89)', *New Zealand Slavonic Journal,* I (1980), pp. 1-15.

46 Letter from Ralston to Aleksandr Onegin-Otto, 26 December 1882, Alekseev and Levin, *Vil'iam Rol'ston,* p. 261. Ralston's crushing anonymous review of *On the Eve* had appeared in the *Athenaeum* (4 February 1871), pp. 135-6.

the publication of *Studies in Russian Literature* (1882), the first of several books (and numerous articles) Turner wrote over the next twenty years, interpreting for British audiences the achievements of modern Russian literature. *Count Tolstoi as Novelist and Thinker* followed in 1888 and two years later, *The Modern Novelists of Russia*. Both these books were based on lectures Turner delivered at the Royal Institution and at the Taylor Institution, Oxford, respectively. His final significant contribution came in 1899 with the publication of *Translations from Poushkin, in Memory of the Hundredth Anniversary of the Poet's Birthday*, published simultaneously in St Petersburg and London and including in addition to verse translations of fifteen lyric poems, *The Gypsies* and *Poltava*, two 'Little Tragedies', *Boris Godunov* and *The Bronze Horseman*.[47]

Instrumental in Turner's invitation to lecture in his *alma mater* had been W.R. Morfill (1834-1909), who himself gave the first Ilchester Lectures in 1870 and became Reader in Russian and Slavonic from 1889 and Professor from 1900. Morfill, a man of enormous erudition and a close friend of Ralston, had a special penchant for Russian literature and indeed had published as early as 1860 his first translations from Pushkin.[48] His book-length publications included *Slavonic Literature* (1883), *A History of Russia from Peter the Great to Alexander II* (1902) and a Russian grammar (1889) but give no real hint of his influence, particularly in the 1890s, of furthering the cause of Russian literature. Like Ralston, he was a constant reviewer for the *Athenaeum* (a journal performing for foreign literature what the *Foreign Quarterly Review* had done for an earlier age), but he was also responsible for engaging two of the foremost Russian Symbolists, Konstantin Bal'mont and Valerii Briusov, to contribute annual reviews of contemporary literature, which he translated for publication in the journal in the years 1898-1906.[49]

Ralston, Turner and Morfill were far from alone in furthering the cause of Russian literature by article, review, book or translation in the post-Crimean War period. In 1865 F.R. Grahame (the pseudonym of Catherine Laura Johnstone) followed a work on the early history of Russia (1860) with *The*

---

47 Turner had included excerpts from most of these translations in his *Studies in Russian Literature* and in a long article devoted to Pushkin in *Fraser's Magazine*, XVI (1877), pp. 592-601, 772-82.

48 *Several Poems Translated from Pushkin by W.R. Morfill* (London: Constitutional Press, 1860). See also 'On the Calumniators of Russia: translated by W.R. Morfill', *Literary Gazette*, V (1860), p. 63.

49 See my 'Konstantin Bal'mont in Oxford in 1897', *Oxford Slavonic Papers*, NS XII (1979), pp. 104-16; S. Il'ev, 'Valerii Briusov i Uil'iam Morfill', in V.S. Dronov *et al.* (eds.), *V. Briusov i literature kontsa XIX-XX veka* (Stavropol', 1979), pp. 90-107.

Progress of Science, Art, and Literature in Russia. It was in truth a summation, but a substantial one, of what the British knew of Russian literature up to the Crimean War rather than a survey of contemporary developments. Miss Johnstone relied significantly on the articles in the *Foreign Quarterly Review* in the 1830s (in ignorance of Leeds's authorship) and copiously reproduced existing English translations by Bowring, Leeds, Shaw and others of poems by Russian poets from Derzhavin to Pushkin. Chapters were devoted to both secular and ecclesiastical writers from the earliest times, but it was essentially literature under Alexander I and authors of the stature of Karamzin and Pushkin that were the centre of detailed attention. There was very little on the novel, apart from Bulgarin and Lazhechnikov, and no mention of such as Gogol and Turgenev. Miss Johnstone, however, made many references to 'a most interesting little book', none other than Sutherland Edwards's *The Russians at Home*, published four years earlier and already noted for its chapter on Krylov. Edwards was among the most informed of British commentators on the Russian literary scene and his 'unpolitical sketches' included a series of chapters under such titles as 'Journalism' with its useful review of contemporary periodicals, 'The Censorship', 'Secret Literature' with much on Ryleev's poem *Voinarovksii* and on Herzen, and, 'Political Comedies' with its detailed résumés of the plots of Gogol's *Revizor* and Griboedov's *Gore ot uma (Woe from Wit)*, and 'The Russian Gypsies' with Edwards's extensive re-telling of, and long translated excerpts from, Pushkin's *The Gypsies*.[50]

In his discussion of Griboedov's play Edwards had referred, with little enthusiasm, to its recent appearance in English (1857), suggesting that 'it certainly conveys an idea of the substance of the original, though the style all but perishes in the double translation from Russian into English, and from verse into prose'.[51] The period up to the accession of Nicholas II in 1894 saw in fact the first appearance of translations from a number of prominent Russian writers of prose and verse. What follows is simply the enumeration of some of the more interesting or curious publications

50 Edwards and his wife Margaret (née Watson) were active as translators: he was among the earliest of British translators of Dostoevskii, translating from the French *Zapiski iz mertvogo doma* as *Prison Life in Siberia* (1887) and she translated Pushkin's prose (1892), including a first translation of *Istoriia sela Gorokhina.*

51 Edwards, *The Russians at Home*, p. 152. Titled *Gore ot Ouma: a Comedy*, trans. from the Russian by Nicholas Benardaky (London and Edinburgh, 1857), it was generally well reviewed (*Macphail's Edinburgh Ecclesiastical Journal and Literary Review* (September 1857), pp. 88-100; *The Literary Gazette and Journal of Archaeology, Science, and Art* (17 October 1857), pp. 992-4.

(published in Britain and not in America or, indeed, in Calcutta) from a fuller list that would include the dramatist and novelist Count Aleksei Tolstoi, Ivan Goncharov, Vladimir Korolenko and Vsevolod Garshin.

In 1861 there appeared *Tchinovniki: Sketches of Provincial Life*, offered as 'from the memoirs of the retired Conseiller de Cour Stchedrin (Saltikow)', a selection from M.E. Saltykov-Shchedrin's *Gubernskie ocherki* (1857) rendered directly from the Russian by 'Frederic Aston', the pseudonym of Francis Adams, a member of the British Embassy in St Petersburg, with the clear intention of revealing a corrupt and inefficient bureaucracy.[52] With the exception of a generally unremarked version of *Taras Bul'ba* and *Noch' pered Rozhdestvom* (*The Night before Christmas*) appearing in 1860 under the title *Cossack Tales*, translated from the Russian by George Tolstoy, Gogol was neglected, although Pushkin (and to a lesser extent Lermontov) received increasing attention. Pushkin's *Kapitanskaia dochka (The Captain's Daughter)*, *Pikovaia dama* (*The Queen of Spades*) and his *Povesti Belkina* (*Tales of Belkin*) were rendered on several occasions from 1858 (when they appeared in Blackwood's London Library and thereafter republished) to 1894 (the version by T. Keane that proved popular well into the 20th century). It was these tales, together with *The Moor of Peter the Great* (*Arap Petra Velikogo*), that were published in 1875 to considerable critical acclaim under the title *Russian Romance by Alexander Serguevitch Poushkin* in the translation of Ekaterina Murav'eva, who was undoubtedly aided by her husband, Commander John Buchan Telfer (1831?-1907), R.N., F.R.G.S., who the following year himself produced a book of travels through southern Russia with interesting references to both Pushkin and Griboedov.[53] It was another military man, Lt-Colonel Henry Spalding (1840-1907), learning his Russian during a spell at the British Embassy in the Russian capital, who made an unexpected appearance in 1881 as the first British translator of *Evgenii Onegin: Eugene Onéguine: A Romance of Russian Life in Verse* and indeed rendered into English verse but of a quality that elicited from Turgenev in conversation with Ralston the verdict that it was 'astonishingly faithful

52 See I.P. Foote, 'Frederic Aston's *Tchinovnicks* and Mr Adams', *Oxford Slavonic Papers*, NS XIV (1981), pp. 93-106.

53 John Buchan Telfer, *The Crimea and Transcaucasia, Being the Narrative of a Journey in the Kouban, in Gouria, Georgia, Armenia, Ossety, Imeritia, Swannety, and Mingrelia, and in the Tauric Range*, I (London, 1876), pp. 148-9, 189. The Telfers spent three years (1873-6) travelling around southern Russia and visited places connected with both writers. At the end of the book is a full-page advert for his wife's Pushkin translations with laudatory quotations from many reviews.

and astonishingly fat-headed'.[54] Lermontov fared somewhat better. His *Demon* had appeared in 1875 in a verse translation by a young Englishman, Alexander Condie Stephens, that also involved Turgenev, to whom the translation was dedicated, and Ralston, who was as ever critical in his review in the *Athenaeum*.[55] Stephens's version with its informative preface went through two more editions in 1881 and 1886, and in 1894 it was considered there was a market for another verse translation by Francis Storr. Finally, mention might be made of yet another verse translation which became available to a British public in 1886 after its initial publication in Calcutta: Thomas Hart Davies's *The Poems of K.F. Relaieff* included as its major piece Kondratii Ryleev's *Voinarovskii*, an epic explicated in 1832 by Leeds and in 1861 by Sutherland Edwards.

However, these were truly the Turgenev decades when his name, in whatever transliteration, 'was on the lips of every self-respecting reviewer'.[56] Visiting England on many occasions between July 1847 and October 1881, Turgenev became a familiar figure in English literary and social circles and was hailed as 'not only the greatest writer of fiction ever produced by Russia, but also one of the greatest of living European novelists' in an anonymous panegyric in the *Saturday Review*, penned in fact by his indefatigable promoter Ralston.[57] By the end of the century some fifty translations had appeared in England in journals and book form, culminating in the first fifteen volumes of Constance Garnett's *The Novels of Ivan Turgenev* (London: Heinemann, 1894-9).[58]

By the time of their appearance Turgenev had rivals for the attention of British critics and readers in Tolstoi and Dostoevskii.[59] The publisher Vizetelly commissioned translations, appearing in 1886-8, of *Crime and Punishment*, *The Idiot*, and other novels, all translated from French and mainly the work of Frederick Whishaw, who, incidentally, probably knew

---

54 Quoted in Patrick Waddington, *Turgenev and England* (London and Basingstoke, 1980), p. 280. See also Morfill's review, 'Alexander Poushkin', *Westminster Review*, CXIX (1883), pp. 420-51.

55 See Chin When, pp. 11-16.

56 Waddington, *Turgenev and England*, p. 12.

57 *Saturday Review* (22 October 1881), pp. 509-10.

58 Major surveys of Turgenev and the English-speaking world include: Royal A. Gettman, *Turgenev in England and America* (Urbana, 1941); Patrick Waddington, *Turgenev and England* (London and Basingstoke, 1980); Glyn Turton, *Turgenev and the Context of English Literature 1850-1900* (London, 1992); Patrick Waddington (ed.), *Ivan Turgenev and Britain* (Oxford, 1995).

59 See Clarence Decker, 'Victorian Comment on Russian Realism', *PMLA*, LII (1937), pp. 542-9.

Russian better than French. The first translation in book form and from the Russian original was, however, *Buried Alive, Or, Ten Years of Penal Servitude in Siberia* (*Zapiski iz mertvogo doma*), that appeared in 1881 and was reprinted three times in the same year: the English title that seeks to emphasize the 'reality' of events is reminiscent of the notorious 'translations' during the Crimean War. Critical comment appearing over little more than a decade virtually ceased, as did new translations, in the 1890s and Dostoevskii awaited Garnett's translations in 1912 to re-awaken an interest that soon became a cult.[60]

Tolstoi, whose *Childhood and Youth*, translated from the Russian, had appeared in England as early as 1862, was infinitely more prominent, for reasons often far from literary.[61] Gareth Jones rightly emphasizes that the Tolstoi first encountered by British critics in the 1880s was the Tolstoi who 'had already abandoned *belles letters* in favour of his newly assumed role as a social, political and religious teacher [...] and reached England all of a piece, novelist, thinker and social commentator combined'.[62] This was certainly the Tolstoi of Matthew Arnold in his seminal essay of 1887, stressing that 'we are not to take *Anna Karénine* as a work of art; we are to take it as a piece of life', but regretting that Tolstoi had 'perhaps not done well in abandoning the work of the poet and artist'.[63] It is significant that Arnold read, and preferred to read, Tolstoi in French and, indeed, Ralston had opined that *Anna Karenina* and *War and Peace* could not be translated into English,[64] but translated they were, as well as a remarkable number of other works. The list of English translations from Tolstoi's *opus* from the late 1880s to early in the following century shows clearly not only how many they were and the numerous translators involved, but their proliferation, particularly the non-fiction, in varied formats, and they were bolstered, as it were, with books on Tolstoi's 'teaching' and descriptions of pilgrimages to see him in Moscow and Iasnaia Poliana, as well as the evidence of Tolstoian colonies in England.

---

60 See Helen Muchnic, *Dostoevsky's English Reputation 1881-1936* (Northampton, 1939); W.J. Leatherbarrow (ed.), *Dostoevskii and Britain* (Oxford, 1995), with an excellent bibliography of 'bibliographies' and of relevant reviews, studies and books, pp. 293-310.

61 See W. Gareth Jones (ed.), *Tolstoi and Britain* (Oxford, 1995), with its bibliography focusing on the theme of Tolstoi's very varied relations with Britain, pp. 279-89.

62 Jones, *Tolstoi and Britain*, p. 10.

63 *Ibid.*, pp. 108, 124.

64 W.R.S. Ralston 'Count Leo Tolstoy's Novels', *The Nineteenth Century*, V (April 1879), p. 651.

Up to this point the emphasis has been intentionally on the reception of Russian literature, with an excursus into early awareness of Russian painting. Before addressing the generally limited impact that Russian music and art had in Britain during the later decades of the 19th century, it is important to examine, however briefly, other factors that coloured British perceptions of Russia during the same period.

The Russophilia that was evident in Britain at the time of Napoleon's defeat was unprecedented, although throughout the 18th century—particularly during the reigns of Peter I, Catherine II and Paul I—there had been periods of rapprochement alternating with hostility. It was, however, to be hostility that was to prevail during the reign of Nicholas I. British reaction to such events as the suppression of the Polish revolt of 1830 was considerably more vehement than it had been to the partitions of that country during Catherine II's reign. Moreover, the crisis in the Near East in 1833 brought on an anti-Russian publicist campaign, spearheaded by David Urquhart and emphasizing Russian expansionist ambitions. Russophobia, despite a degree of political rapprochement in the 1840s, was the order of day and led, almost inevitably, to the Crimean War—a memorable way indeed to mark the tercentenary of Anglo-Russian relations.[65]

The Crimean War left a legacy of suspicion that only intensified over the following decades. Despite all the efforts of the tsar-liberator, Alexander II, internal dissatisfaction with the extent of his reforms led to the emergence of terrorist organizations and a reign that had promised much ended with the assassination of the tsar in 1881. The ensuing reign of his younger son, Alexander III, ushered in a period of unrelenting reaction and 'counter-reforms', moves against the universities and the press, laws against religious minorities, particularly the Jews. These events were reflected most graphically in English fiction to such an extent that by the turn of the century a lecturer to the Anglo-Russian Literary Society, established in 1893 to encourage understanding and sympathy towards Russia, felt obliged to declare that 'what is dark, what is sad, what is tragic in Russian life is mostly dwelt upon in English literature, whether journalistic or fiction, and therefore my efforts are directed here to show you that everybody in the country is not belonging to a secret society, or being sent off to Siberia to endure a lasting exile'.[66]

65 See John Gleason, *The Genesis of Russophobia in Great Britain* (Cambridge, Mass., 1950); Harold N. Ingle, *Nesselrode and the Russian Rapprochement with Britain, 1836-1844* (Berkeley, Los Angeles and London, 1976).

66 F. Toulmin Smith, 'That the Representation of Russian Life in English Novels is Misleading', *Proceedings of the Anglo-Russian Literary Society*, XXV (1899), pp. 88-110.

Although the further suggestion that 'five novels out of six will have a Nihilistic plot' was indeed an exaggeration, it highlighted a British obsession during these decades with the sensational aspects of revolutionary activity in Russia and the music of the very word 'Nihilist'. The word seems to have appeared in a title for the first time in a play, *Vera: or the Nihilists*, by none other than Oscar Wilde (privately published in 1880 but its planned production in 1881 postponed because of the assassination of the tsar), but was soon paraded in a string of novels, such as *A Nihilist Princess* and *Narka the Nihilist,* and including the doyen of boy's fiction, G.S. Henty's *Condemned as a Nihilist: A Story of Escape from Siberia* (1893) that combined Nihilism with the no less popular theme of Siberia.[67]

British Russophobia continued to be fed by the perceived Russian threat in the Near and Far East and Central Asia and the manoeuvrings of the 'Great Game', but it was underpinned to a previously unequalled degree by sympathy for the oppressed and for the persecuted, be they peasant, Stundist or Jew. Poets joined with novelists to condemn the excesses of autocracy. James Thomson's 'Despotism Temepered by Dynamite' (1882) was but a prelude to Algernon Swinburne's 'Russia: An Ode' (1890), in which he claimed 'Night hath none but one red star—Tyrannicide' and which was written to refute the more optimistic view of Siberia and the exile system as presented in recent travel accounts by such as the Rev. Henry Lansdell (1882) and Harry de Windt (1889).[68]

It was in such a context that Russian exiles in London played a significant role not only in propagandizing the revolutionary cause but also influencing British attitudes to Russian literature. In the 1850-60s London had been the home of Alexander Herzen, soon joined by his collaborator Nikolai Ogarev, who engaged in the production of Russian–language journals such as *Kolokol* (*The Bell*), influential in their homeland but far less so in Britain. They attracted a flow of notable travelling Russians such as Turgenev, Nekrasov and Chernyshevskii, but their English circle was very limited. This was far from the case with the next influx of political émigrés in the 1880-90s, several of whom were members of the Populist Chaikovskii circle, headed by N.V. Chaikovskii and including notably Feliks Volkhovskii, Prince Petr Kropotkin and Sergei Kravchinskii.

67 See my *The Russian Theme in English Literature from the Sixteenth Century to 1980: An Introductory Survey and a Bibliography* (Oxford, 1985).

68 See M.P. Alekseev, 'Sibirskaia ssylka i angliiskii poet', *Sibirskie ogni,* IV (1928), pp. 182-93.

Kropotkin, 'the anarchist prince', arrived in England in 1886 and produced over the next twenty years a stream of books on politics and economics and including a *Russian Literature: Ideals and Realities*, based on a 1901 series of lectures and published in 1905, that stressed the significance of the great Russian novelists, Gogol, Turgenev, Goncharov, and Tolstoi, while placing Dostoevskii far below them. It was, however, Kravchinskii, arriving in London two years before Kropotkin and known more widely under his pen name of Stepniak, who was the dominant voice, influencing public opinion by his writing and lecturing and, like Kropotkin, cultivating a circle of friends and acquaintances.

It was on the initiative of Stepniak that in 1890 there was established the Society of Friends of Russian Freedom, attracting to its membership many leading British intellectuals and politicians, including William Morris, Sidney Webb, Kier Hardie and Robert Spence Watson.[69] He then became editor of *Free Russia,* the Society's monthly organ, and was assisted by Ethel Voynich (née Boole). It was Mrs Voynich, the Russian-speaking Irish wife of a Polish émigré and the future author of *The Gadfly*, who not only helped Stepniak in his journalistic and propagandist activities but also contributed to his equally strong and in many ways complementary passion for Russian literature. Under his guidance she brought out in 1893 her versions of *Stories from Garshin* and in 1895 an anthology of translated plays and stories under the title *The Humour of Russia*, to both of which Stepniak contributed introductions. Among Stepniak's other close acquaintances were Constance Garnett and her sister-in-law Olivia Garnett, yet another author of novels about revolutionaries in Russia.

It is a curious fact that that the three greatest Russian novelists of the late 19th century, Turgenev, Tolstoi and Dostoevskii, and the greatest composer, Petr Chaikovskii (hereafter Tchaikovsky), all visited England in 1861-2, Turgenev not for the first or last time, Tolstoi and Dostoevskii for their only visit, and Tchaikovsky for the first of four visits, and all left with differing impressions but generally without regret. Unlike their contemporary Turgenev, Tolstoi and Dostoevskii, even longer, were to wait many years before the British public became truly aware of their work (although even in French translation Dostoevskii exerted influence on British practitioners of the crime genre, as Muireann Maguire suggests). The same was true with Tchaikovsky and it would seem appropriate at

69 See Barry Hollingsworth, 'The Society of Friends of Russian Freedom: English Liberals and Russian Socialists, 1890-1917, *Oxford Slavonic Papers*, NS III (1970), pp. 45-64.

this juncture to update the situation with regard to British awareness of Russian 'progress' (to use Miss Johnstone's word) in music and in art. It is in Sutherland Edwards's book that we find chapters on 'The Moscow Opera House' and 'Operatic and Other Music' in which he demonstrates his knowledge and obvious love for Russian music, particularly Glinka. *The Russians at Home* was published very early in his writing career, which was incredibly productive and led to many works on European music and opera, including a *History of the Opera* (1862) and, most importantly, to the English version (together with his wife) of Konstantin Shilovskii's libretto for Tchaikovsky's *Eugene Onegin*, which was given its first performance in England at the New Olympic Theatre on 17 October 1892.[70]

In the three decades separating that event from the publication of *The Russians at Home* British appreciation of Russian music had but slowly advanced. *The Musical Times*, the pulse of musical life since 1844, included from time to time information about Russian music and musical events, but the only Russian composer, Glinka apart, who enjoyed any reputation in Britain before Tchaikovsky was Anton Rubinstein, who first visited England as a twelve-year old prodigy in 1842 and came another seven times to increasing acclaim both for his playing and for his music, which included concertos, symphonies and operas.[71] It was Rubinstein's *Demon* that was one of three Russian operas—the others were Glinka's *A Life for the Tsar*, and Tchaikovsky's *Mazeppa*—that were performed by a Russian opera company in various British cities in July-November 1888 and whose reception, adventures, and mishaps are examined by Tamsin Alexander in her article in the collection. The three operas were sung in Russian (the first performances of *Demon* and *Life for the Tsar* in 1881 and 1887 respectively had been sung in Italian) and gave audiences the elements of 'the national' assiduously sought in literature, art and music.

In 1871 Turgenev was awarded a D.C.L. by Oxford University; twenty years later in July 1893, Cambridge awarded an honorary doctorate to Tchaikovsky.[72] It heralded a period of his great popularity with British audiences, particularly for his Fifth and Sixth Symphonies. His first

70 *Eugene Onegin a Lyrical Drama, in Three Acts, the Libretto Derived from Pushkin's Celebrated Poem* (London: Printed and Published for Signor Lago's Royal Opera by J. Miles & Co., 1892).

71 See Stiuart Kempbel, '"Sensatsiia za sensatsiei": britanskie zhurnaly o pervykh vstrechakh s russkoi muzykoi i kompozitorami', in N.V. Makarova and O.A. Morgunova (eds.), *Russkoe prisutstvie v Britanii* (Moscow, 2009), pp. 159-66.

72 See Gerald Norris, *Stanford, the Cambridge Jubilee and Tchaikovsky* (Newton Abbot, 1980).

orchestral piece to be performed had been the First Piano Concerto on 11 March 1876 at the Crystal Palace. It was followed by numerous performances of other pieces, including the Serenade for Strings with which the composer made his London debut as a conductor on 22 March 1888 at the St James's Hall, a few months before the visiting opera company gave the first British performance of his opera *Mazeppa*. In October 1892 came the premiere of *Eugene Onegin* (in the Edwardses' translation), which was not a success and in general the Russian's fortunes over the preceding years had been very mixed, eliciting more enthusiasm from audiences than from critics. A year later, the composer was dead, an event recorded and his opus assessed in numerous obituaries in the British press and was followed by a remarkable upturn in his fame in Britain, leading to the first all-Tchaikovsky concert conducted by Henry Wood at the Queen's Hall on 15 May 1897 and the performance of almost all his works over subsequent years. His success led to an interest in the work of other Russian composers, led by Rimskii-Korsakov but also including Borodin, Glazunov and a host of others, on such a scale that *The Musical Times*, always exhibiting some difficulty in digesting Russian music, wrote in February 1899 about the introduction of 'a flood of Russian music—good, bad and indifferent, without discrimination and without mercy'.[73] It was in the following year, however, that Rosa Newmarch produced her *Tchaikovsky: His Life and Works, with Extracts from His Writings, and the Diary of His Tour Abroad in 1888* (London, 1900), a landmark work that was followed by her translation of the biography written by the composer's brother, Modest, in 1906. Philip Bullock, already the author of a monograph on Newmarch and more generally on the reception of Russian music at this period,[74] explores in his contribution to this collection Newmarch's role in interpreting Tchaikovsky—the man and his music—and her subsequent championing of Rimskii-Korsakov. Rimskii-Korsakov was one of the heroes of her influential *Russian Opera*, published in 1914, that offered enthusiastic readings of the operatic works of Glinka through to the works of the 'Mighty Handful', of which Rimskii-Korsakov was a member, but less so of Tchaikovsky's, believing that his 'nature was undoubtedly too emotional and self-centred for dramatic uses'.[75]

---

73 *Ibid.*, p. 495.

74 Philip Ross Bullock, *Rosa Newmarch and Russian Music in Late Nineteenth and Early Twentieth-Century England* (Royal Musical Association Monographs, 18) (Farnham, 2009). See also Lewis Stevens, *An Unforgettable Woman: The Life and Times of Rosa Newmarch* (Leicester, 2011).

75 Rosa Newmarch, *The Russian Opera* (London, 1914), p. 361.

Russian Opera was part of an impressive trilogy of survey volumes that Mrs Newmarch produced within a decade, beginning with *Poetry and Progress in Russia* in 1907 and ending with *The Russian Arts* in 1916. The titles are to a degree reminiscent of Miss Johnstone's work of 1865 but in substance differ markedly. Miss Johnstone confined her review of 'The Fine Arts in Russia' to a mere nine pages, relying on the *Foreign Quarterly Review* and Lady Eastlake for her information and thus effectively ending in the early 1840s, and concluding that 'the names of the Russian Painters and Architects who will be remembered by posterity, until the last thirty years, may be comprised in merely a few lines'.[76] Fortunately, the British public had at last the opportunity to see examples of Russian painting from the age of Catherine the Great to the present at the London exhibition of 1862, when for the first time paintings by such as Levitskii, Borovikovskii, Venetsianov, Fedotov, Briullov, Aivazovskii and others, seventy-eight canvases in all, were on display.[77]

It was the international exhibitions in London and Paris, at which Russian art was exhibited that inspired an English art critic, Joseph Beavington Atkinson (1822-86), to undertake a visit to Russia in the summer of 1870 'for the purpose of judging of the art capabilities of Russia'.[78] He of course spent much time and pages in describing the treasures of the Hermitage—as had done so many visitors before him—but it was his pursuit of Russian art as exhibited and produced in St Petersburg, Moscow and Kiev that form the most original pages in his book, presenting to the British public for the first time detailed information about a whole range of Russian artists, including not only painters but also architects and sculptors, the majority of whom, in truth, he did not highly rate. He does, however, say much in praise of Karl Briullov, even more so of Vereshchagin and somewhat less about Aivazovskii, whom he considered too commercially minded for the good of his art.[79] On his return to London from Russia, Atkinson visited the International Exhibition of 1872 and included in his book impressions about

76 F.R. Grahame, *Progress of Science, Art and Literature in Russia* (London, 1865), p. 403.

77 See L.I. Iovleva, 'O russkom khudozhestvennom otdele na vsemirnoi vystavke 1862 goda v Londone', in *Nezabyvaemaia Rossiia: Russkie i Rossiia glazami britantsev XVII-XIX vek* (Moscow, 1997), pp. 252-6.

78 J. Beavington Atkinson, *An Art Tour to Russia* (London, 1986), p. 6. (This is a reprint of the original edition, entitled *An Art Tour to Northern Capitals of Europe* (London, 1873)).

79 *Ibid.*, pp. 143-5 (Briullov), 171-4 (Vereshchagin), 204-6 (Aivazovskii). The foremost Russian marine artist received a much more enthusiastic appraisal from the eminent naval architect Sir James Reed, who had met him in the Crimea in 1875 (*Letters from Russia in 1875* (London, 1876), pp. 58-61).

the Russian exhibits that had brought a much greater positive response from British art critics than in 1862 and been seen by a million visitors. He declared that 'for the first time, was England made acquainted with the recent movement in the direction of the literal study of nature. Landscapes, domestic scenes, and genre generally, were in the ascendant'.[80]

Atkinson's interests included all aspects of the decorative and applied arts. During his visit to the Hermitage he paid special attention to the Kerch antiquities, anticipating thereby Alfred Maskell's *Russian Art and Art Objects in Russia* (1884). Maskell (d. 1912), who had worked at the South Kensington (later Victoria and Albert) Museum since 1874, spent the year 1880-1 in Russia selecting objects for phototype reproduction, resulting in a handbook to serve a basis for research into Russian art treasures. Unlike Atkinson, Maskell's attention was steadfastly focused on early Russian art, but his opinion that 'Russian art is a subject which has so little occupied public attention, at least in England, so little is known amongst us concerning it, and so scanty is the information to be gathered from the few notices which exist in our language, that the question whether or not there is a Russian art, distinct and national, has probably entered into the minds of very few persons to consider' was more widely applicable and, unfortunately, long-lasting.[81] It was consonant with the views, thirty years later, of Mrs Newmarch, who had set out on her researches 'to trace the common link of nationality through every branch of Russian art, including music and the peasant industries'.[82] Mrs Newmarch, who makes no mention of either Atkinson or Maskell, laments the fact that the British public's acquaintance with Russian art and literature is confined to the very latest developments of the last decades of the nineteenth and first decades of the twentieth centuries; and is unmindful not only of earlier periods but of the realists and *peredvizhniki* on whose works she herself was nurtured—under Stasov's guidance—and was reluctant to discard. She does, however, end with a chapter on 'The New Art' that allows her to discuss artists such as Rerikh, Churlianis, Dobuzhinskii, Bakst, and Kustodiev.

---

80 *Ibid.*, p. 171.

81 Alfred Maskell, *Russian Art and Art Objects in Russia: A Handbook to the Reproductions of Goldsmiths' Work and Other Art Treasures from That Country in the South Kensington Museum* (London, 1884), p. 1. (Extensive reviews of both Atkinson's and Maskell's books were written by the foremost Russian art critic V.V. Stasov, who was, incidentally, the mentor of Rosa Newmarch and the dedicatee of her *Poetry and Progress in Russia* (1907): V.V. Stasov, *Sobranie sochinenii*, II (St Petersburg, 1894), cols. 335-43, 823-43).

82 Rosa Newmarch, *The Russian Arts* (London, 1916), p. v.

She mentions that some of these artists had exhibited in the Second Exhibition of Post-Impressionism at the Grafton Galleries on Bond Street in 1912-13 and 'suffered by being judged in proximity with those belonging to a movement in which, with few exceptions, the Russian artists had taken no part'.[83] Others, however, saw the Russian presence in Roger Fry's famed exhibition, following as it did on the heels of the first Ballets Russes season in London, as evidence of the impact of Russian art on British artistic modernism. Louise Hardiman persuasively argues nonetheless for the importance of the preceding exhibitions of the newly established Allied Artists' Association (A.A.A.) in 1908-11 in a chapter that is one of three devoted to 20th-century exhibitions of vastly differing scope and ambition. Nicola Kozicharow focuses on an exhibition of the work of the by-then Russian émigré Filipp Maliavin that took place in the New Burlington Galleries in 1935, a few months after the great Anglo-Russian exhibition (in which he did not participate) was held at 1 Belgrave Square.[84] This was already nearly two decades into the Soviet period and nearly three more were to elapse before the Soviet Government entered into its own cultural offensive with a series of three mega-exhibitions at Earls Court, beginning with a fanfare in 1961 and ending with a whimper in 1979, as chronicled in detail by Verity Clarkson.

The dawn of the 20th century brought new names to the Anglo-Russian scene, both of Russians, who had previously been neglected or were from an emerging new generation of writers and artists, and of British writers and critics, who increasingly responded positively to Russian culture; it also brought an increasing number of artistic 'events', notably the seasons of the Ballets Russes and exhibitions such as those already mentioned but also, for instance, the International Exhibition in Kelvingrove Park, Glasgow, with its four Russian 'mediaeval' wooden pavilions designed by Fedor Shekhtel to house the Russian exhibits.[85] And all against a background of far-reaching events in the arena of politics, diplomacy and warfare: after years of tension and confrontation that led in the early century to the Russo-Japanese War and British alliance with the Japanese and the Boer

---

83 *Ibid.*, p. 267.

84 See my 'Exhibiting Russia: The Two London Russian Exhibitions of 1917 and 1935', *Slavonica*, XXI (2010), pp. 29-39.

85 See Catherine Cooke, 'Fyodor Shekhtel as a Creator of the Russian "Brand": "The Russian Village" at the International Exhibition of 1901', *Pinakotheke*, 18-19 (2004), pp. 44-51. There was, incidentally, also a mock-up of a Russian village at the 1913 London Ideal Home Exhibition.

War with Russian support for the Boers, there came in 1907 the Anglo-Russian Convention and an new era of benevolence and sympathy (far from universal) that lasted through WWI to the revolutions of 1917.

An amusing reflection of the change in British attitudes towards Russia over the first two decades of the century can be found once more in the themes and subject matter of popular fiction. A purveyor of adventure tales for boys, Captain F.S. Brereton, who began with *A Gallant Grenadier* (1902), a tale about the fearless British troops in the Crimea, quickly moved to embrace the Japanese cause with his *A Soldier of Japan: A Tale of the Russo-Japanese War* (1906), before finishing triumphantly *With Our Russian Allies* (1916). Perhaps a more interesting indication of the change in the mood of public opinion was the well-received publication in 1909 of *The M.P. for Russia: Reminiscences & Correspondence of Madame Olga Novikoff,* edited by the famous journalist W.T. Stead, followed in 1917 by her *Russian Memories,* edited by the bard of 'Holy Russia', Stephen Graham. During the last decades of the previous century Mme Novikoff (Ol'ga Alekseevna Novikova) had been the advocate in England of Russian autocracy and defender of its military and religious policies, but despite all her lobbying of political figures and her own writings, she paled in significance before the persuasive eloquence of Stepniak and his adherents.[86]

If Turgenev and Tolstoi enjoyed the height of their popularity in Victorian Britain, Dostoevskii and Chekhov were the major inspiration for the writers of the new century.[87] They form along with Turgenev and Tolstoi the great highways of Russian literary 'presence' in Britain that have been travelled many times by researchers over the last century since Constance Garnett added to her Turgenev the six volumes of her Tolstoi translations (*Anna Karenina, The Death of Ivan Ilyitch, and Other Stories,* and *War and Peace,* 1901-4) and the twelve volumes of *The Novels of Fyodor Dostoevsky* (1912-20), which were to be joined by another great achievement, the thirteen volumes of her *Tales of Tchehov* (1916-22) and the two-volume *The Plays of Tchehov* (1822-3). The availability of 'the whole Tolstoi' was realized with the publication of Aylmer Maude's twenty-one-volume *Tolstoy Centenary*

86 See Stead's earlier long and interesting essay in *The Review of Reviews* (vol. III, 1891, pp. 123-36), in which he compares her activities with those of Princess Lieven in England in the first part of the century.

87 Gilbert Phelps, *The Russian Novel in English Fiction* (London, 1956) remains a good introduction, despite the proliferation of Anglo-American studies over the last fifty years.

Edition (1928-37), but this was already the consolidation of a 'classic' rather than the response to a vogue.[88]

There was some competition from a younger generation of writers—and over the next twenty years Gor'kii in particular. Artsybashev and Leonid Andreev were much translated and discussed, but Dostoevskii and especially Chekhov were perceived almost as new and their influence spread, touching British writers and thinkers of almost every persuasion and colour. The first collection of Chekhov's stories appeared only in 1903, the year before his death, and another six years were to elapse before the first production in Britain of a Chekhov play, *The Seagull* in Glasgow, in a translation by George Calderon, who did much to promote the Russian's fortunes.[89] 19th-century translations of Dostoevskii had done him less than justice and it was Garnett's 1912 translation of *Brat'ia Karamazovy* (*The Brothers Karamazov*), the first in English, that encouraged, together with the intoxication of the Ballets Russes, an unprecedented explosion of Russomania among the British 'intelligentsia'.[90]

Among the devotees of Dostoevskii were Maurice Baring and Stephen Graham, so distinct in many ways but united in their discovery of the 'real' Russia of orthodoxy and peasant villages and in their pursuit of its soul—it was with a reference to 'the beauty of the Russian soul' that Rosa Newmarch concluded her book in 1917.[91] Baring, initially by his newspaper articles, then by a series of books that included *Landmarks in Russian Literature* (1910), *The Mainsprings of Russia* (1914) and *Outline of Russian Literature* (1915), was highly influential both in guiding English literary taste (cf. his early championing of Chekhov) and explicating Russia's heritage, while, as Michael Hughes shows, Graham 'tramped' around 'Holy Russia' and produced a stream of books beginning with *Vagabond in the Caucasus* (1911) and including *The Way of Martha and the Way of Mary* (London, 1916).

---

88 Aylmer Maude (1858-1938), of course, was one of the most assiduous promoters of Tolstoi and his work from the time of their first meeting in Moscow in 1888. Maude bitterly regretted a twenty-five year delay before he was allowed to undertake what became the centenary edition (*Tolstoy Centenary Edition*, II (London, 1928), p. 397).

89 See Victor Emeljanow (ed.), *Chekhov: The Critical Heritage* (London, 1981); Patrick Miles, *Chekhov on the British Stage 1909-1987: An Essay in Cultural Exchange* (Cambridge, 1987); Patrick Miles (ed.), *Chekhov on the British Stage* (Cambridge, 1993).

90 The word seems to have appeared for the first time in the 1888 translation from the French of Lev Tikhomirov's *Russia, Political and Social*, appearing as '*intelliguentia*' (p. iv). It was much used by Baring and gained common currency in D.S. Mirskii's *The Intelligentsia of Great Britain* (1935).

91 Newmarch, *Russian Arts*, p. 285.

Both Baring and Graham loom large in the opening pages of Svetlana Klimova's contribution, which in its central section looks into the comparative English neglect of the Russian Nobel Prize winning novelist Ivan Bunin and the question of Russian literature in emigration. As she notes, T.S. Eliot's organ of modernism, *The Criterion,* was increasingly begrudging in appreciating the worth of a literature produced far from its homeland. It is *The Criterion*'s engagement with Russian culture from its opening number in 1922 to its close in 1939, as it moves from reviews and comment on the 'old Russia' of Dostoevskii and the Ballets Russes to its assessment of the cultural life of Soviet Russia, that is the subject of Olga Ushakova's article. The English reputation of another leading figure of the emigration, Aleksei Remizov, and the English translators of his works from the 1920s to the 1940s is investigated by Marilyn Smith. Prominent among them was the charismatic figure of the Cambridge don, Jane Ellen Harrison, who back in 1878 had been introduced to Turgenev on his visit to her college, Newnham, and who much later was to immerse herself in the study of Russian and of Russian culture, as described by Alexandra Smith. A figure who loomed large in Harrison's life was Prince Dmitrii Mirskii, who arrived in England in 1922 to teach and write at the School of Slavonic Studies.[92] His books on Russian literature, appearing in rapid succession in 1926-7, won him admirers and friends in the intellectual elite of the capital. He was, however, skeptical about what he regarded as the excesses of the cult of Chekhov in post-WWI England, but believed that 'if Chekhov has had a genuine heir to the secrets of his art, it is in England, where Katherine Mansfield did what no Russian has done—learned from Chekhov without imitating him'. Rachel Polonsky uses this quotation in the course of her fascinating study of John Middleton Murry's editing of his late wife Katherine Mansfield's letters and editing out of virtually all references to Chekhov.

In characterizing, however briefly, the five contributions of Svetlana Klimova, Tatiana Ushakova, Marilyn and Alexandra Smith, and Rachel Polonsky, we have moved seamlessly into a quite different political and historical period, when Russian literature in emigration acquired a colouring and significance distinct from Russian literature promoted by political émigrés during the Victorian age.

92 See G.S. Smith, *D.S. Mirsky: A Russian-English Life 1890-1939* (Oxford, 2000); Ol'ga Kaznina, 'Kniaz' D.P. Sviatopolk-Mirskii: talant i sud'ba', in Makarova and Morgunova, *Russkoe prisutstvie,* pp. 209-20.

The allies of WWI became foes, following the October Revolution and the fiasco of the Intervention between June 1918 and November 1919, although the next two decades up to WWII witnessed many changes in attitudes and policies, often dependent on British party politics but equally often reflecting wider European and global concerns. *De jure* recognition of the Soviet regime on 1 February 1924 seemed a triumph for Labour and the 'Hands off Russia' movement that had been campaigning since 1917 for reconciliation, but a rapid deterioration in relations followed hard on the heels of the Zinov'ev letter in October 1924 and the rupture in diplomatic relations as a result of the 'Arcos Raid' in May 1927.[93] The 1930s, the so-called 'Pink Decade', following on from the Depression of 1929 and ending with the non-aggression pact signed between the Soviet Union and Germany in August 1939, saw the establishing of the *Daily Worker* on 1 January 1930 and of the *Left Review* in October 1934. But it was also the decade of wider ideological confrontation, tragically dramatized in the Spanish Civil War.

For the popular novelist the 20s and 30s remained deeply 'red'. The 'nihilists' in the titles at the end of the previous century gave way to *The Red Tomorrow, The Red Lady, Red Radio, Red Ending* and many others including the obviously menacing *Red Square*. Spy thrillers, from the pens of Walter Le Queux, Edward Oppenheim and John Buchan, alternated with prophetic or 'doom' novels, such as Hugh Addison's *The Battle of London* (1923) and Martin Hussingtree's *Konyetz* (1924), in which the end of the world is preceded by the Bolshevik invasion of Europe and the Black Plague. There were, however, serious fictional attempts to portray life in the Soviet Union in less sensational terms by both writers who had known pre-Revolutionary Russia (Baring, Graham, Hugh Walpole) and a young idealist generation (Ralph Fox). A most interesting contribution came from William Gerhardie (1895-1977), born and bred in St Petersburg, who while a student at Oxford published both *Futility* (1922), subtitled 'a novel on Russian themes' and dedicated to Katherine Mansfield, and in the following year a pioneering study of Chekhov, whose influence on his own writing was pervasive and beneficial.

It was only with the Anglo-Soviet treaty of 1942, following the German invasion of Russia in June of the previous year, that relations warmed. Britain and Russia were allies again, but it was not the uneasy precedent of 1914 that was stressed but 1812 and the similarity of the struggles against

93 See Gabriel Gorodetsky, *The Precarious Truce: Anglo-Soviet Relations 1924-27* (Cambridge, 1977).

Napoleon and Hitler.[94] Just as the English caricaturists, George Cruikshank in the van, had directed their arrows at the French, a whole string of British cartoonists, among them Vicky, Giles and David Low, targeted Hitler and portrayed Soviet exploits with sympathy and humour and encouraged the image of the benign, pipe-smoking 'Uncle Joe'. It was at this time that Soviet literature came into its own in Britain, epitomized in Hutchinson's launching of its Library of Soviet Novels and its International Authors series.[95] 'Understanding our allies' was the slogan, as the blurb to John Rodker's *Soviet Anthology* (1943) makes clear, emphasizing that 'chosen with a special eye to their variety, the stories in this anthology reveal the Soviet citizen in many aspects and particularly in that wherein he is most human'. It is this context of mutual understanding and help that Claire Knight's chapter takes its place. She looks at the phenomenon or practice of gift-giving between the Soviet Union and other governments and, specifically, at the example provided by Clementine Churchill's Red Cross Aid to Russia Fund over the period 1941-5 that culminated in the invitation to her to visit Moscow in 1945. It was also in the spirit of mutual understanding and a desire to shed a favourable light on life in the Soviet Union that, as Emma Minns describes, Isotype (International System Of TYpographic Picture Education), which had been invented by Otto Neurath during his time in Vienna in the late 20s-early 30s, was used for three books, written and published in England in 1945-7.

To promote a positive image of life in the Soviet Union was the aim of the huge exhibitions staged by the Soviets at Earls Court and described in the above-mentioned contribution by Verity Clarkson. The first took place in 1961 and was symbolic of the new era in Soviet relations with the outside world, known as the Thaw and following the harshest years of the Cold War that had ended with the death of Stalin. Evidence of the cultural rapprochement of the 1960s was the great exhibition to illustrate the historical relations between Great Britain and the USSR/Russia that opened at the V&A in February 1967 to coincide with the visit to London

94 See F.D. Klingender, *Russia—Britain's Ally 1812-1942.* Introduction by Ivan Maisky (London, 1942).

95 For a guide to the translation of works from Russian as well as original English-language contributions in the arts in the 20th century up to the end of WWII, see Amrei Ettlinger and Joan Gladstone's *Russian Literature, Theatre and Art: A Bibliography of Works in English Published 1900-1945,* London, 1945). For a more general coverage of books published during the first twenty-five years of the Soviet regime, see Philip Grierson, *Books on Soviet Russia 1917-1942* (London, 1943).

of the Soviet Premier, A.N. Kosygin. Unlike the Exhibition of Russian Art held in London in 1935, which relied on British and European public and private (largely émigré) collections for its rich display, the 1967 exhibition was a unique example of Anglo-Soviet cooperation. The general fragility of Anglo-Soviet relations was, however, soon to be exposed with the cancelling of the Moscow opening of the exhibition, following the Soviet invasion of Czechoslovakia. Nonetheless, despite this and similar confrontations such as the earlier Cuban crisis, cultural interchange continued and developed.

Cultural agreements between the two countries enabled British graduates to spend a year in Russian universities, theatre and ballet companies to perform, art to be exhibited, and eminent literary and artistic figures to meet. The numbers studying Russian language, Russian history, Russian literature, and Soviet studies in British universities went up dramatically and from the consequent supply of able teachers, more and more schools offered Russian.[96] There was a veritable flood of books and articles in journals and newspapers produced by a growing number of Russian specialists, particularly in university departments.[97] Translations from both Russian and Soviet literature proliferated—and were often available in paperback. Intourist arranged tourist visits and the British public's general awareness of political, social and cultural events in the Soviet Union increased immeasurably in comparison with earlier times by the availability of other sources of information—of radio, television and film.

It is to film that the collection's concluding article by Julian Graffy is devoted, more precisely to the attention that Soviet cinema received over a thirty-year period of great historical change from 1960 to 1990 in the widely-read British film journal *Sight and Sound.* Publication had begun in 1932, during the lifetime of *The Criterion*, where, as Ushakova has indicated, the new art form had been duly noted, but for reasons that Graffy explains, it was the Thaw that allowed a greater British acquaintance with Soviet film, which now commands a prime position in university curricula and public interest. He ends his survey on the cusp of the journal's change of editor and transition from quarterly to monthly and, coincidentally, of the demise of the Soviet Union.

---

96 See James Muckle, *The Russian Language in Britain: A Historical Survey of Learners and Teachers* (Ilkeston, 2008).

97 See Malcolm V. Jones, 'Slavonic Studies in the United Kingdom since the Second World War: A Personal View', in Giovanna Brogi Bercoff, Pierre Gonneau and Heinz Miklas (eds.), *Contribution à l'histoire de la slavistique dans les pays non slaves* (Vienna, 2005), pp. 267-301.

This perceptive analysis brings to a close a collection of twenty contributions that have sought to shed light on the processes of one country's reception of and reaction to another country's culture over two centuries. Despite their diversity of focus and subject matter, they find their unity in the contribution they make to a complex picture, adding definition and clarity and understanding where previously there had been little.

2. Byron, *Don Juan*, and Russia

Peter Cochran

Russia posed a problem for Byron when writing *Don Juan*, for although he had never been there, the geographical, historical, and sexual themes of his comic epic dictated that his hero should go there. As a result of his study of Scott's Waverley Novels, he was determined that no episode should pass without a firm backing either in his own experience, or in authentic prose sources. *Don Juan* should have a reality which his Turkish Tales, at least one of which, *Lara*, was, as he confessed to his publisher, set on 'the Moon',[1] manifestly lacked.

There were a number of reasons why Don Juan should visit Russia. Firstly, he was enslaved in Constantinople, and had to escape—and Russia was the nearest stopping-off point on his anti-clockwise trip around Europe. Secondly, Byron knew that no epic in the tradition in which he wrote—the tradition of Pulci, Ariosto and Tasso—was complete without a Christian army besieging a Moslem city, and Suvorov's siege of Ismail, in which Juan takes part, both fitted into his poem's time-scheme, and was a perfect demonstration of that very idea.

A very important subtext for *Don Juan* is a novel by Thomas Hope called *Anastasius, or the Memoirs of a Greek*,[2] which Byron's publisher John Murray had brought out late in 1819, when Byron was writing the third and fourth cantos of his comic epic (the two cantos were originally one). *Anastasius* is a picaresque novel set in the eastern Mediterranean,

---

Quotations from *Don Juan* are from the edition on the website of the International Byron Society www.internationalbyronsociety.org.

1 Byron to Murray, 24 July 1814: text from National Library of Scotland (hereafter NLS) Ms.43488; *Byron's Letters and Journals*, ed. L.A. Marchand (*BLJ*), IV (1975), pp. 145-6.

2 See Peter Cochran, 'Why Did Byron Envy Thomas Hope's *Anastasius*?', in P. Cochran, *Byron's Romantic Politics* (Newcastle, 2011), pp. 221-62.

whose protagonist claims to be either a Turk or a Greek, a Christian or a Moslem, depending on which label seems to give him the best advantage in whatever situation he finds himself. It casts the gravest doubt on the probity of the Greek nation, and upon the philhellenic concept in whose interest Byron was, in the myth, to 'sacrifice his life' five years later. At one point Anastasius finds himself in Bulgaria, near the town of Widin, in the company of General Suvorov. In another, he *contemplates* travelling to St Petersburg to become the toy-boy of Catherine the Great—but does not do so.

Byron's written reaction to *Anastasius* was muted—a sure sign, in one so secretive, that he was studying it assiduously; and indeed we have the word of Lady Blessington that he admired it past reckoning, and envied Hope for having written it.[3] He seems to have taken it with him to Greece in 1823,[4] as if to test out its theories relating to the instability of ethnic barriers there, and the depth of Greek unscrupulousness. If he did, he found ample evidence of both. His own hero, Don Juan, also travels north from Constantinople, passes Widin,[5] fights with Suvorov at Ismail, and (as a reward for his heroism) is sent to Petersburg, where he realises what for Anastasius is a mere ambition, and becomes, indeed, one of the many gigolos of 'Great Catherine, whom glory still adores, / As greatest of all sovereigns and whores'.[6] (Freudian analysts will be delighted when it is pointed out that Catherine was also the name of Byron's mother.)

People have tried to ascribe a political motive to Byron for the writing of the Russian Cantos of *Don Juan*. To his London agent, Douglas Kinnaird, he writes:

> With regard to the D. J.s – in addition to what I have stated within – I would add that as much rolls (in them) upon the White Bears of Muscovy – who do not at present dance to English Music – it is an appropriate moment to introduce them to the discerning public – in all their native intractability. – – Besides – they and the Turks form at the present the farce [after] the Congress melodrame upon Spain. – Their names & qualities are become more familiar household words – than when the D. J.s were written. – I am aware of no inferiority in the four.[7]

---

3 *Lady Blessington's Conversations of Lord Byron*, ed. Ernest J. Lovell jr. (Princeton, 1969), p. 51.

4 See W.N.C. Carlton, *Poems and Letters of Lord Byron Edited from the Original Manuscripts in the Possession of W.K. Bixby, of St. Louis* (Society of the Dofobs, Chicago, 1912).

5 Byron, *Don Juan*, VII, 61, 1.

6 *Ibid.*, VI, 92, 7-8.

7 Byron to Douglas Kinnaird, 29 January 1823: text from NLS Ms.43454; *BLJ*, X (1980), pp. 92-3.

The Anglophobic Byron is not usually concerned when foreign powers refuse to 'dance to English Music': his explanation seems designed for Kinnaird's benefit. However, it is true that throughout 1822, the year in which Byron wrote the Russian cantos, the cavortings of the Holy Alliance, inspired by the mysticism of Madame Krüdener and Alexander I, was very much in European evidence, in its plans to invade Spain and put down the liberal revolt there (in the event, although Russia wanted to invade, it was France who invaded).

In fact, Byron shows little overt interest in any of these issues. His commentary on Russian ambitions was more comical:

But oh thou grand legitimate Alexander!
    Her Son's Son; let not this last phrase offend
Thine ear, if it should reach; and now rhymes wander
    Almost as far as Petersburgh, and lend
A dreadful impulse to each loud meander
    Of murmuring Liberty's wide waves, which blend
Their roar even with the Baltic's; so you be
Your father's son, 'tis quite enough for me. –

To call men love-begotten, or proclaim
    Their mothers as the Antipodes of Timon,
That Hater of Mankind, would be a shame,
    A libel, or whate'er you please to rhyme on,
But people's Ancestors are History's game,
    And if one lady's slip could leave a crime on
All Generations – I should like to know
What pedigree the best would have to show. –

Had Catherine and the Sultan understood
    Their own true interests, which kings rarely know
Until 'tis taught by lessons rather rude,
    There was one way to end their strife, although
Perhaps precarious, had they but thought good,
    Without the aid of Prince or Plenipo:
She to dismiss her Guards, and He his Haram,
And for their other matters, meet and share 'em.

Don Juan, VI, sts.93-5

These stanzas bring us to the last and most important reason for Byron making Don Juan travel to Russia. The main theme of *Don Juan* is not—as in the Molina / Molière / Mozart tradition—the male sexual appetite, but rather the female sexual appetite. Juan is throughout the passive victim of predatory women. And the most famous example in recent history of a woman with not only a large sexual appetite, but the power to satisfy it too, was Catherine the Great. Byron's jest—that she and the Sultan would be far better employed in bed than at war—is an amusing meditation on this theme.

Douglas Kinnaird found Byron's treatment of Catherine unfair:

> With regards to the new Cantos I am delighted with them – the political reflections, the address to Wellington & the Preface are admirable – but why call the Katherine a whore? – She hired or whored others – She was never hired or whored herself – why blame her for liking fucking? If she canted as well cunted,[8] then call her names as long as you please – But it is hard to blame her for following her natural inclinations – She dared do it – others are afraid – She could do it with impunity; & would have been a fool not to have done it – I should be equally a fool to do it, if I could not do it with impunity – I looked for more liberality from you – You must not turn against rogering – even tho' you practise it seldomer ...[9]

This paper will chart Byron's use of what sources he had to hand in making Juan's Russian visit, and his sexual servitude to Catherine the Great, look authentic.

His primary source was William Tooke's *Life of the Empress Catharine II*, (for which I've used the fourth edition of 1800), and his *View of the Russian Empire* (3 vols., 1799). This last is number 184 in the 1827 Sale Catalogue of Byron's library; the absence of the *Life* does not mean Byron did not possess it, for only a remnant of his library was auctioned in 1827, most of it having been 'cherry-picked' by his friends. William Tooke was chaplain to the British merchants in St Petersburg from 1774 to 1792. A frequenter of Catherine's court, he was friends with, for example, Falconet, creator of the famous statue of Peter the Great. His books on Russia bear a complex relationship with those of the French writer Jean-Henri Castéra, who published similar volumes between 1797 and 1800.[10]

However, Byron seems also to have used a different French book, Charles François Philibert Masson's *Secret Memoirs of the Court of St. Petersburg* (1800 English translation); this is not in his library sale catalogue, but again, that does not prove that he did not have a copy. I shall mention other books *en passant*.

---

8 Kinnaird echoes Byron's words to him in a letter of 26 October 1819.

9 Kinnaird to Byron, 15 October 1822: text from NLS Ms.43456. Byron had told Kinnaird on 16 November 1819 that he 'had not now for a year—touched or disbursed a sixpence to any harlotry'.

10 See A.G. Cross, 'The Reverend William Tooke's Contribution to English Knowledge of Russia at the End of the Eighteenth Century', *Canadian Slavic Studies*, III (1969), pp. 113ff.

From Masson, Byron would have formed a very poor view of Russian manners and morals. Here is one of his milder passages:

> Next to drunkenness, the most prominent and common vice of the Russians is theft. I doubt whether any people on earth be more inclined naturally to appropriate to themselves the property of others—from the first minister to the general officer, from the lackey to the soldier, all are thieves, plunderers and cheats. In Russia theft does not inspire that degrading contempt which stigmatizes a man with infamy, even among the lowest of the populace. What the thief dreads most is the being obliged to return his booty, for he reckons a caning as nothing; and, if detected in the act, he cries with a grin: "*Vinavat gospodin! vinavat*; I have done wrong, sir", and returns what he had stolen, as if that were sufficient amends. This shameful vice, pervading all classes, scarcely incurs blame. It sometimes happens that your pocket is picked in apartments at Court, to which none but persons of quality and superior officers are admitted, as if you were in a fair. A stranger, who lodges with a Russian, even a kniaz, will find, to his cost, that he must leave nothing on his dressing-table or his writing-desk; it is even a Russian maxim, that what is not locked up belongs to anyone who will take it. The same quality has been falsely ascribed to the Spartans; but an Englishman, who has published a book on the resemblances between the Russians and the Greeks, after having proved that they eat, sing and sleep like them, has forgotten to add that in stealing they are still more expert.[11]

At Canto IX stanza 70, Don Juan, having been summoned to court and dressed for his new role, comes face to face with the Empress. Byron is mildly facetious:

> And Catherine (we must say thus much for Catherine)
> Though bold and bloody, was the kind of thing
> Whose temporary Passion was quite flattering,
> Because each lover looked a sort of king,
> Made up upon an amatory pattern;
> A royal husband in all save the *ring,*
> Which, being the damn'dest part of Matrimony,
> Seemed taking out the sting to leave the Honey.
>
> Byron, *Don Juan,* IX, st.70

Next he uses a detail with which both Tooke and Masson provided him: the colour of Catherine's eyes. His uncertainty as to what colour they in fact were is a sign that he has consulted both books, and cannot choose between them:

---

11 Masson, *Secret Memoirs of the Court of St. Petersburg,* II (London, 1800), pp. 45-6.

And when you add to this her Womanhood,
In its Meridian; her blue eyes – or Grey –
(The last, if they have Soul, are quite as good,
Or better, as the best Examples say:
Napoleon's, Mary's (Queen of Scotland) should
Lend to that Colour a transcendent ray –
And Pallas also sanctions the same hue,
Too wise to look through Optics black or blue.)

Byron, *Don Juan*, IX, st.71

And indeed we find that Tooke writes of the Empress, 'She has fine large blue eyes';[12] whereas Masson writes of '... her grey eyes'.[13]

Byron now assays a more detailed description:

Her sweet smile, and her then majestic figure;
Her plumpness, her imperial condescension,
Her preference of a boy to men much bigger,
Fellows whom Messalina's Self would pension;
Her – Prime of Life – just now in juicy vigour –
With other *Extras* which we need not mention –
All these – or any One of these – explain
Enough to make a stripling very vain.

Byron, *Don Juan*, IX, st.72

He may still have both Tooke and Masson open on his writing-desk at the same time; but he prefers the greater discretion of the Englishman. Tooke quotes a source from the 1770s, and has:

> She [*Catherine*] is of that stature which is necessarily requisite to perfect elegance of form in a lady. She has fine large blue eyes; her eyebrows and hair are of a brownish colour; her mouth is well-proportioned, the chin round, the nose rather long; the forehead regular and open, her hands and arms round and white, her complection not entirely clear, and her shape rather plump than meagre; her neck and bosom high, and she bears her head with peculiar grace and dignity. She lays on, as is universally the custom with the fair sex in Russia, a pretty strong rouge... Her gait is majestic: in the whole of her form and manner there is something so dignified and noble, that if she were to be seen, without ornament or any outward marks of distinction, among a great number of ladies of rank, she would be immediately esteemed the chief. There is withal in the features of her face and in her looks an uncommon degree of authority and command. In her character

12 William Tooke, *Life of the Empress Catharine II*, II (4th edn, London, 1799), p. 179.
13 Masson, I, p. 78.

there is more of liveliness than gravity. She is courteous, gentle, beneficent; outwardly devout.[14]

Whereas Masson, describing Catherine in the 1790s (Juan's 'period') writes:

If, upon the introduction of a stranger, she presented her hand to him to kiss, she demeaned herself with great courtesy, and commonly addressed a few words to him upon the subject of his travels and his visit: but all the harmony of her countenance was instantly discomposed, and you forgot for a moment the great Catharine, to reflect on the infirmities of an old woman; as, on opening her mouth, it was apparent that she had no teeth. Her voice too was hoarse and broken, and her speech inarticulate. The lower part of her face was rather large and coarse; her grey eyes, though clear and penetrating, evinced something of hypocrisy, and a certain wrinkle at the base of the nose indicated a character somewhat sinister.[15]

Byron doesn't want Juan's ordeal in Catherine's bed to be too onerous, so he leaves these details out. But he has borrowed from Masson in an earlier passage:

Though somewhat large, exuberant, and truculent
    When *wroth,* while *pleased,* she was as fine a figure
As those who like things rosy, ripe and succulent
    Would wish to look on – while they are in vigour;
She could repay each amatory look you lent
    With interest – and in turn was wont with rigour
To exact of Cupid's bills the full amount
At sight, nor would permit you to discount.

Byron, *Don Juan,* IX, st.62

Masson (or rather, his translator) gives the rhyme-word which the gentlemanly Byron implies without using:

She [*Catherine*] was of the middle stature, and corpulent; few women, however, with her corpulence, would have attained the graceful and dignified carriage for which she was remarked.[16]

Another source, still to be mentioned, is not a history book, but a poem: *Il Poema Tartaro,* by Giambattista Casti—a writer Byron admired and imitated, while hardly mentioning him, so risqué was he (few Italians these days have even heard of him). *Il Poema Tartaro* (which as usual is not in Byron's library sale catalogues) was inspired by Casti's time as a diplomat in Russia during the 1770s. He had conceived a great detestation of the place:

14 Tooke, II, pp. 179-80 (quoting a source of 1772-3).
15 Masson, I, pp. 77-8.
16 *Ibid.*, p. I 76.

> Utile insomma sarebbe all'Europa tutta di togliersi dai confini e slontanar più che sia possibile una Potenza rapace, infida, ingannevole, prepotente, inquieta, soverchiatrice, impertinente, pericolosa, insaziabile, che così sarebbe costretta a riconcentrarsi a Mosca e rinunciare a ogni influenza e ingerenza Europea, e ritornare come le altre volte a divenire Potenza asiatica. E così sia amen.
>
> [To sum up, it would be useful if all Europe could combine to confine and keep at a distance more than has hitherto been possible a Power so rapacious, faithless, deceitful, arrogant, turbulent, overwhelming, impertinent, dangerous, and insatiable, so that it would be forced to centre itself again on Moscow, renounce all European influence and interest, and return as in past times to being an Asiatic Power. Let all say Amen.][17]

Il Poema Tartaro travesties Catherine's Russia by moving it a couple of thousand miles north-east, rechristening it 'Mogollia', Catherine 'Cattuna', Peter the Great 'Djenghis-Khan', Potemkin 'Toto', and so on. The joke makes Russia into an Asiatic power. The hero is a young Irishman with a big nose called Tomasso Scardassale, who does what Juan does, and serves 'Cattuna' sexually.

There are numerous echoes of Casti's poem in Byron's:[18] but Byron is much less offensive than the Italian. Byron's joke about Catherine's appetite, just quoted ('She could repay each amatory look you lent / With interest—and in turn was wont with rigour / To exact of Cupid's bills the full amount / At sight, nor would permit you to discount') is a more discreet version of a passage from Casti:

> Me di fibra sensibile [*says Cattuna to Tomasso*], e di vive
> Tempe, come ben sai formò natura
> E diemmi ancor molle, e al piacer proclive,
> Cor, che in van di resistere procura,
> Alle dolci invincibili attrative
> Di bella qual tu sei, maschil figura;
> E o fanciulla foss'io, vedova, o moglie,
> Invan m'opposi all'amorose voglie.
>
> Or perchè sol regnando amar poss'io
> Liberamente, e premiar chi degno
> Parmi de'premii miei, dell'amor mio;
> Perciò sol di regnar formai disegno;

17 Casti, dispatch in Bibliothèque Nationale, MS.1629 ff 152-61; quoted by Antonino Fallico, 'Notizie e appunti sulla vita e l'operosità di G.B. Casti negli anni 1776-1790', *Italianistica*, III (September-December 1972), p. 530.

18 See Cochran, 'Casti's *Il Poema Tartaro* and Byron's *Don Juan* Cantos V-X', *Keats-Shelley Review*, XVII (2003), pp. 61-85.

Ne mai sott'altro aspetto a me s'offrio,
Il Diadèma Real; lo Scettro, il Regno,
E tutto'altro che il Trono ha in se di pregio
Miro con filosofico dispregio.[19]

['As you can tell, Nature has made me of sensitive stuff, and of passionate energies, and has given me tenderness, and a liking for pleasure; my heart, which cannot be resisted, obtains for itself those sweet invincible beauties which you, proud man, know all about; and, whether a maiden, a widow or a wife, it has always been impossible for me to resist my loving inclinations. / Now, since I reign alone, I may love liberally, and choose lovers from amongst the finest around me; and everything else that is offered me – the Royal Diadem, the sceptre, the power, and all of value that the throne offers – I regard with philosophical indifference'.]

One final detail: Catherine was rumoured, before engaging a favourite formally, to have him 'tested' by one of her ladies, Miss Protasoff. Byron, less nauseated and much wittier than Casti, creates far subtler effects. Thus Cattuna turns Tommaso over to Turfana, 'Amazone di Venere, d'Amore':[20] Casti describes the 'testing' in some detail:[21] a section, in fact, entirely verbal (which is perhaps a disappointment). Tommaso gets a good report, so Cattuna installs him as favourite. Byron, on the other hand, affects innocent incomprehension:

An order from her Majesty consigned
    Our young Lieutenant to the genial care
Of those in Office, and all the World looked kind
    (As it will look sometimes with the first stare –
Which Youth would not act ill to keep in mind)
    As also did Miss Protasoff then there,
Named from her mystic office "l'Eprouveuse" – *
A term inexplicable to the Muse. –[22]

Byron, *Don Juan*, IX, st.84

There is in fact very little evidence that Miss, or Mlle., Protasova actually 'proved' the virility of all Catherine's proposed lovers in advance of their taking up residence; all is rumour; but it is such a disgusting idea that posterity has found it impossible to discard it as myth. If she did so, it was a function she shared with another friend of the Empress, the Countess

19 Casti, *Il Poema Tartaro* (2nd edn, n.p., 1796), Canto IV, sts. 76-7.

20 *Ibid.*, Canto IV, st. 17, l.2.

21 *Ibid.*, Canto IV, sts. 20-5.

22 For the term *l'Éprouveuse*, see Masson, I, p. 144n.

Bruce (whom Byron may have met in Geneva in 1816).[23] William Tooke—an Anglican clergyman, anxious to place a dignified interpretation on all things imperial—even goes so far as to assert that the function at least of the later favourites of Catherine was simply decorative:

> For a series of seventy years the monarchs of Russia have always had favourites officially: it is no wonder then that the custom, thus sanctioned for so long a period, should be almost decreed a fundamental law of the empire, and an appendage to imperial grandeur; for the age of the late sovereign latterly gave no room to think that she kept hers for any other purpose than in conformity to established usage, and as a property to the magnificence of the court.[24]

Byron regarded such Anglican cant just as he regarded all Anglican cant (though he can be *almost* as discreet as Tooke): his version of Catherine the Great is much more entertaining, in consequence, than those of his prose sources.

Of all the episodes in *Don Juan*, that at the Russian court is the briefest, and, in terms of action, the barest of incident. As is not the case with Donna Julia in Canto I, or with Haidee in Cantos II to IV, with the Sultana Gulbeyaz and the odalisques in Cantos V and VI, or with the three English ladies in the final cantos, nothing memorable is said by Catherine the Great (in fact she says nothing at all), and no incidents make the story memorable. At this, the lowest and most degraded point in his hero's traversal of Europe, Byron shows the least interest in his tale. Perhaps Tooke, Masson and Casti did not provide him with sufficient compensation for the personal experiences on which he drew for the rest of the poem, or perhaps the Russophobic contempt of Masson and Casti had infected his view of Russia, and made him want not to investigate or portray the country in too much detail. But there is more to the Russian cantos than just Catherine the Great.

Potemkin, who ordered the attack upon Ismail in which Don Juan distinguishes himself, is briefly the subject of Byron's poem:

> There was a Man, if that he was a Man,
> Not that his Manhood could be called in question,
> For had he not been Hercules, his Span
> Had been as short in youth as Indigestion
> Made his last illness, when, all worn and wan,
> He died beneath a tree, as much unblest on

23 See Polidori, *Diary*, ed. Rossetti (London, 1910), pp. 141-3.
24 Tooke, II, pp. 271-2.

The soil of the Green province he had wasted,
As e'er was Locust on the land it blasted.

This was Potemkin—a great thing in days
    When Homicide and Harlotry made great;
If Stars and Titles could entail praise,
    His Glory might half-equal his Estate;
This fellow, being six foot high, could raise
    A kind of phantasy proportionate
In the then Sovereign of the Russian people,
Who measured men, as you would do a Steeple.[25]

Byron, *Don Juan* VII, sts.36-7

Potemkin was a character so much larger than life that one regrets that Byron felt able to devote only 2 stanzas to him. He brings him into the poem suddenly, and drops him in the same way. He derived his description of Potemkin's death (from 'Indigestion… beneath a tree') from the following passage in Tooke:

> As soon as the empress had intelligence that he was sick, she sent off to him two of the most experienced physicians at Petersburg. He disdained their advice, and would follow no regimen. He carried even his intemperance to an uncommon height[;] his ordinary breakfast was the greater part of a smoke-dried goose from Hamburgh, slices of hung-beef or ham, drinking with it a prodigious quantity of wine and Dantzic-liqueurs, and afterwards dining with equal voracity. He never controlled his appetites in any kind of gratification. He frequently had his favourite sterlet-soup, [*a sterlet is a small sturgeon*] at seasons when that fish is so enormously dear, that this soup alone, which might be considered only as the overture to his dinner, stood him in three hundred rubles... With this sort of diet it is no wonder that he perceived his distemper to be daily gaining ground[;] he thought, however, to get well by moving from Yassy. Accordingly he resolved to set out for Nicolayef, a town which he had built at the confluence of the Ingul with the Bogue. Scarcely had he gone three leagues of his journey when he found himself much worse. He alighted from his carriage in the midst of the highway, threw himself on the grass, and died under a tree, in the arms of the Countess Branicka, his favourite niece.[26]

As another of the poem's themes, in addition to sex and imperialism, is feasting and over-indulgence, Potemkin's diet and its consequences are of great relevance.

---

25 'A kind of phantasy proportionate / In the then Sovereign of the Russian people, / Who measured men, as you would do a Steeple': J.J. McGann (Byron, *The Complete Poetical Works*, V (1986), p. 724) comments, 'The lines probably involve an obscene suggestion'.

26 Tooke, II, pp. 322-4.

The Russian character whose depiction gives us the most insight into Byron's preoccupations is Suvorov (or 'Suwarrow' as he is anglicised). Suvorov, a legend in Russia in his own lifetime, and a great Stalinist hero was one of the most successful generals ever—he never suffered a defeat. He was hugely popular with his troops, who happily died under his command. This success, however, is something Byron at first finds mockable:

For on the sixteenth, at full gallop, drew
    In sight two horsemen, who were deemed Cossaques
For some time, till they came in nearer view;
    They had but little baggage at their backs,
For there were but *three* shirts between the two;
    But *on* they rode, upon two Ukraine Hacks,
Till, in approaching, were at length descried
In this plain pair, Suwarrow and his Guide.

-

...Great Joy unto the Camp!
    To Russian, Tartar, English, French, Cossacque,
O'er whom SouwarrowSuvorov shone like a Gas lamp,
    Presaging a most luminous attack;
Or like a Wisp along the marsh so damp,
    Which leads beholders on a boggy walk,
He flitted to and fro, a dancing light,
Which all who saw it followed – wrong or right.

Byron, *Don Juan,* VII, sts. 43 and 46

The detail about the shirts is not merely an inference from Castelnau's *Histoire de la Nouvelle Russie* (the source of Byron's military detail), but comes from the reactionary *Anti-Jacobin* journal (which we know Byron read):

> It is not to be supposed that the toilet occupies any portion of his [*Suvorov's*] time; but when he is not on active service, he is clean in his person, and frequently washes himself in the course of the day. He confines his dress to an uniform, and a kind of close jacket, called a gurtka: but robes de chambre, and riding coats, are banished from his wardrobe, and he never suffers the indulgence of gloves, or a pelisse, but when a winter's march compels him to use them.[27]

However, much more sinister is the comparison of 'Suwarrow' to an *ignis fatuus*: this is one of Byron's most favoured images of pessimism and

27 Frederick Anthing, *History of the Campaigns of Count Alexander Suworow Rymnikski* (London 1799), p. xxx; or a sympathetic review of the above, incorporating all of its biographical introduction, *Anti-Jacobin* (October 1799), pp. 133-8.

doom,[28] and the idea that the devotion shown to Suvorov by his men was a kind of supernatural curse is well in keeping with his use of the idea elsewhere.

Later, Suvorov's 'hands-on' ways of training recruits seem to be mocked, but Byron keeps his best line to the last:

> New batteries were constructed; was held
> A general Council, in which Unanimity,
> That Stranger to most councils, here prevailed,
> As sometimes happens in a great extremity;
> And, every difficulty being dispelled,
> Glory began to dawn with due Sublimity,
> While Souvaroff, determined to obtain it,
> Was teaching his recruits to use the bay'net.*

(* Note: fact; Souvaroff did this in person.)

> It is an actual fact, that He, Commander
> In Chief, in proper person, deigned to drill
> The awkward Squad, and could afford to squander
> His time, a Corporal's duty to fulfil;
> Just as you'd break a sucking Salamander
> To swallow flame, and never take it ill;
> He showed them how to mount a ladder (which
> Was not like Jacob's) or to cross a ditch. –
>
> Byron, *Don Juan,* VII, sts.51-2 and authorial note

Byron's *seeming* disgust, at the idea of a Field-Marshal lowering himself like this, is from Castelnau:

> Le 19 et le 20, Souvarow exerça les soldats; il leur montra comment il fallait s'y prendre pour escalder; il enseigna aux recrues la manière de donner le coup de baïonette: pour les exercises d'un nouveau genre, il se servit de fascines disposées de manière à représenter un Turc. [Note:] J'ai rendu au maréchal de Souvarow toute la justice qu'il appartient à un homme impartial d'exprimer; mais je trouve cet exercise, ces leçons de carnage, au-dessous d'un maréchal; n'y avait-il pas assez de bas officiers dans son armée pour qu'il se crût obligé de remplir la plus inhumaine de leurs fonctions?[29]
>
> [On the 19th and 20th, Suvorov exercised the soldiers; he showed them how to scale a ladder; he demonstrated to the recruits how to use the bayonet; in a new kind of exercise, he dressed up dummies to represent Turks. [Note:] I have written of the Field-Marshal with all becoming justice; but I find this

---

28 See *Manfred,* I i 195, *The Prisoner of Chillon,* l.35, *The Vision of Judgement,* st.105 l.5, *Don Juan,* VII st.46 l.5, VIII st.32 l.5, XI st.27 l.6, and XV st.54 l.6, *The Two Foscari,* III i 172-6, *The Deformed Transformed,* I i 478, or *The Island,* IV l.86.

29 Castelnau, *Histoire de la Nouvelle Russie,* II, pp. 207-8.

> exercise, these lessons in carnage, to be beneath a Field-Marshal: were there insufficient officers of lower rank in his army, that he felt obliged to fulfil the basest of their functions?]

Castelnau cannot see that Suvorov's training methods were the ones best-designed to get his soldiers to bond with him, and to fight well: in his humility lay his success. Byron's mockery at first seems on the same level of impercipient snobbery; however, he concludes (in a passage which shows he has read the above passage from Castelnau):

> Also he dressed up, for the nonce, fascines
> Like men, with turbans, Scimitars and dirks,
> And made them charge with bayonet these machines,
> By way of lesson against actual Turks;
> And when well practised in these mimic scenes,
> He judged them proper to assail the Works;
> At which your wise men sneered in phrases witty;
> He made no answer: but he took the City.
>
> Byron, *Don Juan,* VII, sts.51-3

Suvorov, though an aristocrat himself, was often described as gross and half-mad by those (mainly aristocrats) who disliked his success, and appreciated neither his style nor the pressures under which he worked; and, as he was the exclusive and willing tool of absolutism, liberals were anxious to malign him as well. The following description is typical of the writings about him which Byron could have read:

> A stranger, who has heard the name of Suvarof, wishes, on his arrival [*in St. Petersburg*], to see this hero. An old man is pointed out, of a weather-beaten and shrivelled figure, who traverses the apartments of the palace, hopping on one foot, or is seen in the streets, followed by a troop of boys, to whom he throws apples, to make them scramble and fight, crying himself, "I am Suvarof! I am Suvarof!" If the stranger should fail to discover in this old madman the conqueror of the Turks and the Poles, he will at least, in his haggard and ferocious eyes, his foaming and horrid mouth, readily discern the butcher of the inhabitants of Prague [*Praga, a suburb of Warsaw, attacked by Suvorov's troops in 1794*]. Suvarof would be considered as the most ridiculous buffoon, if he had not shown himself the most barbarous warrior. He is a monster, with the body of an ape and the soul of a bull-dog. Attila, his countryman, and from whom he is perhaps descended, had neither his good fortune nor his ferocity. His gross and ridiculous manners have inspired his soldiers with the blindest confidence, which serves him instead of military talents, and has been the real cause of all his successes.[30]

30 Masson, I, pp. 318-9.

Byron sums up the Field-Marshal thus:

Suwarrow chiefly was on the alert,
Surveying, drilling, ordering, jesting, pondering;
For the Man was, we safely may assert,
A thing to wonder at beyond most wondering;
Hero, buffoon, half demon and half dirt,
Praying, instructing, desolating, plundering;
Now Mars, now Momus. and when bent to storm
A Fortress, Harlequin in Uniform. –

Byron, *Don Juan*, VII, st.55

Byron derived the idea of Suvorov as a clown from Masson:

At Court, he is sometimes seen to run from lady to lady, and kiss the portrait of Catherine which they wear at their breasts, crossing himself and bowing. Catherine told him one day to behave himself more decently.[31]

[…] Frequently he rides through his camp, naked to his shirt, on the bare back of a Cossack horse; and at daybreak, instead of causing the drums to beat the *reveille*, he comes out of his tent and crows three times like a cock, which is the signal for the army to rise, sometimes to march, or even to go to battle.[32]

But Byron would have been more impressed by what he understood to be the way in which Suvorov's destructive talent was wedded to a modest creative bent:

Suwarrow now was a Conqueror – a Match
For Timour or for Zinghis in his trade;
While Mosques and Streets beneath his eyes like thatch
Blazed, and the Cannons' roar was scarce allayed,
With bloody hands he wrote his first dispatch;
And here exactly follows what he said: –
"Glory to God and to the Empress!" (Powers
Eternal!! such names mingled!) "Ismail's ours". *
* In the original Russian –
"Slava bogu! slava Vam!
Krepost Vzala, y iä tam".
A kind of couplet; for he was a poet.[33]

Byron, *Don Juan*, VIII st.133 and authorial note

---

31 Masson, I, pp. 217-8.

32 *Ibid.*, I, p. 326.

33 Suvorov was indeed given to writing simple verse, although it is not clear where Byron got his information from, or how seriously he took it. For another 'poem' by Suvorov, written to Potemkin before Ochakhov in 1788, see Philip Longworth, *The Art of Victory* (London, 1965), p. 148. It was the general's habit to parody the achievements of his

Anyone, not just buffoonish but 'antithetically mixed' (Byron's phrase for Napoleon, no less),[34] able to crow like a cock *and* write poetry, would remind the poet of himself, just as Robert Burns did: in a Journal entry for 13 December 1813, Byron writes:

> Allen... has lent me a quantity of Burns's unpublished, and never-to-be-published, Letters. They are full of oaths and obscene songs. What an antithetical mind! – tenderness, roughness – delicacy, coarseness – sentiment, sensuality – soaring and grovelling – dirt and deity – all mixed up in that one compound of inspired clay![35]

Byron senses an *alter ego* in Burns; and in this analysis the similarly Protean and uncategorisable Suvorov functions in the same way. When he went to Greece in 1824, with a view to forming a battalion and fighting the Turks, Byron may have intended to make Suvorov a role-model: but he died of despair and medical bloodletting before he saw any action.

---

professional enemies—of whom he had many—in the style of Ossian, the Russian translation of which was dedicated to him. For further examples of his doggerel, see A.V. Suvorov, *Pis'ma*, ed. V.S. Lopatin (Moscow, 1986), pp. 6 (in French), 8, 157, 190 (in French), 214, 220, 222, 224, 230, 261 (in French), 287 (to the poet Derzhavin), 293, 349 (in German), 378-9, and 394.

34 Byron, *Childe Harold's Pilgrimage*, III, 36.2.

35 *BLJ*, III (1974), p. 239.

3. William Henry Leeds and Early British Responses to Russian Literature

Anthony Cross

'The *Westminster Review* (*WR*) was the very first English periodical of any kind to give a tolerably complete general sketch of Russian literature in its various departments; and though no more than a mere map of the subject, it may be said to have been drawn up according to 'the latest authorities and discoveries', and to have been well calculated to excite a more powerful interest than that of mere curiosity'.[1] This is the opening sentence of a review that appeared in 1841 in the very same *Westminster Review*, but some thirty-five volumes and seventeen years later than the 'sketch' to which it referred. 'Politics and Literature in Russia', for such was the running title of the sketch, had been written in 1824 for the very first number of the *Westminster Review* by its recently appointed editor, John Bowring, who in 1821 had published to wide acclaim and professed astonishment the first of the two volumes of his *Rossiiskaia antologiia: Speciments of the Russian Poets*. In the introduction to that work Bowring expressed his intention 'to write a general history of Russian literature',[2] which several reviewers, confessing ignorance of all Russian authors with the exception of Karamzin, encouraged him to do. However, he removed the sentence from the second edition of his

1 'Russian Literary Biography, &c'., *Westminster Review*, XXVI (July-October 1841), p. 35. The reviewer, who, as will be shown, was W.H. Leeds, was far less complimentary about Bowring's efforts when writing for a different journal five years earlier, suggesting that 'there was a freedom of interpretation in many passages, that amounted to positive blunders, and those, too, of a most ridiculous kind—quite sufficient to justify the suspicion that it was first of all done out of Russian into some other language before it was done into English' (*Foreign Quarterly Review*, XVI (1836), p. 446).

2 *Rossiiskaia antologiia: Speciments of the Russian Poets*, I (London, 1821), p. i. See my 'Early English Specimens of the Russian Poets', *Canadian Slavic Studies*, IX (1975), pp. 44-62.

anthology published later that year and contented himself on assuming editorship of the *Westminster Review* with a relaying of information taken mainly from the German version of A.A. Bestuzhev-Marlinskii's 'Vzgliad na staruiu i novuiu slovesnost' v Rossii' ('A Look at Old and New Literature in Russia', 1823).[3]

Ignorance of Russian literature, coupled with an unassailable sense of cultural superiority, was a badge worn very lightly by English journalists, authors, travellers, and public at large in the first decades of the 19th century, indeed, up to and beyond the Crimean War, but it was to some extent a case of convenient corporate amnesia. During the reigns of Catherine and Paul there were significant contributions made by a series of knowledgeable and informed writers, notably Rev. William Coxe, Rev. William Tooke and Dr Matthew Guthrie, to provide sound information about Russian cultural, literary and scientific achievements.[4] Coxe's *Travels*, going into six editions between 1784 and 1803, was one of the most widely read and consulted 'guides' and its long chapter on Russian literature and the likes of Lomonosov, Sumarokov and others was used, for instance, as the source for entries in biographical dictionaries towards the end of the 18th century, but it tended to be the hostile and dismissive Edward Daniel Clarke's influence that was the most marked throughout the second decade of Alexander's reign and beyond and helped to create the impression of a continuing Russian cultural wasteland.[5] It was, however, evidence of literary activity precisely during Alexander's reign that was missing and it was indeed Bowring's happy fate to be seen as the discoverer of Russian poetry and literature, adding to his already mentioned anthology and essay another review in July 1825 that initiated British awareness of the art of the fabulist Krylov, who alone (Pushkin, Gogol and Lermontov not excepted) was to become a familiar name in the pre-Turgenev-Tolstoi-Dostoevskii era.[6]

---

3 *Westminster Review*, I (January 1824), pp. 80-101 (pp. 92-100 are specifically concerned with Russian literature).

4 See my 'The Reverend William Tooke's Contribution to English Knowledge of Russia at the End of the Eighteenth Century', *Canadian Slavic Studies*, III (1969), pp. 106-15; 'Arcticus and *The Bee*: An Episode in Anglo-Russian Cultural Relations', *Oxford Slavonic Papers*, NS II (1969), 62-76; 'British Awareness of Russian Culture (1698-1801)', *Canadian-American Slavic Studies*, XIII (1979), pp. 412-35.

5 The Cambridge don travelled through Russia in the reign of Paul, but his account, *Travels through Russia and the Bosphorus*, many times reprinted thereafter, appeared for the first time only in 1810.

6 'J.A. Krilov's Russian Fables', *Westminster Review*, IV (July 1825), pp. 176-8. The work reviewed was *Fables russes, tirées du recueil de m. Kriloff et imitées en vers français et italiens*

It is during the reign of Nicholas I that Bowring's initiative was given new impetus and it is fitting that the journals primarily associated with this development should proclaim their foreign interest in their titles: the *Foreign Review and Continental Miscellany* (*FRCM*), which survived a mere two years from 1828 to 1829, carried in its second volume (1828) an extensive review of Nikolai Grech's *Opyt kratkoi istorii russkoi literatury* (*Attempt at a Brief History of Russian Literature*, 1822),[7] already briefly acknowledged the previous year as a source in the first volume of the *Foreign Quarterly Review* (*FQR*), its infinitely more successful and long-lived rival, in its review of Emile Dupré de Saint Maure's *Anthologie russe* (1823).[8] The author of this second item is generally acknowledged to be the Scottish bibliographer and journalist, John George Cochrane (1781-1852), and soon to be the journal's editor, who was assisted (and one suspects in no small measure) by 'a Russian friend', Ivan Iakovlevich Smirnov, a secretary in the Russian embassy in London and son of its long-serving chaplain. Both articles have excited some interest in modern times for their discussion, however flawed with inaccuracies, of Pushkin and his work and the first of them, in the *Foreign Review and Continental Miscellany*, as further distinguished by the first mention in Britain of *Evgenii Onegin*, about which the reviewer writes:

> Among other points of this poet's resemblance to Byron may be mentioned his facility of composition, and variety of subjects; his "Eugenius Onegin", which, like "Beppo", is designed as a satire on the follies of the fashionable world, is not only curious as a picture of the manners of the higher classes in Russia at the present day, but also attractive for the touches of loftier poetry, and the warmth of feeling which it occasionally displays. Like "Don Juan", this production has been published piecemeal, and is not, we believe, yet completed, so that we cannot judge sufficiently of the plan to express on its merits. (*FRCM*, II, 299)

No less historically significant are the verse translations of passages from 'Ruslan i Liudmila', 'Kavkazskii plennik' and 'Brat'ia razboiniki' (*FRCM*, pp. 296-300), which have justly been acclaimed as 'the first English

---

par divers auteurs (Paris, 1825). See my 'The British and Krylov', *Oxford Slavonic Papers*, NS XVI (1983), pp. 91-140.

7 *Foreign Review and Continental Miscellany*, II (1828), pp. 279-309.

8 *Foreign Quarterly Review*, I (1827), pp. 595-631. An equally influential source of information was the 'Coup d'oeil sur l'histoire de la langue slave, et sur la marche progressive de la civilization et de la littérature en Russie', included in Adrien Balbi, *Introduction à l'atlas ethnografique du globe*, I (Paris, 1826), pp. 321-57. Its unnamed author, Balbi's young Russian friend, was in this instance the Shishkovite N.I. Bakhtin (1796-1869).

translations from Puskin'.[9] The identity of the reviewer, however, has never previously been positively established: Gleb Struve in his important study of Pushkin's early English reputation, published long ago in 1949, alone suggested in a footnote that 'both the style of his article and some of its ideas resemble a later article on *Poltava* in the *Foreign Quarterly Review;* it is quite likely that the two came from the same pen', while Vadim Rak in the most recent revisiting of the subject concluded that 'some Russian, visiting London in 1828, was in all probability involved [*prichasten*] in the extensive review'.[10] The reviewer was in fact William Henry Leeds (1786-1866), a truly significant figure in the early history of British reception and perception not only of Russian literature but also of Russian art and architecture.

The reasons for Leeds's hitherto modest niche may easily be established. Anonymity was the norm for articles in the journals of the early 19th century and very few of his articles were signed, designated if at all with the letter 'L' or sometimes 'HL'. It is only his own compositions or translations that seem to bear his full name. He was unbelievably prolific and his publications were not only contributions to journals but also included books he edited or for which he wrote introductions. His range was very wide and Russian literature was to a degree an avocation. He has no entry in the *Dictionary of National Biography,* although he fully deserves one, and it is in dictionaries of architects and reference works on architecture that his name appears.[11] Only one article on his work as an architectural critic, and then for a single journal, has been published.[12] It is the *Wellesley Index of Victorian Periodicals* that first allowed most researchers to see his contributions to leading journals, but it contains a far from complete list of his articles even in those periodicals it covered[13]—and his work appeared in other journals and publications such as almanacs, albums, and encyclopedias. If we look only at his contributions to Russian literature, then his presence is even less

9 See Gleb Struve, 'Puškin in Early English Criticism (1821-1838)', *American Slavic and East European Review,* VIII (1949), p. 301.

10 *Ibid.,* p. 302; V.D. Rak, 'Prizhizhennaia izvestnost' Pushkina za rubezhom: Angliia', in *Pushkin: issledovaniia i materially,* XVIII-XIX (St Petersburg, 2004), p. 247.

11 *Macmillan Encyclopedia of Architects,* II (London, 1982), p. 654 (entry by R. Windsor Liscombe); James Stevens Curl, *A Dictionary of Architecture and Landscape Architecture* (2nd edn, Oxford, 2006), p. 438; Howard Colvin, *Biographical Dictionary of British Architects, 1600-1840* (4th edn, New Haven and London, 2008), pp. 640-1.

12 Odile Boucher-Rivalain, 'William Henry Leeds (1786-1866), critique architectural et sa contribution à la *Westminster Review* dans les années 1840', *Cahiers victoriens et édouardiens,* LV (2002), pp. 33-41.

13 *Wellesley Index to Victorian Periodicals, 1824-1900,* V (Toronto and Buffalo, 1989), pp. 456-7.

apparent and appreciated, and recognition of his achievement, very partial and fragmentary, is determined by a scholar/researcher's particular areas of study and expertise rather than by interest in the man himself. Thus he was known to some Pushkin scholars, such as the aforementioned Struve and Rak, but not, for instance, to M.P. Alekseev. Because Leeds wrote something, as will be seen, about Gogol, he is included by Karl Lefevre in his study of that writer's early British reception, but he is only referred to as the reviewer 'L'.[14] Several of his articles in *The Foreign Quarterly Review* are briefly cited in Dorothy Brewster's *East-West Passage* of 1954, but Leeds is nowhere named.[15] His achievement in that journal is more widely appreciated by Eileen Curran, but her study is restricted precisely to the journal, while not identifying some of his contributions and without any reference to his other activities.[16]

Who, then, was this elusive and enigmatic man? Leeds was born in Norwich in 1786, but nothing is known of his early years or education and he first surfaces in 1815, when he showed a design for a monument to Admiral Nelson at the Norwich Society of Artists. He subsequently exhibited architectural drawings at the Royal Academy and Society of British Artists but he seems not to have received any formal training as a draughtsman or architect. It is as a frequently controversial and acerbic architectural journalist and critic that he was to earn his reputation, particularly for the series of articles under the pseudonym 'Candidus' that he wrote in the 1830s, when his particular *bête noire* was Greek Revivalism. He worked for the London booksellers Baldwin and Cradock, but small inheritances following the deaths of his brother and sister, augmented by fees for his journalism and editing, allowed him to pursue an independent career. Some insight into his personality and work is provided in an obituary written by the philologist and engineer Hyde Clarke (1815-95), who had known Leeds for more than thirty years, particularly as a colleague on

14 Carl Lefevre, 'Gogol and Anglo-Russian Literary Relations during the Crimean War', *American Slavic and East European Review*, VIII (1949), pp. 106-9.

15 Dorothy Brewster, *East-West Passage: A Study in Literary Relationships* (London, 1954), pp. 52-5.

16 Eileen M. Curran, '*The Foreign Quarterly Review* on Russian and Polish Literature', *Slavonic and East European Review*, XL (1961-2), pp. 209-16. (Curran's discussion is flawed by her failure to attribute to Leeds several articles in the late 1830s that clearly bear his stamp. Equally, her assertion that Leeds 'always appeared ignorant of the pre-19th century Russian literature which had found such favour with Cochrane and Smirnove' (pp. 210-11) is wide of the mark.)

The Building News where it appeared.[17] It is a unique contemporary source, invaluable for what Clarke knew and revealing for ignorance he himself acknowledged of much else.

Conceding that Leeds had 'a fierce disposition', he describes him as a foe of 'humbug', ever ready to cross swords and attracting controversy for his views, committed to the cause of enlightening a wide readership about art and architecture, and refusing to believe that 'architecture was a mystery far beyond the vulgar kin'. He also, amusingly, noted that 'there are many readers of this publication who knew Leeds, in his advanced life, as an old bore, and avoided him accordingly'. He was 'a bookworm', increasingly surrounded by dusty piles of books, leaving at his death in 1866 at the good age of seventy-nine a library of some three thousand books that was sold over four days, although, somewhat surprisingly it contained very few books about Russia or in Russian.[18] Although Leeds suffered from a speech defect, he was an assiduous and talented student of languages, probably not conversing readily or fluently, but reading with ease books in German, French, Italian, and Russian. Precisely when and why he began his study of Russian is unknown, although it would seem to have been in the 1820s, possibly inspired by the example of Bowring to enter into an unknown area of research and probably teaching himself. He certainly never visited Russia and may never have spoken the language or even met a Russian. Leeds, however, had a deep commitment to literature, was widely read, dabbled in verse, and apparently left a number of unpublished dramatic works. He loved to insert the occasional foreign word into his articles, 'an alloy', Clarke suggests, 'by which his anonymous writings can often be known'. He also had a penchant for neologisms and is said, for instance, to have coined in 1843 the phrase 'to Puginise', meaning 'to mix up political and theological speculations with architectural ones'.

Clarke was not really interested in anything other than Leeds's architectural passion and this led him to make patently untrue statements. While he was undoubtedly right in emphasizing Leeds's punctiliousness

17 Hyde Clarke, 'William Henry Leeds, Architectural Critic', *The Building News*, XIV (4 October 1867), pp. 681-2 (11 October), pp. 697-8 (18 October), pp. 717-8.

18 *Catalogue of the Architectural and Foreign Library of the Late W.H. Leeds, Esq. comprising a large collection of books relating to the arts, painting, sculpture, and architecture, works in Russian, Danish, Swedish, German, French, Spanish, and Italian literature [...] which will be sold by auction, by Messrs Puttick and Simpson [...] on Monday, April 29th, and three following days* (London, 1867). There were runs of a few Russian periodicals and dictionaries but the only individual literary works were a two-volume edition of Kheraskov (1820) and a three-volume collection of Karolina Pavlova (1841).

in matters of style (perhaps somewhat convoluted and precious to modern tastes), he could hardly be further from the truth in saying 'he wrote little', when his estimated output is over a thousand items.[19] No less obviously inaccurate is his contention that Leeds's 'acquaintance with Russian [was] kept up for solely for what architectural information he could glean from original sources'.

On 10 January 1831 Leeds wrote an unpublished letter to the famed Scottish publisher John Murray II in which he offered for publication his now lost translation of Ippolit Bogdanovich's famous 'ancient tale in free verse', *Dushen'ka* (1783), 'the first attempt ever made in this country to give an entire version of a Russian poem of any length'.[20] He then suggested that 'within the last three or four years Russian literature has begun to attract a good deal of attention in Germany, & I hope that ere long it will be so in England also. Many things may be found in it worth translating, & I would willingly undertake something of the kind, could I meet with any encouragement to do so'. He then revealed that he had been the author of the anonymous review in the *Foreign Review and Continental Miscellany* in 1828 and expressed the hope that the editor (J.G. Lockhart, Walter Scott's son-in-law) of the House of Murray's *Quarterly Review* would also feel 'disposed to introduce an article on the subject'. Lockhart evidently didn't, and it was instead to the *Foreign Quarterly Review* that he turned and in July 1831 there was published the first of his many 'Russian' contributions to that journal.

Leeds had continued to contribute to the *Foreign Review and Continental Miscellany* during the remaining months of its existence, most notably in volume IV, when he produced a substantial review of the only recently published tale in verse, *Div i Peri* (St Petersburg, 1827) by the young minor poet and acquaintance of Pushkin, A.I. Podolinskii (1806-86).[21] Leeds

19 The estimate is by the late Phoebe Stanton (1915-2003), professor of architecture at Johns Hopkins University. She compiled a sixty-six page typewritten bibliography which is held with her voluminous research materials, mainly on A.W. Pugin (about whom she published a book in 1972), in the archive of the Royal Institute of British Architects, London, StP/1—and to which I am indebted.

20 National Library of Scotland, Edinburgh, Murray Archive, Ms.40685. (There are three other letters from Leeds to Murray, dated 1836 and 1844 (2), but they are concerned solely with architectural matters.)

21 *Foreign Review and Continental Miscellany*, IV (1829), pp. 245-8. Podolinskii's poem received extensive reviews in *Moskovskii telegraf*, XXI (1827) and *Moskovskii vestnik*, XV (1827) and I have been unable to establish whether Leeds's review was an adaptation of either of these.

accompanied his review with long translated excerpts and it is interesting to note that the subject, made famous in Thomas Moore's *Lalla Rookh* (1817), spurred him to creative emulation, publishing in *The Bijou* in 1830 his own poem 'Paradise and the Peri'.[22] This was signed, as was his next publication, which, however, has a historical significance way beyond its intrinsic value. In the first volume of *The Royal Lady's Magazine, and Archives of the Court of St. James's* (1831) there appeared 'Specimens of Russian Poetry', comprising Leeds's versions of a piece from Mikhail Zagoskin's opera *Ivanovskii* (?), a poem entitled 'Children's Youthful Pastimes' by 'Shlaepushkin' (Fedor Slepushkin (1783-1848), whom he calls in a footnote 'the Russian Bloomfield'), and 'The Spanish Serenade' 'from the Russian of Pushkur', which I believe to be the first published English translation of a poem by Pushkin, his 'Ispanskii romans' of 1824, beginning with the repeated refrain: 'Zephyrs of eve / Sport, thro' the air, / And flit o'er the stream / Of Guadulquivér'.[23]

Before we survey Leeds's contributions to the *Foreign Quarterly Review*, we might note not only as further evidence of his prodigious and unflagging activities his keen interest in the progress of the arts in Russia. In the first volume of the *Foreign Review* he had offered a 'notice of the Fine Arts in Russia', derived from an unspecified Russian source which he thought probably overplayed their flourishing state.[24] However, two years later, in 1831, he contributed to the first volume of *Fraser's Magazine* a substantial essay on 'The State of the Fine Arts in Russia' that named many names among architects, painters and their like in frequently mangled transcriptions and essentially confirmed what he had earlier doubted.[25] That same year he began to contribute to another new journal, the *Library of the Fine Arts*, of which under its new title of *Arnold's Library of the Fine Arts* he became editor in November 1832. In 1831 he entered into a controversy aroused by an obituary of the painter George Dawe of the Hermitage 1812 Gallery fame and revealed in a review of Sir William Gell's *Pompeiana* (1832) not only his dislike of Palladio but introduced the sort of reference that was his unique signature, when, praising the advantages

22 *The Bijou: An Annual of Literature and the Arts*, III (London, 1830), pp. 271-88. (Leeds had contributed to the first volume 'The National Norwegian Song' (*ibid.*, I (1828), pp. 173-5. Other contributors to this almanac included Coleridge, James Hogg, Robert Southey, and many other luminaries.)

23 *Royal Lady's Magazine, and Archives of the Court of St. James's*, I (1831), pp. 83-5.

24 *Foreign Review and Continental Miscellany*, I (1828), pp. 338-9.

25 *Fraser's Magazine for Town and Country*, I (April 1830), pp. 276-86.

that glazing had brought to architecture, he wrote 'In his poem *O Polzae Stekla*, Lomonosov has sung the praises of glass—a singular subject, it will perhaps be thought, but the Russian bard was as much a votary of science as of the muse'.[26] In 1832 he translated Zinaida Volkonskaia's 'Project for a Museum of Fine Arts, in the Imperial University of Moscow' and followed it by 'A Visit to the Academy of Arts', an important neglected version of Konstantin Batiushkov's 'Progulka v Akademiiu khudozhestv', as well as providing information in the 'Miscellaneous' section on, for instance, the latest building developments in St Petersburg (St Isaac's, the Alexander Column, the Aleksandrinskii Theatre) and the ill-fated architect Vasilii Bazhenov.[27]

The translation of Batiushkov's essay followed a year or so after a very favourable review of his *Opyty v stikhakh i proze* (*Essays in Verse and Prose*, 2 vols, 1817), together with a version of his poem 'Umiraiushchii Tass' ('The Dying Tasso'), that Leeds had contributed as his second 'Russian' article for *Foreign Quarterly Review (FQR*, IX, 218-22). He had begun the previous year, in volume 8 (1831), with a review of Faddei Bulgarin's historical novel *Dimitrii samozvanets* (*Dimitrii the Impostor*, 2nd edn, 1830) (*FQR*, VIII, 117-39) and over the period 1831-43 he contributed eight review essays, complemented by at least the same number of 'miscellaneous literary notices' that are frequently informative and detailed and indicative of Leeds's continued interest in Russian literature, despite his ongoing and steadily increasing attention to architectural matters.[28]

Bulgarin held a particular place of affection with Leeds, who had indeed already written in the *Foreign Review* in 1828 about the then still incomplete *Ivan Vyzhigin, ili russkii Zhil Blas* (*Ivan Vyzhigin, or the Russian Gil Blas*), as well as translating a long passage from the novel. In what may well have been his last published 'Russian' piece in 1846 he also translated an excerpt from Bulgarin's memoirs, prefacing it with the confession that 'we were before not a little prepossessed in Bulgarin's favour, having formed our acquaintance with him as a writer almost with our very first study of the Russian language itself' and recognizing him as 'almost the very first who

26 *Library of the Fine Arts*, I (April 1831), pp. 229-33; (July), p. 498.

27 *Ibid.*, III (1832), pp. 54-5, 123-32 (Volkonskaia); *Arnold's Library of the Fine Arts*, NS I (1833), pp. 160, 337-8 (Miscellaneous); NS III (1834), pp. 451-6, 522-9 ('Batiashkov', i.e. Batiushkov).

28 Although John Macray (later to become the first librarian of the Taylorian in Oxford) held overall responsibility for this section of the journal, there is little doubt that it was Leeds who supplied all the Russian material.

introduced into it [*Russian literature*] both the modern novel and historical romance'.[29] Nevertheless, Leeds was not prepared to over-praise Bulgarin's efforts, noting his failure 'to display any great power or originality', and was generally unhappy with the picaresque mode of *Ivan Vyzhigin*, which he felt inevitably brought caricature and satire and not a reassuring picture of contemporary society.

By the time Leeds reviewed *Dimitrii samozvanets* an English translation (1831) of *Ivan Vyzhigin* had appeared and was soon followed by an English version (1833) of Mikhail Zagoskin's *Iurii Miloslavskii, ili Russkie v 1612 godu*, both of which were deemed by Leeds as 'eminently unsuccessful' and merit mention merely as the first Russian novels to appear in English dress, however ill-fitting.[30] Leeds's review of Zagoskin's novel (*FQR*, XI (1833), pp. 382-403), which appeared before the publication of the translation, was largely a re-telling of the story, but his overall judgment was that it deserved 'a very respectable place in the fictitious literature of modern Europe', although he was quick to deride efforts to raise Zagoskin to equal status with Sir Walter Scott. He finished with a brief look at Zagoskin's *Roslavlev, ili Russkie v 1812 godu*, but preferred the earlier work that allowed the writer greater freedom in the creation of characters, just as he had opted for Bulgarin's foray into historical romance rather than for his portrayal of the contemporary scene.

At the end of his Zagoskin review, Leeds had signalled his intention to write about 'another Russian novelist, who has risen upon the literary horizon, and to bear our testimony to the merits which seem to announce a distinguished reputation for Lazhetchnikov'. This did not materialize, but Leeds's interest in the long form of the novel which he seemed to regard as a touchstone of a nation's cultural maturity did not diminish. For the next three years, following a change of ownership and editorial policy,[31] he wrote nothing about Russian literature for the journal, but in 1838 he returned to the infant Russian novel in another extensive review that was principally devoted to an historical romance by Rafail Zotov, *Niklas, Medvezh'ia lapa,*

29 'Charles XII and Peter the Great', *New Monthly Magazine and Humorist*, LXXVIII (1846), pp. 17-25. (Leeds, incidentally, elsewhere alludes to a further translation from Bulgarin, entitled 'My First Acquaintance with Karamzin' and published in the old *Monthly Magazine*, that I have been unable as yet to locate.)

30 *Westminster Review*, XXXVI (1841), p. 38. *Ivan Vejeeghen, or, Life in Russia*, 2 vols. (London and Edinburgh, 1831), trans. by George Ross; *The Young Muscovite, or, The Poles in Russia*, paraphrased, enlarged and illustrated by Frederick Chamier and by the author of 'A Key to the Houses of Parliament', 3 vols. (London, 1833).

31 See Curran, '*The Foreign Quarterly Review*', pp. 215-6.

ataman kontrabandistov (*Nicholas Bearspaw, Ataman of the Smugglers,* 1837, and a collection of tales (1837) by Aleksandr Vel'tman (*FQR,* XXI (1838), pp. 56-78). The running title was 'Russian novel writing' and Leeds offered a series of characteristic pieces of advice to practising and budding Russian novelists, observing that 'at present they are pursuing an erroneous course, adhering, as if it were a particular merit, to all the conventional and worn-out forms'. He demands a depiction of 'what really exists around them, so as to convey a faithful portraiture of native society and manners, of actual feelings and passions in their various phases and degrees, not caring whether what was so produced accorded or not with the literary fashions of other countries'. They are too prone to strive for 'incidents fantastic and improbable, and, for the most part also stale and hacknied, without a claim to invention or ingenuity'.

Leeds reacted strongly against French and particularly German models and, not surprisingly, believed that if examples were to be sought, then they should be English: 'we would gladly give up all their historical romances and flashy melodramatic tales for one such narrative as the Vicar of Wakefield, or one clear and vivid picture of domestic lie as exhibited in Miss Austen's novels,—full of vigour and force, yet quiet and perfectly unpretending'. Then finally in 1844, in virtually his last contribution to the journal, the publication of a translation, and a good one, of Ivan Lazhechnikov's *Basurman* as *The Heretic* by none other than Thomas Shaw gave Leeds the opportunity to write, if briefly, about 'a work purely and intensely national' and to assert, after some twenty years of observing its progress, that 'nothing could be more erroneous than the commonly received opinion, that Russia has no indigenous literature, none that has its root in native popular ground, that her writers put forth only translations or imitations of foreign works' (*FQR,* XXXIII, p. 242).

Whether he was writing about prose or poetry Leeds was ever aware of the presence of Pushkin. It was as if he felt obliged to introduce some mention or discussion of a writer so renowned in his homeland but about whom he always had some niggling reservations. In his very first article for the *Foreign Review* in 1828, which has already been highlighted, he devoted some 5 pages to the poet, generally positive and informative, but the sting was in the tail: 'this apparent fertility is rather a matter of regret than congratulation, for instead of sending forth so many slight compositions, we should be better pleased to find him applying his talents to some work of varied and sustained interest, worthy of his powers, and redeeming the promise of excellence given in his Ruslan and Liudmila' (*FR*, II, p. 300). It was much in the spirit of a headmaster's report on a bright pupil who could do better. It became a perpetual criticism that Pushkin frittered his time on minor pieces in verse and prose when he should have concentrated on the epic and the sustained narrative. In his review of Bulgarin he strikes the same note, declaring that Pushkin 'instead of concentrating his talents in some undertaking of at least tolerable magnitude, has preferred exhibiting his versatility and—his indolence' (*FQR*, VIII, p. 118). The same volume for 1831 contained among its 'Miscellaneous Literary Notices' news of the publication of *Boris Godunov* and of another chapter of *Evgenii Onegin* (*FQR*, XV, pp. 256, 519) and would seem to give the lie to Leeds's accusations both of idleness and little ambition, but Leeds had not as yet seen the tragedy and *Evgenii Onegin*, 'a poetical romance', was for him still a work in progress, but with which he never really came to terms. It was, nevertheless, obviously time for Leeds to face Pushkin full square and it was the publication of *Poltava* in 1829 that gave him the pretext for a major review that was the only English contemporary critique of the poet's work of real substance and significance (*FQR*, IX (1832), pp. 398-416).

Leeds begins by tackling the inevitable comparison of Pushkin and Byron and 'although we could wish that Pushkin did not remind us quite so much of Byron, we consider his productions as affording evidence of indisputable genius and power; they exhibit many masterly touches, much vigour of hand, and not a few beauties and traits of detail, together with that peculiar hue which is derived from the language in which they are expressed' (p. 398). He goes into considerable detail to identify what he considers 'Byronic' in Pushkin's manner before he embarks on a survey of the poet's work. Beginning with the early lyric poems, he discusses *Ruslan i Liudmila* and, no longer regretting that Pushkin had moved on to a different form of composition, reviews the southern poems, where he finds plot cedes to 'the workings of the feelings alone, and the emotions of the human heart' (p. 404). Out of sequence, he had earlier mentioned *Evgenii Onegin* as demonstrating Pushkin once again as 'an emulous follower of Byron' but 'a satiric narrative [...] unquestionably very inferior' to both *Beppo* and *Don Juan* (pp. 400-1), but then prefers to say no more about a 'still incomplete' production, before turning to *Poltava*. This is a poem he inevitably also views in a Byronic context, but he is largely impressed by evidence of Pushkin's growing maturity as a poet, his 'greater vivacity and variety of colouring, more graphic force and richness'. Nevertheless,

Leeds's final judgment seems strangely misplaced, for while reiterating his call for 'something for enduring fame', he warns that Pushkin's place might otherwise be 'among the *poetae minores* of his country' (p. 416). The running title of the review is 'Pushkin and Rilaeev' and Leeds devotes the final two pages to a tribute to a poet 'who, like Pushkin, may be considered as belonging to the Byron school, and who, if he had not been prematurely cut off, there is every reason to suppose would have proved himself no mean rival to him' (pp. 416-7) and translates a passage from Ryleev's *Voinarovskii*.[32]

In 1839 there appeared the last of Leeds's major reviews for the *Foreign Quarterly Review*, a very detailed account of Ksenofont Polevoi's *Mikhail Vasil'evich Lomonosov* (1836), an example of *biographie romancée* he clearly would have preferred as straight biography (*FQR*, XXIII, pp. 316-39). His penultimate contribution to the *Foreign Quarterly Review* came 4 years later in 1843, and was an interesting table of 18th- and 19th-century Russian literature by date of death of authors from Kantemir (1744) to Kachenovskii (1842), followed by an alphabetical listing of living authors (*FQR*, XXX, pp. 242-50). By authors, he understood not only poets, dramatists and prose writers but also practitioners in the other arts, and therefore there are noted architects such as Starov and Bazhenov, painters such as Losenko and Alekseev, sculptors such as Kozlovskii and Martos, and musicians such as Berezovskii and Bortnianskii. In his introduction he declared, and not without reason and no little vanity, that the *Foreign Quarterly Review* had 'done more than any other publication, in communicating intelligence relative to Russian Literature and Art'. He suggested that the table was also partly an index to the articles that had earlier appeared in the *Foreign Quarterly Review* and that it also showed that 'there are other names besides those of Lomonosov and Sumarokov, Karamzin and Pushkin, who claim notice in biographical works'.

Some years earlier, he had already made a strong case for Krylov in a detailed two-part analysis with numerous translations of fables that appeared in *Fraser's Magazine* in 1839 and 1842.[33] Here, as in many of his reviews, he went consciously and happily beyond the confines of his original brief, mocking in the opening pages of the second part the inadequacies of the recently published *History of Russian Literature, with a Lexicon of Authors*

---

32 Leeds did not forget Ryleev. See his praise in 1836 for Ryleev's *Dumy* (*FQR*, XVI, p. 446).

33 'Russian Fabulists, with Specimens', *Fraser's Magazine for Town and Country*, XIX (February 1839), pp. 153-63; XXV (February 1842), pp. 237-50. On Leeds's treatment of Krylov, see my 'The British and Krylov', pp. 96-8.

(Oxford, 1839, translated by George Cox from the German of Friedrich Otto), emphasizing how out-of-date it was and pointing to his own work and other reliable works of reference.[34] He made specific reference to the *Entsiklopedicheskii leksikon*, 'fourteen very thick and closely printed octavo volumes' already published but only the third letter of the alphabet reached. It was these volumes, together with the first volume of the *Slovar' russkikh svetskikh pisatelei* (*Dictionary of Russian Secular Authors*), that were the point of departure for a provocative article on 'Russian Literary Biography' in the *Westminster Review* in 1841 (the opening lines of which were quoted to begin this paper). Regretting that the works under review have not yet reached 'the more interesting and important names in Russian literary biography', he himself supplied 'a chronological list of some of the principal literary figures etc who have died in the last twenty-five years', which looks directly to his 'Table' of Russian literature appearing in the *Foreign Quarterly Review* the following year.

The article in the *Westminster Review* commands interest for any number of reasons. One is the obviously heartfelt complaint about the difficulties of obtaining Russian books, for 'no Russian works are imported by any of the foreign booksellers', and the attack on the British Museum, which is 'so very scantily provided with Russian books, as to afford scarcely any assistance whatever', adding in a footnote that the absence of a classified catalogue makes it virtually impossible to locate what foreign books it has anyway. Another is yet another contribution to his ongoing engagement with Pushkin, here said to 'have transformed himself into a Russian version of Byron, with some admixture of Goethe, and the novelty of the shape thus assumed procured for him, with his countrymen, the credit of originality'. Once again he voices the regret that there was not more 'substance and stamina' in the poetry, while continuing his dismissal of the prose works as 'poor and meagre in themselves, and in a puerile and extravagant taste, abounding with the worst faults of the German school, out-Germanized' (*WR*, XXVI, pp. 40-1). His critique of Pushkin pales, however, before his astonishing attack on Gogol, provoked by his reading of the very positive appraisal provided by Heinrich König in his *Literarische Bilder aus Russland* (1837).[35] The previous year, Leeds had spoken warmly of Gogol's essay 'Ob arkhitekture' from his collection *Arabeski* (*Arabesques*) (*FQR*, XXIV, 311-2),

34 *Ibid.*, XXV, pp. 237-40.

35 König was essentially conveying the opinions of N.A. Mel'gunov, a professor at Moscow University, who was very pro-Pushkin and Gogol and very anti-Bulgarin and Grech,

but here he launched into a scathing demolition of various stories from *Mirgorod* and ended with a rejection of 'such writers as Gogol and Co., who dive down to celebrity, by writing down to the level of the lowest capacity and the lowest taste, and whose seeming strength is no better than feebleness in hysterics, whose liveliness is that of St Vitus's dance' (*WR*, XXVI, pp. 42-4, 47-8).

Concurrent with these journalistic activities at the end of the 1830s Leeds had been contributing entries to the *Penny Cyclopaedia*, produced by the Society for the Diffusion of Useful Knowledge over the years 1833-43. It was a project close to his heart and he took the opportunity to insert up-to-date biographies, based on the latest Russian dictionaries and encyclopedias, of some twelve writers from Kantemir to Pushkin and of the architect Voronikhin, as well as his final long essay on Russian literature that named many more.[36] His hitherto unremarked essay on Pushkin, appearing in 1841, was his final appreciation of 'certainly the most distinguished poet of Russia in the present century'. He refers readers to what he had said in his earlier reviews about the long poems, but is much more positive in his overall appraisal of the poetry, while remaining dismissive about 'a few tales and essays'.[37]

Merely on the basis of his acquaintance with his writings on Pushkin in the *Foreign Quarterly Review*, Gleb Struve suggested that Leeds's article on *Poltava*, while not of the quality of the much more widely acknowledged Thomas Shaw's articles and translations that began to appear in *Blackwood's Magazine* in 1845,[38] was 'for its time amazingly comprehensive and understanding'.[39] He finished with the hope that 'more will be found out about this pioneer of Russian studies in England, who seems to me to be, in some ways, more interesting than Bowring'. Indeed, he is. While it is understandable that 'Leeds on Pushkin' has been the centre of attention,

---

which also did not endear him to Leeds. On König/Mel'gunov, see R. Iu. Danilevskii, *'Molodaia Germaniia' i russkaia literatura* (Leningrad, 1969), pp. 138-44.

36 *Penny Cyclopaedia*, V (1836), pp. 51-2 (Bogdanovich); VIII (1837), p. 430 (Derzhavin); IX, p. 42 (Dmitriev); XIII (1839), pp. 177 (Kantemir), 178 (Karamzin), 207 (Khemnitser and Kheraskov); XV, p. 109 (Lomonosov); XIX (1841), pp. 136-7 (Pushkin); XXII (1842), pp. 105-15 (Russian language and literature); XXIII, pp. 268-9 (Sumarokov); XXVI (1843), pp. 391-2 (Fonvizin), 430 (Volkov), 453 (Voronikhin).

37 *Ibid.*, XIX, p. 137.

38 On Shaw, see L.M. Arinshtein, 'Tomas Shou—angliiskii perevodchik Pushkina', in A.S. Bushmin *et al.* (eds.), *Sravnitel'noe izuchenie literatur* (Leningrad, 1976), pp. 117-24; Patrick Waddington, 'Shaw, Thomas Budge', *Oxford Dictionary of National Biography*, L (Oxford, 2004), pp. 127-8.

39 Struve, 'Puskin in Early English Criticism', p. 314.

it represents only a part, and a very small part, of his total 'Russian' output over the 18 years it has been possible to trace his work (1828-46). Leeds was a dedicated chronicler of contemporary Russian literature, providing information about publications and authors that is remarkably comprehensive. Despite the difficulties in obtaining books, he was very much up-to-date and increasingly relied on direct information from Russian sources rather than via German or French reviews. Over the years there is a distinct maturing and growing self-confidence in his writing and judgments about Russian literature, accompanied by his sense that he was witnessing its coming of age and the emergence of a new generation of authors. He undoubtedly had his blind spots, his strange prejudices, and likes and dislikes that frequently run counter to modern tastes and judgments. He perhaps suffered by championing such as Bulgarin and not being fulsome enough in his praise of Pushkin and nonplussed by Gogol. Nevertheless, it is to be regretted that what he achieved did not penetrate more deeply into the consciousness of the British reading public, but his anonymity, his contributions to so many different journals and the absence of good translations (other than his own!) in book (or any) form of almost all of the authors he discussed did not help his cause in the years up to the Crimean War. In a letter to John Murray in 1844 he had suggested that a useful volume could be made out of his scattered and various articles on architecture, but nothing of this nature ever appeared. There is, however, a strong case to be made for the publication of Leeds's articles on Russian literature with the aim of establishing his significance as the first major English critic of Russian literature.

4. Russian Icons Through British Eyes, *c.* 1830-1930

Richard Marks

The plot of Nikolai Leskov's famous short story, *Zapechatlennyi angel* (*The Sealed Angel*), centres on an icon of a Guardian Angel, painted in the 16th century by the Stroganov school and the most venerated of a large number of icons in the possession of a group of priestless Old Believers employed to build a bridge under the direction of an Englishman, James Jameson. In this tale Jameson and his wife develop a sympathetic interest in ancient icon-painting. Leskov first published *The Sealed Angel* in the January 1873 issue of the *Russian Messenger*.[1] Later the same year, *An Art Tour to Northern Capitals of Europe* by Joseph Beavington Atkinson appeared. Atkinson was an art critic who *inter alia* wrote two books on English painters. His attitude to the religious art in general, and icons in particular, which he encountered in Russia oscillated between the unsympathetic and the downright hostile. This is a sample:

> Here in the cathedrals of the Kremlin [...] I observed, what I had long noted in Munich, that the modern art, which aims to be true in its drawing and grammatical in its construction, has much less spell over the multitude than the so-called miraculous pictures, though coarse and common as sign-boards. One of such works, the Holy Virgin of Vladimir, said, of course, to have been painted by St. Luke, and now absolutely black, and with features obliterated, receives, as one of the most ancient images in Russia, countless kisses and genuflexions. Here is an instance where Mr. Ruskin's 'lamp of

I am indebted to Tony Cross for his very helpful comments on this text. Also to Wendy Salmond who kindly read a draft and provided some valuable corrections.

1 Nikolai Leskov, *The Sealed Angel and Other Stories*, ed. and trans. K.A Lantz (Knoxville, TN, 1984), pp. 5-72.

sacrifice'—a precept fine in humanity but false in art—is made to burn most brightly [...] No reasonable being will contend that this is art: nothing further need be said, for this one example represents the whole.[2]

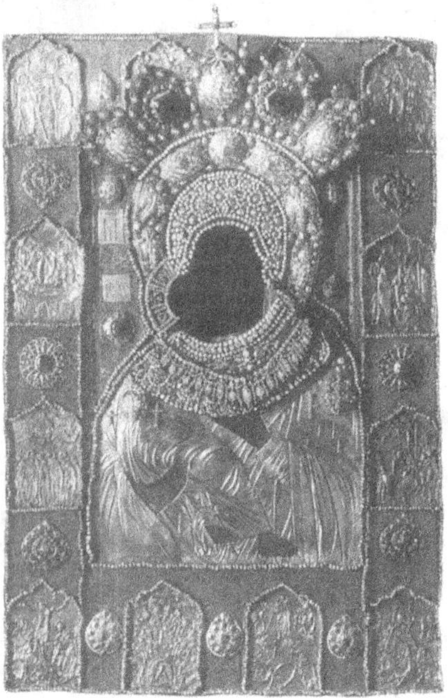

Fig. 4.1 *Mother of God of Vladimir* icon (before 1918). Kremlin Museums.

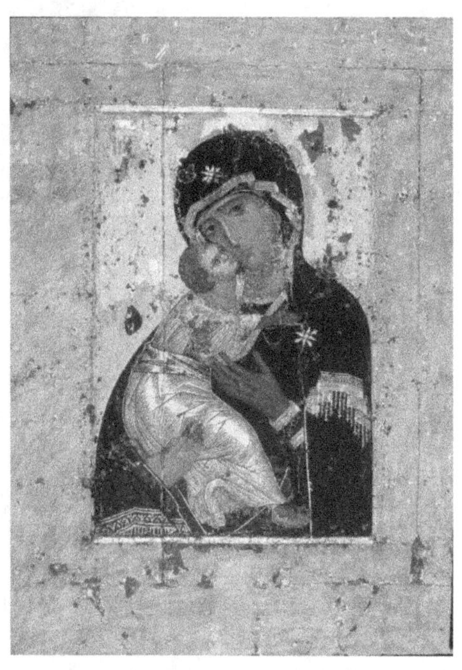

Fig. 4.2 *Mother of God of Vladimir* icon, after cleaning and removal of *oklad*. Tretyakov Gallery.

Here we have utterly divergent assessments of British attitudes to Russian icons in Victorian times expressed simultaneously by a Russian novelist and an English critic. Which of them most accurately reflects British perceptions of these objects at the time? 1873 marks almost the halfway point in the period this paper covers—the 100 years between *c.*1830 and 1930. The rationale behind this date-span is that it post-dates the Enlightenment, which in respect of western responses to Russian icons—and Orthodoxy as a culture—has attracted scholarly attention;[3] the *terminus ante* is the exhibition of Russian icons held at the Victoria and Albert Museum at the end of 1929 and the book on the subject published

2 John Beavington Atkinson, *An Art Tour to Northern Capitals of Europe* (London, 1873), pp. 243-4.

3 Larry Wolff, *The Enlightenment and the Orthodox World* (Athens, 2001).

soon afterwards under the title *Masterpieces of Russian Painting*. Together they mark a seminal moment in British experience of icon-painting.[4] (Figs. 5, 6) To cover a century invites generalisation, and it is impossible to do more than open up the subject to further and more detailed research.

Until the end of the period under consideration, to all intents and purposes Russian icons could only be experienced in Russia. A rare instance of an icon being brought to England is the 18th-century St Nicholas icon presented in 1834 to Christ Church College Oxford by William Fox-Strangways, later 4th Earl of Ilchester, a noted collector of early Italian paintings who had served as an attaché at the British Embassy in St Petersburg.[5]

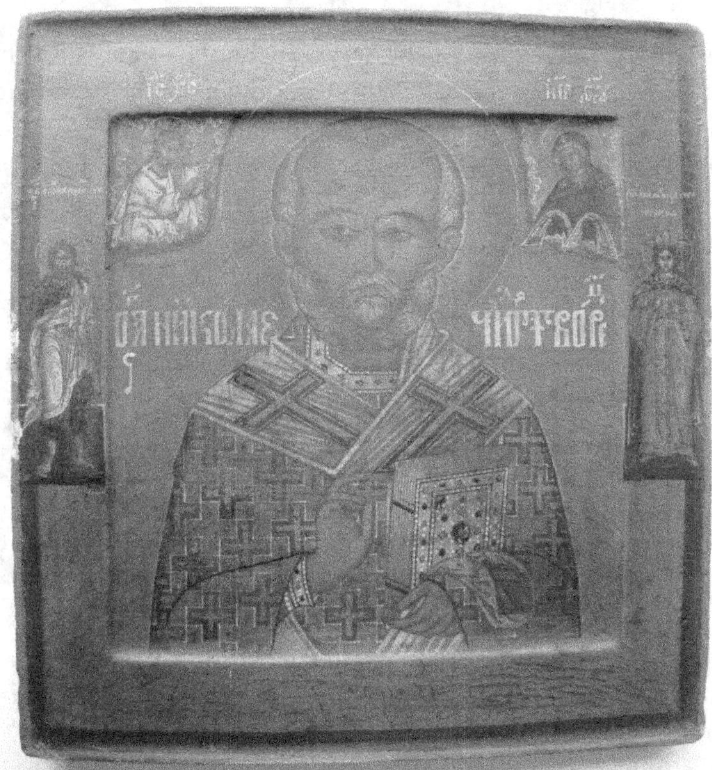

Fig. 4.3 St Nicholas icon (18th century), Christ Church College, Oxford.

---

4 Russian Ikon Exhibition (Victoria & Albert Museum, 18 November-14 December 1929); *Ancient Russian Icons* (Victoria & Albert Museum Exhibition Catalogue, 1929); Michael Farbman (ed.), *Masterpieces of Russian Painting* (London, 1930).

5 I am indebted to Dr Georgi Parpulov for bringing this icon to my attention.

Those who travelled in Russia and left records of their impressions were for the most part drawn from the upper strata of society: diplomats and aristocrats like Fox-Strangways, gentry, clergy and army and naval officers. Into the last category falls Captain C. Colville Frankland RN, who visited Russia in 1830-1. His comments on the icon of the *Mother of God of Vladimir* in Moscow are very similar to those of Beavington Atkinson forty years later:

> This cathedral boasts of a Virgin... painted by St Luke [...] This black ill-looking idol is decorated with a superb solitaire, valued at 80,000 roubles: the frame containing her ladyship's portrait is estimated at 200,000 more. Money badly spent, thought I. There are so many holy pictures of Saints, Martyrs, etc. here, miraculous as well as ludicrous, that I cannot attempt to name them.[6] (Fig. 4.1)

Much the same tone is evident in the observations of Edward Pett Thompson, who travelled in Russia in 1848. Whilst acknowledging the splendour of the iconostasis in the Dormition Cathedral in the Kremlin, his description of the *Mother of God of Vladimir* icon was followed by this dismissive remark:

> The number of these miraculous pictures in Russia is quite inconceivable, and the readiest faith is bestowed on them although the priests, like their heathen brethren of old, themselves prepare the fraud, to which it is impossible that they can be dupes [...].[7]

Thompson had aesthetic as well as religious objections to the visual manifestations of the Orthodox faith:

> [...] the Greek church prostrates itself before pictures which are a libel on humanity, and much more on a saint. I can imagine fanaticism bowing before the sublime conception of a Thorwaldsen, or worshipping the representations of a Murillo or a Raphael, but I cannot conceive the genuineness of even mistaken devotion when its objects are either a caricature or a burlesque [...].[8]

The skepticism evinced by Frankland and Thompson was consonant with the critical stance taken by western observers of the Enlightenment and even earlier, notably Giles Fletcher (1591) and Samuel Collins (1671)—the latter describing Russian icons as 'very pitiful painting, flat and ugly, after

6 Captain C. Colville Frankland, *Narrative of a Visit to the Courts of Russia and Sweden in the Years 1830 and 1831*, II (London, 1832); extract published in *Moscow. A Travellers' Companion*, selected and intro. by Laurence Kelly (London, 1983), p. 121.

7 Edward Pett Thompson, *Life in Russia: or, The Discipline of Despotism* (London, 1848), p. 272.

8 *Ibid.*, p. 273.

the Greek manner'.[9] Collins's dismissive remarks about the quality and nature of Russian painting were echoed a century later by the Rev. John Glen King, who served as Chaplain to the British Factory in St Petersburg, in his *The Rites and Ceremonies of the Greek Church in Russia*:

> It might be expected that valuable paintings should also make a part of the riches of a church, in which religious pictures are not only an indispensable ornament, but are necessary in its worship [...] but though the number of these pictures is so great, and though religion was the cause which called forth such excellency and perfection in painting and sculpture in popish countries [...] yet the same cause has not been so lucky as to produce one good painter or one capital picture in Russia: on the contrary these are the most wretched dawbings that can be conceived, some of them notwithstanding are said to be the work of angels.[10]

The aesthetic sensibilities of King were framed by the conventions of contemporary taste, expressed within an Anglican theological context, as the book's dedication (to George III) makes clear: 'One reflection of great moment [...] arises from the similarity between the burthensome ceremonies of the Greek and the Romish church [...] whence every protestant may learn to set a just value on that reformation which is established in his own'.[11]

Whether clerical or lay, those British commentators who made observations on the quality of Russian icon-painting were (like Collins and King) nurtured within a Protestant ideology opposed to imagery and devotional gestures associated with it. Even in the case of Beavington Atkinson, who was writing from the point of view of an art critic, his strictures were as much religious as aesthetic.

Such attitudes were not confined to Russia. As in the Enlightenment, the antipathy towards the visual manifestations of Russian religious practices and beliefs applied to Eastern Christianity as a whole. The discourse was that of a superior faith which deemed the culture of Orthodoxy in its various manifestations to be ignorant and idolatrous and hence belonging to the world of the Other.[12] Here, for example, is the dismissive comment of the Rev. John Hartley, who travelled in the newly independent Greek state and

---

9 Samuel Collins, *A Survey of the Present State of Russia* and Giles Fletcher, *Of the Russe Common Wealth*, in Marshall Poe (ed.), *Early Exploration of Russia*, I (London, 2003), p. 88 (see also pp. 410, 411, 421-2).

10 John Glen King, *The Rites and Ceremonies of the Greek Church, in Russia* (London, 1772), p. 33.

11 *Ibid.* (dedication page); for British taste in this period, see Francis Haskell, *Rediscoveries in Art: Some Aspects of Taste, Fashion and Collecting in England and France* (London, 1976).

12 Wolff, *Enlightenment;* Robin Cormack, '"A Gentleman's Book": Attitudes of Robert Curzon', in Robin Cormack and Elizabeth Jeffreys (eds.), *Through the Looking Glass.*

the Ottoman Empire for the Church Missionary Society in 1826 and 1828: 'These objects of religious regard [i.e. icons] are, invariably, most wretched performances, destitute of all taste and beauty'.[13] The archaeologist/explorer Austen Henry Layard, although well-disposed to the Nestorian Christians he encountered in present-day Iraq, took the same line as Hartley when it came to their religious images: '[...] the hideous pictures, and monstrous deformities which encumber the churches of Mosul'.[14]

Not everyone though, even in the early 19th century, danced to this negative tune. The Rev. Robert Pinkerton, who visited Eastern Europe and Russia on behalf of the British and Foreign Bible Society, published in 1814 a description of Russian churches, their frescoes, iconostases and principal icons which was largely free from value-judgments, apart from a passing comment that they were 'overloaded with decorations'—and a social distinction. At the end of a lengthy exposition by Metropolitan Platon on Orthodox theology, which comprises the major part of the book, Pinkerton comments that the illiterate peasants were unable to comprehend the dogma on icon veneration, '[...] observing the idolatrous ideas which thousands of them actually entertain about the pictures and powers of departed saints'.[15] Robert Curzon, later 14th Baron Zouche, who travelled extensively through the Ottoman Empire during the 1830s, while asserting that Byzantine and Coptic art lacked the 'purity and angelic expression so much to be admired in the works of Beato Angelico, Giovanni Bellini, and other early Italian masters', also acknowledged that 'the earlier Greek artists in their conceptions of the personages of Holy Writ sometimes approached the sublime'.[16]

From the middle of the century a positive attitude becomes more widespread, a by-product of the emergence of the ritualist movement within the Church of England. In 1850 John Mason Neale, one of the founders of the Cambridge Camden Society and a High Churchman, published *A History of the Holy Eastern Church*; although only a brief section is devoted to a description of an iconostasis, the tone throughout is anything but hostile.[17]

Byzantium through British Eyes (Papers from the 29th Spring Symposium of Byzantine Studies, London, March 1995) (Aldershot, 2000), pp. 147-59.

13 John Hartley, *Researches in Greece and the Levant* (2nd edn London, 1833), p. 55.

14 Austen Henry Layard, *A Popular Account of Discoveries at Nineveh* (London, 1851), p. 143.

15 Robert Pinkerton, *The Present State of the Greek Church in Russia* (Edinburgh, 1814), pp. 22, 231.

16 Robert Curzon, *Visits to Monasteries in the Levant* (London, 1849), pp. 299-300. For Curzon, see also Ian Fraser, *The Heir of Parham: Robert Curzon 14th Baron Zouche* (Harleston, 1986).

17 John Mason Neale, *A History of the Holy Eastern Church* (London, 1850), pp. 191-202.

Just over a decade later appeared *Lectures on the Eastern Church*; its author, Arthur Penrhyn Stanley, Dean of Westminster, was less of a ritualist than Neale but shared his interest in Orthodoxy. Like Neale, his work spanned the Orthodox world, but he had observed the Russian church at first-hand during a stay in Moscow. Prefacing his remarks with a Russian proverb he saw displayed at a residence of Metropolitan Platon ('Let not him who comes in here carry out the dirt that he finds within') did not inhibit Stanley from indulging in ethnic superiority when it came to defining the nature of Russian Orthodox religious practice: '[...] the great Empire of which we are speaking, if it has not been civilised, has unquestionably been kept alive, by its religious spirit'.

Notwithstanding this exercise in Otherness, Stanley invokes neither superstition nor idolatry in his account. He observes that icons are at the core of the Russian faith and sees them as didactic as well as sacred: '[...] a passion for pictures, not as works of art but as emblems, as lessons, as instructions, is thus engendered and multiplied in common life beyond all example elsewhere'. He also underlines the place of miracle-working icons like the *Mother of God of Vladimir* in Russian history and identity: 'And when we remember that some of these pictures have beside their interest as the emblems of truth to a barbarian and child-like people, acquired the historical associations involved in the part they have taken in great national events, it is not surprising that the combination of religious and patriotic feelings [...] should have raised their veneration to a pitch to us almost inconceivable'.[18] This more enlightened approach is evident in the second edition of Curzon's *Visits to Monasteries in the Levant*, published in 1865. By then he had read Alphonse Didron's translation of the *Painter's Manual* by Dionysios of Fourna; the result was the inclusion of a passage in the Introduction which showed greater familiarity with the conventions governing Orthodox iconography. Curzon understood the devotional rather than the purely aesthetic appeal of (Greek) Orthodox images:

> They are all painted in the stiff conventional manner which tradition has handed down from remote antiquity. No one who has had the opportunity of improving his good taste by a careful study of these ancient works of art can fail to appreciate and reverence that high and noble spirit which animated the pencils of those saintly painters, and irradiates the composition of their sublime conceptions with a dignity and grandeur which is altogether

18 Arthur Penrhyn Stanley, *Lectures on the History of the Eastern Church* (London and Oxford, 1861), pp. viii, 341, 362, 365.

wanting in the beautiful pictures of Rubens, Titian, Guido, Domenichino, and other great artists of more mundane schools.[19]

Most of the British commentators discussed so far were men of the cloth and their books were primarily intended for a pious readership, hence the interest in icons as religious artefacts. Already, however, by the middle of the 19th century the taste for foreign travel had given rise to the expansion of the guidebook genre aimed at a wider public. The most enduring and prominent of these was the series of red handbooks produced by the publishing house of John Murray (whose imprint included *Visits to Monasteries in the Levant*)—the authors of which were almost entirely drawn from outside the ranks of the clergy.[20] The firm published a handbook for Russia as early as 1839, edited by Thomas Denman Whatley and with information on Russia supplied by Layard, who had visited the country in the previous year. In 1848 the first edition of the *Handbook for Northern Europe* appeared, under the editorship of Captain W. Jesse. The Russian section was largely confined to St Petersburg, Moscow and their environs, but as communications improved with the construction of railways, in subsequent editions more places became accessible and were included (although the focus remained on the two main cities).

As with the entire series, the *Handbook for Northern Europe* has a factual description of the principal historical, architectural and artistic attractions. Icons are rarely specifically listed, except for those on the iconostases of the most important churches and those deemed to be miracle-working, including of course the *Mother of God of Vladimir* with its 'dark, almost black' face.[21] (Fig. 4.1) Several expanded, revised and up-dated editions were published from 1865 onwards, all by Thomas Michell, FRGS, an attaché at the British Embassy in St Petersburg. The later versions incorporated material provided by others, but as Michell points out in the 1868 edition, it was 'the result of personal travel and observation during a residence of many years in Russia'.[22] As with all of the series, the later editions are more impersonal, with the eschewing of negative value-judgments found in the earlier volumes, such as the characterization of the frescoes in the principal

19 Robert Curzon, *Visits to Monasteries in the Levant* (2nd edn, London, 1865), p. 34; see also Cormack, '"A Gentleman's Book"', p. 158.

20 I am indebted to Tony Cross for information on the early Murray's handbooks to Russia. For the series in a wider context see John Vaughan, *The English Guide Book c.1780-1870* (Newton Abbot, 1974), esp. Chapter 2.

21 *Handbook for Northern Europe*, II (new edn, London, 1849), p. 544.

22 *Handbook for Travellers in Russia, Poland and Finland* (2nd revised edn, London, 1868), p. vi.

church of the Donskoi monastery as 'miserable productions'.[23] They are often more detailed, as in the case of the description of the *Mother of God of Vladimir* icon, where the reference to the opaque face is replaced by a brief account of its origins in Constantinople and subsequent history in Russia. Observation in conjunction with familiarity with Russia's historical treasures is exactly what the *Handbooks* comprise. Although they rarely attract scholarly attention, their significance in disseminating information on a little-known country in an easily digestible form should not be overlooked; for long they were a *sine qua non* for British travellers.

Notwithstanding the *Handbooks*, there is little evidence that Russian icons, any more than Byzantine or post-Byzantine ones, made any impact on Victorian Britain. The Rev. William Sparrow Simpson, an antiquary and historian of Old St Paul's Cathedral, published two articles in the *Journal of the British Archaeological Association* for 1867 and 1869. They were not, however, concerned with painted icons but with what he labelled 'Russo-Greek portable icons of brass', in other words the small cast-metal icons which were made in vast quantities during the 18th and 19th centuries, especially by Old Believer communities.[24]

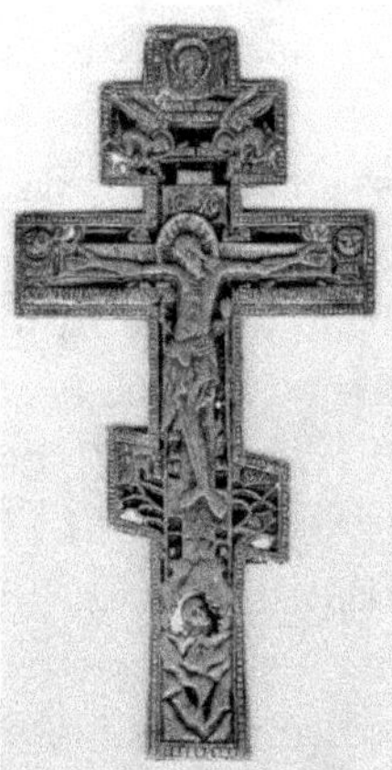

Fig. 4.4 Cast-metal and enamel Old Believer cross (19th century). Private collection

23 *Handbook for Northern Europe*, II (new edn, London, 1849), p. 557; Vaughan, *English Guide Book*, p. 47.

24 W. Sparrow Simpson, 'Russo-Greek Portable Icons of Brass', *Journal of the British Archaeological Association*, XXII (1867), pp. 113-23, *idem*, XXV (1869), pp. 179-85. For these artefacts see *Neizvestnaia Rossiia. K 300-letiiu Vygovskoi staroobriadtsesskoi pustyni* (State Historical Museum exhibition catalogue, Moscow, 1994), pp. 37-58; Richard Eighme Ahlborn and Vera Beaver-Bricken Espinola (eds.), *Russian Copper Icons and Crosses from the Kunz Collection: Castings of Faith* (Smithsonian Studies in History and Technology, LI, 1991).

Sparrow Simpson's interest in these artefacts came about as a result of the Crimean War, when a number of them found their way to England, either taken from the bodies of dead Russian soldiers by their British counterparts or from prisoners of war held in Lewes gaol. Although fifty years previously the Rev. Pinkerton had noted that the Vyg Old Believer community was a centre for the production of cast-metal icons, and although they had been mentioned in the *Gentleman's Magazine* for 1802, Sparrow Simpson's articles (as far as I am aware) were the most detailed studies of Russian icons to appear in England to date.[25] They consist principally of catalogue entries for 29 examples mainly in his possession plus a few in other British collections, compiled with the assistance of a member of the staff of the Russian Embassy.

The other late 19th-century British publication which covered the pre-Petrine period was also principally concerned with metalwork, but not cast icons. This is *Russian Art and Art Objects in Russia*, one of the South Kensington Museum Handbooks, written by Alfred Maskell and published in 1884. As the Introduction observes, 'In the whole range of catalogues and handbooks published in English treating of the arts of all countries and of all periods, the mention made of Russian might perhaps be summed up in a score of pages'.[26] The book is primarily a guide to the collection of reproductions of goldsmiths' work and jewelled ornaments in the South Kensington Museum, but also provides a very well-informed, factual chronological survey of Russian art from pre-history onwards, including icons and their function as devotional objects. There is a detailed account of the interiors of the Dormition and St Michael cathedrals in the Moscow Kremlin; the emphasis is less on the icons as paintings but on their gold and silver covers, which Maskell and until quite recently, many others, considered to be a comparatively recent development.[27]

Inevitably Maskell's reference points were Italian Renaissance painters, but like Curzon he understood the conventions which governed icon-painting: 'As a rule, the conception of ideas was diametrically opposed to the sentiment of the Italian School, nor was there any room for the genius of a Raphael. His beautiful faces would have amounted to little short of rank heresy'. He was also aware that distinctive styles of icon-painting

---

25 Pinkerton, *Present State*, p. 331.

26 Alfred Maskell, *Russian Art and Art Objects in Russia* (South Kensington Museum Handbook, London, 1884), p. 2.

27 *Ibid.*, p. 159.

were associated with Moscow, Novgorod and the Stroganov family and was even familiar with the work of Semen Ushakov.[28] Although in general he was not impressed by the kind of painting practised in the 16th and 17th centuries, he allowed that there were exceptional icons of the Mother of God, 'full of tender grace and beauty', and recognized that in subject-matter Russia did not slavishly follow Byzantine iconography; he even praised the quality of contemporary icons for sale at the Trinity-Sergei monastery.[29]

What begins to emerge in the observations of Curzon, Maskell and even the Murray's *Handbooks* is the treatment of icons not merely as works of Orthodox devotion but as art objects, even if Beavington Atkinson rejected them as such. A highly pertinent factor is that only from the middle of the century, and as a by-product of the Slavophile movemement, was there a burgeoning of interest within Russia itself in the preservation and study of ancient church art in general and icons (Byzantine as well as Russian) in particular. In 1846 the Russian Archaeological Society was founded, followed in 1859 by the establishment under Alexander II of the Imperial Archaeological Commission, in 1863 by the Society of Lovers of Religious Education and a year later by the Society of Early Russian Art in Moscow. A key moment was the founding in 1895 of the State Russian Museum in St Petersburg, which in the following decades amassed large and important holdings of icons, a process which accelerated after 1917. These came not only from churches but also from private collectors, above all the scholar Nikolai Likhachev; in Moscow Pavel Tret'iakov, like other wealthy Old Believers, also had icons amongst his enormous art acquisitions. Outside St Petersburg and Moscow local archaeological societies were formed and regional museums established.[30]

Apart from their being largely unknown and inaccessible, a major obstacle to the study and appreciation of ancient icons which undoubtedly

28 *Ibid.*, pp. 169, 203.

29 *Ibid.*, pp. 167-9, 187.

30 The literature on this subject is immense. See for example, Olga Etinhof, 'Pyotr Ivanovich Sevastianov and his activity in collecting Byzantine objects in Russia', in Cormack and Jeffreys, *Byzantium Through British Eyes*, pp. 211-20; *idem*, *Vizantiiskie ikony VI—pervoi poloviny XIII veka v Rossii* (Moscow, 2005); Gerold Ivanovich Vzdornov, *Istoriia otkrytiia i izucheniia russkoi srednevekovoi zhivopisi: XIX vek* (Moscow, 1986); *idem*, *Restavratsiia i nauka: ocherki po istorii otkrytiia i izucheniia drevnerusskoi zhivopisi* (Moscow, 2006), esp. pp. 11-56; Kari Kotkavaara, *Progeny of the Icon: Émigré Russian Revivalism and the Vicissitudes of the Eastern Orthodox Sacred Image* (Åbo, 1999), pp. 124-96; Aleksandr Evgenevich Musin, *Vopiiushie Kamni* (St Petersburg, 2006), esp. Chapter 2; Liudmila Likhacheva, 'The Medieval Collection of the State Russian Museum', in Roderick Grieson (ed.), *Gates of Mystery. The Art of Holy Russia* (exhibition catalogue, Victoria & Albert Museum, 1992), pp. 309-13.

coloured British attitudes was their condition. Either the painted surfaces were largely hidden by the *oklads, rizas* and other embellishments or, as Captain Frankland and Beavington Atkinson noted, they had become opaque as their linseed oil varnish darkened, or were concealed beneath later layers of painting. From the middle of the 19th century new methods evolved for cleaning and removing repainted layers to reveal the original.[31] To what extent British observers were aware of these developments is uncertain, as nothing to match Maskell's book was published in English until 1916—and that was in a general survey of Russian arts by Rosa Newmarch, a feminist, poet and specialist on music. This, like *The Soul of Russia,* edited by Winifred Stephens, which appeared in the same year and was sold in aid of the Fund for Russian Refugees, was no doubt prompted by Russia's role as an ally of Great Britain in World War I, an event which had a dramatic impact on the historiography of the Russian icon.[32] Although both publications had something to say about icons, the subject was scarcely treated as mainstream.

The October Revolution in the following year was to prove a landmark in the history of Russian icon-painting. Both the old regime and the Orthodox Church were accused by the new Soviet government of neglecting (and misusing) its artistic treasures and from the outset church buildings, together with their valuable and historic contents, were subject to nationalisation. A decree was issued on the Recording and Protection of Ancient Church Monuments and the Commission for the Preservation and Identification of Monuments of Ancient Russian Painting (Narkompros) was established; similar provincial and district commissions followed. Led by the painter, museum director, art critic and historian Igor' Grabar', the Commission embarked on a series of expeditions to churches and monasteries, in the course of which many major new discoveries were made.[33]

Prior to the Bolshevik Revolution very few, if any, of the most important early icons, especially those like the *Mother of God of Vladimir* deemed to be miraculous, had been touched. In Soviet ideology, they were now liberated

31 Vzdornov, *Istoriia otkrytiia; idem, Restavratsiia i nauka;* Evgenii Nikolaevich Trubetskoi, *Icons: Theology and Color* (1917; Crestwood, NY, 1973), pp. 41-3, 93-4; Olga Lelekova, 'Icon Restoration and Research in Russia', in *The Art of Holy Russia: Icons from Moscow 1400-1660* (Royal Academy of Arts exhibition catalogue, London, 1998), pp. 87-92 (esp. p. 87).

32 Rosa Newmarch, *Russian Arts* (London, 1916); Winifred Stephens (ed.), *The Soul of Russia* (London, 1916), pp. 65-8. For Newmarch, see Philip Ross Bullock, *Rosa Newmarch and Russian Music in Late Nineteenth and Early Twentieth-Century England* (Farnham, 2009).

33 Vzdornov, *Restavratsiia i nauka*, pp. 57-88; for Grabar' see *ibid.*, pp. 307-26; Kotkavaara, *Progeny,* pp. 157-8; Lelekova, 'Icon Restoration', pp. 88-90.

and treated as monuments of Russian artistic achievement. A major cleaning campaign was undertaken by the Commission's team of restorers, led by the icon-painter Grigorii Chirikov; in 1924 the Commission became the Central State Restoration Workshops. The policy was not merely to remove accretions of dirt, but also successive layers of painting in order to expose the original. The result was the revelation of numerous hitherto unknown masterpieces, above all perhaps the famous *Trinity* icon by Andrei Rublev and the *Mother of God of Vladimir*, the latter shown to be Byzantine in origin and of the 12th century.[34] (Figs. 4.1, 4.2) Both were star attractions in the exhibition Methods of Restoring and Preserving Monuments of Early Russian Art, Architecture and Fine Arts held in Moscow in 1920. This was followed 6 years later by another Moscow exhibition, at the State Historical Museum, on Early Russian Icon-Painting.[35]

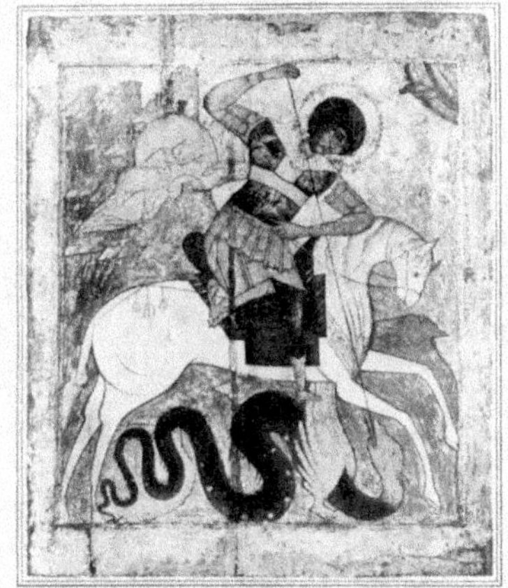

Fig. 4.5 Russian Ikon Exhibition poster, Victoria & Albert Museum (1929).

34 Vzdornov, *Restavratsiia i nauka*, pp. 89-136 and on Chirikov, pp. 161-76; Lelekova, 'Icon Restoration', pp. 88-90; Lindsey Hughes, 'Inventing Andrei: Soviet and Post-Soviet Views of Andrei Rublev and his Trinity Icon', *Slavonica*, IX (2003), pp. 83-90 (esp. p. 85); Aleksandr Ivanovich Anisimov, *Our Lady of Vladimir* (Prague, 1928).

35 For a review of the 1920 exhibition, see N. Levinson, 'The Restoration of Old Russian Paintings', *The Slavonic Review*, III (1924-5), pp. 350-5 (this article was first published in Russian in *Russkoe Iskusstvo* in 1923).

These exhibitions, plus growing awareness in western European circles of the work of the researchers and restorers, prompted the Soviet government to organize the most important display of icon-painting yet seen outside Russia. This toured Brussels, Vienna, Berlin and other German cities in 1929; the venue at the end of the year was the Victoria and Albert Museum under the title 'Russian Ikon Exhibition'.

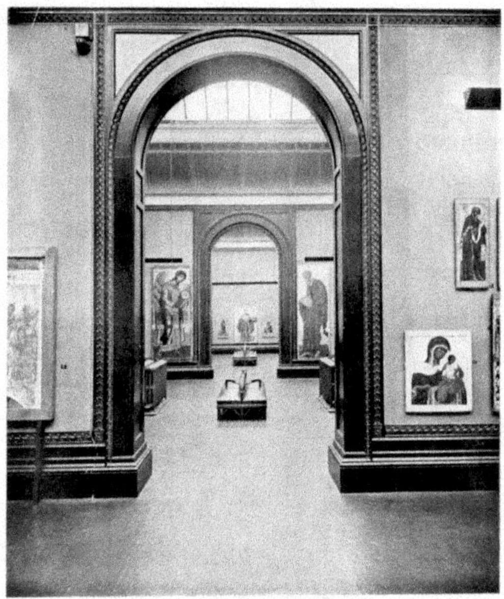

Fig. 4.6 General view of the Russian Ikon Exhibition, Victoria & Albert Museum (1929).

Subsequently the exhibition travelled to the United States. Almost 150 icons were shown, together with a selection of metal *oklads* and other elements which had been removed as part of the cleaning process for the painted surfaces; there was also a section devoted to the techniques used by the restorers. The exhibits ranged in date from the 12th to the early 19th centuries and included major artefacts drawn from the Central Restoration Workshops and museums in Moscow, St Petersburg and provincial centres. Masterpieces such as the Rublev *Trinity* or the *Mother of God of Vladimir*, which it was not feasible to lend, were represented by high-quality copies painted by the foremost members of the Restoration Workshops.[36] The

36 For the exhibition, see note 4 above and Vzdornov, *Restavratsiia i nauka*, pp. 111-7; see also L.A. Olsufiev, 'Russian Ikons at South Kensington', *Burlington Magazine*, LV, no. 321 (Dec.

selection of exhibits and the catalogue were prepared under the direction of Igor' Grabar' and his colleague Professor Aleksandr Anisimov, a past student of Nikodim Pavlovich Kondakov (1844-1925), the founder of modern art-historical scholarship on icons.[37] As might be expected, the discourse of the catalogue was no longer framed in terms of Orthodox belief and worship, but firmly located within the current formalist methodology of art history—with its emphasis on connoisseurship and the concept of a national style which was deemed to have attained a pinnacle of excellence in the 15th century through Rublev's inspiration.[38]

While the London exhibition and its catalogue were primarily the work of Grabar' and Anisimov and their associates, two British figures were involved: Sir Martin Conway (1856-1936) and Sir Ellis Hovell Minns (1874-1953). In his varied career Conway was a mountaineer and explorer, politician and museum curator, as well as the founder of the photographic archive at the Courtauld Institute of Art which bears his name. He was not primarily an academic, although he held the Slade Professorship of Fine Art at Cambridge between 1901 and 1904 and published a number of books on art. One of these, entitled *Art Treasures in Soviet Russia*, appeared in 1925 and included a section on icons which drew attention to the achievements of the Central State Restoration Workshops. Conway was chairman of the committee for the Victoria and Albert Museum icons exhibition and wrote the Introduction to the catalogue; presumably he played a significant part in securing the exhibition for Britain.[39]

Sir Ellis Minns, Disney Professor of Archaeology at Cambridge University and a Fellow of Pembroke College, was a member of Conway's exhibition committee and translated the catalogue entries. A genuinely academic polymath whose best-known work is his monumental *Scythians and Greeks* (1913), he played a crucial role in fostering interest in Russian

1929), pp. 284-9. For the reception of the exhibition in the United States, see Wendy R. Salmond, 'How America Discovered Russian Icons: The Soviet Loan Exhibition of 1930-1932', in Jefferson J.A. Gatrall and Douglas Greenfield (eds.), *Alter Icons. The Russian Icon and Modernity* (Pennsylvania, 2010), pp. 128-43.

37 Much has been written on Kondakov: see Viktor Lazarev, *N.P. Kondakov, 1844–1925* (Moscow, 1925); *Nikodim Pavlovich Kondakov 1844-1925* (State Russian Museum, St Petersburg, 2001); Vzdornov, *Restavratsiia i nauka*, pp. 291-306; Kotkavaara, *Progeny*, pp. 143-51, 212-24 and *passim*. For Anisimov, see Irina L. Kizlasova, *Aleksandr Ivanovich Anisimov (1877-1937)* (Moscow, 2000); Vzdornov, *Restavratsiia i nauka*, pp. 139-60 and Shirley A. Glade, 'Anisimov and the Rediscovery of Old Russian Icons', in Gatrall and Greenfield (eds.), *Alter Icons*, pp. 89-111.

38 *Ancient Russian Icons* (Victoria & Albert Museum exhibition catalogue).

39 William Martin Conway, *Art Treasures in Soviet Russia* (London, 1925).

icon-painting. Minns's direct activities were confined to translating Russian texts, but as a reviewer noted, he was 'the first introducer to this country of the art of old Russia'.[40] Minns's first and most substantial contribution in this capacity came in 1927 with the publication of *The Russian Icon* written by his lifelong friend Kondakov.[41] He did more than render the author's text into English: his own annotations, which sometimes diverged from the views of the author, are testament to his own expertise in the field. The following year saw the publication of his revision of the English translation of Anisimov's monograph on the icon of the *Mother of God of Vladimir*.[42]

The Russian Icon and *Our Lady of Vladimir* for the first time made available the fruits of Russian scholarship to English-speaking audiences. They were quickly joined by a third major publication, in which both Minns and Conway were again involved. Within a year of, and inspired by, the Victoria and Albert Museum exhibition there appeared *Masterpieces of Russian Painting*. In the words of the editor, in this handsomely produced and illustrated book, 'the art historian and the amateur have the first opportunity that has been offered to them of forming some idea of what, with all its limitations both of subject and treatment, must yet be accounted a highly important chapter in the history of art'.[43] *Masterpieces* in every sense is a much more profound work of scholarship than the exhibition catalogue. The latter is little more than a booklet, with very few illustrations and catalogue entries comprising a summary description, in which the most substantial element is Grabar's six-page essay.[44] By contrast, *Masterpieces* is of quarto size and with no fewer than sixty plates, many full-page and in colour. The text too is far more substantial.

As with the catalogue this was a Russo-English collaboration. Anisimov and Grabar' respectively contributed an outline history of icon-painting in Russia to the late 17th century and an account of the work of the Central Restoration Workshops; members of the latter provided the material for

---

40 D.S. Mirsky in his review of Kondakov, *The Russian Icon* in *The Slavonic Review*, VI (1927), pp. 471-4 (p. 471); see also the obituaries of Minns by Elizabeth Hill in *idem*, XXXII (1953), pp. 236-8 and Ethel John Lindgren in *Man*, LIII (1953), pp. 172-4.

41 Nikodim Pavlovich Kondakov, *The Russian Icon* (Oxford, 1927); Minns also wrote an appreciation of Kondakov in celebration of his 80th birthday, 'N.P. Kondakov: The Father of Russian Archaeology', *The Slavonic Review*, III (1924), pp. 435-7.

42 Anisimov, *Our Lady of Vladimir*.

43 Farbman, *Masterpieces*, no pagination; see also the review in the *Burlington Magazine*, LVII, no. 332 (Nov. 1930), pp. 247-8.

44 Igor Grabar, 'Ancient Russian Painting', in *Ancient Russian Icons*, pp. 5-10.

the descriptions of the illustrated icons, which are far more detailed than those in the exhibition catalogue. Conway wrote an overview covering much the same ground as both Anisimov and Grabar'; Minns on the other hand, while no text appears under his name, provided advice to the editor and read the proofs. In terms of profile the most significant contributor was the foremost British art critic of the day, Roger Fry.[45] Fry had a long-standing interest in Russian art, but this exhibition brought him into contact with an aspect he had never previously encountered. His essay, entitled 'Russian Icon-Painting from a Western-European Point of View', focuses on identifying the underlying aesthetic values of Russian icons, which he saw as different from their Byzantine and western counterparts. For Fry, like Curzon before him, their qualities were transcendent and also abstract and remote, unconcerned with rendering the external world: 'the painters of Russia [...] were bent exclusively on the inner vision which the contemplation of divine beings and sacred histories aroused within them'.[46] He was nevertheless alive to the painterly qualities of decorative inventiveness and harmonious use of colour as well as the significance of facial expressions, especially ocular, as agents of meaning.

The Russian Ikon Exhibition and *Masterpieces of Russian Painting* were a celebration of the achievements of Russian scholars and restorers after the 1917 Revolution. Overlooked, ignored or suppressed were the distinctly less positive features of Soviet policy. Although briefly acknowledged by Grabar', the icon cleaning and restoration carried out prior to 1917 were downplayed.[47] Secondly, the speed at which icons were treated and the craft-based methodologies employed in the years immediately after the Revolution resulted in irreversible damage in some cases; it was only with the establishment of the Central State Restoration Workshops in 1924 that x-rays, scientific analyses and microscopes came into use and conservators rather than former icon-painters were trained to adopt minimal interventionist methods of treatment.[48]

---

45 Andrei Rogachevskii, 'Samuel Koteliansky and the Bloomsbury Circle (Roger Fry, E.M. Forster, Mr and Mrs John Maynard Keynes and the Woolfs)', *Forum for Modern Language Studies,* XXXVI (2000), pp. 368-85; see also Frances Spalding, *Roger Fry: Art and Life* (London, 1980).

46 Roger Fry, 'Russian Icon-Painting from a Western-European Point of View', in Farbman, *Masterpieces,* p. 36.

47 Grabar, 'Ancient Russian Painting', p. 6; *idem,* 'The Scientific Restoration of Historic Works of Art', in Farbman, *Masterpieces,* p. 96.

48 *Idem,* 'Scientific Restoration', pp. 95-105; see also Lelekova, 'Icon Restoration', pp. 88-92; Vzdornov, *Restavratsiia i nauka,* pp. 89-136.

If criticism of the cleaning of icons after (as well as before) 1917 has the benefit of hindsight (and would also apply to western practices common at this time), this does not apply to the scale of destruction of church buildings and artefacts in the aftermath of the Revolution. As we have seen, the most important monuments and works of art were preserved through appropriation. Subsequently, and as a result of a severe famine in the Volga region, all church valuables were forfeited and, despite the efforts of national and local museums, much was lost. Contemporary Western observers were aware of these events. In his chapter in *Masterpieces,* Sir Martin Conway alluded to confiscations but accepted at face-value what he was told, namely that the vast majority of icons and other works of art were neither of value nor importance and that in any case many had been returned to their churches. He also defended the Soviet regime on the grounds that its treatment of ancient Russian art compared favourably with that of its predecessors. Less sympathetic was an article by Klepinin which appeared in the *Slavonic and East European Review* in 1930.[49] In contrast Grabar' remained silent on the subject in both his *Masterpieces* chapter and in the *Russian Ikons Exhibition* catalogue. Undoubtedly a *raison d'être* of the exhibition was to demonstrate the positive aspects of Soviet policy in the hope that destruction would be overlooked.[50]

There was also another hidden agenda to the exhibition. The cash-strapped government hoped to use it as a showcase for the sale both of the facsimiles and the original icons to western collectors. Early in 1930 word reached Minns of this plan and he immediately drew attention to it in print.[51] This attempt had tragic consequences for one of the key figures in the preservation of Russia's ancient art and Grabar's co-organizer of the exhibition. Aleksandr Animisov had maintained his contacts with the émigré community of scholars grouped around his old mentor Nikodim Kondakov in Prague, which after his death formed the Seminarium Kondakovianum; this institute's publication in 1928 of his *Our Lady of Vladimir* translated by Minns aroused the ire of the Soviet authorities. Before the exhibition came to London Anisimov was charged with profiting from

49 *Masterpieces,* p. 18 (see also Conway's remarks on p. 3 of the *Ancient Russian Icons* catalogue); Nicholas Klepinin, 'The War on Religion in Russia', *Slavonic and East European Review,* VIII (1930), pp. 514-32.

50 Kotkavaara, *Progeny,* pp. 156-8.

51 *Ibid.;* Ellis Hovell Minns, 'The Exhibition of Icons at the Victoria and Albert Museum', *Slavonic and East European Review,* VIII (1930), pp. 627-35 (p. 635); see also Glade, 'Anisimov', p. 100 and Salmond, 'How America Discovered Russian Icons', pp. 129-32.

sales of icons while it had been travelling in Europe; he was stripped of his posts and arrested in October 1930. The final charges did not mention icon sales, but included having extensive contacts with foreigners and émigrés. There followed an investigation of the Central State Restoration Workshops in which Chirikov and others, but evidently not Grabar', came under suspicion. Sentenced to ten years' imprisonment, Anisimov was sent to the notorious labour camp (and former monastery) of Solovki, where he helped in the museum before being transferred to the White Sea-Baltic Canal camp and eventually executed in 1937.

He was not the only member of the team involved in the Russian Ikon Exhibition to fall victim to Stalin's terror: Olsuf'ev, a co-compiler of the catalogue and co-contributor to the descriptions of the icons in *Masterpieces*, also perished.[52] Anisimov and Olsuf'ev were but 2 of the thousands of victims of the anti-intellectual and anti-religious repression which was already underway while the exhibition was perambulating around Europe and England. Of this the British figures involved in promoting the exhibition and encouraging interest in Russian icon-painting were blissfully unaware.

When all is said and done, while the Russian Ikon Exhibition and the flurry of publications in the late 1920s provided a more scholarly understanding of Russian icons than hitherto, they did not generate a wider interest within the United Kingdom. The cause continued to be espoused by Tamara, the Russian-born wife of David Talbot Rice, Watson Gordon Professor of Fine Art at Edinburgh University and a noted Byzantinist.[53] A steady stream of publications by leading scholars, notably Viktor Lazarev, with good-quality colour reproductions and English translations has flowed in from Russia since the 1970s and 80s. During these decades London was the centre of the auction market for Russian icons and it remains the domain of a few specialist dealers. Nonetheless, the Victoria and Albert Museum icon exhibition was the most significant display on the subject in Britain until the 1990s when Gates of Mystery and The Art of Holy Russia, both major loan shows, were held in London.[54] While a few scholars, notably Robin Cormack, Robin Milner-Gulland and the late

52 Shirley A. Glade, 'Dispelling the 'Fog of Half-Forgotten History'', *The Russian Review*, 63 (2004), pp. 130-3; *idem*, 'Anisimov', pp. 100-4; Kizlasova, *Anisimov*. For Anisimov's last years see also Dmitry S. Likhachev, *Reflections on the Russian Soul: A Memoir* (Budapest, 2000), pp. 125-7. For Olsu'ev see Vzdornov, *Restavratsiia i nauka*, pp. 177-214.

53 Tamara Talbot Rice, *Icons* (London, 1959), *idem* and David Talbot Rice, *Icons. The Natasha Allen Collection Catalogue* (Dublin, National Gallery of Art, 1968).

54 *Gates of Mystery* (1992); *The Art of Holy Russia* (1998) (see above, nn. 30, 31).

Lindsey Hughes, have continued to fly the flag, Russian icon-painting as an academic subject continues to reside outside the canon of art history within the United Kingdom. In some respects, though, the wheel has come almost full circle: what began primarily as an interest largely confined to Anglican clergymen now has widespread popular appeal for the devout, as is evidenced by the quantity of reproductions of Rublev's *Trinity* and the *Mother of God of Vladimir* and other icons to be found for sale in cathedrals and shops purveying religious items—and also in use as devotional images in churches other than Orthodox.

5. The Crystal Palace Exhibition and Britain's Encounter with Russia

Scott Ruby

The Great Exhibition of the Works of Industry of all Nations, sometimes referred to as the Crystal Palace Exhibition, was the first World's Fair Exhibition and focused on culture and industry. This international exhibition took place in Hyde Park, London, from 1 May to 15 October 1851 in an enormous fantastical glass and reinforced iron structure, from whence the 'Crystal Palace' designation derives. The grandeur of the exhibition was enhanced immediately upon entrance as the visitor was met by an enormous glass fountain designed by Osler of Birmingham. The fountain contained iron bars embedded within the glass for support. Although the Exhibition was intended as a platform on which countries from around the world could display their achievements, Great Britain was a dominant force and in fact occupied the entire western section of the exhibition.

In 1851 foreign goods were not as familiar as they are today and the exhibition provided a vicarious way of travelling the globe. 'The exhibition offered cultural diversity and geographic scope during a period when people's lives were still highly localised'.[1] There was enormous uncertainty prior to the exhibition opening as to the extent of the foreign participation in the exhibition. In many cases the distances involved were such that no information was available about what was being sent until it actually arrived. This was certainly the case with Russia's Great Exhibition, the United States's and others.

1 John R. Davis, *The Great Exhibition* (Trowbridge, 1999), p. 71. Davis and Fisher (note 3) provide the general informational background to this essay and will only be footnoted hereafter when directly quoted.

Two Great Exhibition catalogues were produced, the first was intended as a smaller guide priced at 1 shilling The other was the 'Official Descriptive and Illustrated Catalogue' of the exhibition and was conceived as something much more monumental, costing the substantial sum of £3.3s. This cost provided the purchaser with 'a record of the most varied and wonderful collection of objects ever beheld, and [...] a book of reference to the philosopher, merchant, and manufacturer'.[2]

The organizers were counting on various exhibits for their crowd-pulling power. The Russian and Austrian exhibits were considered highly important in this regard and were referred to as the 'Lions of the Exhibition'. These exhibits included works from royal collections and works of art. Also included were works that depicted royalty or politicians, which proved extremely popular in a simpler age less used to mass-produced imagery.

Most foreign displays were organized by state governments. The foreign sections had an emphasis on luxury, splendour and magnificence and wealth. The Russian and Austrian displays in particular seemed to be produced in order to show to the outside world the power of the imperial state in terms of art and artefacts. The exhibition allowed direct comparison between countries and the way was opened for governments to begin competing with one another. However, there was some fear as to what this competition might mean. In Britain, many producers had viewed the Exhibition suspiciously, as an event that would allow foreign manufacturers to spy on British production techniques. For a conservative power such as Russia, participation in the Exhibition was an extremely sensitive matter. At the beginning of April 1851, foreign secret police reports began to show that notorious revolutionaries were using the Exhibition as an excuse to travel to London and proselytise among their countrymen. Russia immediately stopped issuing passports and stepped-up its efforts to prevent certain elements of Russian society from travelling to London.

Russia's goals in participation, as stated in the Russian press, were not to compete with other countries but to educate foreigners about Russian agriculture and industry.[3] While the tsar established an imperial commission to organize Russian participation, other government institutions were

2 Davis, p. 102.

3 David C. Fisher, quoting *Ob'iavlienie ot vysochaishe i uchezhdennoi v s.-Peterburge komissii o Londonskoi vystavke* (St Petersburg, 1850), in his 'Russia and the Crystal Palace in 1851', in Jeffery A. Auerbach and Peter H. Hoffenberg (eds.), *Britain, the Empire, and the World at the Great Exhibition of 1851* (London, 2008), p. 126.

appealed to directly for participation. For example, the Ministry of the Imperial Court was asked to contribute examples of decorative art produced at the Imperial factories specializing in porcelain, lapidary and cut stone. However, like many of the agricultural interests involved in the exhibition, these artistic manufacturers worried that their European colleagues might regard their work as inferior. By early September 1850 the Russian Imperial Commission had begun preparations for shipping exhibits to England. Approximately 376 exhibitors were involved, including well-known industrialists such as the Demidov Brothers, whose display of malachite decorative objects dominated the Russian display. Few proposed exhibits were turned down, though displays considered odd were rejected, such as an unusually large ear of rye and the idiosyncratic work of a peasant clock-maker who turned elements of agricultural machinery into clocks.

At the time of the Great Exhibition writers regularly expressed fear and distrust of foreigners. Real or perceived, the differences between foreign people and the British were thought of as of immutable national characteristics. *The World's Fair: Or, the Children's Prize Gift Book* even used national characteristics as a theme. The English were industrious and persevering; Indians were poor and simple; Turks were a handsome race of people, but prone to a fiery temperament. Italians were beggars and bandits and not particularly industrious, although their country had a good climate. Germans were thoughtful, romantic and well-educated; the Dutch industrious and tidy. Northern Europeans were held in highest regard, followed by southern Europeans, with Russians, Asians, Africans and American Indians bringing up the rear.

Some writers used a country's 'otherness' as a jumping-off point for a story. One example which features English people encountering Russians was Thomas Onwhyn's *Mr. & Mrs. Brown's Visit to London to see the Great Exhibition of All Nations. How they were astonished at its wonders, inconvenienced by the crowds, and frightened out of their wits by the Foreigners.* In the Crystal Palace the Browns meet a Don Cossack who has bushy hair, is dressed in military garb and carries a sword. The caption for this meeting reads 'A good natured Don Cossack takes notice of Anna Maria, much to her terror'.[4] For many in Britain, Russia represented an unknown; it conjured up images of a barbaric people living in arctic cold and ruled by tyrannical despots—a view established by English travel accounts of the 16th century,

4 Fisher, pp. 173-4.

which remained remarkably powerful into the Victorian period. In many ways the presence of a Russian display at the Great Exhibition was an attempt to combat Russophobia and the Russian stereotypes commonly held in the Western mind.

Alexis de Valon seemed to capture in a few words what many British people felt about Russia and its image problem at the Great Exhibition. He wrote: 'I do not know Russia and this causes me much regret. It seems that there is not another country in the entire world about which such a false understanding is held'.[5] When the British invited all nations to the Great Exhibition, Russian officials viewed this as an opportunity to put right misconceptions about the Empire and to demonstrate Russia's rich natural resources, industrial achievements and her native ingenuity. Since Britain was also the major purchaser of Russian exports, Russia regarded participation in the exhibition as a wise strategy in terms of maintaining a favourable public opinion.

Like France, the United States and many other foreign exhibitors, Russia's display was largely incomplete on the opening day. The shipment from Odessa and one shipment from St Petersburg had arrived in the autumn of 1850. However, a second shipment from St Petersburg was delayed by ice floes in the Baltic Sea and a third shipment had not even set sail by the opening of the exhibition. The display was finally completed and opened to the public on 7 June 1851. The Russian commissioner, Gavril Kamenskii, performed most of the installation with help from the Ministries of State Domains and Finance. He and his colleagues worked day and night to make sure the display was complete. There were four galleries in the Russia section, which neighboured the United States to the east and the exhibits of pre-unification Germany (Zollverein) to the west.

Among the avid visitors to the exhibition was Queen Victoria. She recorded her impressions of the visit:

> 11 June. To the Exhibition: with our relatives. We went first to look at the Russian exhibits, which have just arrived and are very fine: doors, chairs, a chimney piece, a piano as well as vases in malachite, specimens of plate and some beautifully tasteful and very lightly set jewelry [...] we came home at a quarter to 12 and I felt quite done and exhausted, mentally exhausted.[6]

In some ways the Russian display was a more extreme version of Austria's. There was almost a complete absence of machine-produced goods. Instead,

5 Fisher, p. 123.

6 C.H. Gibbs-Smith, *The Great Exhibition of 1851* (London, 1964), p. 21.

raw materials formed a large part of the display. Art was used to demonstrate wealth and power, and colossal vases and architectural elements in stone (such as malachite and jasper) helped to make this point along with costly jewellery. Industrial produce, including cast iron, was also of a gigantic scale, as though size were a substitute for complexity. Almost all of these works were created by state-producers, from the Imperial copper works of Bogoslovskii and Perm', the Aleksandrovskii cannon foundry and the metal works of Artinsk, Narnoulsk and Koushvinsk, to name but a few. The power of the state was clearly the watchword for the Russian display.

The Russian exhibition was divided into two halves by the exhibition's main aisle. Machinery, manufacturers' goods and fine art were on the north side, while raw materials were on the south. The raw materials section was divided into four sections. First: silk, chintz and yarn; second: hemp, flax hides, leather and felt. Ores and ingots from Russian mines formed the third, and the fourth was dedicated to chemical products. The northern section contained one large room hung with pomegranate-red cloth. Pieces from the Demidov's malachite factory were on display in the centre, along with porcelains, mosaics and other *objets d'art* from the imperial factories and private craftsmen. Along the sides of the rooms were galvanized medals designed by Count Tolstoi to commemorate Russia's 1812 victory; tools, cutlery and other objects, specimens of decorative paper, ornamental arms, and inlaid wood ornamented the walls. Ten-foot tall bronze candelabra stood alongside the columns at the entryway. At the back of the gallery there was machinery for making sails, as well as three carriages and two sleighs. On the second floor the Russian display continued with furs, mohair, shawls, lace and other miscellaneous items.

The Russian sections created an absolute sensation with the public. According to *The Times*, the beauty of the Russian section was phenomenal. *The Illustrated London News* gushed that 'only a fairy palace could be furnished with such incredible malachite [...] brilliant green [...] malachite with its curled waviness like the pattern of watered silk and its perfect polished surface [...] heightened by the burnished gold of the paneling and ornaments.'[7] The gilt bronze candelabra by Moscow maker Krumbigel were deemed 'impossible to excel'.[8] Further, an ebony cabinet decorated with an arrangement of fruit was cited by *The Times* as 'one of the chief

7 Fisher, p. 136, quoting 'The Russian Court', *Illustrated London News*, 18/496 (1851), p. 597.

8 *Ibid.*, quoting *Illustrated London News*, 19/515 (1851), p. 304.

wonders of the exhibition'.[9] The Prince of Wales said of this piece that the amethyst currants depicted on its lid were delectable enough to eat. These successes were matched by the poor reception given to the grains and ores, which were judged 'unattractive' by the press.

One of the prize objects on display in the Russian section was a magnificent lidded silver beaker made by the firm of Sazikov. The celebrated silver making company was started by Pavel Sazikov (d. 1830) in Moscow in 1810. In 1837 Pavel was succeeded by his son Ignatii (1796-1868), who opened a branch in St Petersburg in 1837. The firm became one of the best known in Russia and was one of the first to employ a mechanized process in the production of silver. By the 1840s, Sazikov had machines for rolling, guilloché and polishing. He had also started to divide his workers by tasks so they could work more efficiently and faster. In 1844 Sazikov received the Imperial warrant and a year later established a school for training young students, one of the first of its kind in the country.[10] The firm was particularly adept at working in the new 'Russian style', which became popular after the publication of Fedor Solntsev's monumental tome recording the antiquities of the Russian state, *Drevnosti Rossiiskago gosudarstva* (1849-53). The newly rediscovered vocabulary of Russian design galvanized decorative arts in the country by bringing to light ancient decorative patterns that were commented upon in the media. In 1849 a correspondent with the St Petersburg newspaper, *Severnaia pchela* (*Northern Bee*), described this usage:

> The St Petersburg public was full of admiration for Mr. Sazikov's... [objects] in the new Russian style, based on ancient designs and forms of jewelry in the Kremlin's Palace of Facets. Mr. Sazikov has resurrected and firmly established in Russia the art of Benvenuto Cellini.[11]

Sazikov's prestige in St Petersburg and his commissions from the Imperial family undoubtedly influenced his selection to participate in the Crystal Palace Exhibition in London. For this event he sent 29 objects, mostly in the Russian style. Eleven are illustrated in the Official Catalogue, among which was a tall, lidded cup now at Hillwood Museum in Washington DC. Interlace patterns embellish the cup, which is further ornamented by raised spheres and ellipses.

---

9 Fisher, p. 136, quoting *The Times*, 9 June 1851, p. 8.

10 Anne Odom, *Russian Silver in America: Surviving the Melting Pot* (London, 2011), p. 150.

11 Odom, p. 180, quoted by Zavadskaia, in 'Gold and Silver in St. Petersburg, 1830-1850', in Géza von Habsburg, *Fabergé: Imperial Craftsman and His World* (London, 2000), p. 51.

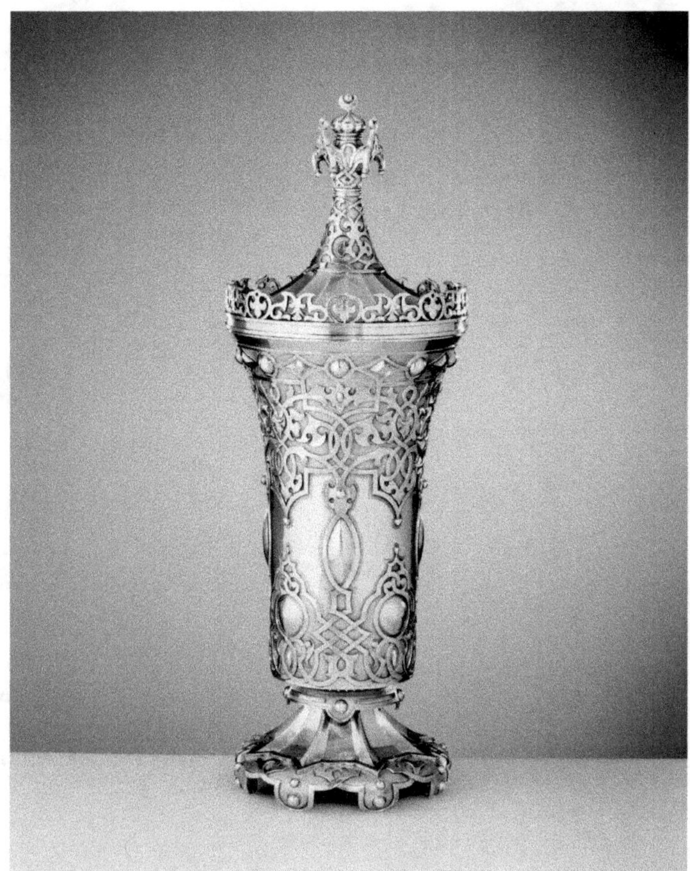

Fig. 5.1 Ignatii Pavlovich Sazikov (1796-1868), Covered Cup, 1851, St Petersburg, Russia. Silver gilt. Hillwood Estate, Museum, & Gardens, Washington, D.C. Photography: Edward Owen.

One writer commenting on Sazikov's pieces remarked:

> The Russian contributions to the Crystal Palace evince a large amount of costly splendour combined with quaint and characteristic design, showing much fantasy in the Art-manufactures who have been engaged in their fabrication... There is a very free and fanciful taste prevalent in these articles, which gives them a strong individuality of character.[12]

In many ways world exhibits such as the Russian display in 1851 replaced the ceremonies surrounding royal weddings, coronations, and diplomatic receptions as opportunities to show off the latest style. The challenge to

12 *Crystal Palace Exhibition Catalogue* (London, 1851), pp. 266-7.

Russia was to present positively a largely unknown 'other' to the world. This attempt was successful. As a later reviewer, commenting generally about the Great Exhibition, noted 'a taste for art is largely aided by exhibitions'.[13] In the case of Russia, the Great Exhibition had the effect of pulling aside a veil that had obscured Russia's artistry; now her achievements were displayed for the world to appreciate.

13 Prof. Archer, 'The Influence which the Exhibition of 1851 and Those Held Subsequently Have Had in the Diffusion of a Knowledge of Art', *The British Architect* (1875), pp. 306-7.

6. An 'Extraordinary Engagement': A Russian Opera Company in Victorian Britain

Tamsin Alexander

> Exactly a year ago this weekend, the press was full of encomiums for the Kirov Opera. It was hailed as 'the best opera company in the world' in all quarters after its visit to Covent Garden, when it brought a programme consisting entirely of Russian works [...] This time, though, reactions to its two-week Verdi celebration at the Royal Opera House have been very different [...] When we have heard them before here, [...] it has almost invariably been in Russian opera. There was something revelatory about many of those productions—the real sense of witnessing a performing tradition that was beyond our normal experience (Andrew Clements, *The Guardian*, 21 July 2001).
>
> [...] if the Russian singers will keep to Russian music, they deserve and may meet with every encouragement (*The Times*, 9 October 1888).
>
> [...] as we listen, we are sensible of being transported to a far greater extent than we had anticipated into a world of art of which we have little experience (*Manchester Guardian*, 4 July 1888).

While the story of Sergei Diagilev's touring *saisons russes* of the early 20th century is well known, that of the first visit of a Russian opera company to Britain has not yet been told. In 1888, a Russian troupe[1] performed in cities across the country, exhibiting a wealth of vocal talent and performing three Russian grand operas that depicted the country's historical triumphs and colonial acquisitions. At a time when still little was known of Russian

1 The company will be referred to simply as the Russian opera company throughout, since such a variety of names appeared in papers, e.g. Grand Russian Opera Company, the Russian National Opera Company, the Moscow Opera Company, the Imperial Opera Company, that it seems they did not advertise themselves with a specific title.

opera (see Appendix A), when Britain was insecure about its lack of home-grown opera and singers and when the countries were colonial rivals, the press presented the tour as a spectacular exhibition, thus encouraging ethnographic engagement with the operas, despite the more serious aims of the company. This generated an image that, though sensational, was not conducive to the future endorsement of the repertoire in Britain.

In June 1886, Giuseppe Truffi, a conductor of the Imperial Theatre in Moscow, began seeking venues for an opera tour. His search excited much interest in British music periodicals. Rumours appeared that his troupe would soon be visiting such fashionable destinations as Paris, New York, Vienna and Milan. However, when the company eventually departed in April 1888, it would be for a very different set of cities. Having visited Berlin and Copenhagen, they arrived in Britain in July ready to perform in Manchester, Birmingham, Huddersfield, Liverpool, Nottingham and Cardiff (see Appendix B). Their repertoire was made up of operas that were popular in Russia at that time: Glinka's *A Life for the Tsar*, Rubinstein's *Demon*, Tchaikovsky's *Mazeppa* and Verdi's *La Traviata* and *Rigoletto*. Despite performing out of season,[2] from July to September, the press in most cities recorded a resounding success; the company was even asked to return to Manchester and Birmingham for repeat performances.

In October, the company travelled to London for a series of concerts in the Royal Albert Hall. The venture was a failure and critics unanimously urged the company to give a performance of a complete opera instead. Having been rejected by Covent Garden, despite the theatre being empty, they eventually managed to secure the Jodrell Theatre. The theatre, known previously as 'The Novelty', had been closed for a year and was described by one critic as 'a kind of extra theatre to be hired for charitable entertainments and amateur performances'.[3] Its low profile, meagre size and limited resources did not help the company's cause. Poor reviews and suspicions of corrupt management followed and the season was abandoned early. None of the operas performed in the tour would be seen in Britain for another century.[4]

---

2 The main musical season, based on that in London founded on the tradition of high society coming to town for the opening of parliament, lasted from April to July.

3 *The Belfast News Letter*, 15 October 1888. (All newspaper reviews were anonymous. Possible authors' names are given in parentheses. These names are those of the main music critic of the paper for that time.)

4 Next would be *Mazeppa* at the English National Opera, 1984, though extracts and unstaged versions of *Demon* and *Life for the Tsar* have been performed since 1888.

Sensation and Spectacle: 'Nobody should miss this rare opportunity of seeing this marvellous company in works which are of a peculiarly fascinating nature'.[5]

Interviews, illustrations, gossip and advertisements published in papers during the tour, particularly in the provinces, promoted a highly sensationalised image of the Russian troupe that was at times more akin to a visiting circus than a serious opera company. In 1887, Francis Hueffer of *The Times* wrote despairingly that 'English people like serious music and like the stage, but they do not care for serious music on the stage'.[6] During the 1880s, many of the leading music critics were calling for reforms in British musical life in a movement that came to be dubbed the 'English Musical Renaissance'.[7] In opera, it was hoped that the Italian-dominated repertoire would be revitalised with new works, particularly by British composers, and that the public could be encouraged to appreciate 'serious' opera. In spite of this, music halls, vaudevilles, burlesques, pantomimes and operettas remained the most popular forms of musical theatre. This can be seen in the types of entertainment advertised at the time of the Russian company's visit. At the Birmingham Grand Theatre, for instance, they were followed by a burlesque of *Aladdin*. Andrew Melville, the theatre manager who accommodated the troupe, went on to assist an American circus at the Queen's Theatre. In Liverpool, competition came in the form of a 'Red Hungarian Band' which performed at the Bijou Theatre in the same week.

However, touring opera had gained a popular following in the provinces. Cities outside London did not have their own opera companies and so relied on such tours. Tickets were sold at relatively low prices, making performances more widely accessible, in contrast to the more elite scene still found in London. [8] When the Russian company arrived in Birmingham, people flocked to the train station to welcome them and Ioakim Tartakov, the lead baritone, was presented with a laurel crown after the first performance of *Demon* there.

This excitement over visiting companies, combined with a taste for sensationalist entertainment, heavily shaped the style of advertising used for the company's visit, as shown below:

---

5 *Dart: The Midland Figaro*, 27 July 1888.

6 Francis Hueffer, *Half a Century of Music in England, 1837-87* (Cambridge, 2009), pp. 79-80.

7 See Leanne Langley, 'The Musical Press in Nineteenth-century England', *Notes*, XLVI, no. 3 (March, 1990).

8 Dave Russell, *Popular Music in England: 1840-1914* (Manchester, 1997), p. 69.

MONDAY, 24TH SEPTEMBER, 1888.

EXTRAORDINARY ENGAGEMENT, FOR TWELVE NIGHTS ONLY, OF THE GRAND

RUSSSIAN NATIONAL OPERA COMPANY.

The first time upon record that the Original Members have been allowed to leave their own country, Special Permission having been obtained from His

IMPERIAL HIGHNESS THE CZAR OF RUSSIA.

120 PERFORMERS, BAND OF 40

ORIGINAL RUSSIAN, CIRCASSIAN, AND TARTAR COSTUMES, SCENERY, PROPERTIES AND EFFECTS.

TO-NIGHT MONDAY, WEDNESDAY, FRIDAY,
SEPT. 24th. SEPT. 26th. SEPT. 28th.

RUBINSTEIN'S GRAND OPERA,

THE DEMON.

TUESDAY, THURSDAY, AND SATURDAY,
SEPT. 25th. SEPT. 27th. SEPT. 29th.

VERDI'S OPERA,

RIGOLETTO.

SATURDAY MORNING, SEPTEMBER 29TH,

GRAND SPECIAL PERFORMANCE AT 2.30 OF RUBINSTEIN'S OPERA,

THE DEMON.

During this Engagement the Prices will be as follows:—Private Boxes, £1 11s. 6d. and 10s. 6d. Dress Circle, 5s.; Stalls, each, 4s. (reserved); Upper Circle, 3s. (reserved); Pit, 1s.; Gallery, 6d.

Box Plan now open at Messrs. Thompson and Shackell's (Limited).

Doors Open at 7 o'clock, Opera at 7.30.

Fig. 6.1 Advertisment for the Russian Opera Company, *Western Mail,* Cardiff (24 September 1888). © The British Library.

The promise of 'original Russian, Circassian, and Tartar costumes, scenery, properties and effects', before even mentioning the title of the opera, shows that exotic visual effect was a principal point of appeal. The subtitle—'an extraordinary engagement'—and the idea that the singers had for 'the first time on record' been 'allowed to leave their own country' evoked an air of intrigue, the latter tapping into age-old stereotypes about Russian despotic leadership; in fact, the company had been gathered especially for the tour. The huge numbers of performers projected, again appealing to the public taste for the spectacular, were also inaccurate. There was no band with the company at all and certainly not 120 singers.[9] As these performances were held at the more prestigious theatres of each town, advertising always took a prominent place in theatrical listings. The contrast in London could not

9 Advertisements requesting players for these performances in each town show that bands were collected there and then, and did not arrive with the opera company. As for the '120 singers', according to the police report sent to the London (e.g. *Lloyd's Weekly Newspaper* (11 November 1888)), there were 36 members of the company stranded in London in November.

have been greater. The Jodrell Theatre's announcement appeared at the bottom of the listings and gave scant information in comparison with the provincial notices; there is no mention that *Demon* was an opera, let alone that the performances were by a Russian company. These advertisements alone indicate how differently the company were received in and outside of London.

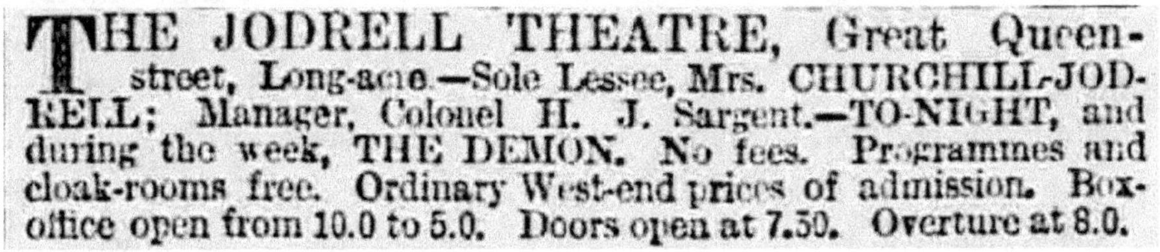

THE JODRELL THEATRE, Great Queen-street, Long-acre.—Sole Lessee, Mrs. CHURCHILL-JODRELL; Manager, Colonel H. J. Sargent.—TO-NIGHT, and during the week, THE DEMON. No fees. Programmes and cloak-rooms free. Ordinary West-end prices of admission. Box-office open from 10.0 to 5.0. Doors open at 7.30. Overture at 8.0.

Fig. 6.2 The Jodrell Theatre's announcement, *The Standard* (22 October 1888). © The British Library.

A further aspect of the press response which shows the interest the tour excited was the number of scandals reported surrounding the company during the tour—a feature which was becoming typical of the late-Victorian press.[10] Rumours surfaced of financial problems resulting from a previous director abandoning them in Berlin, and of an impending court case between a chorus member and Vladimir Liubimov, a baritone and organiser of the tour, over unpaid wages of £10.[11] The most widespread story, however, was of the company's early dismissal from the Jodrell Theatre, which left them unable to finance their journey home and stranded in London for 3 weeks. This led to a court case between William Ralston, an eminent Russian scholar of the time who intervened on the company's behalf, and George Saville, the theatre administrator. Ralston attended multiple performances of *Demon* at the Jodrell and suspected that Saville had not been passing on the correct takings to the proprietor. Their original confrontation on the matter, in the theatre foyer, had led to an assault by Ralston on Saville, over which another court case was also being held. This, and Ralston's arrest a week later for drunken and disorderly behaviour following an unsuccessful benefit concert (that he had organised for the company), largely discredited his attempts to help. Court cases were still being

10 See Michael Diamond, *Victorian Sensation: Or the Spectacular, the Shocking and the Scandalous in Nineteenth-Century Britain* (London, 2003).

11 *Birmingham Daily Post* (11 September 1888) (Stephen Stratton).

held over owed wages even after the company had managed to travel home through funds raised by the National Vigilance Association and a campaign in *The Star*.[12] As well as numerous police reports, emotive headlines such as 'The Starving Russian Artistes' appeared in papers nationwide; sad tales emerged of the company's living conditions and fears for the safety of the women were frequently voiced. To make matters worse, their stay happened to coincide with the infamous Whitechapel murders. The letters printed in a range of papers shows that the story gripped the nation. The following is typical for its expression of sympathy coupled with an assertion of British superiority:

> Well, as we have, many of us, in speech and song, so often expressed our determination to do something dreadful to Russia and the Russians,[13] here is a glorious opportunity. Let us conspire to send these, our supposed national and natural enemies, back to their own country with a lively and grateful sense of how Britons can treat a foeman in distress, and perhaps, though in a very small way, it may tend to foster that 'union of hearts' which we should like to see binding together all the nations of the world in a common band of brotherly love.[14]

Thus, at a time when sensation sold, the lasting image of the company would be of their failure and criticisms of the Russian government's inefficiency in helping them, rather than the artistic achievements of the enterprise.

Further evidence of the troupe's sensationalist appeal can be found in the images and articles printed during their visit. The Birmingham *Dart* printed sketches from *Demon* with suitably wistful, melancholic images of the soprano and baritone below, once again tapping into popular stereotypes of Russian national character held at the time. The Cardiff *Evening Express* published short biographies and portraits of some of the soloists, in which the ladies were invariably described as 'beauties'.[15] The author further endeared his readers to the singers by writing that 'of strong individuality and palpable brain power, even in the matter of religion [the tenor, Bogatyrev] thought for himself to leave the orthodoxy in which he had been trained by his parents'.[16] This statement qualified

12 Yet another court case over the company's visit was held between the theatrical agent, Macheon, and the Jodrell, though his grievances were really against the Russian Opera Company, who he claimed owed him £142 in unpaid commission fees.

13 See Russell, pp. 146-8 for examples of such songs.

14 *Morning Post* (13 November 1888) (W.A. Barrett).

15 *Evening Express*, Cardiff (4 October 1888).

16 *Ibid.*

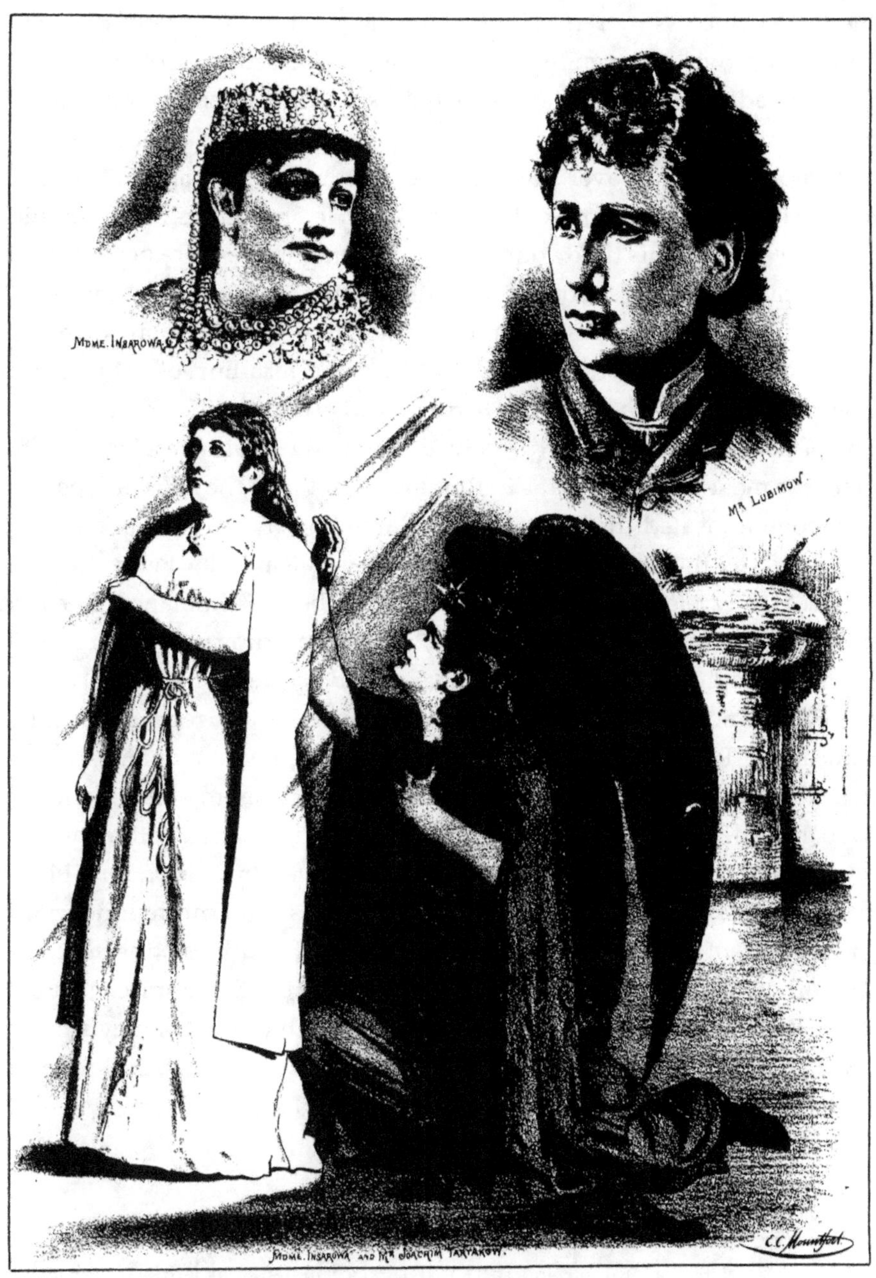

SKETCHES AT THE RUSSIAN OPERA.

(New Grand Theatre, Birmingham).

Fig. 6.3 'Sketches at the Russian Opera', *Dart: The Midland Figaro*, Birmingham (27 July 1888).

the tenor's success by removing one of the primary sources of difference and disapproval between Britain and Russia. The article also hinted at the widespread view that Russia was a suppressed and underdeveloped nation. For instance, some of the singers' biographies reported that they heroically supported their impoverished families through their singing, and the conductor, Truffi, was presented in this article and others as a tyrannical leader rehearsing his tired company into the night to ensure perfection.

Despite this sensationalised presentation, the opera company's repertoire shows a serious attempt to demonstrate that Russian performers and composers were on a par with those in Western Europe, as well as to present operas with the potential to become internationally popular.[17] *Demon* and *A Life for the Tsar*, which received the most performances on the tour, were the most popular operas in Russia at that time. The chosen repertoire also communicated that Russia was a large and united European power. *Mazeppa* tells the story of a Ukrainian rebel defeated by Peter the Great and *A Life for the Tsar* depicts the rescue of the first Romanov tsar from a Polish attack. The story of *Demon*, with its portrayal of the beautiful, conquerable Georgian princess Tamara, sold by her father and seduced by the Demon, gives a colonialist depiction of the recently acquired Caucasus.[18] Rubinstein's setting, through its employment of emasculating oriental colouring for background effect and for the impotent Caucasian hero, Prince Sinodal, enforces this. These locations—Ukraine, the Caucasus and Poland—were three of the four regions visited by Alexander III in his first (and only) official extensive tour of the Russian Empire, undertaken in 1888, to enforce his policy of Russification.[19] In addition, the singers of the company had been brought together from across the Empire, including Kiev, Brest and Kazan, exhibiting the wide reach of the country's talents. Thus, Russia presented itself through the tour as an empire-builder equal to Britain, via an operatic tradition that exceeded its colonial rival.

---

17 See Daniel Fisher, 'Russia and the Crystal Palace in 1851', in Jeffrey Auerbach and Peter Hoffenberg (eds.), *Britain, the Empire, and the World at the Great Exhibition of 1851* (Aldershot, 2008) for another example of a failed attempt by Russia to introduce Britain to a more accurate picture of the country.

18 Susan Layton, *Russian Literature and Empire* (Cambridge, 1994), pp. 201-9.

19 See Richard Wortman, *Scenarios of Power: Myth and Ceremony in Russian Monarchy from Peter the Great to the Abdication of Nicholas II* (Princeton, 2000), p. 282.

Ethnographic Insight: *'It is an instructive form of entertainment'.*[20] Despite these serious aims, music critics were more interested in the potential for the performances to unveil the secrets of the mysterious Empire. This was not the first visit of a Russian musical troupe to Britain. A Russian horn band had visited in 1831 and a Russian choir, under Slavianskii d'Agrenev, in 1886. Both had performed popular, folk and sacred music from Russia in quasi-national dress, thus giving the ventures a distinctly ethnographic feel. Continual assurances by critics in 1888 that the 'costumes were all true to the country and period',[21] that the singers' vocal production was 'entirely united to the weird effects of their native music'[22] and that these were true 'specimens' of Russian national operas suggest that the Russian opera company's performances were expected to serve a similar purpose. The term 'specimen' was used frequently by critics as if describing a museum exhibit, thus transforming the audience into tourists observing foreign culture.

This expectation of encountering a foreign novelty led to bewilderment over the company's performances of *Rigoletto* and *La Traviata*. Hueffer wrote for the *Times* that 'if the Russian singers will keep to Russian music, they deserve and may meet with every encouragement. If they should rashly venture on *Rigoletto* or *La Traviata* the result will probably be the reverse of agreeable'.[23] The patronising promise of 'encouragement', characterisation as 'rash' and menacing litotes ('the reverse of agreeable') gives this the tone of a warning to a young child, asserting British superiority and stressing the importance of restricting Russian musicians to Russian music. However, the company's performances of these operas showed that they were far from being on the peripheries of performance practice. For instance, they staged *La Traviata* in evening-dress, a recent Parisian venture in keeping with Verdi's original intentions, which had only just been attempted in Britain.[24]

Some critics even took the Russian operas performed to be representative of contemporary Russian life. This reaction to Russian culture in Britain was already common. For instance, Lermontov's *A Hero of Our Time* had been taken for a travelogue and published as *Sketches of Russian Life in the Caucasus*

20 *Aberdeen Weekly Journal* (11 October 1888).
21 *Manchester Guardian*, 11 July 1888 (George Freemantle).
22 *Liverpool Daily Post*, 15 August 1888.
23 *The Times*, 23 October 1888 (Francis Hueffer).
24 The first British staging of *La Traviata* in modern dress was in June 1888 under Augustus Harris at Covent Garden (See 'Inartistic Opera', *Musical Times*, June, 1888, p. 341).

(1853)[25] and the 1881 translation of Dostoevskii's *House of the Dead*, depicting prison-life in Siberia, had been widely enjoyed for its documentary value.[26] A South Kensington Exhibition of Russian Art and Art Objects in 1884 presented ornaments, vases, plates, scabbards, armour and sacred objects, rather than paintings, further encouraging a museum-style reception of Russian culture. In 1888, critics saw *A Life for the Tsar* in particular as representative of contemporary Russian life, despite being set almost 300 years in the past and the plot being largely fictional. One reviewer described it as an opera 'than which perhaps nothing is a more faithful representation of Russian patriotic life' and that would give 'insight into the inner life of the 'mysterious empire'.[27]

As supposedly representative of national practices, a primary motive of reviews was to seek out moments of 'national' music.[28] Carl Engel's popular *Literature of National Music* (1879) defined this as designating 'any music which, being completed in the peculiar taste of the nation to which it appertains, appeals more powerfully than other music to the feelings of that nation'.[29] Engel continued that it was important to study this music, since it 'reveals the character and temperament of different races'. Thus, by reading the operas performed by the Russian company as 'national', critics immediately indicated that they could only be truly enjoyed, performed and understood by others from Russia. Engel's definitions also exemplify the common belief at this time that nationality, personality and musical style were all inextricably linked, which meant that listening to the music of other nations could provide information about national character. In a comparison of the Russian company's performance of *Demon* with that of the Royal Italian Opera in 1881, *The Times* reported that 'it is in the rendering of [...] *couleur locale* that the Russian artists have a marked advantage over their predecessors at Covent Garden'.[30] This treats moments of '*couleur locale*' as glimpses into Russian folk practice, despite Rubinstein mostly employing oriental colour, as exotic to Russian audiences as it was to British ones.

---

25 Philip Bullock, *Rosa Newmarch and Russian Music in Late Nineteenth and Early Twentieth-century England* (Aldershot, 2009), p. 21.

26 Helen Muchnic, 'Dostoevsky's English Reputation (1881-1936)', in William Leatherbarrow (ed.), *Dostoevskii and Britain* (Oxford, 1995), p. 24.

27 *Western Mail*, Cardiff (2 October 1888).

28 Just a few examples from many: '[In *Demon*] the imitations of Russian national tunes are excellent' (*Weekly Dispatch* (28 October 1888)); '[*Life for the Tsar* is] strongly impregnated with local colour' (*Birmingham Daily Post* (26 July 1888)).

29 Carl Engel, *Literature of National Music* (London, 1879), p. 1.

30 *The Times*, 23 October 1888 (Francis Hueffer).

Some critics' focus on national melody also weakened the operas' value by associating them with popular entertainment. The critic for the *Manchester Guardian* described *Demon* as being imbued with '*local colour* which so easily appeals to the popular mind',[31] while the *Birmingham Daily Post* wrote of *Life for the Tsar* that 'native melodies [...] are never without a freshness and charm which speak touchingly to every ear'.[32] Examples such as these, in locations where the company were most enthusiastically received, written in the cities' most august newspapers, undermined their success by implying that the operas were only popular because of their accessible musical language. Effeminate terms such as 'charming', 'pretty', 'delicate' and 'quaint' abounded in reviews,[33] further indicating surface beauty. In the *Academy*'s description of *Demon*, the employment of local colour was presented as an artificial, unsophisticated practice: 'Rubinstein gives local colour by means of augmented intervals and quaint harmonies and peculiar rhythms. Thus interest was imparted to many portions of the work'.[34] These simple sentences and use of a list sound more like a recipe than a method of composition. Therefore, the term 'national' was dissociated from the serious national opera ideal which the English Musical Renaissance called for and ensured that the Russian operatic tradition was not seen as an example to British composers.

A Learner: '[Russia] is young, so far as civilisation goes'[35]

A fundamental problem that shaped the response to the Russian opera company was the persisting idea that Russia was culturally and politically a youthful nation that was still in the process of learning from its westerly neighbours. This image was applied to all aspects of the visit, including the singers' voices, the sets and their administrative procedures. However, it was the idea that the composers of the operas performed were

---

31 *Manchester Guardian*, 4 July 1888 (George Freemantle).

32 *Birmingham Daily Post*, 27 July 1888 (Stephen Stratton).

33 A few examples from many: 'freshness and charm [...] touching' (*Birmingham Daily Mail*, 27 July 1888); 'The chorus of male voices sang with great delicacy and charm in the pretty and characteristic evensong' (*Academy*, 27 October 1888, p. 280); 'A charm which cannot be verbally described' (*Manchester Guardian*, 4 July 1888).

34 *The Academy*, 27 October 1888, p. 280.

35 '[Russia] is young, so far as civilisation goes, and as it possesses a distinct nationality in feeling, it is only natural to find this feature reflected in the music that its subjects put forth. Most of this is marked by what may be called the vigour of youth, mingled with accents, unusual rhythms, quaint turns of melody and novel harmony, such as is not current in the more southerly nations' (T.L. Southgate, *The Musical Standard* (31 March 1888), p. 196).

simply imitators that would make long-term critical success unlikely. The idea that 'great' composers were defined by their originality and innate genius was deeply ingrained in music criticism by this period.[36] Focus on imitation refuted both of these important credentials. Of Rubinstein, for instance, the *Liverpool Mercury* reported that 'like other composers of the Slav race, he betrays here and there [...] some token of submission to German influences'.[37] Tchaikovsky's *Mazeppa* was criticised for being a poor imitation of Wagnerian writing, while Rubinstein's conservatism in *Demon* was deemed backward. One critic reviewing *A Life for the Tsar* wrote that its most 'musical' part was the 'fugal number' in Act I, since it reached 'almost a Handelian vein in breadth and development'.[38] This, the critic continued, could be attributed to Glinka's German training. Thus, not only was Glinka's musicality merely learnt, but, like Tchaikovsky's Wagnerisms, it was not quite fulfilled, his music only 'almost' reaching Handelian levels.

This image of Russia as a 'learner'[39] is conveyed especially by the following extract from a review which compares *Demon* with Gounod's *Faust*:

> As compared with Goethe's devil [...] [the demon] is a mere abstraction [...] [Tamara is] a tender and loving woman of Russian nationality, but with no pretensions to figure side by side in the same portrait gallery as Goethe's Gretchen. [...] [*Demon*] may be described as very charming and very uncommon, but without the fibre or real dramatic quality of Gounod's work. [...] In Rubinstein the fluency [of melody] is sometimes so obvious as to give his music the character of an improvisation, and the composer apparently has not known how to exercise the reserve and polish and severe self-discipline which have made so many of Gounod's airs enduring gems of melody. Both composers possess strong dramatic instincts, but those of the Russian are not so carefully penned and directed as those of the French musician.[40]

The description of the Demon as 'a mere abstraction' and Tamara's exclusion from the 'portrait gallery', a symbol of public endorsement and permanent acknowledgment, indicate a lack of faith in their enduring power. The iteration of Tamara's 'Russian nationality' in this statement, paired with the idea that she has 'no pretensions' to hang next to Gretchen, also suggests her provinciality. By calling these 'Goethe's' characters, not Gounod's, the author reminds his

---

36 Bennett Zon, *Music and Metaphor in Nineteenth-Century British Musicology* (Aldershot, 2000), p. 184.
37 *Liverpool Mercury*, 7 August 1888.
38 *Liverpool Daily Post*, 10 August 1888.
39 This term is taken from Iver Neumann, *Uses of the Other* (Manchester, 1999), pp. 108-12.
40 *Birmingham Daily Post*, 24 July 1888 (S.S. Stratton).

reader that *Faust* is part of a broader European tradition—a French opera based on a German plot—thus creating a division between Russia and its westerly neighbours. To enforce this divide, the contrast between the two composers is portrayed as a binarism of controlled learning and a lack thereof. Rubinstein's 'charming' and 'uncommon' music is juxtaposed with Gounod's 'fibre and real dramatic quality'. 'Charming' and 'uncommon' denote something Other, mysterious, even magical. 'Fibre' and 'real', by contrast, suggest music of substance and sincerity. Next, Rubinstein's 'obvious' and 'improvisatory' melodies are placed in opposition to Gounod's 'reserve', 'polish' and 'severe self-discipline' which enable him to create 'enduring gems of melody'. This links Rubinstein's melodies to a popular and oral tradition, while Gounod's 'gems' become part of a written-down, educated tradition. This idea is enforced by the following sentence which tells us that Gounod's drama is 'carefully penned'. Thus, the imagery assigned to *Faust*—the gems, the portrait gallery—indicate wealth, beauty, power and endurance. *Demon*, however, is defined and analysed via a series of negatives: an 'abstraction [...] no pretension [...] without [...] not known [...] not so'. Its identity is shaped by what it is *not* in comparison to the Franco-German *Faust*.

In conclusion, the critics' reluctance to accept Russian opera into the canon paralleled and was influenced by the reluctance of Britain to accept Russia as an enlightened world power at the time. The 1880s were a period of uneasy Anglo-Russian relations; the Russo-Turkish war (1877-8) had recently seen Russia threaten British naval supremacy in the Mediterranean and the Penjdeh crisis of 1885 had brought the countries to the brink of war over Russia's expansion into Afghanistan. The colonial rhetoric that presented these performances as exotic, ethnographically interesting and lagging behind the Western world thus undermined Russia's position as a rival to Britain. It also detracted from the idea that Russia may be in possession of a flourishing and internationally competitive operatic tradition at a time when Britain was struggling to find one of its own. The discussion of the company being ethnically attached to music written by their countrymen, and thus best-suited to performing it, created a barrier that damaged prospects of repeat performances. However, the success in the provinces, albeit prompted by sensationalised media attention and the lack of other entertainment in the summer months, shows that the public were willing to support these operas. Reviewers often commented that people attended the same opera night after night, indicating that novelty was not the only source of appeal. But, without the provinces having their own opera companies, and following the damning response in London, little more could come of this. Excluded from the portrait gallery, Russian opera was confined instead to the museum or the international Exhibition, to be given a display case as spectacular as any, but not to be touched, to be labelled 'Russian' and to be learned *about,* certainly not *from.*

Appendix A: Table showing all performances of Russian Opera in Britain, 1881-92

Date	Opera	Language	Company, Venue, People
21, 25, 30 June, 15 July 1881	*Demon* Rubinstein	Italian	Royal Italian Opera, Covent Garden **Director** Frederick Gye **Conductor** Anton Rubinstein, Enrico Bevignani
12, 16 July 1887	*A Life for the Tsar* Glinka	Italian	Royal Italian Opera, Covent Garden **Director** Antonio Lago **Conductor** Enrico Bevignani
2 July-4 November 1888*	*A Life for the Tsar* *Demon* *Mazeppa* Tchaikovsky	Russian	**Director** Vladimir Liubimov, Aleksandr Aleksandrov **Administrator** Bogatyrev **Conductor** Giuseppe Truffi
17, 20, 21, 24, 26, 28, 31 October 1892	*Eugene Onegin* Tchaikovsky	English	Royal Italian Opera, Olympic Theatre **Director** Antonio Lago **Conductor** Henry Wood

* See Appendix B for further details.

Appendix B: Timeline of the tour.

Venue	Date (1888)	Opera
Berlin, Victoria Theatre	6-18 May	*Life for the Tsar* (x8) *Demon* (x5)
Copenhagen, Folketheatret	2-19 June	*Life for the Tsar* (x3) *Demon* (x8) *Rusalka* (x2) *Rigoletto* (Act III) Tartakov Miscellany
Manchester, Comedy Theatre	2*-21 July	*Demon* (x12) *Life for the Tsar* (x6)
Birmingham, Grand Theatre	23-28 July	*Demon* (x5) *Life for the Tsar* (x2)
Huddersfield, Theatre Royal	30 July-3 August	*Demon* (x3) *Life for the Tsar* (x2)
Liverpool, Alexandra Theatre	6-18 August	*Demon* (x5) *Life for the Tsar* (x3) *Rigoletto* (x2) *Mazeppa* (x2)
Manchester, Comedy Theatre	20 August- 1 September	*Demon* (x4) *Rigoletto* (x3) *Mazeppa* (x5)
Birmingham, Grand Theatre	3-15 September	*Demon* (x6) *Rigoletto* (x4) *Mazeppa* (x2) Lubimov Benefit
Nottingham, Grand Theatre	17-22 September	*Demon* (x4) *Rigoletto* (x2)
Cardiff, Grand Theatre	24 Sep-6 October	*Demon* (x6) *Rigoletto* (x 4) *Life for the Tsar* (x2) *La Traviata* (x2)
London, Royal Albert Hall	8-13 October	Variety concerts
London, Jodrell Theatre	22 Oct-4 November	*Demon* (x14) (every night + Saturday matinees)

* All visits in British cities began on a Monday and included performances every night except Sunday, sometimes with Saturday matinees.

7. Russian Folk Tales for English Readers: Two Personalities and Two Strategies in British Translations of the Late 19th and Early 20th Centuries

Tatiana Bogrdanova

Introduction

More than a century-long tradition of British translators' creative efforts has resulted in Russian folk narratives becoming an integral part of European children's literature and culture. But who were the main contributors to this process of cultural and textual communication? In the initial stages two personalities, with their own individual styles, were of key importance, but the full extent and significance of their contribution has not as yet been fully appreciated.

The role of William Ralston in the popularization of Russian folklore and literature has long been recognized in Russia, where his translations were indeed appreciated during his lifetime. The only biography of him was published in Russian, and due attention has been paid by Russian researchers to his works, for instance, in recent studies on the British reception of Krylov, Turgenev and other great Russians. However, Ralston's collection of *skazki* (1873), published in London at a time when the 'discovery' of Russian literature was yet to be made, has been largely overlooked and no works have been specifically devoted to its study. Hence I offer here an analysis of his translation strategy and techniques in the context of the existing European translation tradition. These translations, part of a heated scholarly discussion of folklore issues at the time and accompanied by detailed commentaries of a specialized character, appealed to experts rather than the general reader. They were no doubt an excellent first introduction to the new and fascinating world of the Russian oral tradition, but the task of reaching the most receptive audience for the genre—British children—fell to Arthur Ransome, whose retelling of favourite *skazki* in *Old Peter's Russian Tales* (1916) marked the beginning of his distinguished career as a children's author. The style of this publication, which appeared in the heyday of Russian literature in Britain, was quite distinct from that of his major predecessor, chiefly because Ransome's premises were of a different nature: in the golden age of folk narratives he had chosen to follow the popular style of Andrew Lang, famous for his adaptations of international folktales for British children.

William Ralston Shedden Ralston (1828–1889)

Given the important role Ralston played in the popularization of Russian folklore and literature in the West, it is only natural that he still attracts the attention of Russian scholars interested in Anglo-Russian literary and cultural interaction, especially in its early stages. In the only study devoted to Ralston and his works published in Russia, M.P. Alekseev and Iu.D. Levin assert that he was one of the most important mediators between the Russian and British literary worlds in the second half of the 19th century, his activity as 'an indefatigable popularizer of the Russian language and literature in England' (which lasted more than twenty years) attracting attention in Western Europe, America and Russia itself.[1] There is also a recent instance of interest in Ralston in his homeland. It is for this reason that Professor W.F. Ryan devoted his presidential address before the Folklore Society (4 April 2008) to 'the librarian William Ralston, an interesting and rather tragic figure', the Society's vice-president or a member of its Council for some twenty years until his death in 1889.[2] Notably, Ralston's name was mentioned among other founders of the Society, characterized by Ryan as 'a mixed bag of enthusiasts'.

1 Mikhail P. Alekseev and Iurii D. Levin, *Vil'iam Rol'ston—propagandist russkoi literatury i fol'klora. S prilozheniem pisem Ralstona k russkim korrespondentam* (St Petersburg, 1994), p. 7.

2 W.F. Ryan, 'W.R.S. Ralston and the Russian Folktale: Presidential Address Given to the Folklore Society, 4 April 2008', *Folklore,* CXX (August 2009), p. 123.

Both British and Russian authors point out that Ralston's interest in the Russian language was first prompted by his duties as a librarian in the British Museum. He was unusual in that he was one of few Englishmen who had a good command of the Russian language, and of still fewer interested in Russian literature.[3] His written work suggests that Ralston was 'gifted linguistically and was widely read in many areas of literature and scholarship'.[4] In fact, Ralston learnt the language by 'memorising a Russian dictionary page by page'.[5] His interest gradually turned into his most important field of expertise and creative effort; he became 'known in a quiet way in literary, artistic and intellectual circles in London'. As Ryan notes, Ralston's Russian interests were at first literary and political—he enjoyed translating and was of a liberal and philanthropic turn of mind: between 1865 and 1868 he wrote half-a-dozen pieces in periodicals on the poor in Russia, the wrongs suffered by the Poles and other liberal causes of the day.[6]

According to Ryan, it was during Ralston's visit to Turgenev's country estate in 1868 that his interest in Russian folklore seems to have been seriously aroused. In December 1868, immediately after his return from Russia, he published in the family journal *Good Words* several articles on Russia, including one entitled 'Glimpses of Russian Village Life'. There followed a gradually increasing number of articles and reviews on Russian folklore, legends and folktales, and later, as his confidence grew, on folklore and folktales in general.[7] Ralston met and made friends with many famous Russian folklore scholars of the day, whose works he studied and relied on in his translations. He had a lively correspondence with quite a number of Russians: Alekseev and Levin included in their study 158 letters by Ralston to Russian correspondents.

It seems no accident now that Ralston's first success as a translator should be associated with the name of a famous Russian literary figure, the fabulist Krylov. Following the first edition (London, 1869) of 93 prose translations of fables, accompanied by a short biography of Krylov based on the works of Russian scholars of the day, three expanded editions appeared in 1869, 1871 and 1883. According to Alekseev and Levin the book, which

3 Alekseev and Levin, p. 8.
4 Ryan, p. 123.
5 *Ibid.*, p. 124.
6 *Ibid.*
7 *Ibid.*

in its final form included 148 of the most important fables with detailed commentaries, proved to be seminal in familiarizing the British reader with Russian literature and the Russian people.[8] In his study of the Russian fabulist's English translations Anthony Cross points out that Krylov became 'firmly established in the English consciousness through the efforts of one of the first genuine scholars of Russian literature',[9] namely Ralston, who 'opts for a 'faithful prose rendering'. In fact, 'Krylov makes his first significant impact in England, shorn of the form and poetry which are so essential a part of his work but which had been palely preserved by his earlier translators into verse'.[10] One of the recent Russian studies devoted to the English tradition in question also pays due attention to Ralston's work as the author points out that 'thanks to their utmost accuracy and scrupulous faithfulness to the original, Ralston's translations—amply provided with explanations of historical character and commentaries—turned into something like 'a guidebook' to the strange northern country'.[11]

Ralston's work on Krylov marked the beginning of his career as a translator and scholar of Russian folklore. He gradually acquired a serious scholarly reputation and in 1871 he was invited to deliver the second series of Ilchester Lectures at the Taylorian Institution of the University of Oxford. The three lectures were given the overall title 'On the Songs and Stories of the Russian People', and along with other material gathered in their preparation became *The Songs of the Russian People as Illustrative of Slavonic Mythology and Russian Social Life* (1872). Later, using more of his lecture material, he published *Russian Folk Tales* (1873). The latter also appeared in several editions in the USA and in French translation as *Contes populaires de la Russie* in 1874.[12] Alekseev and Levin assert that 'responsibility, great industry, perseverance and scrupulous attention to every detail combined with readiness zealously to pursue any question of interest to him were characteristic of the translator in the highest degree'. They state that it was thanks to his efforts that the European reader became familiar with the riches of the Russian oral tradition, Western scholars for the first time being presented with detailed information about Russian

8 Alekseev and Levin, pp. 24-5.

9 Anthony Cross, 'The English and Krylov', *Oxford Slavonic Papers*, NS XVI (1983), p. 104.

10 *Ibid.*

11 Nadezhda Kritskaia, 'Ob osobennostiakh vosproizvedeniia basen Krylova V. Rol'stonom', in *Russkaia literatura v kontekste mirovoi kul'tury*, I, 1 (St Petersburg, 2008), p. 36, http://sun.tsu.ru/mminfo/000349796/000349796.pdf [accessed 29.8.2012].

12 Ryan, pp. 125-6.

folklore.[13] Ryan also stresses the English enthusiast's contribution to the study and popularization of Russian folklore, highlighting that, unlike the other publications of Russian folktales in English that would follow in the next few decades, 'Ralston's book was not really for the general reader or for children—it was a serious scholarly exercise', being 'the most extensive collection of Russian tales in English until the publication in New York in 1945 of the misnamed *Russian Fairy Tales* translated by Norbert Guterman'. He adds that 'up to that time Ralston's book was widely quoted in scholarly literature and was treated as authoritative; and it is still quoted with respect'.[14] Moreover, as Ryan notes, Ralston employed all his talents to promote the cause. He was a very successful public storyteller with Russian folktales as part of his repertoire, and 'he can fairly be said to have introduced the Russian dimension into western folktale studies, and in his own writing on the subject to have made a genuine contribution to the scientific study of folktales'.[15] Thus, Ralston's folklore translations marked an important stage in introducing the English (and European) reader to the Russian oral tradition, contributing to the growth of literary and cultural ties between the countries. They received a positive response in Russia, where critics highlighted the author's sympathy with the Russian people and his genuine appreciation of Russian folklore.[16] Ryan also points out that 'Ralston's scholarship was recognised in Russia and he was elected to a fellowship of the Imperial Russian Academy and to the Ethnographic Section of the Russian Geographical Society'.[17]

However, to my knowledge, Ralston's book of Russian folktales has never been studied specifically in terms of its translation strategy and practice, though its relevance would seem obvious from what has been discussed above. The present work aims to contribute to filling the gap.

The English scholar and translator dedicated his book to the memory of Aleksandr Afanas'ev, whom he had met while on a visit to Russia and held in great esteem as a foremost folklore scholar. Most of the 51 stories Ralston translated in full came from Afanas'ev's collection of *skazki*, together with short retellings of many others. The book includes extended commentaries which show the author's sophisticated interest in the subject, for instance when he touches on the question of possible sources of some of the most

13 Alekseev and Levin, pp. 39, 42.

14 Ryan, p. 128.

15 *Ibid.*, p. 129.

16 Alekseev and Levin, pp. 43-5.

17 Ryan, p. 125.

popular plots and parallel texts found in both European and non-European countries. However, he avoids discussing in detail the controversial issue of the origin of the folktales, instead focusing his readers' attention on their individual character. Thus he writes in his introduction: 'For the present, we will deal with the Russian folktale as we find it, attempting to become acquainted with its principal characteristics to see in what respects it chiefly differs from the stories of the same class which are current among ourselves, or in those foreign lands with which we are more familiar than we are with Russia, rather than to explore its birthplace or to divine its original meaning'.[18]

He specifically stresses the importance of *mythological* folktales and devotes three out of six chapters to them as, in his opinion, this predominant category of Russian folktales is remarkably distinct from their Western European counterparts. These *skazki* give an idea of the unique character of mythological supernatural beings characteristic of the Russian (Slavic) wonderworld such as the Snake, Koshchei the Deathless, the Water King and the Baba Iaga. Some of them deal with such 'singular beings' as One-Eyed Likho, Woe, Friday, Wednesday and Saturday as female spirits, the Leshii (a forest spirit), Morozko (Frost) and even rivers. Others are associated with magic objects—such as dolls and magic water—that have either a unique character or characteristics not found elsewhere.

Ralston's translation strategy, in general, can briefly be described in his own words. He writes that he rendered the 51 stories he translated at length 'as literally as possible', thus trying to produce a photograph of the Russian storyteller and not an idealized portrait.[19]

In fact, this translation philosophy conforms to his scholarly interests, as Ralston seems to have the folklore expert in mind rather than the general reader as his addressee. Besides, one should not exclude the influence of the European translation tradition, namely, that of German folklore scholars (for example, Bernhard Jülg, whom Ralston cites in his work on more than one occasion). Throughout the 19th century Germany was recognized as the leading translating country in Europe, and the general tendency of German translators was to follow the original as closely as possible, especially as far as folklore translations were concerned.[20]

---

18 *The Project Gutenberg EBook of Russian Fairy Tales,* by W.R.S. Ralston, p. 18, http://www.gutenberg.org/files/22373/22373-h/22373-h.htm [accessed 29.8.2012].

19 Ralston, p. 9.

20 Lev L. Nelyubin and Georgi T. Khukhuli, *Nauka o perevode (istoriia i teoriia s drevneishikh vremen do nashikh dnei)* (Moscow, 2008), p. 130; Bernhard Jülg, *Mongolische Märchen-*

Thus, as the first guide to the fascinating world of the Russian oral tradition, Ralston was at his best. In fact, one could hardly have found anyone more interested or knowledgeable in the subject than he. His collection of Russian folktales has been of great interest and importance for specialists in folklore and Slavic studies, but it is also the first serious effort in the field of Russian folklore translations; it established the tradition and paved the way for those who followed him.

Arthur Michell Ransome (1884–1967)

Arthur Ransome's *Old Peter's Russian Tales* (1916) marked the next important step in familiarizing the English reader, this time the young English reader, with Russian folklore. The book appeared in a different cultural situation, for it was published in the period before World War I, the heyday of Russian culture and literature on the British Isles.[21] It also marked the turning point in the literary career of an author who was to become an outstanding children's writer. Ransome's first-hand knowledge of the country and its folklore tradition was acquired when he was the foreign correspondent of British newspapers in Russia during its most turbulent period, the October Revolution.

In a brief note to his book the author leaves no doubt as to his addressee, pointing out that it is not 'for the learned, or indeed for grown-up people at all', as it is 'written far away in Russia, for English children'.[22] Old Peter and his grandson and granddaughter, the audience for the 21 tales, are fictional characters introduced by the author both to narrate the stories in their most natural way and to introduce the necessary explanations about culturally specific words and concepts, avoiding commentaries of a more scholarly character. The difference in approach between Ralston with his appeal to the scholar and Ransome with the child as his audience is clearly marked. Ralston is selective in choosing stories for translation, trying to present the most interesting samples with the intention of rendering their

---

Sammlung. Die neun Märchen des Siddhi-Kür nach der ausführlicheren Redaction and die Geschichte des Ardschi-Bordschi Chan. Mongolisch mit deutscher Uebersetzung und kritischen Anmerkungen herausgegeben von Bernhard Jülg (Innsbruck, 1868), p. xvi.

21 Tatiana Krasavchenko, 'Zagadka, zavernutaia v tainu i pomeshennaia vnutr' golovolomki', *Otechestvennye zapiski,* V (37) (2007), http://strana-oz.ru/2007/5/zagadka-zavernutaya-v-taynu-i-pomeshchennaya-vnutr-golovolomki [accessed 29.8.2012].

22 *The Project Gutenberg EBook of Old Peter's Russian Tales* by Arthur Ransome, p. vi, http://www.gutenberg.org/files/16981/16981-h/16981-h.htm [accessed 29.8.2012].

distinct character, while Ransome's guiding principle is his personal taste. Hence the difference in their translation strategies: Ralston follows the original as closely as possible, which is appropriate to a scholarly style of folklore translation, while Ransome transforms the tales to appeal to his young readers, conforming to the English tradition of folklore adaptations in the style of Andrew Lang (his favourite read as a child).

Lang was closely associated with the golden age of the folktale in Britain at the end of the 19th century, playing a crucial role in transforming folktales from all over the world into standard children's literature. Lang—folklorist, classicist, romantic poet, literary scholar, journalist, historian, parapsychologist, author of 120 books and contributor to 150 more—is chiefly remembered today as the editor of a coloured series of folktales for children, a role that earned him the soubriquet 'the Master of Fairyland'.[23] In fact, Lang was one of the first specialists who promoted folktales, adapting them to the needs and interests of children, and was obliged to bear the criticism of his colleagues. 'Lang's scholarly reputation suffered from the connection with children's literature, and despite the scholarly introductions available in limited editions for the *Blue* and *Red Fairy Books* where Lang motivates the enterprise, he drew a lot of fire'.[24] Published between 1889 and 1910, the twelve anthologies of folktales collected from around the world were 'enormously popular in their day and can be found gracing the shelves of better bookstores today'.[25] The name of the editor and the uniform style of the stories were among the main factors contributing to the edition's success.

With children as their target audience, the editing practice of the books was focused on transforming oral narratives from all over the world into a specific genre of English children's literature. The stories were far from being literal, as they were adapted in many ways to conform to the strict tastes of the Victorian age. According to Sundmark, already in *The Blue Fairy Book* (1888) Lang established principles that over time became normative: the intended child audience, the eminence of the wonder tale, the international approach, the uniform language and style. The tales were chosen to please

23 J. David Black, *David Andrew Lang: Master of Fairyland* (Waterloo, Ontario), p. 25,. http://digitalcommons.mcmaster.ca/cgi/viewcontent.cgi?article=1038&context=nexus [accessed 29.8.2012].

24 Björn Sundmark, *Andrew Lang and the Colour Fairy Books* (2004-11-18), pp. 1-2, http://dspace.mah.se/dspace/bitstream/handle/2043/8228/Lang%20present.pdf [accessed 29.8.2012].

25 Black, p. 27.

rather than to instruct or to convey a utopian, moralizing, or religious message. Thanks to the efforts of Lang and Leonora, his wife, who did most of the translations, the tales were 'steeped in the same linguistic and cultural mold'.[26] Thus, the canons of international folktales for children in the English language were largely established by Andrew Lang, a major influence on Ransome's literary retellings of the Russian folklore. However, there was also an important difference, as the latter tried to preserve the culturally specific character of the original.[27]

The British tradition of Russian folktale translations was established by two different personalities living at different times (more favourable for British–Russian interactions in the case of Arthur Ransome) and professing different translation strategies in accordance with their aims, principles and cultural influences. To complete the picture let us now look at their translation practice, best illustrated with the help of a contrastive textual analysis of parallel English texts.

Ralston versus Ransome: Translation Strategies and Practices

Let us begin with an analysis of the translations of a short folktale that well illustrates the respective translation strategies and practices under discussion (the text on the left is Ralston's, that on the right Ransome's):

VAZUZA AND VOLGA	The Vazouza and the Volga
Volga and Vazuza had a long dispute as to which was the wiser, the stronger, and the more worthy of high respect. They wrangled and wrangled, but neither could gain the mastery in the dispute, so they decided upon the following course:-	The Vazouza and the Volga flow for a long way side by side, and then they join and flow together. And the Vazouza is a little river; but the Volga is the mother of all Russia, and the greatest river in the world. And the little Vazouza was jealous of the Volga. **'You are big and noisy'**, she says to the Volga, **'and terribly strong; but as for brains'**, says she, **'why, I have more brains in a single ripple than you in all that lump of water. 'Of, course the Volga told her not to be so rude**

26 Sundmark, pp. 1-2.

27 Tatiana Bogrdanova, 'Rol' Andriu Langa v transformatsii folklornoi skazki dlya detei', *Nauchnaia mysl' Kavkaza*, no. 4, Part II (2010), p. 76.

'Let us lie down together to sleep', they said, 'and whichever of us is the first to rise, and the quickest to reach the Caspian Sea, she shall be held to be the wiser of us two, and the stronger and the worthier of respect'.

So Volga lay down to sleep; down lay Vazuza also. But during the night Vazuza rose silently, fled away from Volga, chose the nearest and the straightest line, and flowed away.

When Volga awoke, she set off neither slowly nor hurriedly, but with just befitting speed. At Zubtsof she came up with Vazuza. So threatening was her mien, that Vazuza was frightened, declared herself to be Volga's younger sister, and besought Volga to take her in her arms and bear her to the Caspian Sea. And so to this day Vazuza is the first to awake in the Spring, and then she arouses Volga from her wintry sleep.[28]

and said that **little rivers should know their place and not argue with the great. But the Vazouza would not keep quiet,** and at last she said to the Volga: 'Look here, we will lie down and sleep, and we will agree that the one of us who wakes first and comes first to the sea is the wiser of the two'. And the Volga said, 'Very well, **if only you will stop talking**'. So the little Vazouza and the big Volga lay and slept, white and still, all through the winter. And when the spring came, the little Vazouza woke first, **brisk and laughing** and hurrying, and rushed away as hard as she could go towards the sea. When the Volga woke the little Vazouza was already far ahead. But the Volga did not hurry. She woke slowly and shook the ice from herself, and then came roaring after the Vazouza, a huge foaming flood of angry water. And the little Vazouza listened as she ran, and she heard the Volga coming after her; and when the Volga caught her up—a tremendous foaming river, whirling along trees and blocks of ice—she was frightened, and she said,—'O Volga, let me be **your little sister. I will never argue with you any more. You are wiser than I and stronger than I. Only take me by the hand and bring me with you to the sea**'. And the Volga forgave the little Vazouza, and took her by the hand and brought her safely to the sea. And they have never quarrelled again. But all the same, it is always the little Vazouza that gets up first in the spring, and tugs at the white blankets of ice and snow, and wakes her big sister from her winter sleep.[29]

---

28 Ralston, p. 215.
29 *Ibid.*, pp. 322-3.

That the story is in fact about a dispute between rivers is explained by Ralston in a short introduction, though the absence of articles before their names in the title and text seems to be deliberate, as this better serves their personification and accords with the original. The effect is further enhanced by the choice of lexical items. For example: *mien*, defined in Merriam-Webster as 'air or bearing especially as expressive of attitude or personality'.[30] A contrastive textual analysis of the original story[31] with Ralston's translation has shown that it may serve as a substitute for the Russian folktale, its copy or photograph, so close is it to the original: it may therefore be further contrasted with the second English parallel text to continue our analysis.

In the chapter entitled 'Christening in a Village'[32] Ransome's variant is preceded by a long introduction that describes for the reader village life in pre-revolutionary Russia. As Old Peter and his grandchildren return from the village, they have a discussion about rivers and about which of them is the first to wake up in spring, and so the grandfather tells the story about the Vazouza and the Volga. The beginning of the story contains an explanation that leaves no doubt that these are rivers which nevertheless, according to Ransome's interpretation, behave like little children and grown-ups. The stereotypical situation of an argument is created with the help of appropriate lexis (marked above in bold). Thus, the story becomes more explicit but also somewhat trivial. In accordance with his adaptive strategy, Ransome transforms the original story, adding details and expanding on the themes that he thinks are important, mostly those that may educate as well as entertain. He never forgets his little reader, changing the linguistic features of the text according to their level of understanding and emotionality. One such characteristic marker of children's speech is the word *little*, which is repeated several times throughout this short piece of narrative. Direct speech, used quite extensively, also helps to enliven the narrative, making it more emotional and expressive. Whereas Ralston, following the original as closely as possible, nevertheless fails to render such prominent stylistic characteristic of the original Russian tale as its rhythmical character and almost melodious tone based on numerous repetitions, Ransome employs them to the full. For example, one cannot fail to notice the frequency with which most sentences begin with the

30 Merriam-Webster Online, http://www.merriam-webster.com [accessed 29.8. 2012].

31 'Vazuza i Volga', in *Narodnye russkie skazki A.N. Afanas'eva,* I (Moscow, 1984), p. 112.

32 Ransome, pp. 316-34.

conjunction *and,* as well as the parallel use of syntactic constructions. The important feature of Ransome's interpretation of the original story is that its events are rendered in a dramatic and emotional way, which is achieved by both syntactic and lexical features of the text as discussed above.

It may therefore be concluded that the difference in translation practices of both authors in question may be accounted for primarily by the difference in their translation strategies—which are, in their turn, to be understood within the framework of the cultural and translation traditions of their times.

8. 'Wilful Melancholy' or 'a Vigorous and Manly Optimism'?: Rosa Newmarch and the Struggle against Decadence in the British Reception of Russian Music, 1897-1917

Philip Ross Bullock

In the late 19th century, Russian music came to enjoy a particularly prominent place in orchestral concerts in London, especially in the wake of Tchaikovsky's visit to Cambridge and London in 1893.[1] In particular, Tchaikovsky's Sixth Symphony (the 'Pathétique') soon became one of the most regularly performed works of modern symphonic music. Colourful, passionate, seductively orchestrated and with an apparent sense of narrative and drama, it rapidly came to enjoy great popularity with the growing audience for modern orchestral works. Yet not all commentators were happy with this development. The composer Hubert Parry, then Professor of Music at Oxford, used his position to write about Slavonic music with undisguised hostility, and his accounts mix racial superiority and Darwinian evolutionary theory with a general disdain for the emotional intensity of such compositions:

> One of the most noteworthy features of recent music has been the increase of the taste of the works of semi-civilized peoples; not, indeed, their folk-music, but the imitation of types of classical art by composers who have by habit or descent a great deal of the 'untutored Indian' in their natures. The old

1 See, in particular, Gareth James Thomas, *The Impact of Russian Music in England, 1893-1929* (unpublished PhD dissertation, University of Birmingham, 2005).

> classical forms [...] seem to be infused with new life by the temperamental qualities of Slavs and Czechs and such races. But the products are strangely mixed. It is obvious that when the most cultured audiences prefer the music of the less developed races to their own, a lowering of the standard of their artistic perception and taste is implied, and a lessening of their sympathy with the productions of the best of their own composers is sure to follow.[2]

Parry's most consistent target was Tchaikovsky. In keeping with many British prejudices about music, Parry described Tchaikovsky as having an 'abnormally sensitive nature', and detected in the colours and harmonics of the Sixth Symphony 'the very profoundest mental gloom', as well as 'the despair which must accompany the admission of incapacity of self-mastery'.[3] A particular factor soon complicated Tchaikovsky's British reception. Although it would be some time before news of Tchaikovsky's homosexuality became widely known in Britain,[4] British attitudes to music were predisposed to see music as a dangerously effeminate and morally dubious occupation. An article published in *The Musical Times* in August 1889 and entitled 'Manliness in Music' amply reveals the kinds of prejudices that faced anybody wishing to embark the serious pursuit of music as a career:

> Few things have contributed more effectively to perpetuate in this country the prejudice against the musical profession [...] than the impression that musicians are a class wanting in the manlier quantities. In a country like England, where devotion to athletics forms a cardinal tenet of the national creed, such an impression cannot fail to have operated greatly to the prejudice of the art—indeed, of all arts, for there are many excellent people with whom the term 'artist' is simply a synonym for 'Bohemian' or 'black sheep.' They are so firmly persuaded that exclusive devotion to the study of music is inevitably attended by a weakening of moral and physical fibre that they avoid all personal contact or association with such persons.[5]

The article provoked a reply from one particularly John Bull-ish character:

> My own experience has taught me that immediately after that excess of feeling which has of its own force taken shape in the poem or tone-picture,

---

2 C. Hubert H. Parry, *Style in Musical Art* (London, 1911), p. 128.

3 *Ibid.*, pp. 206, 241.

4 Malcolm Hamrick Brown, 'Tchaikovsky and His Music in Anglo-American Criticism, 1890s-1950s', in Alexander Mihailovic (ed.), *Tchaikovsky and his Contemporaries: A Centennial Symposium* (Westport and London, 1999), pp. 61-73, republished (in revised form) in Sophie Fuller and Lloyd Whitesell (eds.), *Queer Episodes in Music and Modern Identity* (Urbana and Chicago, 2002), pp. 134-49.

5 'Manliness in Music', *Musical Times and Singing Class Circular* (1 August 1889), pp. 460-1.

> the gun, the bicycle, the football or cricket ball, the rod and line, or the gloves are the best possible antidotes to the poisons of sedentary occupation and passions that alternately feed and waste the energies of life.[6]

Seen as either an activity for itinerant foreign musicians or as a form of feminine domestic accomplishment, music was often interpreted as un-British and effeminate. Men who wished to take up musical careers were obliged to project virile identities and write strongly nationalist music; Elgar would be the prime example here, as the work of recent scholars has amply demonstrated.

The link between music, sentiment and homosexuality became a key concern for many turn-of-the-century writers. Edward Carpenter, for instance, argued that 'the defect of the male Uranian, or Urning, is *not* sensuality—but rather *sentimentality*. The lower, more ordinary types of Urning are often terribly sentimental; the superior types strangely, almost incredibly emotional'.[7] This sentimentality was, according to Carpenter, crucial in turning the homosexual towards the arts as a mean of self-expression and personal satisfaction. The homosexual, he argued, had 'the artist's sensibility and perception', and was 'often a dreamer, of brooding, reserved habits, often a musician, or a man of culture, courted in society, which nevertheless does not understand him'.[8] Of all the arts, it was in fact music that marked out the modern homosexual, and Tchaikovsky in particular:

> As to music, this is certainly the art which in its subtlety and tenderness—and perhaps in a certain inclination to indulge in emotion—lies nearest to the Urning nature. There are few in fact of this nature who have not some gift in the direction of music—though, unless we cite Tschaikowsky, it does not appear that any thorough-going Uranian has attained to the highest eminence in this art.[9]

The potency of this discourse was such that anybody writing about Tchaikovsky was obliged to address the question of the emotional quality of his music, and—by implication—its ability to function as marker of modern sexuality. Moreover, stereotypes linking the emotions, sexuality and music were strongly linked to issues of national identity that tended to portray Russia in terms of a feminised, emotional oriental culture.

---

6 Lennox Amott, 'Manliness in Music', *The Musical Times*, 1 October 1889, p. 620.

7 Edward Carpenter, *The Intermediate Sex: A Study of Some Transitional Types of Men and Women* (London and Manchester, 1908), p. 13.

8 *Ibid.*, p. 33.

9 *Ibid.*, p. 111.

The impact of these ideas can be seen particularly in the writings of Rosa Newmarch—Tchaikovsky's first English-language biographer and the most prominent, consistent and successful advocate of Russian music in turn-of-the-century Britain.[10] In many respects, Newmarch subscribes to the dominant view of Tchaikovsky's music as excessively emotional. In her 1900 biography, she gives the following assessment of Tchaikovsky's ambiguous status in Britain:

> Another source alike of weakness and popularity in Tchaikovsky's music is his sympathy with the *maladie du siècle*; his command of every note in the gamut of melancholy. 'A poet of one mood in all his lays,' his monotony of pessimism, though it must at times weary the sane-minded individual, seems to engage the public and draw them to him most persistently in his moods of blackest despair.[11]

Specifically she claims that:

> In the Sixth, Tchaikovsky seems to have concentrated the brooding melancholy which is the most characteristic and recurrent of all his emotional phases. Throughout the whole of his music we are never far away from this shadow. Sometimes this mood seems real enough; sometimes it strikes us as merely artificial and rhetorical. But melancholy in some form constitutes the peculiar quality of his genius, and nowhere does it brood more heavily or with more tragic intensity than in the last movement of this symphony.[12]

Furthermore, she faults his songs for their 'monotonous vein of sentimental melancholy', arguing that 'the great preponderance of the 'tearful minor' in his songs suggests an unhealthy condition of mind'. Her description of Tchaikovsky as 'this gentle and sensitive artist, possessed with an almost feminine craving for approval and encouragement' even hints at the link between melancholy and sexuality that was so prevalent at the time, as does her reference to 'his tender-heartedness and the almost feminine sensibility of his nature'.[13]

Newmarch's writings are significant because of the way she handles this particular discourse in seemingly contradictory ways. On the one hand, she downplays the importance of melancholy and morbidity in his music—a crucial strategy if establishment doubters such as Parry were to be

---

10 Philip Ross Bullock, *Rosa Newmarch and Russian Music in Late Nineteenth and Early Twentieth-Century England*, Royal Musical Association Monographs, 18 (Farnham, 2009).

11 Rosa Newmarch, *Tchaikovsky: His Life and Works, with Extracts from his Writings, and the Diary of his Tour Abroad in 1888* (London, 1900), pp. 2-3.

12 *Ibid.*, p. 106.

13 *Ibid.*, pp. 30, 25 and 69.

converted to appreciating a music that Newmarch valued highly. Rejecting rumours about the Sixth Symphony as some sort of autobiographical confession, Newmarch criticised British audiences for their interested in a limited range of Tchaikovsky's works, and suggested that his reputation for morbidity said more about his listeners than about the composer himself:

> We who in England know Tchaikovsky so well—so much too well—by his *Sixth Symphony*, are disposed to interpret the whole trend of his character by this one dark-toned work, which may reflect—for all we know—as much the tragic historical destinies of his country as the shadow of a personal sorrow. [...] I think we shall never appreciate the true greatness of Tchaikovsky until we have forgotten, for a time, the over-wrought emotion of the *Sixth Symphony* [...]. Then perhaps we shall turn with pleasure to the wholesome vigour and dramatic interest of *The Tempest*; to the poetic sentiment, the intense passion, the poignant—but controlled—melancholy of *Francesca da Rimini*, one of the most beautiful examples of programme music ever written; and the numerous other interesting works of his best and most robust period. Meanwhile it is good to see Tchaikovsky in a sober, business-like capacity, sane and clear-headed, exercising his critical faculties with a discretion and reserve that goes far to correct any false impressions of his extreme morbid subjectivity.[14]

As with so many aspects of her work, Newmarch derives her vocation as a writer on Russian music from countering the lazy stereotypes and ingrained prejudices that she encountered.

One the other hand, Newmarch strikingly accepts—albeit partially—the interpretation of Tchaikovsky as an overly subjective composer since she believed that his emotional range was something that British composers could learn from. At the time Newmarch was writing, British music was undergoing what is often termed a renaissance, and Newmarch was keen to play a part in shaping that process:

> As to the influence exerted by foreign music on the revival, she thinks that some of our composers have submitted too much to the influence of Brahms, who, although a sincere and natural composer, produces on his disciples the curious effect of making them wearisome, even though he gives them academic respectability. As to young composers, the influence of Russian music has been extensive and salutary. They have learned from Tchaikovsky a certain emotional pessimism and in general the art of effective orchestration.[15]

---

14 *Ibid.*, pp. 112-3.

15 M., 'Mrs. Rosa Newmarch', *The Musical Times*, 1 April 1911, pp. 226-7.

Elsewhere, her argument was yet clearer:

> The recent cult of Tchaikovsky's music in this country may have been over-emphasised, but side by side with much imitation of his mannerisms it has left us with a distinctly emotional gain, our younger composers losing under his influence some of the Englishman's self-conscious horror of 'giving himself away'; while familiarity with the Russian school in general has imparted immense style and brilliance to our orchestration during the last ten years.[16]

The 'emotional pessimism' of Tchaikovsky's music was, in Newmarch's eyes, not a marker of a morbid sensibility, let alone an indication of sexual deviance. Rather, it was a vital and generative influence on the limited emotional range of British music, which was constrained by durable prejudices against music as an art form likely to encourage moral degeneracy.

If Newmarch's writings on Tchaikovsky show her negotiating astutely between rejecting and endorsing such accounts of music, then her less well-known statements about Rimsky-Korsakov show a more determined attempt to defend Russian music against its British detractors, and to reject accounts of modern Russian music as dangerously melancholic and even worse. Newmarch in fact wrote about Rimsky-Korsakov more than nearly any other figure—there are at least 6 articles or chapters devoted to him in her output, dating from 1897 to 1914.[17] Moreover, Rimsky-Korsakov is often held up as the direct opposite of Tchaikovsky on a number of important grounds. Writing in 1905, Newmarch claimed that 'With a nature to which the objective world makes so strong an appeal, impassioned self-revelation is not a primary and urgent necessity. In this respect he is the antithesis of Tchaikovsky'. Later, she makes the same point a greater length:

> Rimsky-Korsakov does not correspond to our stereotyped idea of the Russian temperament. He is not lacking in warmth of feeling which kindles to passion in some of his songs; but his moods of exaggerated emotion are very rare. His prevailing tones are bright and serene, and occasionally flushed with

16 Rosa Newmarch, 'Chauvinism in Music', *The Edinburgh Review* (July 1912), pp. 101.

17 Rosa Newmarch, 'Rimsky-Korsakov: A Biographical Sketch', *The Musical Standard* (6 March 1897), pp. 152-3; (13 March 1897), pp. 166-8; 'Rimsky-Korsakov', *Zeitschrift der internationalen Musikgesellschaft*, VII, no.1 (October 1905), pp. 9-12; 'The Development of National Opera in Russia: Rimsky Korsakov', *Proceedings of the Musical Association*, XXXI (1904–5), pp. 111-29; 'Rimsky-Korsakov, Nicholas Andreievich', in J.A. Fuller Maitland (ed.), *Grove's Dictionary of Music and Musicians*, IV (London, 1908), pp. 102-5; and 'Rimsky-Korsakov: Personal Reminiscences', *Monthly Musical Record*, XXXVIII (August 1908), pp. 172-3.

glowing colour. If he rarely shocks our hearts into a poignant realisation of darkness and despair, neither has he any of the hysterical tendency which sometimes detracts from the impressiveness of Tchaikovsky's *cris de cœur*.[18]

By admitting the intensity of Tchaikovsky's emotional range, Newmarch creates a space where Rimsky-Korsakov can instead be held up as a composer of interest to British audiences. Aware that Russian music was so closely identified with Tchaikovsky (and especially his Sixth Symphony), Newmarch seeks to establish a different account of Russian music that would accord more closely with British taste at the same time as challenging widespread preconceptions. For Newmarch, 'his music is entirely free from that tendency to melancholy unjustly supposed to be the characteristic of all Russian art',[19] and British composers and critics would do well to listen to his music.

The high point of Newmarch's espousal of Rimsky-Korsakov, both as a significant figure in his own right and as an acceptable representative of the Russian school, came in her brief 1908 memoir, written after the composer's death. Her article began by summarising his role in the 1905 Revolution and describing him as 'a man of the highest ethical ideals, a liberal in the best sense of the word'.[20] It ends with her most explicit rejection of the ideas and ideologies that had shaped the reception of Russian music in Britain, against which she sets her own endorsement of Rimsky-Korsakov in strikingly explicit terms:

> Of late years English critics have expended a good deal of censure upon the morbid and melancholy tendencies of modern composers. Death and sorrow, unhappy passion—all kinds of impolite and indiscreet tragedy — have incurred their displeasure and caused much shaking of heads over the decadence and pessimism of the younger generation. The influence of Tschaïkowsky has not altogether unjustly been held accountable for some of this wilful melancholy. That being the case, it is strange how few good words have been said in this country on behalf of a composer who combines in his music poetic interest with a vigorous and manly optimism. Rimsky-Korsakov was the embodiment of all those qualities which stage literature and a misinformed Press have taught us *not* to look for in the Russian character: sincerity, unpretentiousness, refinement, gaiety, and a sweet and healthy outlook upon life.[21]

18 'Rimsky-Korsakov', p. 10, and 'The Development of National Opera in Russia: Rimsky Korsakov', p. 115.

19 'Rimsky-Korsakov, Nicholas Andreievich', p. 104.

20 'Rimsky-Korsakov: Personal Reminiscences', p. 172.

21 *Ibid.*, p. 173.

Throughout Newmarch's writings, we see an attempt to link a composer's biography with an awareness of his musical language. The 'vigorous and manly optimism' of Rimsky-Korsakov's music were allied, in her mind, to the engaged liberalism of his public politics, and offered an alternative account of Russian music that otherwise accorded too great a degree of attention to the supposedly pathological qualities of Tchaikovsky's music. Moreover, in recommending Rimsky-Korsakov's music as the embodiment of a kind of liberalism that would not have been out of place in Edwardian Britain, Newmarch was promoting a view of Russia that stressed its proximity to and similarity with values that were wholly and uncontroversially British, and thus set herself against Russophobic view that saw Russia as nothing more than an oriental, barbarian, half-developed interloper within modern Europe.

Ultimately, Newmarch's attempts to downplay the deviant melancholy of Tchaikovsky and to advocate Rimsky-Korsakov as an alternative figure of interest to modern British critics and composers were unsuccessful. The forces of received opinion were just too strong to be resisted by one woman, however determined. As news of Tchaikovsky's sexuality because common knowledge, he rapidly lost what little critical favour he had once enjoyed (even if popular audiences remained loyal to his works). Neither did the day come when Rimsky-Korsakov's works (and especially his operas) began to enjoy the prominence Newmarch felt they deserved. Nonetheless, Newmarch's writings constitute an important strain not only in writings on Russian music in turn-of-the-century Britain, but also in the development of discourses on the emotions that would continue to shape the theory and practice of music in Britain for some time to come, and indicate the complex interaction of gender, sexuality, emotion and national identity that was so central to the musical renaissance in a country that had long been held to be 'ohne Musik'.

9. 'Infantine Smudges of Paint… Infantine Rudeness of Soul': British Reception of Russian Art at the Exhibitions of the Allied Artists' Association, 1908–1911

Louise Hardiman

The many-faceted artistic displays of the Ballets Russes, first seen in London in 1911, together with the Russian section of Roger Fry's famed Second Post-Impressionist Exhibition of 1912, are often cited as the prime instances of when Russian art first made its mark upon the scene of British artistic modernism.[1] Too little attention has been paid, however, to another important forum for the display and reception of Russian art in Britain which dates from several years earlier, namely, the exhibitions of the newly established Allied Artists' Association (A.A.A.).[2] These

I would like to thank Rosalind P. Blakesley and Jesco Oser for their comments on earlier drafts of this chapter. I am also grateful to Oser for his help in sourcing the illustrations of Princess Mariia Tenisheva's enamels which accompany this chapter.

1 Literature discussing the reception of the Ballets Russes in Britain is too extensive to list here. However, for a concise account, see Lynn Garafola, *Diaghilev's Ballets Russes* (New York; Oxford, 1989), pp. 300-29. On Fry's exhibition, see *Catalogue of the Second Post-Impressionist Exhibition* (exhibition catalogue, London, Goupil Galleries, 1912), and, in particular, Boris Anrep, 'The Russian Group' in the catalogue introduction; Anna Gruetzner-Robins, *Modern Art in Britain 1910-1914* (London, 1997), pp. 105-7; Boris Anrep, 'Po povodu londonskoi vystavki s uchastiem russkikh khudozhnikov', *Apollon*, II (1913), p. 47.

2 The only significant scholarly discussion of the topic to date is contained in two articles by Adrian Glew. See Adrian Glew, 'Every Work of Art is the Child of its Time, Often it Is the Mother of our Emotions', *Tate Etc*, VII (Summer 2006), pp. 39-43 and 'Blue Spiritual

exhibitions, staged in London from 1908 onwards, are equally important to our understanding of the history of British-Russian cultural exchange during this period, in that they offered audiences interpretations of modern trends in Russian art which differed from those which would be showcased later by Fry, Sergei Diagilev and their respective collaborators. Moreover, these ground-breaking displays were promoted by other less well-known mediators of Russian culture in Britain: Frank Rutter, the A.A.A.'s founder, and the Russian artist and patroness Princess Mariia Tenisheva, who worked with him on a special Russian section for his inaugural exhibition. This chapter summarises the content of Russian art seen at A.A.A. exhibitions between 1908 and 1911 and briefly considers the critical reaction. Furthermore, it adds additional context to the ongoing scholarly debate as to how British responses to Russian culture were shaped by existing perceptions of Russia, in particular, as to its 'barbarism' or 'primitiveness'.

When Rutter set up the A.A.A., his aim was to create a British platform for the display of modern artistic trends akin to that established by the Salon d'Automne and the Salon des Indépendants in Paris. Billed as the 'London Salon', the first exhibition took place in the Royal Albert Hall from 11 July to 6 August 1908 (fig. 1). Although a limit of five works per artist was imposed, there were some 4 000 entries, mostly British.[3] However, signalling his modernist credentials, Rutter had also decided to include a separate display of foreign art in each annual event. For maximum impact in the opening year, he chose the little-known art of Russia. As he wrote in the catalogue:

> Following the precedent of the Salon d'Automne [...] the committee of management hopes to make each year a special display of the art of some foreign country, and this year a commencement is made with a representative collection of the modern national art of Russia. This special section has been entirely organised by Princess Marie Tenicheff, who has done so much to encourage and develop the distinctive arts and crafts of her country.[4]

Sounds: Kandinsky and the Sadlers, 1911-16', *The Burlington Magazine*, CXXXIX, no. 1134 (September 1997), pp. 600-15. It should also be mentioned, however, that there was some brief critical discussion of the inaugural A.A.A. exhibition in Russian journals of the period. See, for example, I. Kirillov, 'Khudozhestvennye vesti', *Rech'*, 1/14, No. 155 (July 1908), p. 5.

3 In subsequent years, the limit upon entries per artist would be reduced to three.

4 Frank Rutter, 'Introduction', in *Catalogue to the First Salon of the Allied Artists' Association* (London, 1908).

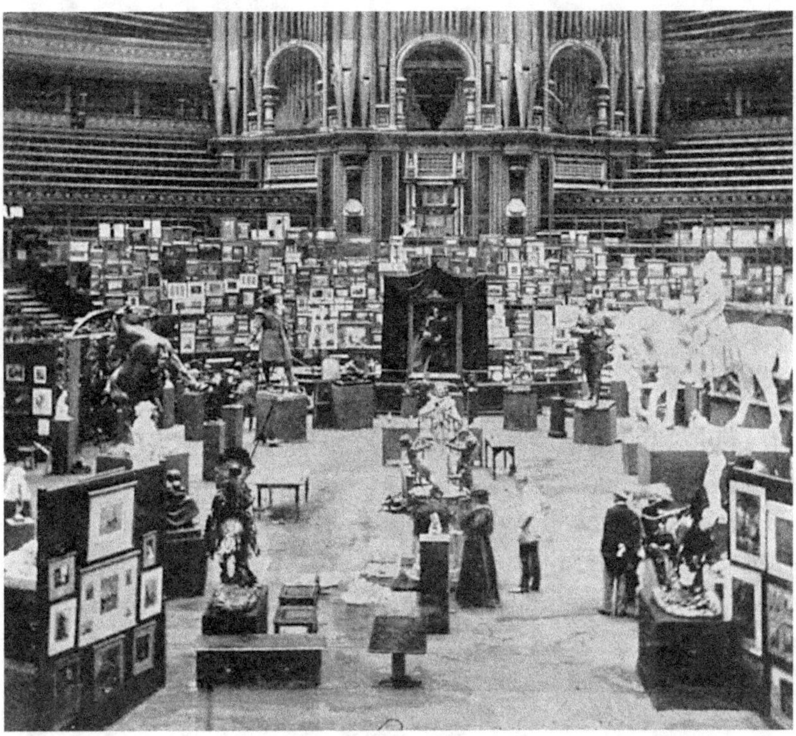

Fig. 9.1 Photograph of the 1908 Exhibition of the Allied Artists' Association at the Royal Albert Hall in London, *Illustrated London News* (18 July 1908). © Illustrated London News Ltd/Mary Evans.

The reasons as to why Rutter chose Russia and 'Princess Marie Tenicheff' (Mariia Klavdievna Tenisheva (1858-1928) are not documented. However, Russian entries at the Paris Salons in recent years had been particularly successful, and he may have been aware of previous events organised by Tenisheva in the French capital. Specifically, between 1907 and 1908 there had been two major exhibitions of works from the artists' colony at Talashkino, near Smolensk, which she had founded at around the turn of the century.[5] In their wake, a handful of articles on Talashkino had

5 On Tenisheva and the Talashkino workshops, see A. Abramova, *Talashkino* (Smolensk, 1950); John A. Bowlt, 'Two Maecenases: Savva Mamontov and Princess Tenisheva', *Apollo* (December 1973), pp. 444-53 and John A. Bowlt, *The Silver Age: Russian Art of the Early Twentieth Century and the 'World of Art' Group* (Newtonville, Massachusetts, 1979), pp. 39-46; and Wendy R. Salmond, *Arts and Crafts in Late Imperial Russia: Reviving the Kustar Art Industries, 1870-1917* (Cambridge, 1996), pp. 115-43. Tenisheva's two Paris exhibitions of this period were held at the Musée des Arts décoratifs at the Louvre and the Galerie des Artistes modernes. For the catalogues, see *Objets d'art russes anciens, faisants parties*

featured in British art publications.[6] Yet, it seems unlikely that Rutter knew Tenisheva personally, as she had few links to London artistic circles at that time. Indeed, he states that he was assisted in the organisation of the foreign section by the Polish artist Jan de Holewinski, 'who had been requested by Tenisheva to organise for her in London an exhibition of Russian arts and crafts'.[7]

In appointing Tenisheva as curator, Rutter was unwittingly participating in the prevailing debate in Russia about the future of Russian art and its relationship to Western art. The arrangement afforded her another opportunity to expand the international reputation of Talashkino, and, more importantly, to gain exposure for the version of modern Russian art which she wished to promote. For the Talashkino project had established Tenisheva as the latest standard-bearer for the 'neo-national' school, in which Russian art that principally reworked Slavic themes was favoured over that which sought to acknowledge the influence of a more European tradition.[8] It was these trends which she would also showcase in London. Evidencing his ignorance of the subject, Rutter's catalogue introduction described the section as a 'representative collection of the modern national art of Russia', but this was far from the case. Most tellingly, it revealed little of the avant-garde movement already well underway in Russia by 1908. Furthermore, though there were 175 Russian works, only a handful of professional artists were represented. The narrow range of the display is illustrated by the fact that, of Tenisheva's contributors, only Ivan Bilibin (1876-1942) and Nikolai Rerikh (1874-1947) already had well-established artistic reputations by this time. Moreover, both remained for the most part outside the avant-garde camp. The selection thus displayed only one of the many co-existing strands of Russian modernism; indeed, it contrasted sharply with the more broadly constituted array of Russian art recently presented by Diagilev at the 1906-7 Salon d'Automne.

---

des collections de la Princesse Marie Tenichef exposés au Musée des Arts Décoratifs du 10 mai au 10 octobre 1907 (exhibition catalogue, Paris, 1907) and *Exposition d'art russe moderne* (exhibition catalogue, Paris, 1907).

6 C. de Danilovich, 'Talashkino: Princess Tenisheva's School of Russian Applied Art', *International Studio*, XXXII, No. 126 (August 1907), pp. 135-9; 'Talashkino', *Studio*, XXXII (October 1907), pp. 328-30.

7 Frank Rutter, *Since I Was Twenty-five* (London, 1927), p. 182.

8 For a detailed account of the history of the Russian neo-national school, see Evgeniia Kirichenko, *Russian Design and the Fine Arts 1750-1917* (New York, 1991), pp. 135-273.

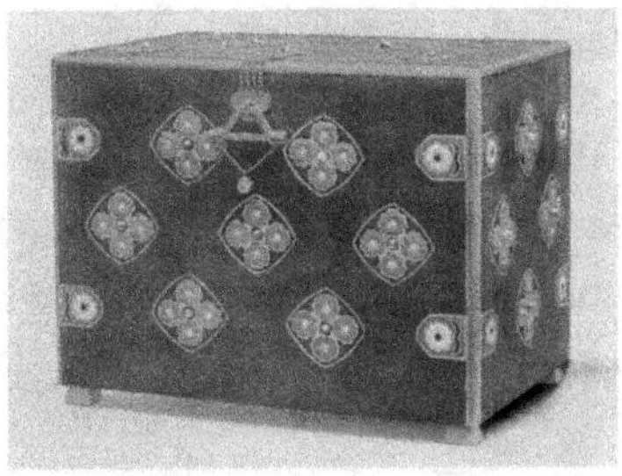

Fig. 9.2 Mariia Tenisheva, *Enamelled Amaranth Chest* (*c.*1907). Reproduced in Denis Roche, *Les émaux champlevés de la princesse Marie Ténichév* (Paris, 1907).

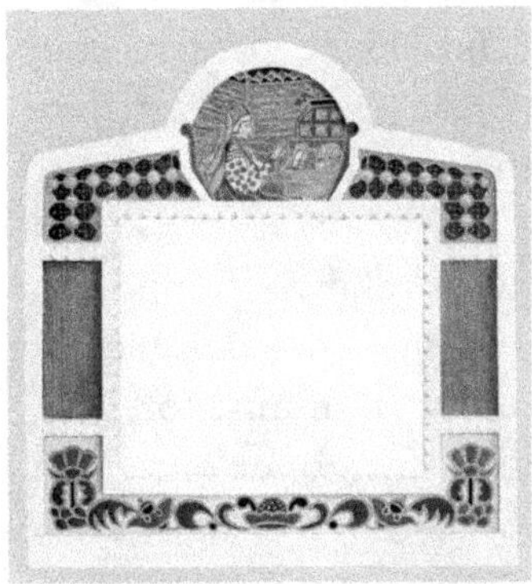

Fig. 9.3 Mariia Tenisheva, *Enamelled Mirror Frame* (*c.*1907). Reproduced in Denis Roche, *Les émaux champlevés de la princesse Marie Ténichév* (Paris, 1907).

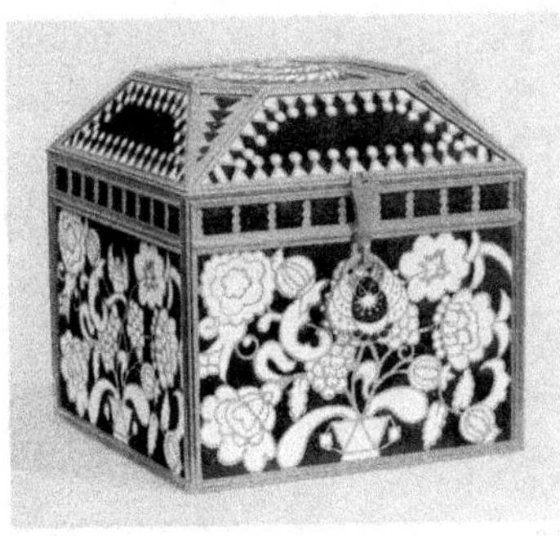

Fig. 9.4 Mariia Tenisheva, *Ornamental Chest* (*c.*1907). Reproduced in Denis Roche, *Les émaux champlevés de la princesse Marie Ténichév* (Paris, 1907).

Nevertheless, it was extremely useful for Rutter's inaugural exhibition that the 'neo-national' works were known to appeal to Western audiences—Tenisheva's success in Paris had already demonstrated this. 'Russian-ness' was clearly highlighted, playing to Edwardian tastes for the exotic and unusual. Among the works exhibited were various of Bilibin's illustrations for Russian folk tales, including 'The Golden Cockerel', 'The King Saltan' (Tsar Saltan) and 'Volga'.[9] Works by Rerikh comprised the majority of exhibits, with a remarkable 87 paintings and 2 sets of book illustrations including those 'For Rouslan and Ludmila (Pushkin)'.[10] As in Paris, Tenisheva placed Rerikh centre-stage, in a direct challenge to Diagilev's relegation of the artist to the margins in his Salon d'Automne exhibition.[11] Also sharing the neo-Russian style were the exhibits of her own enamel work, displayed alongside a selection of Talashkino peasant crafts[12] (Figs. 9.2-9.4). Finally, there were sculptures by Konstantin Rausch von Traubenberg (1871-1935), and architectural designs by Alexei Shchusev (1873-1945) and Vladimir Pokrovskii (1871-1931).

Though the Russian works shown formed a tiny proportion of the 4 000 works displayed, they attracted considerable attention, and reviews were generally positive. A weekly columnist for *The Observer* thought that the Russian section was 'the only harbour of rest' in a sea of wildly differing works; it was, he added, 'an engrossingly interesting display'.[13] He was apparently so impressed that he devoted the most part of the following week's column to it. Tenisheva's enamels, he thought, had 'more than a hint of barbaric splendour and [were] clearly derived from medieval Byzantine models'.[14] As to the paintings and sculpture, 'the strangeness of it all is certainly attractive and fascinating'; however, 'the aesthetic code upon which this art is based is so alien to the Western spirit that it is difficult to feel much sympathy with it'.[15] Though he was attracted to the 'decorative spirit' which he found in the art of Bilibin and Rerikh, he puzzled over the lack of evidence of any modern European artistic tradition, and saw only the hallmarks of a Byzantine legacy. The lack of an identifiably European

9 *Catalogue to the First Salon of the Allied Artists' Association* (London, 1908), nos. 1-44.

10 *Ibid.*, nos. 64-171.

11 Salmond, p. 141.

12 *Catalogue to the First Salon of the Allied Artists' Association*, nos. 172-3.

13 P.G. Konody, 'Art Notes: Allied Artists' Association at the Albert Hall', *The Observer* (12 July 1908), p. 12.

14 P.G. Konody, 'Art Notes: Russian Art at the Albert Hall', *The Observer* (19 July 1908), p. 5.

15 *Ibid.*

style was also remarked upon by other commentators. One observer was also particularly struck by the art of Bilibin:

> M. Bilibin's [books] will come as a delightful novelty. They are absolutely Russian in sentiment and feeling with an occasional trace of Oriental influence [...]. They are so unlike anything yet seen in this country.[16]

Such responses provide yet another example of how Russian culture was seen by Britons not only as different, but also through an 'orientalist' lens. Moreover, the association with Byzantine art was one which, in due course, would be taken up by Roger Fry, when he invited the emigré mosaic artist and Byzantinist Boris Anrep to curate the Russian section of his Second Post-Impressionist Exhibition in 1912. Writing much later, Rutter seemed keen to assert that he had been one step ahead of Fry, suggesting that his first A.A.A. exhibition 'revealed to London the continued existence of the Byzantine tradition at a time when historical schools had not yet revived interest in Byzantine art'.[17] However, the claim is difficult to justify. Although Tenisheva, in her enamels, was to some extent reworking ideas from the Byzantine tradition, the art of Bilibin and Rerikh frequently dealt with Slavic, pre-historic or highly national themes in which this influence is non-existent or barely discernible—Rerikh's images of pagan Rus', to cite one example.

In subsequent years, Rutter did not repeat the concept of a dedicated foreign section; a Polish exhibition was mooted for 1909, but never materialised. Nevertheless, the display of Russian art in 1908 set a precedent for subsequent years, and, significantly, the exhibitions of 1909 and 1910 heralded the first British appearances of the art of Vasilii Kandinskii. Adrian Glew has suggested that Kandinskii might have been introduced to the A.A.A. by Tenisheva, who, he claims, was a member of the Selection Committee in 1909.[18] The contact was more likely to have been Rerikh, whose ethnographic interests and predilection for Slavic

---

16 W.R., 'A Russian Book-Illustrator: M. Ivan Bilibin', *Athenaeum*, 4218 (29 August 1908), pp. 247-8. More recent scholarship suggests the possibility that, contrary to this reviewer's assertion, Bilibin may have been influenced by the work of English artists such as William Morris and Walter Crane. See Anna Bronovitskaya, 'An Accidental Similarity?: British Art and Russian Artists in the late 19th and early 20th Century', *Pinakotheke*, 18-19 (2004), pp. 104-10 (p. 107).

17 Frank Rutter, *Art in My Time* (London, 1933), p. 136.

18 See Glew, 'Every work of art', p. 40. Yet, the 1909 catalogue does not list Tenisheva as a committee member, and my research thus far has found no evidence of her involvement in the second Salon. Moreover, Kandinskii was not a member of the Talashkino circle nor it is clear that he ever visited there. Neither Salmond, Zhuraleva nor Tenisheva herself

pre-historical themes in his art were shared by Kandinskii.[19] However, Kandinskii himself may have taken the initiative—he was now based in Munich and had already exhibited elsewhere in Europe. By 1909, the artist had progressed from the neo-impressionistic style characterising his earlier works, in which historical Russian motifs were clearly discernible, to what were now highly abstract canvases. His works of this period can be seen as bridging both the neo-national movement and the emergent avant-garde, and their appearance in London signalled a decisive shift in the style and content of Russian art on display at the A.A.A. Salon. This shift was confirmed by the participation of the modernists Il'ia Mashkov (1881-1944) and Petr Konchalovskii (1876-1956) in the exhibition of 1911. Moreover, the critical response to these later exhibitions also made clear that another version of Russian art was now being seen, one quite different from the 'engrossingly interesting' display curated by Tenisheva.

Rutter later recalled that the first British showing of Kandinskii's art excited 'a large amount of interest and heated controversy'.[20] That year, the artist entered 3 works: *Jaune et Rose* and *Paysage* in the paintings section, and *Frame with 12 Engravings* in the etchings section.[21] Identifying them, in order to assess why they were so controversial, is difficult—the catalogue was not illustrated and the titles referenced do not clearly correspond with Catalogue Raisonné entries for the relevant dates.[22] By contrast, the works Kandinskii entered for the 1910 Salon—*Composition No. 1, Improvisation No. 6* and *Landscape*—are easier to identify (albeit tentatively, as, again, there were no catalogue illustrations), and thus provide a more useful case study on reception.[23] *Composition No. 1* (1910) is a known work among the artist's extensive series of *Compositions*.[24] It seems likely that *Landscape* was the second *Composition*, as one scholar has mentioned that Kandinskii also referred to this as 'Paysage (Landscape)'.[25] Unfortunately, the first 3

---

mention any relationship between the two (See Salmond; M.K. Tenisheva, *Vpechatleniia moei zhizni* (Paris, 1933); L. Zhuravleva, *Kniaginia Mariia Tenisheva* (Smolensk, 1994)).

19 On the ethnographical aspects of Kandinskii's art and his interest in pre-history, see Peg Weiss, *Kandinsky and Old Russia: The Artist as Ethnographer and Shaman* (New Haven and London, 1995).

20 Frank Rutter, *Art in My Time*, p. 137.

21 *Catalogue to the Second Salon of the Allied Artists' Association* (London, 1909), nos. 1068-9 and 1923.

22 Hans K. Roethel and Jean K. Benjamin, *Kandinsky: Catalogue Raisonné of the Oil Paintings*, I: 1900-1915 (London, 1982).

23 *Catalogue to the Third Salon of the Allied Artists' Association* (London, 1910), nos. 961-3.

24 Jelena Hahl-Koch, *Kandinsky* (London, 1993) (trans. Karin Brown *et al.*), p. 166.

25 *Ibid.*, p. 163, citing a letter from Kandinskii to Gabriele Münter of 5 November 1910.

Compositions were destroyed during WWII, but there are extant sketches for both the exhibited works: *Sketch for Composition No. 1* (Musée National d'Art Moderne, Centre Georges Pompidou, Paris), showing the central motif, and *Sketch for Composition No. 2* (1910) (Solomon Guggenheim Museum, New York). The third work, *Improvisation No. 6* (1910) is one of the series of *Improvisations* which date from 1909 onwards.

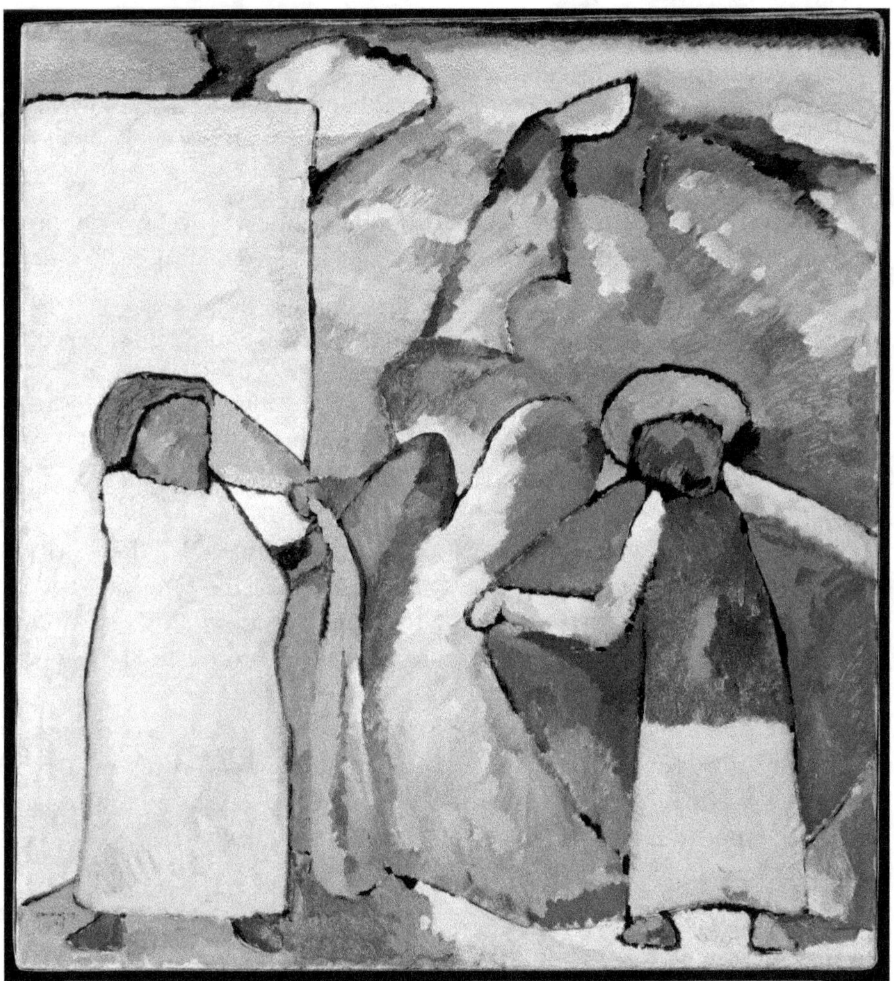

Fig. 9.5 Vasilii Kandinskii, *Improvisation No. 6 ('Afrikanisches')* (1910).
Oil on canvas, 107 x 95.5cm.

Rutter described all three works as 'abstract' and, in further confirmation of the theory that *Paysage* was *Composition No. 2*, specifically mentions a 'so-called landscape, nearly as non-representative as the other two'.[26]

Some evidence of the reception in the British press illustrates the degree of shock among the critical community upon first seeing these non-representational artworks. For one reviewer, the paintings clearly were not worthy of exhibition:

> Wassily Kandinsky offends from malice aforethought. Shapeless patches of garish colours, strung together in meaningless juxtaposition by bold, black lines, are dignified by the names of 'Composition No. 1', 'Improvisation No. 6', and, save the mark! 'Landscape'. These atrocities are really only suitable for the badge of the Wagner Society.[27]

Another commentator merely conveys his bafflement as to how he might interpret a work of abstract art:

> In the case of Kandinsky [...] I entirely failed to unearth his secret. [...] [T] hough I laid my hand upon the motive, which I held to be candles, crowned by flames of a supremely decorative yellow, yet that did not help the clouds to break [...]. I was unable to understand anything except that I was confronted by an apparently promiscuous medley of colour; colour pure and strong and fervid; wherein I could detect the adumbrations of strange forms, reminiscent of the nursery [...].[28]

Yet another resorted to the nursery analogy, describing one of the works as 'three archaic wooden dolls on hobby horses, whilst the blue cabbage on a winding red snake may possibly be intended for a tree'.[29] Thus, in their different ways, each of these writers allude to the primitivism of the works, the prioritisation of colour, and the absence of realism.

In 1911, Kandinskii contributed a set of works called 'Six Woodcuts and an Album with Text' and, again, these exhibits evidenced his continued explorations into new artistic territory.[30] However, it was the other Russians who participated that year who attracted the larger share of the critical

---

26 Rutter, *Art in My Time*, p. 143.

27 Wilfred H. Myers in *The Onlooker* (22 July 1910), cited in 'Press Opinions on the 3rd London Salon 1910', *The Art News* (4 August 1910), p. 258. The reference to the Wagner Society picks up on the already well-established reputation of the German composer Richard Wagner as a modernist.

28 'How it Strikes a Contemporary', *The Art News* (4 August 1910), p. 255.

29 'Art Notes: The London Salon', *The Observer* (10 July 1910), p. 9.

30 *Catalogue to the Fourth Salon of the Allied Artists' Association* (London, 1911), no. 1201. These were the first of Kandinskii's works to be sold to a British collector, and their buyer, Michael Sadler, would go on to build a substantial collection of the artist's work (Glew, 'Blue Spiritual Sounds', p. 603, note 30).

opprobrium. Kandinskii had very likely encouraged his compatriots, Il'ia Mashkov (1881-1944) and Petr Konchalovskii (1876-1956) to enter the Salon. Both were founder members of the 'Bubnovyi valet' ('Knave of Diamonds') artists' group recently established in Moscow and had already exhibited at the Paris Salons. Rutter had certainly seen Mashkov's work; he had written a favourable review of the artist's 'heroic still-life' paintings seen at the Salon des Indépendants:

> His grapes are the size of plums, his plums the size of apples, and his apples the size of cannonballs. Not only is their size enlarged, but their colour is also intensified. These 'fruits of the Gods' (pace Wells) are summarily expressed with undeniable power, and are not without a certain barbaric splendour as decorations.[31]

Even Rutter, it seems, erstwhile champion of Russian art, was not immune from making racially motivated judgments, with his reference to 'barbaric splendour'.

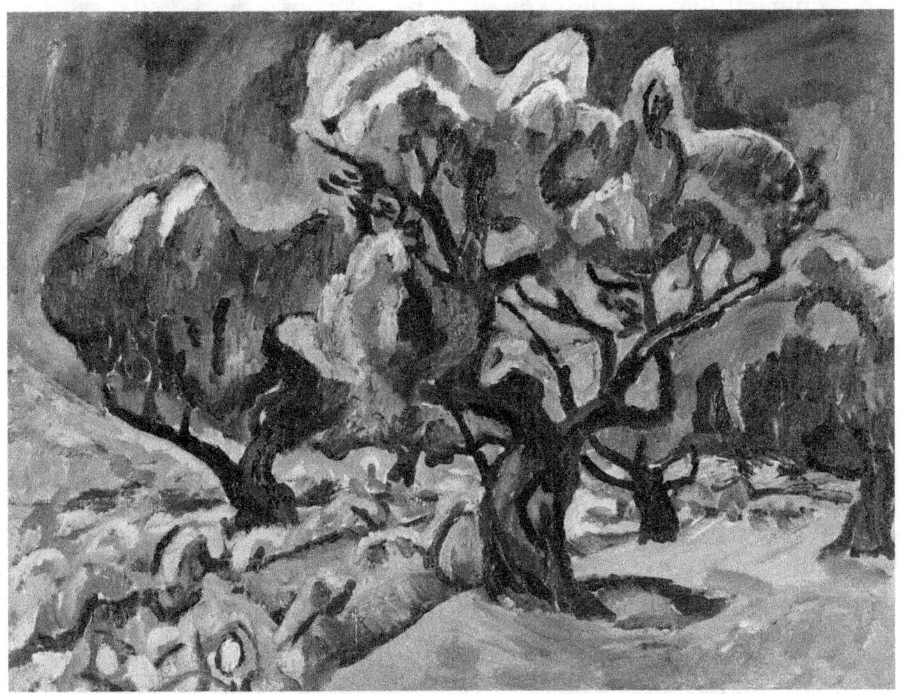

Fig. 9.6 Petr Konchalovskii, *Les oliviers* (1910). Oil on canvas, 70.5 x 90.2cm. Private Collection. Reproduced by permission of Sotheby's.

31 Frank Rutter, 'Salon d'Automne', *The Art News* (15 October 1910).

The Mashkov entries in 1911 (listed under 'Ilia Machkoff') were 'Portrait' and two 'Nature Mortes', one in the paintings section, and another in 'Large Paintings and Decorative Works'.[32] Konchalovskii (listed under 'Pierre Kantchalovsky') entered three works: *Amateur de Courses de Taureaux, Les Oliviers* and *Nature Morte*.[33]

The critical response was mixed. One writer commented enthusiastically that the Mashkov and Konchalovskii works, which were hung side by side, were 'examples of a very interesting and growing school of painting, upon which few in this city are qualified to form a critical opinion'.[34] He added that:

> In the arena we have an opportunity of seeing M. Machkoff's 'Nature Morte' [...], such as could be enjoyed in no other gallery in London, from across the Hall the amazing qualities of the picture can be seen to full advantage. In strength of colour and 'carrying power' it has no rival among its present company [...].[35]

The comment that the Mashkov work had 'carrying power' suggests that this still-life was of a similar kind to those 'larger than life' paintings in Paris which Rutter had reviewed. This commentator does not appear to base his remarks upon any notions of 'Russian-ness' in the paintings, but in singling them out it was clear that he had found something distinctive and novel about these works compared to the surrounding entries.

Not all reviewers responded so positively. For one, Mashkov's 'Portrait' was 'a Byzantine vision of a monstrously deformed human being', while a 'Nature Morte' was less '*morte*' than '*vivante*': 'alive with an uncanny, unnatural vitality [...] and testif[ying] to a frenziedly passionate colour sense'.[36] Yet again, these comments raise similar themes: Byzantine and primitive. This reviewer also singled out Konchalovskii's *Amateur de Courses de Taureaux* (*Fan of the Bullfight*) for attack, calling it 'revolting' and chiding the artist's 'contempt of the imitation of nature'.[37] But the most extreme reaction came from Arthur Lynch, a Member of Parliament and evidently a fierce and conservative critic. Calling his piece 'Artistic Rebels', he seems initially to praise the artists' novelty, referring to: 'audacity,

32 *Catalogue to the Fourth Salon of the Allied Artists' Association* (London, 1911), nos. 46, 47 and 951.
33 *Ibid.*, nos. 48-50.
34 Malcolm C. Drummond, 'Another Member's View', *The Art News* (15 July 1911), pp. 76-7.
35 *Ibid.*
36 'Art and Artists: The London Salon', *The Observer* (9 July 1911), p. 4.
37 *Ibid.*

intensity of feeling, high, impetuous spirit'. But his attack on the Russians was blunt:

> The 'Amateur de Courses' was by Mr Pierre Kantchalovsky and the Slav was not tamed there. [...] I am not quite sure [...] whether Pierre Kantchalovsky is an incorrigible humourist poking fun at the public, or whether he is the austere apostle of a new movement in art. His 'Amateur de Courses' sits in my mind when many excellent things are forgotten—sits in its infantine simplicity, sits in its infantine smudges of paint, sits in its infantine rudeness of soul.[38]

Amateur was one of an extensive series of paintings of matadors, the bullfighting ring and other genre scenes painted by Konchalovskii during a long sojourn in Spain. As with his other works of this period, the style is Fauvist—bright swathes of colour, primitive black outlining of motifs and an obvious disregard for realism.[39] Yet, in its Western subject-matter and its apparent adoption of French modernist trends, arguably this work was not so obviously Russian. Lynch clearly linked its primitivism with the artist's nationality, for not only does he scorn its 'infantine simplicity' and 'infantine smudges of paint', this work, he decrees, 'sits in its infantine rudeness of soul'. On the surface it is the comment of a conservative on the rebellious outlook of the modernist artist and his perceived lack of refinement. However, the additional layer of patronising xenophobia is made clear by the suggestion of 'taming' the 'Slav' in the bullring. That an MP, presumed to be well-off and well-educated, was making such observations confirms that prejudiced attitudes toward Russians were

---

38 Arthur Lynch, MP, 'Artistic Rebels: A Souvenir of the Allied Artists' Association', *The Art News* (15 December 1911).

39 'Amateur de Courses de Taureaux' would appear to correspond with a work of 1910 ('Liubitel' boiia bykov') listed in the catalogue of works in the monograph by V.A. Nikolskii (see V.A. Nikolskii, *Petr Petrovich Konchalovskii* (Moscow, 1936)). In addition, a work entitled 'Fan of Bullfight' (1910) is reproduced in the catalogue on the website of the Petr Konchalovsky Foundation (see www.pkonchalovsky.com). Other works from the Spanish period are illustrated in the monographs of Nikolskii and Neiman, such as 'Boi bykov', 'Matador Manuel' Garta', and 'Ispanskaia komnata' (all 1910) (see Nikolskii, and M. L. Neiman, *P. P. Konchalovskii* (Moscow, 1967)). Nikolskii also lists a 1910 work with the title 'Olivkoyve derev'ia', which appears to correspond with the other work exhibited in London, 'Les Oliviers'. 'Les Oliviers' was auctioned by Sothebys in 2006 (see http://www.artfact.com/auction-lot/petr-petrovich-konchalovsky-1-c-vxa0sq4x7c [accessed 15.10.2012]). It has not been possible to identify the third work, as both Russian monographs list numerous still life works of 1910-11. Interestingly, Neiman mentions that a 1912 work, 'Natiormort–Samovar', was in a London collection at the time of his publication, which could indicate that the exhibition led to a purchase the following year.

held at all levels of society. Indeed, Lynch was not the only commentator to reveal racial prejudice. Another lamented that:

> It is useless for English gentlemen painters to tell these Russians that they must not do it, they must conform to English nice ideas of beauty. You might just as well tell Niagara to behave more like Virginia Water and not to make such a splash.[40]

The quirky comparison of the Russian temperament to a mighty, unstoppable waterfall could perhaps be seen positively as a reference to Russia's expanse. Nevertheless, it repeats the idea that the Russians lacked refinement, were not gentlemen, and, in essence, were barbaric.

In subsequent A.A.A. exhibitions, the number of Russian paintings entered was overtaken by the number of Russian sculptures. Konchalovskii did not participate after 1911, but Mashkov entered three more works in 1912 (*Nature–Morte de la Paque, Nature-Morte,* and *Le Modele Vivante*).[41] The 1912 catalogue also lists Kandinskii as a contributor, though no titles are listed. He made a more significant contribution in 1913, showing three major works (*Improvisation (No. 29), Improvisation (No. 30),* and *Landscape with River Pappeln*).[42] Discussion of these later exhibitions is outside the scope of this chapter. Nevertheless, Russian participation was to be, in the end, short-lived, as no Russian artists entered works after 1913.

In conclusion, the mixed response to the Russian works displayed in these early years of the A.A.A. Salons suggests, as would be expected, that the British artistic and critical community was divided into conservatives and modernists. The conservatives tended to invoke traditionally negative reactions to Russia and Russians, using terms such as 'simplicity', 'barbaric', and, most damning of all, 'infantine rudeness of soul'. Yet, even the so-called modernists, such as Rutter and Fry, who admired recent developments in Russian art for their innovation, still revealed their prejudices and preoccupations about Russia: Fry's focus on the Byzantine tradition, for example, and Rutter's remarks as to 'barbaric splendour'. Nevertheless, through Rutter's initiative, the summer of 1908, rather than the arrival of the Ballets Russes almost exactly three years later, can be seen as the turning point after which Russian art gained a considerably greater prominence in Britain. The A.A.A. Salons provided a forum for its display in a wide range of different media, and thus a showcase for its considerable diversity in

40 C. Lewis-Hind, *The Daily Chronicle* (24 July 1911), cited in *The Art News* (15 August 1911).
41 *Catalogue to the Fifth Salon of the Allied Artists' Association* (London, 1912), nos. 746-8.
42 *Catalogue to the Sixth Salon of the Allied Artists' Association* (London, 1913), nos. 285-7.

content and style. Between Tenisheva's extensive Russian section of 1908 and Kandinskii's final participation in 1913, the varied exhibits of paintings were supplemented by book illustrations, works of applied art, Talashkino artefacts, woodcuts, and in the latter years, sculpture. However, although these shows highlighted the contrast between the neo-national school of modernism favoured by Tenisheva and the art of the emerging avant-garde artists Kandinskii, Mashkov and Konchalovskii, the brief examples of reception discussed in this chapter indicate that British audiences made little distinction between these competing versions of Russian modernism. To them, all of these artists were Russians, thereby invoking stereotyped responses based on their nationality.

Yet, at the same time, Kandinskii's frequent participation at the A.A.A. provided a channel for British artists to be exposed to his pioneering forays into abstraction.[43] His ideas were taken up enthusiastically by the Vorticists and other British modernist groups, and, arguably, were so influential that his art has since come to define Russian art in British eyes for the entire century to follow. On the other hand, Tenisheva's Russian section at the inaugural London Salon has long since disappeared from the historical picture. Yet, her role should not be overlooked. If 1908 was indeed a turning point for British attitudes to Russian art, establishing a momentum that would be so capably exploited by the Ballets Russes in the years to follow, then, in Britain at least, it was she, rather than Diagilev, who was initially more influential in what Wendy Salmond has termed their 'bitter competition [...] to determine the true nature of Russian art in the European imagination'.[44] The early A.A.A. exhibitions provide an extremely important case-study in the display and reception of Russian art in Britain, and, more importantly, one which adds weight to an overarching hypothesis that British cultural engagement with modernist trends in Russian art began earlier in the 20th century than has generally been acknowledged.

---

43 On the links of Kandinskii to British modernism, see: Glew, '*Blue Spiritual Sounds*'; Gruetzner-Robins, pp. 130-4; Paul Edwards (ed.), *Blast: Vorticism 1914-1918* (Burlington, 2000), p. 114; Norbert Lynton, *The Story of Modern Art* (Oxford, 1980), p. 44.

44 Salmond, p. 142.

10. Crime and Publishing: How Dostoevskii Changed the British Murder

Muireann Maguire

Leonid Grossman acutely called Dostoevskii's *Crime and Punishment* 'a philosophical novel with a criminal setting';[1] the Irish novelist George Moore dismissed the same work as 'Gaboriau with psychological sauce'.[2] Whether one chooses to exaggerate or minimize the crime narrative inside Dostoevskii's novel, it exercised considerable influence on the subsequent development of the genre in Britain. Most historians of crime fiction mention *Crime and Punishment*, if only in passing and with an apology for tarnishing Dostoevskii's genius by association. Julian Symons writes, '[i]n a way Dostoevsky *was* a crime novelist, with the true taste for sensational material, but in his single case the results far transcend anything the crime novelist achieves or even aims at'.[3] William Godwin's *Caleb Williams* (1794) has endured an analogous critical fate, recognized as a major novel of ideas yet also frequently claimed as the 'first detective novel'.[4] Yet Dostoevskii's novel can be appropriated by the crime genre with greater justice than Godwin's. *Crime and Punishment* was written in the same decade as Émile Gaboriau's first *romans policiers* and Wilkie Collins's foundational novels of detection; its author had steeped himself in Eugène Sue's *Les mystères*

1 Leonid Grossman, *Dostoevskii: A Biography*, trans. Mary Mackler (London, 1974), p. 357.

2 Cited by W.H. Leatherbarrow, 'Introduction', in *Dostoevskii and Britain*, ed. W.H. Leatherbarrow (Oxford, 1995), pp. 1-38 (p. 25).

3 Julian Symons, *Bloody Murder: From the Detective Story to the Crime Novel: A History* (London, 1972), p. 58.

4 Michael Cohen, *Murder Most Fair: The Appeal of Mystery Fiction* (London, 2000), pp. 35-40.

de Paris (1843), and had recently read and reviewed Edgar Allan Poe's classics of criminal psychopathology, *The Tell-Tale Heart* and *The Black Cat* (both 1843).[5] In the context of such antecedents and contemporaries, there is every reason to regard *Crime and Punishment* as part of a generation of experimental, highly influential murder mysteries.[6]

This chapter analyses how *Crime and Punishment* influenced British fiction *as a crime novel*, arguing that Dostoevskii's model effected substantial changes to the construction of the fictional British murder. Interesting as it would be to pursue a structural comparison between *Crime and Punishment* and fiction by professional mystery writers like Agatha Christie and Josephine Tey, any such attempt founders on the lack of evidence indicating that these nominally 'low-brow' authors actually read Dostoevskii. I will therefore look at three British authors who are known to have engaged with Dostoevskii's novel in its first French and English translations: Robert Louis Stevenson, George Gissing and G.K. Chesterton. I will discuss how each of these writers adapted an aspect of Dostoevskii's criminal plot. My first topic is the murder itself; second, the criminal type; and third, the criminal investigator.

Stevenson: Murder in Cameo

Crime and Punishment first appeared in French translation in Dérély's version in 1884;[7] two years later, the first English translation, by Frederick Whishaw, followed. Considering Whishaw's verbosity, it was probably fortunate that Robert Louis Stevenson first read the novel in French. His immediate enthusiasm was evinced in these much-quoted lines to his friend John Addington Symonds: 'Raskolnikoff is easily the greatest book I have read in ten years; I am glad you took to it. Many find it dull: Henry James

5 For Joan Delaney Grossman's fascinating discussion of how Poe's tales may have influenced *Crime and Punishment* (providing a prototype for Raskol'nikov's masochistic compulsion to flaunt his guilt), see her *Edgar Allan Poe in Russia: A Study in Legend and Literary Influence* (Würzburg, 1973), pp. 31-4. Dostoevskii reviewed Poe's tales in 1861 for his journal *Vremia*.

6 For more conventionally themed analysis of how Dostoevskii's novels influenced British literature, see, for example, Gary Adelman, *Retelling Dostoyevsky: Literary Responses and Other Observations* (London, 2001); Colin Crowder, 'The Appropriation of Dostoevsky in the Early Twentieth Century: Cult, Counter-cult, and Incarnation', in *European Literature and Theology in the Twentieth Century*, eds. Colin Crowder and David Jasper (London, 1990), pp. 15-33; and Peter Kaye, *Dostoevsky and English Modernism, 1900-1930* (Cambridge, 1999).

7 Plon published a second edition of Dérély's translation, cited below, in 1885.

could not finish it: all I can say is, it nearly finished me. It was like having an illness'.[8] When he read *Crime and Punishment*, Stevenson was gestating two lurid tales of murder that would make him notorious: the short story 'Markheim' (written 1884, published 1885) and the novella *The Strange Case of Dr Jekyll and Mr Hyde* (1886). As long ago as 1916, Edgar Knowlton made the case that 'Markheim' is a 'cameo version' of Dostoevskii's novel.[9] Not only do many details of the two plots correspond, Stevenson has attempted to integrate a medley of Dostoevskian stylistic effects—flashbacks, delirium, unexpected visitors, even a Svidrigailov-like double—in order to replicate the confusion of a novice murderer's mind. Knowlton overlooks one or two discrepancies: Markheim is a genteel ne'er-do-well, rather than a student; his victim is a niggardly antiques dealer, rather than a pawnbroker; and the weapon is a poignard rather than an axe.

Nonetheless, the essential *murder* is little different:

> Markheim bounded from behind upon his victim. The long, skewer-like dagger flashed and fell. The dealer struggled like a hen, striking his temple on the shelf, and then tumbled on the floor in a heap.[10]

Contrast Dérély's *Le Crime et le Châtiment*:

> 'Aléna Ivanovna, selon son habitude, avait la tête nue. Ses cheveux grisonnants, clair-semés, et, comme toujours, gras d'huile, étaient rassemblés en une mince tresse, dite queue de rat, fixées sur la nuque par un morceau de peigne de corne. Le coup atteignit juste le sinciput, ce à quoi contribua la petite taille de la victime. Elle poussa à peine un faible crie et soudain s'affaissa sur le parquet; toutefois elle eut encore la force de lever les deux bras vers sa tête. [...] Alors Raskolnikoff, dont le bras avait retrouvé toute sa vigueur, asséna deux nouveaux coups de hache sur le sinciput de l'usurière.'[11]

In each case, the fatal blow falls from behind while the victim is distracted by a pretext devised by the murderer: Raskol'nikov tricks Alena Ivanovna into unwrapping what she believes is a silver cigarette-case; Markheim persuades the elderly dealer to look for an engagement present for an imaginary fiancée. Immediately afterwards, both murderers proceed to search their victim's bloody corpse for keys to his or her savings-box and

8 Cited by Edgar C. Knowlton in 'A Russian Influence on Stevenson', *Modern Philology*, XIV, 8 (1916), pp. 449-54 (p. 450).

9 Knowlton, 'A Russian Influence on Stevenson', p. 449.

10 Robert Louis Stevenson, 'Markheim', in his *The Complete Short Stories*, ed. Ian Bell, II (Edinburgh and London, 1993), pp. 86-101 (p. 89).

11 Fedor Dostoevskii, *Le Crime et le Châtiment* (2nd edn), trans. Victor Dérély (Paris, 1885), pp. 96-7.

both are interrupted by the unexpected arrival of a late customer, demanding admittance. Muchnic disputes these similarities, discounting them as mere situational parallels; she argues that Stevenson's self-conscious devotion to the '[b]eautiful phrase' prevents the reader from fully entering into Markheim's state of mind.[12]

Granted that Stevenson could not match Dostoevskii's ability to convey emotional disturbance, it surely remains beyond argument that Dostoevskii's novel taught Stevenson how to write a murder. Not only are the correspondences between 'Markheim' and *Crime and Punishment* undeniable (despite Muchnic), the physical horror that informs *Dr Jekyll and Mr Hyde* may be more tentatively attributed to the same influence. In the opening pages of this novel, an eyewitness reports how a man later known to be Jekyll 'trampled calmly over [a] child's body and left her screaming on the ground'.[13] Jekyll retreats into his den in a 'sinister block of building' with 'marks of prolonged and sordid negligence', recalling Raskol'nikov's equally squalid *kamorka* in a Petersburg tenement.[14] Later, another witness reports the 'audible shattering' of the bones of the genteel Sir Danvers Carew, beaten to death by Jekyll; this transport of sadistic violence recalls Raskol'nikov's graphic dream of the horse flogged to death in *Crime and Punishment*.[15] Jekyll's first episode of violence, targeting a female child, may reveal the influence not only of *Crime and Punishment* but also of its predecessor *The Insulted and Injured*, which Stevenson had also read in French translation with almost equal delight, where the child Nelly is a victim of casual adult brutality and lust.

Gissing: Hero as Murderer

George Gissing first encountered Dostoevskii in the late 1880s; like Stevenson, he read *The Insulted and Injured* and *Crime and Punishment* in French translation. His reaction was overwhelmingly positive: *Crime and Punishment* was 'magnificent [...] one of the greatest of modern novels' he

---

12 Helen Muchnic, *Dostoevsky's English Reputation (1881-1936)* (Northampton, MA, 1939), p. 173.

13 Robert Louis Stevenson, *The Strange Case of Dr Jekyll and Mr Hyde*, in his *The Strange Case of Dr Jekyll and Mr Hyde and Other Tales of Terror* (London, 2002), hereafter *Jekyll and Hyde*, pp. 2-70 (p. 7).

14 Stevenson, *Jekyll and Hyde*, p. 6.

15 *Ibid.*, p. 22.

wrote in 1887.[16] Two years later, the book was still a 'marvellous' triumph of psychology and realism; Gissing felt himself to be 'deeply in sympathy with Dostoievsky'.[17] Later, he told his friend Eduard Bertz: 'The more I read of him, the more I want to read; he appeals to me more distinctly than the other Russians, & more perhaps than any modern novelist'.[18] In 1899, only 4 years before his death, he still considered *Crime and Punishment* to be 'marvellous'.[19] The career of this Yorkshire-born novelist, best known for his portrayal of the suffering of the working classes and lower-middle-class outsiders in London's Victorian slums, was thus influenced by Dostoevskii throughout his career. In his important 'character study' of Dickens in the context of 19th-century European realism, published in 1898, Gissing argues that Dostoevskii's accuracy, humour, and sense of the grotesque all exceed Dickens's. There are obvious thematic convergences between Gissing and Dostoevskii, such as the recurrence of prostitute characters, the fixation on economic hardship and social isolation, even the thread of sympathy for Russia that runs through Gissing's novels: in *The Crown of Life* (1899), the wealthy heroine demonstrates her inclination for her lower middle-class suitor by learning to read Tolstoi in Russian. I turn now to Gissing's most famous adaptation of a Dostoevskian motif: the hero of *Born in Exile* (1892), who is essentially the same type of moral transgressor as Raskol'nikov.

Although George Orwell considered *Born in Exile* potentially Gissing's best novel, he also confessed that he had never read it.[20] This was regrettable: Orwell had much in common with Gissing's hero Godwin Peak. All three—Orwell, Gissing, and Peak—were scholarship boys who narrowly missed the chance to attend university and were forced to define themselves on their own merits against a financially punishing, rigidly hierarchical, and frequently hypocritical class system: all were 'proud natures condemned to solitude'.[21] There is a real, if facile, parallel here with Raskol'nikov's

---

16 George Gissing, undated letter to Mary E. Carter, in *The Collected Letters of George Gissing*, eds. Paul F. Mattheisen, Arthur C. Young, and Pierre Coustillas, III (Athens, Ohio, 1992), p. 160.

17 Gissing, letter to Eduard Bertz, 4 November 1889, in *Collected Letters*, IV, pp. 139-41 (p. 140).

18 Gissing, letter to Eduard Bertz, 16 December 1891, in *Collected Letters*, IV, pp. 342-4 (p. 343).

19 Gissing, letter to Eduard Bertz, 22 October 1899, in *Collected Letters*, VII, pp. 388-90 (p. 389).

20 George Orwell, 'George Gissing', in Pierre Coustillas (ed.), *Collected Articles on George Gissing* (London, 1968), pp. 50-7 (p. 54).

21 George Gissing, *Born in Exile* (London, 1985), p. 51.

situation at the beginning of *Crime and Punishment*. Godwin Peak, from wounded pride, spurns the chance of an academic career; Raskol'nikov rejects his friend Razumikhin's practical plan to earn his own way through university. Instead, the maximalist Raskol'nikov decides on murder in order to gain the money necessary to underwrite his family's security and his own path to social distinction: he is convinced that the benefit to society will outweigh the initial crime. Additionally, he will thus prove himself to be a Napoleon, rather than a 'louse'. Peak's crime is less bloody but, on a personal level, equally destructive. Having earned a place in the lower middle classes and gained a reputation as a polemical Radical, he still covets the luxury and leisure enjoyed by higher social ranks. As he reflects after meeting an old school-friend's family, the Warricombes:

> This English home, was it not surely the best result of civilisation in an age devoted to material progress? Here was peace, here was scope for the kindliest emotions. Upon him – the born rebel, the scorner of average mankind, the consummate egoist – this atmosphere exercised an influence more tranquillising, more beneficent, than even the mood of disinterested study. [...] Heroism might point him to an unending struggle with adverse conditions, but how was heroism possible without faith? Absolute faith he had none; he was essentially a negativist, guided by the mere relations of phenomena. Nothing easier than to contemn the mode of life represented by this wealthy middle class; but compare it with other existences conceivable by a thinking man, and it was emphatically good. It aimed at placidity, at benevolence, at supreme cleanliness, – things which more than compensated for the absence of higher spirituality.[22]

Peak thus convinces himself that the greater good—that is, the intellectual attainment made possible by material comfort—lies through a minor and ultimately meaningless ethical compromise. His rhetoric echoes Raskol'nikov's insistence that the evil of murder committed for gain (a murder that is virtually ethically neutral, since the victim was a parasite on society) will be cancelled out by the future benefit to humanity from Raskol'nikov's subsequent career. The irony, of course, is that neither man possesses the opportunity—nor the moral resilience—to sustain their defiance of accepted ethics.

Peak's route to the greater good lies through marriage with the eldest Warricombe daughter, Sidwell. Convinced that she will only overlook their class difference if he becomes a parson, Peak announces his intention to

22 Gissing, *Born in Exile*, pp. 170-1.

study for Holy Orders—thus framing his own hypocrisy for inevitable public exposure. Like Raskol'nikov, Peak suffers intense attacks of self-doubt and self-contempt in which he passionately repents his moral relativism; also like Raskol'nikov, Peak confesses his crime to the woman he loves (although Sidwell forgives him, she does not follow him into his subsequent 'exile'). But unlike his Russian predecessor, Peak is a sexual trophy-hunter: Sidwell, as a delicately reared English rose, is both his true love and the supreme symbol of social success. Both men are sent into exile: Raskol'nikov's Siberia is echoed by Peak's voluntary year of low-paid work in a 'vile manufacturing town' in the North of England.[23] Peak's crime is self-conscious 'charlatanism', by Adrian Poole's definition, making his duplicity both more conscious and less ideological than Raskol'nikov's.[24]

Gilbert Phelps and others have identified traces of both Raskol'nikov and Sonia in some of Gissing's earlier novels;[25] Jacob Korg has discussed the thematic overlap between *Crime and Punishment* and *Born in Exile* in some detail, arguing that in the case of both Raskol'nikov's crime and Peak's charade, 'ostensible motivation was far less important than the 'theory' behind it'.[26] Both critics overlook, however, the evidence that Gissing, like Stevenson, has also adapted other significant aspects of Dostoevskii's narrative. Peak and his equally underprivileged former schoolmate Earwaker, who becomes a newspaper editor, replicate the relationship between Raskol'nikov and Razumikhin. Earwaker chooses Razumikhin's path of gradualism and hard work, with commensurate reward; he is also the closest equivalent to a confidant that Peak permits. Both Raskol'nikov and Peak are betrayed by an article. Peak is outed as an atheist when his authorship of an anonymous, pro-evolutionary piece in *The Critical Review* is revealed to the Warricombes; Raskol'nikov's Napoleon complex is quoted back to him by Porfirii Petrovich, who has read his article on moral elitism in *The Periodical Review*. In a final, melodramatic scene from *Born in Exile*, a minor character intervenes to stop a carter from forcing a horse to 'drag a load beyond its strength' and is accidentally killed by a blow from

23 Gissing, *Born in Exile*, p. 482.

24 For Adrian Poole's discussion of 'charlatanism' in the context of Peak, Raskol'nikov and Dickensian hypocrites, see his *Gissing in Context* (London, 1975), pp. 171-3.

25 Gilbert Phelps, *The Russian Novel in English Fiction* (London, 1956), p. 164; see also Muchnic, *Dostoevsky's English Reputation*, p. 171.

26 Jacob Korg, 'The Spiritual Theme of 'Born in Exile'', in Pierre Coustillas (ed.), *Collected Articles on George Gissing* (London, 1968) pp. 131-42 (p. 138).

the animal's hooves; this obviously echoes both Raskol'nikov's dream of the horse and the death of Marmeladov.[27]

While the majority of Gissing's protagonists face social exclusion and some degree of poverty, Peak's resort to charlatanry is exceptional among them. Piers Otway in *The Crown of Life,* for example, overcomes problems almost identical to Peak's through hard work and rigid honesty. Of all Gissing's fiction, only *Born in Exile* is unambiguously in dialogue with *Crime and Punishment*; Godwin Peak is his response to Raskol'nikov.

Chesterton: the Knight-errant Detective

Although G.K. Chesterton did not mention Dostoevskii in print until a 1912 article in the *Illustrated London News,* he had probably been familiar with the Russian author's works since the 1890s. Chesterton read prolifically, and maintained close links with Dostoevskii's admirers and promoters, including Gissing and Edward Garnett. In 1903 he co-wrote a pamphlet on Tolstoi with Garnett. Dostoevskii was inescapable in 1910, when Irving's popular stage production of *Crime and Punishment* at the Garrick Theatre (as *The Unwritten Law*) inspired Everyman to reprint the Whishaw translation of the novel; this was also the year when Chesterton's first Father Brown story, 'The Blue Cross', appeared. Heinemann's publication of Constance Garnett's translations soon ushered in the so-called 'Dostoevsky cult' of 1912-21.[28] It is therefore entirely feasible, albeit speculative, to posit *Crime and Punishment* as an influence on Chesterton's detective stories, including the Father Brown series and other crime mysteries such as *The Man Who Was Thursday* (1908), *The Man Who Knew Too Much* (1922), and *The Poet and the Lunatics* (1929).[29] Mark Knight convincingly indentifies major themes in both writers' fiction—the use of the grotesque and of doubles, a fascination with insanity, and an 'emphasis on the centrality of human freedom', that is, on free will.[30] One Chesterton biographer has pointed out that Chesterton never created a character infused with the bitter existentialism of a Raskol'nikov or an Ivan Karamazov: 'Raskolnikov is

27 Gissing, *Born in Exile,* p. 471.

28 Muchnic, *Dostoevsky's English Reputation,* pp. 62-110. See also Olga Ushakova, 'Russia and Russian Culture in *The Criterion* (1922-39)' in this volume.

29 Mark Knight has traced a detailed timeline of Chesterton's potential encounters with Dostoevskii in his article 'Chesterton, Dostoevsky, and Freedom', in *English Literature in Transition, 1880-1920,* XLIII, no. 1 (2000), pp. 37-50 (37-41).

30 Knight, 'Chesterton, Dostoevsky, and Freedom', p. 42.

not found lurking in Flambeau'.[31] Yet, if we cannot find Raskol'nikov in Chesterton's most famous criminal, we can with greater justification find Porfirii Petrovich, the chief criminal investigator in *Crime and Punishment*, lurking within the British author's various detective heroes. I contend that Porfirii Petrovich represents the inauguration, and Chesterton's detective the continuation, of a particular archetype: the investigator who solves crimes by a combination of incongruity, perspicacity, intuition and surprise, besides more conventional police methods, without resorting to sensational tactics or egoistic posturing. In both Dostoevskii's novel and the majority of Chesterton's mysteries, crime is solved through a fixed alternation of pretence and recognition. Initially, the detective and the criminal each misrepresents himself: the criminal pretends innocence, while the detective manifests a chaotic or incompetent persona. The criminal 'misreads' the detective's pretence as genuine, while the detective correctly 'reads' the criminal's attitude as false. When, at the moment of exposure, the criminal finally 'reads' or interprets the detective correctly, punishment is suspended while both men experience the temporary equality—and intimacy—of mutual recognition.

Here is how Razumikhin describes Porfirii Petrovich to a suspicious Raskol'nikov:

> 'He is a nice fellow, you will see, brother. Rather clumsy, that is to say, he is a man of polished manners, but I mean clumsy in a different sense. He is an intelligent fellow, very much so indeed, but he has his own range of ideas.... He is incredulous, sceptical, cynical... he likes to impose on people, or rather to make fun of them. His is the old, circumstantial method.... But he understands his work... thoroughly... Last year he cleared up a case of murder in which the police had hardly a clue. He is very, very anxious to make your acquaintance!'[32]

Here Razumikhin has identified the essential traits in the character of the Chief Investigator: Porfirii's unusual combination of social polish with assumed 'clumsiness' (amply evidenced by his rapid changes of tone or apparent loss of the thread of a conversation), his desire to 'make fun' of people, and his thorough grasp of circumstantial evidence. At his first meeting with Raskol'nikov, Porfirii is inappropriately garbed in a dressing-gown, and his appearance is deliberately unprepossessing:

---

31 Gary Wills, *Chesterton: Man and Mask* (New York, 1961), p. 51.

32 Fyodor Dostoevsky, *Crime and Punishment*, trans. Constance Garnett (London, 1914, 1979), hereafter *Crime and Punishment*, p. 226.

> He was a man of about five and thirty, short, stout even to corpulence, and clean shaven. He wore his hair cut short and had a large round head, particularly prominent at the back. His soft, round, rather snub-nosed face was of a sickly yellowish colour, but had a vigorous and rather ironical expression. It would have been good-natured except for a look in the eyes, which shone with a watery, mawkish light under almost white, blinking eyelashes. The expression of those eyes was strangely out of keeping with his somewhat womanish figure, and gave it something far more serious than could be guessed at first sight.[33]

While Porfirii is 'womanish' ('bab'e'),[34] Father Brown is repeatedly characterized as 'childlike'. He is also short, round and stout, and he enlarges on Porfirii's clumsiness to the point of helplessness: 'The little priest [...] had a face as round and dull as a Norfolk dumpling; he had eyes as empty as the North Sea; he had several brown paper parcels, which he was quite incapable of collecting'.[35] Like Porfirii, Father Brown's deceptively harmless appearance is belied by his eyes. A murderer opens his confession to the priest: 'damn your eyes, which are very penetrating ones';[36] elsewhere, Father Brown stares at a murder suspect 'so long and steadily as to prove that his large grey, ox-like eyes were not quite so insignificant as the rest of his face'.[37] Porfirii Petrovich and Father Brown (and, indeed, all of Chesterton's detectives) unerringly identify their suspects by a combination of observation and intuition, supported by painstakingly accumulated evidence. Porfirii, for example, has Raskol'nikov's room searched, interviews everyone with whom the student has had contact, and retains, as he claims, 'a little fact' of solid evidence (never disclosed).[38] Yet it is intuition, rather than evidence, which allows Porfirii to accuse Raskol'nikov unequivocally after only three informal meetings. The casual laughter Raskol'nikov artfully produces at their first encounter does not deceive Porfirii for an instant: forewarned by intuition, he correctly interprets it as a disguise. Similarly, the unworldliness, vulnerability, and distraction manifested by Chesterton's detectives are disguises designed

33 *Crime and Punishment*, p. 230.

34 Dostoevskii, *Prestuplenie i nakazanie*, in his *Polnoe sobranie sochinenii v XVIII tomakh*, VII (Moscow, 2004), p. 174.

35 G.K. Chesterton, 'The Blue Cross', in Chesterton, *The Annotated Innocence of Father Brown*, ed. Martin Gardner (Oxford, 1988), pp. 15-41 (p. 18).

36 Chesterton, 'The Wrong Shape', in *The Annotated Innocence of Father Brown*, pp. 138-59 (p. 156).

37 Chesterton, 'The Hammer of God', in *The Annotated Innocence of Father Brown*, pp. 179-96 (pp. 189-90).

38 *Crime and Punishment*, p. 412.

to unbalance and disarm the criminal. Porfirii ingenuously calls his plan to startle Raskol'nikov into confessing by confronting him with a witness his 'little surprise';[39] in 'The Face in the Target', Horne Fisher unexpectedly confronts his suspect with a caricature of the victim to confirm his guilt; in 'The Blue Cross', Father Brown bamboozles Flambeau by behaving outrageously in public.

Dostoevskii's and Chesterton's detectives understand their suspects' motives and urge them to redemption by 'taking their suffering' (the Old Believer penance that Porfirii encourages Raskol'nikov to emulate).[40] Porfirii allows Raskol'nikov time to confess, because moral regeneration is pendant on confession; Father Brown prevents a repentant murderer from committing suicide because 'that door leads to hell';[41] Horne Fisher refrains from exposing certain criminals to avoid harming innocent people. It is not quite true, as one critic writes, that 'Porfiry Petrovitch goes beyond understanding Raskolnikov to identifying with him in some respects';[42] Porfirii recognizes and admires, but does not necessarily share, the ideas raised in Raskol'nikov's article. *The Man Who Was Thursday*'s Gabriel Syme, an undercover detective posing as an anarchist to win a seat on the Anarchist Council, exemplifies the extreme of deliberate identification with one's moral opposite. Yet, ironically, the plot reveals that there are no real anarchists on the Council: each member is an undercover detective.

While one must not over-emphasize Chesterton's debt to Dostoevskii, it is worth stressing that each deploys the same distinct type of detective. Dostoevskii, possibly inspired by Gaboriau, made Porfirii an ordinary police official at a time when professional investigators (as opposed to amateur or accidental sleuths) were highly unglamorous ancillary figures.[43] There is doubt whether Dostoevskii had yet encountered Dickens's charismatic Inspector Bucket in *Bleak House* (1852-3), although he certainly acquired a copy after 1871.[44] Chesterton's detectives are all marginal, superficially insignificant individuals, pursuing undistinguished professions, with the

---

39 *Crime and Punishment*, p. 317.

40 *Ibid.*, p. 415.

41 Chesterton, 'The Hammer of God', p. 195.

42 Michael Cohen, *Murder Most Fair: The Appeal of Mystery Fiction* (London, 2000), p. 73.

43 See Julian Symons, *Bloody Murder: From the Detective Story to the Crime Novel: A History* (London, 1972), pp. 40-55.

44 See N.M. Lary, *Dostoevsky and Dickens: A Study in Literary Influence* (London and Boston, 1973), p. 10. For an argument that Dostoevskii *did* read *Bleak House* while still in exile, see Veronica Shapalov, 'They Came From Bleak House', *Dostoevsky Studies*, IX (1988), http://www.utoronto.ca/tsq/DS/09/201.shtml [accessed 15.10.2012].

single exception of Gabriel Syme, who is a kind of professional amateur, a detective dilettante rather than a dilettante detective. Father Brown is a Catholic priest; Horne Fisher is a private secretary; and Gabriel Gale is a minor poet on the brink of being committed to the lunatic asylum. Despite their marginality, all four emerge, like Porfirii Petrovich, as dedicated defenders of humane behaviour. As Chesterton wrote in 1901, the detective story reminds us 'that civilization itself is the most sensational of departures and the most romantic of rebellions', and that 'the agent of social justice... [is]... the original and poetic figure...[...] The romance of the police force is thus the whole romance of man'. This was a view with which Porfirii Petrovich, as the forerunner of Chesterton's 'successful knight-errantry' of 'noiseless and unnoticeable police management',[45] would certainly have concurred.

Conclusion: the Isosceles Triangle

In his study of Dickens, Gissing summarizes *Crime and Punishment* as 'a story of a strange murder, of detective ingenuity'. Significantly, Gissing understood Dostoevskii's novel primarily as crime narrative, even as he strove to excuse Dickens for failing to reach Dostoevskii's heights of psychology, social realism, or stylistic innovation. Dickens was simply too obedient to decorum, in Gissing's view, to create an English Sonia; and as for Raskol'nikov, 'his motives, his reasonings, could not be comprehended by an Englishman of the lower middle class'.[46] Ironically and apparently unwittingly, Gissing thus excluded himself also from fully understanding Raskol'nikov. As Phelps has noted, Stevenson shows comparable selectivity by borrowing Dostoevskian 'melodrama' and neglecting psychological method; the motifs of serial murder and malign doubling in *Dr Jekyll and Mr Hyde* owe, in all probability, more to Hogg's Gil-Martin than to Dostoevskii's Svidrigailov.[47] In the cases of both Gissing and Stevenson, their categorization of *Crime and Punishment* as crime fiction actually

45 G.K. Chesterton, 'A Defence of Detective Stories', in *The Defendant* (London, 1901), pp. 118-23 (pp. 122-3).

46 George Gissing, *Charles Dickens: A Character Study*, in *Collected Works of George Gissing on Charles Dickens*, ed. Simon James, II (Surrey, 2004), pp. 17-191 (pp. 177-8).

47 See Phelps, *The Russian Novel in English Fiction*, pp. 166-8; for more on Stevenson's Scottish influences, see Christopher Maclachlan, 'Murder and the Supernatural: Crime in the Fiction of Scott, Hogg, and Stevenson', in *Clues: A Journal of Detection*, XXVI: 2 (2008), pp. 10-22.

impeded its reception as a novel of ideas. Dostoevskii's contribution to enriching the British murder may have compromised his reputation as a serious writer.

On the philosophical level, G.K. Chesterton—the least substantiated of the three Dostoevskian imitators discussed here—is also the most faithful. In the short story 'The Yellow Bird', part of the *Poet and the Lunatics* collection, Gabriel Gale asks a friend: 'Were you ever an isosceles triangle?' Gale is curious 'whether it would be a cramping sort of thing to be surrounded by straight lines, and whether being in a circle would be any better'.[48] This apparent irrelevance in fact expresses Gale's insight into the mind of a (coincidentally) Russian anarchist, whose delight in exploding barriers has become a dangerous fixation. As Gale explains, 'What exactly is liberty? First and foremost, surely, it is the power of a thing to be itself. [...] Then I began to think that being oneself, which is liberty, is itself limitation. We are limited by our brains and bodies; and if we break out, we cease to be ourselves, and, perhaps, to be anything'.[49] Raskol'nikov is a close moral relative of Dostoevskii's Underground Man; the latter's determination to defy geometry and arithmetic is transformed into Raskol'nikov's compulsion to shatter the barriers of conventional ethics. But like Gale's anarchist, Raskol'nikov lacks the strength to survive within self-ordained limits, after 'breaking out' of the cage of society. The triangle of British interpretations discussed above demonstrates that Dostoevskii's fiction, at least, was capable of surviving beyond the boundaries of national identity.

48 G.K. Chesterton, 'The Yellow Bird', in *G.K. Chesterton: Selected Stories*, ed. Kingsley Amis (London, 1972), pp. 226-45 (pp. 233-4).

49 *Ibid.*, pp. 242-3.

11. Stephen Graham and Russian Spirituality: The Pilgrim in Search of Salvation

Michael Hughes

The name of Stephen Graham (1884-1975) is familiar to every student of Anglo-Russian relations in the early years of the 20th century. Graham was, in the words of his obituary in *The Times*, 'probably more responsible than anyone else in this country for the cult of Holy Russia and the idealization of the Russian peasant that was beginning to make headway here before 1914 and during the years immediately after'.[1] In a series of books including *A Vagabond in the Caucasus* (1911) and *Undiscovered Russia* (1912), he painted an idealised picture of the way in which the spirit of Russian Orthodoxy had shaped the character of modern Russia, describing how on Easter Eve in Moscow 'even the air is infected with church odours and the multitudinous domes of purple and gold rest above the houses in enigmatical solemnity'.[2] Although he acknowledged that the Russian peasants he met during a long series of 'tramps' through the Tsarist Empire were not interested in abstruse questions of doctrine, he was struck by their natural piety, describing how they lived in a God-saturated world in which a sense of the divine permeated every aspect of their daily life. Graham always denied that he took an idealised view of Russian life, and in books like *Changing Russia* (1913) he certainly showed how the growth of industry and urban living was eroding the spirit of 'Holy Russia', but his claim to offer a realistic picture of modern Russia did not convince all his readers.

1 *The Times*, 20 March 1975.

2 Stephen Graham, *Vagabond in the Caucasus* (London, 1911), p. 111.

Several years later, in 1916, Maksim Gor'kii penned a piece in his journal *Letopis'* (*Chronicle*) condemning Graham—in the thinly disguised *persona* of one 'William Simpleton'—for seeing in Russia a reservoir of spiritual richness where there was in reality only huge amounts of poverty and despair.[3]

Although Graham was struck by the extent of popular piety in Russia during his first two or three years living in the country, following his arrival there in 1908 he was also deeply interested in the cultural ferment of Russia's silver age (among other things he attended a number of meetings of the Moscow Religious-Philosophical Society where he met luminaries ranging from Nikolai Berdiaev to Viacheslav Ivanov). He was also a huge admirer of the painter Mikhail Nesterov, even collecting material for a biography, although it is not clear whether Graham ever really grasped the full subtleties of Nesterov's art.[4] Graham was certainly interested in the whole phenomenon of Russian symbolism—he later translated stories by Fedor Sologub—but he never really understood its complexities and contradictions. What instead intrigued him was the 'symbolist' insight that the material world represented a series of signs pointing to deeper and more fundamental realities.[5] There is in fact something of a paradox here. Graham was—as will be seen later—often at his best as a writer when providing his readers with lively pen-pictures of the human and natural landscapes he encountered during his long tramps across Russia. Many of his books contained a strange juxtaposition of vivid sketches and abstruse philosophising. Most pages of *A Vagabond in the Caucasus*, for example, focus on detailed—if picturesque—descriptions of its author's hikes through the remote wilderness area between the Caspian and Black Seas.

The book nevertheless contains an astonishing confessional epilogue, written shortly after Graham's return to London, in which he stood back from his travel narrative to reflect on how his physical journey had become for him something closer to a pilgrimage:

> A youth steps forward on the road and a horizon goes forward. Sometimes slowly the horizon moves, sometimes in leaps and bounds. Slowly while mountains are approached, or when cities and markets crowd the skies to heaven, but suddenly and instantaneously when summits are achieved or

3 'Pis'ma znatnogo inostrantsa', *Letopis'* (April 1916), pp. 288-99.

4 For the draft of an unfinished biography of Nesterov by Graham, see Florida State University, Strozier Library, Special Collections, Stephen Graham Papers, Box 576.

5 On Russian Symbolism, see Avril Pyman, *A History of Russian Symbolism* (Cambridge, 1994).

> when the outskirts dust of town or fair is passed. One day, at a highest point on that road of his, a view will be disclosed and lie before him—the furthest and most magical glance into the Future. Away, away in the far-distant grey will lie his newest and last horizon, in a place more fantastic and mystical than the dissolving city, which the eye builds out of sunset clouds.[6]

The sense of travel as pilgrimage—a search for meaning and insights that would help to reorient his life—was to become a powerful motif in several of Graham's later books.

Gor'kii was not alone in disliking Graham's frequent descents into a purple prose that one of his English reviewers described scathingly as 'high-brow baby talk'.[7] He also attracted controversy from time to time back in Britain, where he was sometimes seen in liberal circles as an apologist for a brutally anti-Semitic government, particularly in the months following the outbreak of World War I, which threw Britain and Russia together as uneasy allies in the war against the central powers.[8] Graham's prose was sometimes marred by a kind of mystical obscurantism which, although designed to capture in language emotions and insights that defied logical analysis, at times read as little more than an incoherent ramble. It is nevertheless worthwhile trying to make sense of what might—perhaps rather generously—be termed his poetic metaphysics. A little biographical detail can help to facilitate this analysis.

Graham was the son of the writer and journalist Peter Anderson Graham, who for quarter of a century edited *Country Life*, which following its establishment in 1897 sold its readership a vision of a *faux* rural life characterised by wood-panelled houses and country sports rather than mud and poverty. Anderson Graham was nevertheless genuinely concerned about the impact of economic change in the English countryside, writing at length about the flight of the rural population to the towns.[9] He also penned numerous articles praising 19th-century writers and poets, like Wordsworth and Jeffries, who had in their writings articulated a kind of nature-mysticism that saw in the natural environment intimations of profound truths about the world. The burgeoning tradition of nature-

6 Graham, *Vagabond*, p. 288.
7 *Times Literary Supplement*, 26 May 1927 (in a review of Stephen Graham, *The Gentle Art of Tramping*).
8 For a report of a public meeting at the National Liberal Club, where Graham faced sharp criticism for his supposedly negative views towards Russian Jews, see *The Guardian*, 19 January 1915.
9 P. Anderson Graham, *The Rural Exodus* (London, 1892).

writing in Victorian and Edwardian Britain was of course in large part a reaction to the challenges of urbanisation and industrial development. The idealisation of the countryside, seen not merely as a counterpoint to the soulless urban sprawl, but also as a repository of values more profound than any that shaped the contemporary world, was a common response to the unsettling challenges of modernity. Stephen Graham inherited much of his father's distaste for the modern world, along with Anderson Graham's shrewd assessment that there was likely to be a market for books and articles that provided an urban audience with a taste of the exotic and the pastoral, a fantasy world remote from the prosaic rhythms of life in cities like London or Manchester.

Stephen Graham himself grew up in the suburban sprawl of north London, and from the age of 15 he commuted daily into London, where he worked for a number of years as a civil service clerk, spending his leisure hours reading Browning as he walked alone through the lanes of rural Essex. In his autobiography, which was not published until he was 80, he recalled how his interest in Russia was first piqued when he bought a second-hand copy of Dostoevskii's *Crime and Punishment*, which the youthful Graham found much 'more profound' than a simple 'murder story'. He was instead mesmerised by a book that had 'a hidden *x* in it. Let *x* be the soul of man, or let *x* be the meaning of life, something not familiar to the Western mind but, once sensed, forever haunting. I was on the trail of a religious philosophy more inspiring than Carlyle or Ibsen or Nietzsche'.[10] In the years that followed he learned Russian, heading to the country for a month-long visit in 1906, where he was briefly detained on suspicion of being involved in revolutionary activities, before deciding in 1907 to move to Russia permanently where he planned to earn his living through writing.

Graham was determined to use his pen to show readers back home that contemporary Russia was not simply a country of revolutionaries, but also a land where (as he later wrote) the people lived 'as Ruskin wanted the English to live... true to the soil they plough', forsaking 'machine-made things', preferring to 'fashion out of the pine all they need'.[11] Russia quickly became for Graham not only a land where the coruscating effects of modernity had not yet succeeded in ripping apart old ways of living. It was also a kind of sacred space, where the traditions and rituals of everyday life embodied in their very substance a set of deeper spiritual truths. It

10 Stephen Graham, *Part of the Wonderful Scene* (London, 1964), p. 14.
11 Stephen Graham, *Undiscovered Russia* (London, 1912), p. ix.

was doubtless for this reason that Graham chose as the frontispiece of his second book, *Undiscovered Russia*, a copy of Mikhail Nesterov's '*Holy Russia*'. It depicted a group of pilgrims seeking spiritual healing from Christ in a landscape that fused together a typically Russian background with more celestial elements designed to suggest the immanence of the divine presence. Russia appealed to Graham not only as a place freed from the commercialism and industrialisation of the West. It was also a place where the material and spiritual worlds came together in a way that made 'Holy Russia' a country fundamentally different in character from any other.

There is amongst Graham's papers a youthful manuscript that helps to illuminate his early reactions to Russia following his move there at the beginning of 1908. The unpublished book was titled *Ygdrasil*, the name of the immense ash tree central to Norse mythology, which according to legend bound together heaven, earth and hell.[12] Although Graham failed to mention the book in the published version of his autobiography, in which he worked hard to conceal his youthful interest in the esoteric and occult, many of the themes that emerge in this rambling 'book on religion and philosophy' shaped his ideas for many years to come. He made a distinction between two forms of knowledge—'one is dead fact [whilst] the other is living power'—and argued that only the latter was truly worthwhile. Although his language was often convoluted and obscure, Graham in effect sought to articulate what would in later times be considered a form of existentialist epistemology, in which the truths of *Ygdrasil* could be encountered either as 'dead fact' or appropriated to provide a particular personal meaning. Two themes recur through the sometimes tortuous pages of the book. The first is that all creeds and dogmas are lifeless things, seeking to lay down artificial formal truths, whereas in reality 'God has given to each person separate pairs of eyes'. This in turn set the scene for confusion 'between what Christ is and what Christ is to me'. And, as a result, Graham argued that whilst it was true that there was one religion for all, the fact that 'there is one for each is more important'. The second (and for our purposes more significant) theme in *Ygdrasil* was the distinction Graham drew between the 'Little World' and what he termed elsewhere the 'somewhere-out-beyond'.[13] The 'Little World' was the humdrum world of everyday life. The 'somewhere-out-beyond' represented a set of truths that could only be

12 All the following quotations are taken from the manuscript of *Ygdrasil*, located in the Graham Papers held at the Harry Ransom Centre (University of Texas).

13 Stephen Graham, *A Tramp's Sketches* (London, 1913), p. 206, hereafter *TS*.

glimpsed from time to time, either through art, or via a dim sense that 'we are in part substance of the immortal Gods'. The aim of for each individual was to enter metaphorically into the Garden of Asgard—which Graham not altogether accurately identified as the place where *Ygdrasil* grew—in order to 'see the world as a whole, all the worlds as a whole, and from without the universe behold the interdependence of all'.

There is no space here to review the youthful Graham's philosophy in any further depth, except perhaps to note that it was clearly inspired by the writings of Carlyle on the German Romantics. Although many of the ideas articulated in *Ygdrasil* are at best derivative, and at worst incoherent, its author's search for a language capable of articulating his instincts and ideas helped to shape his views about Russia in the years that followed. Russia became—at least potentially—a place where supermundane truths were embedded in time and place. The paradox of many of Graham's early travel books, to return to a point made earlier, is that he was as a writer skilled at painting pictures of the 'Little World'. Some of his best pieces are concerned with such apparently mundane subjects as describing the seaside holidays taken by visitors to the Black Sea resort of Sochi. There is indeed often a profound disconnection in his writing between his views on the nature of 'Holy Russia' and his description of the day-to-day scenes he encountered during his long tramps through the country. Sometimes the 'philosopher' in Graham insisted on seeing Russian life through the prism of *Ygdrasil*—a kind of representation in time of principles and ideals that sat outside time—whilst on other occasions he simple described what he saw. A brief review of three of his books can provide some further insight into these various tensions and contradictions.

A Tramp's Sketches was first published by Macmillan in 1912, based in large part on material collected by Graham during a tramp along the northern shore of the Black Sea, although an earlier version had been rejected by his previous publisher John Lane on the grounds that it was unlikely to find a sufficient market. The book is at times difficult to read and understand, for although it contains a number of sketches of daily life in the towns and villages of southern Russia, it was in Graham's own words less about Russia and more about 'the life of the wanderer and seeker, the walking hermit, the rebel against modern conditions and commercialism who has gone out into the wilderness' (*TS*, p. 7). *A Tramp's Sketches* begins with a diatribe against life in the 'evil city'—in practice London but intended as shorthand for every major urban centre—which in time:

> drove me into the wilderness to my mountains and valleys, by the side of the great sea and by the haunted forests. Once more the vast dome of heaven became the roof of my house, and within the house was rebuilded that which my soul called beautiful. There I refound my God, and my being reexpressed itself to itself in terms of eternal Mysteries. I vowed I should never again belong to the town (*TS*, p. 20).

Whilst Graham's two previous books had been full of stories about the people he met on the road, he now presented himself as a kind of solitary pilgrim, seeking to enter 'into a new relationship with the world', submitting to 'the gentle creative hands of Nature [in order] to re-shape his soul' (*TS*, p. 23). The figure of the tramp was for Graham one of 'the rebels against modern life', seeking 'a little more living in communion with Nature [...] whoever has known Nature once and loved her will return again to her'. He also insisted that the tramp—or perhaps better the pilgrim-tramp—was best-placed to understand how the joys of rural life were linked to more fundamental questions about the nature of existence: 'Whoever has resolved the common illusions of the meaning of life, and has seen even in glimpses the naked mystery of our being, finds that he absolutely must live in the world which is outside city walls' (*TS*, p. 57).

The theme of Holy Russia did not loom large in *A Tramp's Sketches*, although the book does contain a lengthy description of daily life at the monastery of New Athos, along with a number of other monasteries where Graham was given shelter. The informing philosophy was instead that of *Ygdrasil*: that the everyday world was a series of signs that showed the way out of the 'Little World' and into a place of deeper meaning. The final chapters of the book are at times almost incomprehensible, as Graham struggled to convey to his readers a sense of a universe that was irreducible to neat formulae or description. He told the story—or rather the fable—of a young woman called Zenobia whose youth and beauty were corrupted when she moved to the city and entered into local society. Her looks faded to grey as a result of a life lived with a 'lack of sun' and a 'lack of life', leaving Graham to lament how 'in one place flowers rot and die; in another, bloom and live. The truth is that in this city they rot and die' (*TS*, p. 250). The figure of Zenobia—whether real, mythical, or something in between—served for Graham as a symbol of the way in which true beauty and liveliness were crushed by the man-made world of cities. It is worth quoting at some length the passage that ended the main part of *A Tramp's Sketches*, since it conveys more clearly than anywhere else in Graham's writings his understanding of the universe, couched in terms that owe more to early 20th-century Theosophy than to any formal Christian doctrine:

> But beyond the universe, no scientist, not any of us, knows anything. On all shores of the universe washes the ocean of ignorance, the ocean of the inexplicable. We stand upon the confines of an explored world and gaze at many blank horizons. We yearn towards our natural home, the kingdom in which our spirits were begotten [...]. Some day for us shall come into that blank sky-horizon which is called the zenith, a stranger, a man or a god, perhaps not like ourselves, yet having affinities with ourselves, and correlating ourselves to some family of minor gods of which we are all lost children. We shall then know our universal function and find our universal orbit (*TS*, p. 326).

The only hint in this passage of a specifically Christian understanding of these perplexities comes at the very end with the words—which are frankly a *non sequitur*—that 'It is written, "When He appears we shall be like Him"'.

A Tramp's Sketches was not the only book to come out of Graham's tramp along the Black Sea coast in 1911-12, although *Changing Russia* (1913) was so different in tone that it might almost have been written by another author. The first book was designed to articulate its author's sense that there were complex truths that lay beyond the confines of the material world. The second book was designed to show readers how the process of social and economic change sweeping through Russia was threatening to undermine the country's unique vocation as a sacred space where the boundary between heaven and earth was more porous than elsewhere in the world. Graham bitterly complained how in cities like Rostov-on-Don the population was abandoning the Church for the new 'electric theatre', where they watched 'bloodthirsty, gruesome murder stories, stories of crime, of unfaithful husbands and wives, and of course the usual insane harlequinades'.[14] Nor was the situation much better at other towns like Novorossisk with its 'cement factories and soap-works'. Some of the most vitriolic passages in *Changing Russia* were reserved for the Russian bourgeoisie, which Graham believed was the defining product of the new economic and social order:

> The Russian bourgeois [...] wants to know the price of everything. Of things which are independent of price he knows nothing, or, if he knows of them, he sneers at them and hates them. Talk to him of religion, and show that you believe in the mystery of Christ; talk to him of life, and show that you

---

14 Stephen Graham, *Changing Russia* (London, 1913), p. 28, hereafter *CR*.

> believe in love and happiness; talk of woman, and show that you understand anything about her unsexually; talk to him of work, and show that though you are poor you have no regard for money and the bourgeois is uneasy. He would like to deny your existence there as you face him. He will deny your faith and belief the moment your back is turned (*CR*, p. 117)

Graham was particularly concerned at the bourgeoisie's growing social and political influence, which he feared was 'beginning to clamour in the press, to write, to define, to censure. It calls itself the democracy, and points out that it will pay for its likes, and that its sort of art and life will 'pay'. That a thing 'pays' is to the bourgeois the test of democratic approval' (*CR*, p. 121). Graham by contrast remained convinced that:

> Russia has an extraordinary greatness to be attained through her Church, through her national institutions, and by virtue of her national landscape. It is a greatness that starts from the peasant soul, that draws out of all the store of national tradition and belief and experience, as the harvests grow rich out of the black mould that was once her forests... For the peasant is the root, and the root draws up mysteriously from those depths that which is its own, that which God has provided (*CR*, p. 210)

Although Graham bitterly lamented the changes which he feared were sweeping away the old Russia he had come to love, *Changing Russia* shows how adept he was at providing his readers with a sense of the 'Little World' through which he travelled, for the book contained numerous lively sketches of the individuals and scenes he encountered along the way.

By the time *A Tramp's Sketches* and *Changing Russia* were published, some reviewers in Britain were starting to weary both of Graham's philosophical ruminations, as well as his constant lament for an idealised Holy Russia supposedly fading in the face of an unforgiving rush of modernisation and decay. This may partly have accounted for the rather different tone of his next book—*With the Russian Pilgrims to Jerusalem*—which described a journey he took with several hundred Russian pilgrims to celebrate Easter in the Holy Land. The book's Prologue contained the kind of confessional *cri de coeur* that had characterised much of Graham's earlier writing. Graham told his readers that he had for many years wished to undertake a pilgrimage, noting that 'Whoever has wished to go has already started on the pilgrimage. And once you have started, every step upon the road is a step toward Jerusalem. Even steps which seem to have no meaning are taking you by byways and lanes to the high-road [...] The true Christian is necessarily he who has the wishing heart'. He went on to recall how he had even as a child looked 'wistfully' at religious processions, seeing in them some kind of echo of a longer journey, adding that for years his heart had responded more readily to 'march music' than to 'all the other melodies in the world'.[15] Although Graham did not spell it out explicitly, he had begun to acknowledge that his years of tramping in the wilderness had themselves been a kind of pilgrimage, a restless search for some form of personal epiphany capable of resolving the personal sense of dissonance and longing that had first led him to Russia. The journey to Jerusalem seemed to him to have brought together the two main elements in his life: his love of the Russian peasantry and his sense of the incompleteness of human existence when lived purely in the material world.

Although the Prologue echoed many of the themes that had run through Graham's earlier work, the main text of *With the Russian Pilgrims* was very different in tone, allowing a sense of the religious passion and individual idiosyncrasies of the pilgrims to emerge from a series of detailed pen-portraits. Nor did he seek to hide the fact that many of the pilgrims were flawed in both their spiritual character and behaviour. There was, for example, Philip, a peasant from a Ukrainian village close to the Austro-Hungarian border, who was making his fourteenth trip to Jerusalem. The extent of his piety was nevertheless called into question by the fact that he made a good deal of money by acting as 'a tout for ecclesiastical shop-keepers' on arrival in the Holy Land (*RP*, p. 152). Typical of his victims was another pilgrim, to whom Graham gave the name Liubomudrof, a man whose simple piety could not be doubted, even though he cheerfully acknowledged that he had earlier in his life been an alcoholic and an adulterer. Graham also wrote at length of a monk who was travelling with the pilgrims, Father Evgenii, who although honest and pious was often imperious in his treatment of those with whom he travelled. Graham made no effort to hide the human frailty of his companions, nor did he try to sentimentalise his description of the Holy Land itself, which appeared at first sight to be 'a place where every stone has been commercialised either by tourist agencies or by greedy monks'. He nevertheless continued to believe in Jerusalem as an ideal—an 'existence independent of material appearance' (*RP*, p. 6)—and was convinced that this ideal could not be tainted by the omnipresent corruption and dilapidation. It was this same principle that ran through his description of many of his fellow-pilgrims. Whilst Graham openly acknowledged their faults, he also believed that the

---

15 Stephen Graham, *With the Russian Pilgrims to Jerusalem* (London, 1913), pp. 3, 11,. hereafter *RP*.

instinct to pilgrimage was driven by a genuine spiritual hunger, which was powerful enough to bring them to Jerusalem, even if it was not always strong enough to transform their behaviour.

Graham himself played a full part in the celebrations and rituals of the Russian pilgrims. He went to the Church of the Holy Sepulchre in Jerusalem, 'not to look but to pray', and was profoundly moved by the experience of entering the burial chamber. He also travelled to Nazareth with dozens of other pilgrims, passing through the Moslem town of Nablus, before arriving at the 'shabby' birthplace of Christ. During the Holy Week celebrations he attended a Palm Sunday service at the Church of the Holy Sepulchre, whilst on Good Friday he joined the procession to Golgotha, re-enacting the last journey of Christ. On Easter Day he went to the Russian Cathedral, along with thousands of other pilgrims visiting the city, and although he had been present at Orthodox Easter celebrations before he was still thrilled by the intensity of the experience:

> Then at one in the morning we passed [...] into the Russian cathedral, now joyously illuminated with coloured lights, and we heard the service in familiar church Slavonic. And we all kissed one another again. What embracing and kissing there were this night; smacking of hearty lips and tangling of beards and whiskers! The Russian men kiss one another with far more heartiness than they kiss their women. In the hostelry I watched a couple of ecstatical old greybeards who grasped one another tightly by the shoulders, and kissed at least a score of times, and wouldn't leave off (*RP*, p. 296).

With the Russian Pilgrims is altogether more satisfying as travel literature than most of Graham's earlier work. Graham himself was praised by the *Athenaeum* for 'throwing off the bonds of society' so that he could report 'with a clear-eyed simplicity the story of a pilgrimage',[16] whilst the *New York Times* praised him as 'the best modern writer of the saga of vagabondage'.[17] The book was effective precisely because its author allowed the spirituality of the pilgrims to emerge from skilful pen portraits of their foibles and their piety, rather than seeking to link it to his more abstruse ideas about 'Holy Russia', or to complex pseudo-metaphysics, as in *A Tramp's Sketches*. It was an approach that he successfully repeated in his next book, *With Poor Immigrants to Americ*a (1914), which described a journey across the Atlantic with hundreds of émigrés bound for the New World from Eastern Europe.

16 *Athenaeum*, 20 September 1913.
17 *New York Times*, 9 November 1913.

Both *Russian Pilgrims* and *Poor Immigrants* contained numerous photographs, most of them taken by Graham, which allowed readers to see for themselves the people and sites he described. Graham had not abandoned the spirit of *Ygdrasil*—if it can be so called—and he was throughout his life convinced that a genuine understanding of people and places required an 'idealism' that allowed insights that eluded those who adopted a materialistic view of the world. His early books on Russia cannot be fully understood without realising how his vision of the country was shaped by his ideas about the relationship between the 'Little World' and the 'somewhere-out-beyond'. Much of Graham's best work was, though, characterised by his sharp observation of the things he saw rather than his more convoluted ideas about Holy Russia and the nature of Russian spirituality. The 19th-century critic Dmitrii Pisarev once said of the Slavophile writer Ivan Kireevskii that 'he was born an artist but for some reason imagined himself to be a thinker'. They are words that might usefully be applied to Stephen Graham as he sought to explain Russia for his readers back home in Britain.

12. Jane Harrison as an Interpreter of Russian Culture in the 1910s-1920s

Alexandra Smith

Jane Harrison (1850-1928), a British classical scholar, belongs to the first generation of British women academics whose contribution to the intellectual history of the modernist period was highly praised by her friends and fellow scholars and writers, including Virginia Woolf, Gilbert Murray, Francis Cornford and Prince Dmitrii Sviatopolk-Mirskii. Harrison knew 16 languages, including Russian, and had a broad interest in many aspects of European culture. These included Orphic mysticism, ancient Greek art and drama, Freud's interpretation of dreams, and Russian culture, albeit she is especially known for her contribution to the interpretation of Greek religion and art and her use of anthropological theory in Classical studies. Julie Peters praises Harrison's role in the history of the avant-garde theatre and performance. In Peters's view, Harrison's approach to ritualist anti-theatricality continues to be highly valid for neo-avant-garde performance today.[1] Harrison's interest in surviving primitive rituals stemmed from her disillusionment with the museum culture, which was based on hierarchical principles, and her growing Bergsonian belief in the power of the living creative impulse that, through performance, might be experienced in an ecstatic collectivity and an act of transcendence of both beauty and theatre.

1 Julia Peters writes: 'Frazer can arguably be seen as one of the first to place ritual at the centre of investigations of the history of religion, and he was unquestionably the most influential. But Harrison's earliest discussions of ritual precede the publication of *The Golden Bough*, and she and Frazer were developing their ideas about the role of drama more or less simultaneously' (Julia Stone Peters, 'Jane Harrison and the Savage Dionysus: Archaeological Voyages, Ritual Origins, Anthropology, and the Modern Theatre', *Modern Drama*, LI, no. 1 (2008), p. 32.

Harrison produced numerous comments on Russian culture and published a book on the Russian language and literature. She taught Russian at Cambridge from 1917 to 1922 and from 1922 to 1925, lived in Paris where she befriended many Russians, including the prominent Russian writer Aleksei Remizov and the Russian religious philosopher Lev Shestov. Together with Hope Mirrlees, her long-standing friend and pupil, Harrison published her English-language version of Archpriest Avvakum's autobiographical book *The Life of the Archpriest Avvakum* (1924) and a collection of translations of several Russian fairy tales (both folk stories and literary ones) as *The Book of the Bear* (1926). According to Gerald Smith, *The Book of the Bear* 'retains great value because of the literary quality of translations'.[2] Smith also thinks that it brings together Harrison's strong interest in totemism and her Russophilism in an effective manner. It is not surprising that she described Russian folk traditions and performances as being truly beautiful. Harrison's enthusiasm for Russian folk drama is especially felt in her portrayal of Russian *Vertep* plays: the rites that take place on 23 June, the Eve of John Baptist's day and the worship of the pagan spring-god Iarilo. By concluding her account of the above mentioned performances with the statement that the reader should thank the Russian peasant for all the artefacts, Harrison encourages her readers to appreciate the universal aspects of Indo-European cultures and languages.

Harrison's empathy for Russian peasant culture stands in striking contrast to James Frazer's approach to the primitives: in the words of Martha Carpentier, Frazer 'could vent an astonishing disdain for the peasant class whose religious customs he analysed so closely'.[3] According to Carpentier, Harrison's disagreement with Frazer and other scholars who were involved in rationalising religion and hierarchical thought stems from her belief in the mystical aspects and vitalism of early pre-intellectual religious experience. 'For Harrison,' says Carpentier, 'primitives were not "purblind" as for Frazer, but visionary'.[4] To this end, Harrison's interest in the personal experience and the sense of immediate intuitive revelation is especially strongly felt in her understanding of magic as the borderline between man and beast and a form of the spiritual protoplasm which 'gives rise to

2 Gerald Stanton Smith, *D.S. Mirsky: A Russian-English Life, 1890-1939* (Oxford, 2000), p. 99.
3 Martha C. Carpentier, *Ritual, Myth, and the Modernist Text: The Influence of Jane Ellen Harrison on Joyce, Eliot, and Woolf* (Amsterdam, 1998), p. 51.
4 *Ibid.*, p. 52.

Religion and other "civilised' things"'.[5] Harrison developed a strong bond with the young writers who rebelled against the rational and patriarchal values of the Victorian generation. She sought to promote a psychological approach to the manifestations of creativity and spirituality, suggesting that true religious experience is not rationalised theology (Omega) but rather a lived, experienced thing (Alpha)—as in the mysticism of various matriarchal cults, especially the ones related to Dionysus. In Harrison's view, primitive people participate in the natural cycle of life through performing magical dancing. She believed that the example of primitives should teach 20th-century intellectuals to overcome their positivism and embrace the essence of religious life, including secular religiosity, rejecting thereby 'the intellectual attempt to define the indefinable'.[6]

The growing interest in Russian and Slavonic studies found in Harrison's works in the 1910s-20s coincides with the wider scholarly and political engagement with Eastern European and Oriental studies at the beginning of the 20th century. For example, the Deutsche Gesellschaft zum Studium Osteuropas was created in 1913; the School of Slavonic and East European Studies was established in 1915 at the University of London; the first Institut d'Études Slaves was opened in Paris in 1919; and in the United States, a Society for the Advancement of Slavonic Study was founded in 1919. Commenting on the rapid formation of the East European discourse in France after World War I, Ezequiel Adamovsky points out that 'the beginnings of Euro-Orientalism are to be found in the second decade of the 20th century, especially after World War I, when the Western powers had to redraw the map of Eastern Europe. In that context, interest in Slavonic studies spread to different universities in Europe and specialised institutes and periodical publications were established, forming a network of supporting institutions for the new discourse'.[7]

In the light of the growing interest in Eastern Europe as the exotic 'other' in the 1910s-20s, it is not surprising to see that Harrison focuses on the magic qualities of Russian pagan beliefs linked to the tradition of equating word with deed: 'Nowhere so clearly as is St John the Baptist's year aspect not only known but felt. He is essentially a Solstice Saint—the rites of St John's Eve, with its magical bathing, its magical Firewheel, and its magic

5 Jane Ellen Harrison, *Alpha and Omega* (London, 1915), pp. 162-3.

6 *Ibid.*, p. 205.

7 Ezequiel Adamovsky, 'Euro Orientalism and the Making of the Concept of Eastern Europe in France, 1810-1880', Journal of Modern History, LXXVII, no. 3 (2005), p. 609.

flower gathering, are too obviously of the Solstice to need further stress'.[8] The *Vertep* theatre, and a collection of marionettes, including the one with a head of Satan resembling a Gorgon mask, located in the Museum of the Imperial Academy of Sciences at Petrograd, appear of special appeal to her because they represent objects of the living tradition she so cherished. Harrison also defines a reference found in Nikolai Gogol's story featuring the head of a roast ram served at supper as a remnant of the ritual myth. In Harrison's opinion, Russian performances related to 'the loathsome story of the Head and the dance' displayed a sense of 'a new ritual dignity'.[9]

In her 1925 memoir, Harrison demonstrates the notion of ritual dignity embodied by her dream (seen soon after the 1917 Bolshevik Revolution) about her imaginary dance with huge bears in a vast ancient forest. Harrison calls the space of her fantasy a 'dreaming wood', linking the visionary nature of her dream to the archetypal qualities of the subconscious. The description of the dream in the memoir suggests that the bears refused to learn from her how to dance the Grand Chain in the lancers and shuffled away instead, 'courteously waving their paws, intent on their own mysterious doings' which she felt obliged to learn and invoked in her an ecstasy of humility.[10] This dream invokes Nikolai Rerikh's 1912 painting 'Forefathers' that some scholars view as a possible sketch for the opening of Igor' Stravinskii's 1913 ballet *The Rite of Spring*. As Peter Hill notes, Rerikh's painting presents Orpheus-like primitive man who charms with his piping a circle of bears, 'reflecting the Slavic tradition that bears were man's forefathers'.[11] In similar manner to Aleksandr Blok's historiosophical beliefs in the redeeming aspects of the Bolshevik revolution and the importance of Scythian traditions to the Russian identity, Harrison said to her friends: 'The Bears revolution has made me so happy—it is the best and biggest thing the War has brought and does justify our faith in them and it is splendid that there has been so little bloodshed'.[12] The dream described in Harrison's book might be interpreted as an omen for a better social order to evolve.

Arguably, Harrison's mythologised image of Russia—entwined with deeply personal overtones—articulates her own sense of displacement into

---

8 Jane Harrison, 'The Head of John Baptist', *Classical Review*, XXX, no. 8 (1916), p. 218.
9 *Ibid.*, p. 219.
10 Jane Ellen Harrison, *Reminiscences of a Student's Life* (London, 1925), pp. 77-8.
11 Peter Hill, *Stravinsky: The Rite of Spring* (Cambridge, 2000), p. 5.
12 Jessie G. Stewart, *Jane Ellen Harrison: A Portrait from Letters* (London, 1959), p. 176.

the space that enables creativity and transcendence. The dream of bears invokes Harrison's definition of the Dionysian dithyramb as a leaping inspired dance and her understanding of pantomimic dancing as a ritual bridge 'between actual life and those representations of life that we call art'.[13] According to Harrison, not all rites might be defined as art. Harrison gives an example from Russian peasant life that lacks artistic imagination: 'In some parts of Eastern Russia the girls dance one by one in a large hoop at midnight on Shrove Tuesday. The hoop is decked with leaves, flowers and ribbons, and attached to it are a small bell and some flax. While dancing within the hoop each girl has to wave her arms vigorously and cry, "Flax, grow", or words to that effect. When she has done she leaps out of the hoop or is lifted out of it by her partner'.[14] Harrison suggests that such a practice (related to superstitions and primitive beliefs) constitutes neither art, nor ritual, since it is carried privately and not performed for public good by the authorised collective body.

According to Harrison, in order for acts of sympathetic magic to be considered art, they need to be subordinated to the imitation of life and go beyond the function of uttering emotion: 'We must not only utter emotion, we must represent it, that is, we must in some way reproduce or imitate or express the thought which is causing us emotion. Art is not imitation, but art and also ritual frequently and legitimately contain an element of imitation'.[15] By contrast, Harrison's interpretation of the *Hymn of the Kouretes to Zeus*, in which god and worshippers leap together to bring fertility and ensure communal transcendence, points to the expression of ritualistic beliefs and communal experience of the divine. Harrison's examples of the acts of theatricality that occur both through a performer's relocation of the quotidian space that he occupies and through a spectator's gaze framing a quotidian space that he does not occupy, testify to her acute awareness of the necessity to revive the social function of culture as a counterpoint to the highly pessimistic modern world view. It is such a view that she felt led to the disintegration of morality into the plurality of subjective values. That is why Harrison praised the novels of Katherine Mansfield and John Galsworthy for reviving the novel's social function. As Carpentier stresses, Harrison valued 'the collective emotional experience of primitive ritual

---

13 Jane Ellen Harrison, *Ancient Art and Ritual* (London, 1913), p. 28.
14 *Ibid.*, p. 32.
15 *Ibid.*, p. 35.

and hoped to see art in her own generation assuming a similar socially cathartic function'.[16]

Viewed in the light of her disillusionment with the novel's diminished role in a modern society, Harrison's dream about dancing with bears might be seen as a manifestation of theatricality as alterity that emerges through a split in the quotidian space. The dream of dancing with bears is reproduced in Harrison's memoir, and can be interpreted as a special kind of monodrama that gives the reader a sense of shared experience. Harrison's theatrical gesture might be compared to the views of Russian modernist critic Aleksandr Kugel', especially to his idea that every work environment, social group, and manifestation of ordinary life corresponds to certain rhythmical patterns, and his vision of drama as an artistic rendering of psychic life seen as the intuitively comprehensible flow of existence. As Kugel' points out, 'the task of art is to cognise life in such a way that it would be possible to capture its rhythm'.[17] Kugel's vision of monodrama as a manifestation of psychic life was developed in Nikolai Evreinov's book *Introduction to Monodrama,* which claims that the appropriate relationship between audience and performance in the theatre is one of sympathy; therefore, complete unity between character and audience is achievable if everything happening on stage can be subjectively perceived by one main character.[18] By offering her readers a description of a dream of dancing with bears, Harrison moulds herself into the image of a modern artist and a religious-like figure capable of sharing her emotional experience with the audience and aspiring to represent psychological time in a Bergsonian manner.

In addition to creating her own image of Russia and Russian culture, Harrison claimed that the Russian language provided her with a refuge in the same way as painting, music and literature, thereby enabling her to have a parallel existence. Harrison writes of the Russian language in a very intimate manner and says that she fell in love with it in the same way she fell in love with the Greek language.[19] According to Harrison, language is an artefact and 'the *un*conscious or at least subconscious product of the group, the herd, the race, the nation'.[20] Having praised the aesthetic qualities of the

16 Carpentier, *op.cit.,* p. 66.
17 A.R. Kugel', '*Utverzhdenie* teatra', *Teatr i iskusstvo* (1923), p. 170.
18 Nikolai Evreinov, *Vvedenie v monodramu* (St Petersburg, 1909), p. 9.
19 Jane Ellen Harrison, *Aspects, Aorists and the Classical Tripos* (Cambridge, 1919), p. 5.
20 *Ibid.*

Russian artistic imagination that appealed to her, in her 1919 book on the Russian language she admits that her encounters with Russian culture were highly valuable for her own personal development, insisting that the study of Russian language and folklore enriched her understanding of Ancient Greek culture. 'To study the folk-epos of Russia alive in the mouths of the people up to and beyond the time of Peter the Great', Harrison maintains, 'is to look at Homer with new and wider opened eyes'.[21]

Harrison's interpretation of Russian artistic imagination testifies to a special trait in her character—namely, her instinctive pacifism that over the war years grew into a coherent philosophy resembling Lev Tolstoi's vision of peaceful co-existence of all nations. By drawing examples from Russian culture related to the expression of communal ties, Harrison articulated an alternative to the view found in Gilbert Murray's pamphlet *How Can War Ever Be Right?*, asserting that 'war is not all evil'.[22] In this book, Murray welcomes war as an opportunity for heroism that enables common man to elevate themselves to the status of Homeric heroes and writes, 'But, when all allowances are made, one cannot read the letters and dispatches without a feeling of passionate admiration for the men about whom they tell [...]. They were just our ordinary fellow citizens [...]. Yet, now under the stress of war, having a duty before them that is clear and unquestioned and terrible, they are daily doing noble things'.[23] Murray's notion of 'the common necessary heroism of the average men' is presented in his pamphlet as anti-Tolstoian. Commenting on a Russian officer described by the media as a person who had discovered a sense of freedom through war, and who claimed that all his fellow officers were fighting with tears of joy in their eyes, Murray suggests that there are seldom opportunities in everyday life that enable ordinary citizens to find the same sort of happiness. According to Murray, 'this is the inward triumph that lies at the heart of the great tragedy'.[24]

One of Harrison's letters to Murray states otherwise. Harrison feels strongly about the notion of individual freedom that should not be imposed upon people. Opposed to both the dark side of the herd instinct and the artificially constructed sense of community in the name of patriotism uncovered by the war, Harrison thinks that any power structures inflicted

21 *Ibid.*, p. 36.
22 Gilbert Murray, *How Can War Ever Be Right?* (London, 1914), p. 24.
23 *Ibid.*, p. 25.
24 *Ibid.*, p. 27.

upon individuals lead to conformity. She writes, 'I am beginning to feel as if the curse all over was the curse of a dominant *class*, a governing class, which I used to think it so natural and fine to belong to. No one—except perhaps you—is to have power over anyone else. I mean power to compel'.[25] Harrison's 1914 essay 'Epilogue on the War' also denounces the outbreak of war and the propaganda articles that justify military actions.

According to Harrison's model of a new social order, a modern subject should be able to overcome the fragmented state of mind through a universalist and comparativist outlook: 'An accurate knowledge of the Greek and Russian languages together with an intimate understanding of the two civilisations should furnish a humanistic education at once broad and thorough'.[26] Yet it would be wrong to say that Harrison had developed such a model single-handedly. Harrison's belief in the value of an anthropological approach to culture was shaped by various studies penned by the evolutionists, including E.B. Taylor, whose book *Primitive Culture* (1871) had a significant impact on the artistic imagination of many British modernist writers searching for a new world of religious meaning beyond Christianity. Harrison was also inspired by Nietzsche's *The Birth of Tragedy* (1871) that presented the Apollonian and Dionysian principles of Greek religion in a new light. Harrison challenged Nietzsche's conception of the dominance of male archetypes in Hellenic religion and pursued a study of the Hellenic matriarchal goddesses.

It seems that Harrison's research into Dionysian rituals and Dionysian song and pantomime as manifestations of early Greek drama made her aware of the emergence of similar approaches to myth and ritual articulated by Russian scholars and thinkers, including Russian Symbolist poet Viacheslav Ivanov, whose article 'The Spiritual Face of Slavs' portrays Russians as true followers of the Dionysian principle of transcendental unity. Ivanov's poems and essays were well known in the West in the 1900s-10s and admired for their presentation of Dionysus as a powerful mystical god and dying god, the prototype of Christ. Clarence Manning's following words about Ivanov can easily be applied to Harrison herself: 'Christ and Dionysus, mystery and drama, the theatre and the Church, all the forces from all directions which agitated the ancient world in the great crises of its history were felt by Ivanov' in such an intense manner that 'he summed

25 Quoted in Annabel Robinson, *The Life and Work of Jane Ellen Harrison* (Oxford, 2002), p. 262.
26 Murray 1914, *op.cit.*

up religion, art, and thought in the ancient symbols' in order to present 'a sympathetic and appealing figure of the dying god'.[27]

As Sandra Peacock maintains, 'at the end of her life Jane perceived that neither individualism, nor collectivism alone could be the best way to live in the world. As she grew older she internalised Bergson's concept of life as change no longer felt threatened by the gap between youth and age'.[28] Given Harrison's profound interest in Bergsonian thought that may have reflected a general modernist fascination with various aspects of a neo-Romantic organic outlook, it is not surprising that Harrison felt attracted to manifestations of intuitivism found in Russian religious thought and literature.[29] In the obituary he wrote at the time of Harrison's death, Prince Sviatopolk-Mirskii (a passionate admirer of Bergson himself) says that by the time Harrison wrote *Themis: A Study of the Social Origins of Greek Religion* (1912) (hereafter *Themis*), 'primitive religion had become for her a starting point for a general study of the human soul', suggesting that she passed to the Russians from Freud and Bergson who 'attracted her by their broad and spontaneous humanity'.[30] Mirskii's commentary invokes Bergson's criticism of neo-Kantian critical rationality.

Indeed, Jane Harrison's matriarchal anti-Kantian theories shaped Woolf's ideas about group psychology. Patricia Cramer points out that in her book *Between the Acts* (1941) Woolf 'contrasts patriarchal with matriarchal configurations in order to provide a model for an alternative 'family of origins'—centered on women's values rather than on violent, dominating men'.[31] Cramer's article maintains that both Harrison and Woolf wanted to encourage women's active participation in the construction of a new culture opposed to heroic violence, male domination and war conflicts. Harrison's interest in memory studies and reconstruction of the past in the present (through the re-enactment of ritualistic activities or re-definition of tradition) is also comparable to T.S. Eliot's concept of tradition as a process of constant internal adjustment. According to K. Phillips, T.S. Eliot shared Harrison's vision that modern artists need to transmute

27 Clarence A. Manning, 'A Rebirth of Dionysus: In Russia', *Classical Weekly*, XVIII, no. 4 (27 October 1924), p. 29.

28 Sandra Peacock, *Jane Ellen Harrison. The Mask and the Self* (New Haven and London, 1988), p. 242.

29 Hilary Fink, *Bergson and Russian Modernism* (Evanston, 1999), p. xv.

30 D.S. Mirsky, 'Jane Ellen Harrison. Died 15 April 1928', *Slavonic and East European Review*, VII, no. 20 (1929), p. 415.

31 Patricia Cramer, 'Virginia Woolf's Matriarchal Family of Origins in *Between the Acts*', *Twentieth Century Literature*, XXXIX, no. 2 (1993), pp. 167.

their private personalities in the style of ancient ritualists.[32] Eliot's 1919 pronouncement that 'the progress of an artist is a continual self-sacrifice, a continual extinction of personality'[33] echoes Harrison's description of ancient dancers who 'sink their own personality, and by the wearing of masks and disguises, by dancing to a common rhythm, above all by the common excitement, they become emotionally one, a true congregation, not a collection of individuals'.[34]

Other contemporaries also valued Harrison's contribution to the elaboration of modernism in general. Harrison's interest in Russian culture and literature stems from her profound understanding of the modern individual's alienated position in social structures and a need for a compensatory staging of the self as a unified body. By drawing on examples from Russian culture and literature, Harrison produces a compelling argument that the organic work offers compensatory images and enables the decentred modern subject to discover a sense of wholeness. Harrison's preoccupation with emotion, evoked by ritualised actions and effects, positions her alongside many European avant-garde expressionists who were opposed to conventional organic work (due to its affirmative ideological function and reconciliatory use of social integration). According to Richard Murphy, one of the main goals of the avant-garde critique of the institution of art is to expose realism 'as an institutionally-supported code which serves to legitimise only a certain concept of reality, and which lives out of account large areas of human experience that fall outside of this sanctioned category'.[35]

Arguably, Harrison's reading of realist texts (including Russian 19th-century literature) through a prism of modernist experience is comparable to the attempts of Russian theoreticians, including Ivanov and Viktor Shklovskii, to address the problem of overcoming the shift towards hermeticism, so it can help transform everyday life. In her 1915 book Harrison presents herself as the representative of the generation of art lovers fond of music-halls and Russian ballets.[36] In her 1913 book *Ancient*

32 K.J. Phillips, 'Jane Harrison and Modernism', *Journal of Modern Literature*, XVII, no. 4 (1991), p. 468.

33 T.S. Eliot, 'Tradition and the Individual Talent', *The Sacred Wood: Essays on Poetry and Criticism* (London, 1920), p. 47.

34 Jane Ellen Harrison, *Themis: A Study of the Social Origins of Greek Religion*, pp. 45-6.

35 Richard Murphy, *Theorizing the Avant-Garde: Modernism, Expressionism, and the Problem of Postmodernity* (Cambridge, 1998), p. 15.

36 Harrison, 'Crabbed Age and Youth', *Alpha and Omega* (London, 1915), p. 10.

Art and Ritual Harrison writes proudly about the new aesthetic sensibilities developing in Great Britain:

> We English are not supposed to be an artistic people, yet art, in some form or another, bulks large in the national life. We have theatres, a National Gallery, we have art-schools, our tradesmen provide for us 'art-furniture,' we even hear, absurdly enough, of 'art-colours.' Moreover, all this is not a matter of mere antiquarian interest, we do not simply go and admire the beauty of the past in museums; a movement towards or about art is all alive and astir among us. We have new developments of the theatre, problem plays, Reinhardt productions, Gordon Craig scenery, Russian ballets. We have new schools of painting treading on each other's heels with breathless rapidity: Impressionists, Post-Impressionists, Futurists. Art—or at least the desire for, the interest in, art—is assuredly not dead.[37]

According to Harrison, Diagilev's Ballet Russes stands out as an exciting influence on the British audience.

The overwhelming fascination of British audiences with Diagilev's experiments can be exemplified by Ellen Terry's book *The Russian Ballet* that presents Russian modern dance as a tool of transgression and transformation of everyday life. Terry's vision of a new art resembles Harrison's understanding of Russian literature and culture as a model of transnational unity exemplified by the works of Fedor Dostoevskii and Vladimir Solov'ev. To illustrate, Terry praises Russian ballet performances for their ability to re-invent the old forms and embrace the universal aspects of aesthetic experience thus:

> I think they rather transport us into a country which has no nationality and no barriers, the kingdom of dreams. The Russian ballet has transformed itself in a little over a decade because its guiding mind has been more than national. The musicians, artists, dancers and ballet-masters have depended more on invention than on reality. Many stories of widely different character have been drawn on for the new ballets, but all have been treated with an imagination which is neither the property of a nation nor the result of patriotism.[38]

The emphasis on the dream-like qualities of Russian modern dance conveyed by Terry and Pamela Colman Smith's illustrations, which featured Vladislav Nijinskii's androgynous self-representation, is akin to Harrison's description of an emotional and intimate appeal of the Russian verb, especially because of its aspects. In her 1917 book Harrison describes

---

37 Harrison, *Ancient Art and Ritual*, pp. 207-8.

38 Ellen Terry, *The Russian Ballet* (London, 1913), p. 15.

the Russian aspects in Bergsonian terms. In her view, while the imperfective aspect denotes internal time and can be visualised as a line because it has 'duration, continuity, extension in space', the perfective aspect 'is like a dot, a moment, as soon it is begun, it finished'. Harrison suggests to perceive the imperfective aspect as the open hand and snowfield and associates the perfective aspect with a snowball,[39] thereby poeticising Russian linguistic behaviour. In the same vein, Harrison draws the reader's attention to the irrational aspects of the Russian novel, which in her view emerges not from abstract concepts, but from lived experience: 'The Russian novel is written in the imperfective, written from within not without, lived not thought about'.[40]

Similar pronouncements about the ability of Russian modernist and proto-modernist artists to overcome the fragmentation of modern life can be found in Harrison's *Themis*. In this work, she situates the origin of religion in collectively held emotion, and outlines the relevance of ancient rituals to contemporary re-evaluations of humanist values and ideas of national identity. In her book *Alpha and Omega* Harrison argues that the excesses of nationalism emerging in the 1910s stemmed from two major causes: collectivism, which had turned into a fashionable dogma; and the triumph of emotion over reason, which led those who favoured war. She offered Dostoevskii as an antidote to these excesses—a model of how a national identity could be defended without recourse to the kind of nationalism that, she believed, held sway in Britain. Harrison saw Dostoevskii's works as an embodiment of Russian transnational and dialogic thinking that differed from Russian imperialism, suggesting the English could profit by emulating it in order to embrace the patriotism 'that is own sister to Peace'.[41] While Harrison's 1913 book *Ancient Art and Ritual* develops some of Tolstoi's ideas manifested in his 1897 treatise *What is Art?*, in her 1921 book *Epilogomena to the Study of Greek Religion* Harrison refers to Vladimir Solov'ev, whose ideas shaped her own world-view and inspired her to publish two books on Russian grammar. They contain several innovative cognitive approaches to the expression of Russian beliefs and customs through language—*Russia and the Russian Verb: a Contribution to the Psychology of the Russian People*

39 Harrison, *Aspects, Aorists, and the Classical Tripos*, p. 10.
40 *Ibid.*, p. 25.
41 Harrison, 'Epilogue on the War', *Alpha and Omega*, p. 245.

(1915) and *Aorists and the Classical Tripos* (1919). The latter was defined by Mirskii as 'most remarkable studies of Russian linguistic mentality'.[42]

Harrison's analyses of the Russian language display her scholarly interest not only in the mythopoetic qualities of Russian imagination but also her awareness of the role of metaphor in the construction of the sense of continuity between the past and the present. Given Harrison's belief that it is emotion that binds object and beholder, it seems that her interest in the psychology of the creative process and commemorative qualities of Russian language and traditions stems from acute realisation of the crisis of the European novel as a manifestation of the social ills of modernity. According to Boris Eikhenbaum's 1924 assessment of the crisis of the novel, 'The modern novel was thus simultaneously deprived of both plot, that is, of the individual acting in accord with his sense of time, and psychology, since it could no longer support action of any sort. The future development of the novel will be no less than the history of the atomization of biography as a form of personal existence; what is more, we shall witness the catastrophic collapse of biography'.[43] The loss of generic integrity reflects the severed relationship between the individual and the setting that either diminished or became arbitrary. Harrison's belief that the novel embodies a particular fullness of human experience implies that a broader context related to the fate of the individual in the social and historical milieu should be reassessed with the help of a study of ritual. Harrison writes:

> The commemorative dance does especially re-present; it reproduces the past hunt or battle; but if we analyse a little more closely we see it is not for the sake of copying the actual battle itself, but for the emotion felt about the battle. This they desire to re-live... The habit of this mimesis of the thing desired, is set up, and ritual begins. Ritual, then, does imitate, but for an emotional, not an altogether practical, end.[44]

Drawing on Tolstoi's emphasis on the unifying function of art and Ivanov's notion of collective identity, Harrison offers her own model of art. Like Ivanov, Evreinov, and Eikhenbaum, she called for the restoration of the collective self through the re-enactment of universal experiences and collective commemorative acts: 'Art is in its very origin social, and social means human and collective. Moral and social are, in their final analysis, the

42 Terry, *op.cit.*

43 Quoted in Alyson Tapp, ''Kak byt' pisatelem?': Boris Eikhenbaum's Response to the Crisis of the Novel in the 1920s', *Slavonica*, XV, no. 1 (2009), p. 35.

44 Harrison, *Ancient Art and Ritual,* p. 23.

same... "Art", says Tolstoy, "has this characteristic, that it unites people"'.[45] Arguably, Harrison's study of the Greek and Russian cultures not only broadened her own vision of herself as upholder of humanist values but also restored her sense of belonging to the European cultural tradition.

45 *Ibid.*, p. 129.

13. Aleksei Remizov's English-language Translators: New Material

Marilyn Schwinn Smith

Aleksei Remizov, even more so than other writers of the post-revolution emigration, relied on both competent translators *and* prestigious promoters for entry into the British book market. His works did not fall within the genres familiar to British readers from either English or Russian literature. His unique language was a challenge even to Russian readers. As one of his translators said, 'After all, to translate Remizov is not the same as translating some Turgenev or Tolstoy'.[1] The story of Remizov's introduction to British audience—the transit of the émigré's manuscript to a bound volume distributed to British booksellers—follows, almost like a script, the process described by Olga Kaznina.[2]

The Remizov story also incorporates a vignette of British modernists, who looked to the Russian 'moderns' for inspiration and direction. Virginia Woolf's interest in the Russians is but one example of the increasing intellectual

1 Alec Brown to Aleksei Remizov, 5 January 1925, Aleksei and Serafima Remizova-Dovgello Papers, The Amherst Center for Russian Culture (Amherst College, Amherst, MA), hereafter Remizov Papers). I express my gratitude to Dr. Stanley J. Rabinowitz, for his assistance in working with the Center's holdings.

2 The categories, promoters and translators, are abstracted from criteria for successful entry into the Anglophone book market laid out by Olga Kaznina. The first criterion, exposure to British readers through English-language publications, might take the form of positive comparison with authors already known to and appreciated by the British, mention in introductions to works by those authors or in surveys of contemporary Russian literature. Such publicity was but the first step toward establishing a presence in the British market and attracting competent translators. The second criterion was well-reviewed and good translations, even reviews of books translated into languages commonly known among the English, such as German or French. See Olga Kaznina, *Russkie v Anglii* (Moscow, 1997), especially pp. 365-6 and 385.

awareness of Russian culture in Britain. Remizov's English-language translators add another dimension to this period of British engagement with Russia. Drawing together a large cast of characters interesting in their own right, the effort to introduce Remizov to a British audience is broadly representative of an important movement in British culture and consciousness. The cast is composed of Russian émigrés, commonwealth immigrants, native Britons and individuals of dual national heritage. As a whole, these translators and promoters, whose individual paths intersect in sometimes surprising ways, testify to the expansion of British interests beyond the confines of an insular culture into a pan-European modernism.

The time-span of this cross-cultural episode is, broadly, 1914-1947. The prime movers include Harold Williams, Dmitrii Mirskii, Lev Shestov, George Reavey and Stefan Schimanski among the promoters; John Cournos, Alec Brown, Jane Harrison, Hope Mirrlees and Beatrice Scott among the translators. The initial phase consists of Williams's and Cournos's early work during the Great War—a period of intense interest among the British in their new ally. Next, a concentration of effort on Remizov's behalf occurs during the mid-1920s—a decade characterized by a coming-to-terms with post-war reality. Mirskii and Brown sought to alter the taste of the 'British Public'—to replace British enthusiasm for Tolstoi, Dostoevskii and Chekhov with a modernist taste for Remizov. Harrison, meanwhile, translated Remizov's animal tales as a counter to the extremes of rationalism she saw behind the catastrophe of modern warfare. Later, in the aftermath of World War II, Scott, Reavey and Schimanski, variously involved in the small magazines of an international modernism, brought out the final Remizov translation discussed in this chapter. Much is already known about the figures involved in the first two groups, for whom I supply a few previously un-remarked details. Less information has been gathered about the last. Finally, I introduce a new constellation of figures, adding a new dimension to the picture of Remizov and his English-language translators at the heart of European modernism.

Cournos is in many ways exemplary of Remizov's English-language translators. Born Ivan Grigor'evich Korshun (Johann Gregorevich in his own version) in Zhitomir in 1881, his first language was Yiddish; he studied Russian with a tutor at home, together with German and Hebrew. At age ten, he emigrated to Philadelphia, where English became his primary language. In June 1912, Cournos moved to London, where he gained immediate entry to the literary and art worlds, freelancing as an interviewer and critic for

American and, later, British newspapers, and launching his own literary career as a poet among the British Imagists, later, as a novelist. Cournos was not alone among Remizov's promoters and translators to be bi- or multi-lingual, or to have spent his earliest childhood in Russia, or to be deeply involved in a pan-European, modernist culture.

Pride of place goes to Cournos, whose claim to have 'introduced [Remizov] to the English-reading public with *The Clock*'[3] refers to his having been the first to translate a novel. Remizov had, technically, been introduced to British readers by Harold Williams with his encomium to Remizov—'the most interesting of contemporary Russian writers of fiction' in his influential *Russia and the Russians* (1914).[4] Cournos first remarked on Remizov in the context of the wartime debate over German 'civilization' versus Russian 'barbarity'. In the 24 July 1915 issue of *Harper's Weekly*—thus roughly contemporaneously with Williams's book—Cournos offered a précis and translated the final three paragraphs of Remizov's tale 'The Guest'. Cournos asserted that, more than Dostoevskii or Tolstoi, Remizov's tale best represented the Russian characteristic of thinking with one's conscience, in contrast to the German habit of mind—a penchant for efficiency and thoroughness.[5] In February 1916, Cournos published his translation of Remizov's tale ('The Betrothed') and a brief essay on Remizov's style (again contrasting Remizov with Dostoevskii) in the Imagist periodical *The Egoist*, thus introducing the Russian author to the journal's influential modernist contributors, who included James Joyce, Ezra Pound, H. D. and T. S. Eliot.[6]

That same year, Cournos drafted a translation of *The Clock*. When the two men met during the revolutionary winter of 1917-18 in Petrograd, Cournos received 'authorization' to publish his translation,[7] and possibly received a copy of 'Beloe serdtse', a story whose publication reflects the personal connection between author and translator, and their shared experience of

3 John Cournos, *Autobiography* (New York, 1935), p. 305; Aleksei Remizov, *The Clock* (London, 1924).

4 Harold Williams *Russia of the Russians* (London, 1914), p. 217. See also Charlotte Alston, *Russia's Greatest Enemy?: Harold Williams and the Russian Revolutions* (London, 2007).

5 John Cournos, 'Kultur and the Russian Conscience', *Harper's Weekly* (24 July 1915), p. 82.

6 Aleksei Remizov, 'The Betrothed,' trans. John Cournos, *The Egoist*, III, no. 2 (1 February 1916), p. 23; John Cournos, 'Aleksei Remizov' (with woodcut of Aleksei Remizov by Roald Kristian), *ibid.*, pp. 28-9.

7 'I had wished to tell you that there is a good prospect of my finding for my translation of 'Chasy' which I made in 1916 and which I had told you about when I was in Petrograd during 1917-18' (Remizov Papers, John Cournos to Aleksei Remizov, 30 May 1924).

war-time, revolutionary Petrograd.[8] Another consequence of this visit was Cournos's fantasy re-creation of his experiences in the city. 'London under the Bolsheviks' (1919) contains a composite portrait of Russian writers under the Bolsheviks.[9] The revised versions of this portrait, appearing in the 1924 introduction to *The Clock* and in Cournos's 1935 autobiography, make clear that the composite portrait had been based largely on what Cournos observed during his visits to Remizov's flat.[10] Publication of *The Clock* concluded Cournos's relationship with Remizov. Remizov, however, may not have finished with Cournos. In 1932, he composed one of his handwritten and illustrated albums, copying out Cournos's English translation. Remizov titled this album 'Kourinas', a word related to neither '*chasy*' nor 'clock', but rather to the name of its translator. Remizov annotated the text: 'Byessinia—Devil's land; Kourinassi— Hen-noses. Play on words'.[11] Cournos himself pointed to the malapropism of his adopted surname, Cournos (short nose, French) as opposed to the physically more appropriate birthname, Korshun (hawk, Russian). The title 'Kourinas' may be Remizov's sly commentary on his failure to receive royalties for *The Clock* from his ill-named translator.[12]

---

8 Cournos's translation appeared in the January 1921 issue of *The Dial*, which raises the question of how he obtained the text. Hélène Sinany says the following of *Shumy goroda*: 'Il est probable qu'une partie de ces texts a été publiée entre 1918 et 1921 en périodiques. Malheuresement on n'a pu retrouver *toutes* les references'. Hélène Sinany, *Bibliographie des Oeuvres de Alexis Remizov* (Paris, 1978), p. 54.

9 John Cournos, *London under the Bolsheviks: A Londoner's Dream on Returning from Petrograd*, (London [1919]), (Russian Liberation Committee's publications, no. 4), pp. 3-12, and Foreword (pp. 11-12). In all probability, fellow journalist with the Anglo-Russian Commission in Petrograd and long-time friend of Remizov, Harold Williams had introduced Cournos to Remizov. Cournos remained in touch with the Williamses, Harold and Ariadna, who had evacuated from Petrograd, arriving in London, via Newcastle, just a week after Cournos in 1918. Ariadna played a leading role in the Russian Liberation Committee and edited their publications.

10 The 1924 publication of *The Clock* reprinted the three previously published short pieces: 'The Betrothed' (*The Egoist*), 'Easter' (*The Westminster Gazette*) and 'A White Heart' (*The Dial*). 'Easter' ('Svetlo-Khristovo-Voskresenie') was first published in *Rus'* (a daily newspaper) on 11 December 1903 and re-issued in *Sochineniia*, VII, 'Otrechennye povesti' in 1912, where Cournos is most likely to have found it. 'The Betrothed' ('Suzhenaia') first appeared in *Sketing-rink* (a weekly sports, literary and arts, and humour magazine) in 1910 and was re-issued in *Dokuda i balagur'e* (*russkie zhenshchiny*) in 1914, where Cournos is most likely to have found it. 'A White Heart' ('Beloe serdtse') first appeared in *Shumy goroda* (Revel', 1921). See Sinany, *Bibliographie*.

11 See *Images of Aleksei Remizov. Drawings and Handwritten and Illustrated Albums from the Thomas P. Whitney Collection* (Amherst, MA, 1985), p. 69.

12 'As soon as I know how the book is selling I will try to send you a few pounds. What little I have received in advance does little more than pay for the typing of the book, my agent's commissions, and odd expenses. I did the translation in 1916, and spent no little

The émigré Slavist, Dmitrii Mirskii began negotiations with Chatto & Windus in May 1924 for a translation of *The Fifth Pestilence* and sent his chosen translator, the 24-year-old Alec Brown, to Remizov in Paris. Negotiations were complicated by the poor sales of *The Clock*, the possibility of censorship and the relative shortness of the text. When the book eventually appeared in 1927, it included a second novella, *Stratilatov*, and was distributed by another press.[13] Throughout these difficulties, Brown shuttled between England—where he consulted with Mirskii—and his home in Belgrade—where he consulted with Remizov's close friend, Evgenii Anichkov—visiting Remizov in Paris when possible. All the while, the two maintained a prolific correspondence on the subject of Brown's translations and other literary ventures which continued into the 1930s. That same spring of 1924, Mirskii met two Englishwomen, the British classicist and Slavophile Jane Harrison and her companion-in-Russian Hope Mirrlees, thus initiating the much noted and productive friendship between Harrison and Mirskii.[14]

The back-story to these friendships and consequent publications can be dated to 1916, when Harrison wrote: 'I am now embarking on the lives of Russian Saints. [...] There is a modern Remezov [*sic*], I am taken by—but he uses too many hard words'.[15] That same year, Middleton Murry and S. Kotelianskii translated and published a collection of Shestov's essays, from which Harrison cited approvingly Shestov's remark: 'we want not so much a science as an art of life'.[16] After retiring from Newnham College,

---

in sending it around. Then again I revised it, and had the manuscript retyped. However, if I make anything out of the book, you will have a share' (Remizov Papers, John Cournos to Aleksei Remizov, 24 November 1924).

13 Aleksei Remizov, *The Fifth Pestilence together with The History of the Tinkling Cymbal and Sounding Brass. Ivan Semyonovitch Stratilatov*, trans. Alec Brown (London, 1927). See also A.B. Rogachevskii, 'Neizvestnye pis'ma D.P. Sviatopolka-Mirskogo serediny 1920-kh godov', *Diaspora: Novye materially*, II (St Petersburg, 2001), pp. 349-67; Robert Hughes, "... S Vami Beda – ne Perevesti'. Pis'ma D.P. Sviatopolka-Mirskogo k A.M. Remizovu. 1922-1929', *Diaspora: Novye Materialy*, V (Paris and St Petersburg, 2003), pp. 335-401.

14 See G.S. Smith, 'Jane Ellen Harrison: Forty-Seven Letters to D.S. Mirsky, 1924-1926', *Oxford Slavonic Papers*, NS XXVIII (1995), pp. 62-97.

15 Jane Harrison to Gilbert Murray, 22 January 1916. Harrison Papers 1/1/33, Newnham College Archive, Cambridge University. I thank Anne Thomson for her assistance in using the Harrison Papers. Harrison does not mention which Remizov text she has been reading, but since his name comes up in association with lives of the Saints, she may have been reading from his 1907 *Limonar'*—a modernist re-working of saints' lives and medieval apocryphal texts. During World War I Harrison studied Russian with Paul Boyer at the École des langues orientales in Paris.

16 Lev Shestov, *Anton Tchekhov and Other Essays by Leon Shestov*, trans. J.M. Murry and S.S. Koteliansky (London, 1916); Jane Ellen Harrison, *Aspects, Aorists and the Classical Tripos*

Cambridge, and moving to Paris in 1922, Harrison met Shestov. They were socializing actively by April 1923. Shestov enlisted Harrison's financial assistance for Remizov's move from Berlin to Paris at the end of the year. Remizov arrived in Paris on 8 November 1923 and Shestov introduced Harrison to Remizov on 3 February 1924.[17]

At the end of March 1924, Mirrlees and Harrison lunched in the London home of Logan Pearsall Smith. Among the guests were Raymond Mortimer and 'Prince Mirsky'. Mirrlees writes: 'Logan & the Prince were very anxious to persuade Jane & me to translate some Russian books; but we refused with an oath. However, Jane thought better of it & sent a p.c. to say she'd be willing to do some Remizov, one of the writers the Prince is particularly anxious should be known in England'.[18] The pair began, however, with a translation of the 17th century *Life of Archpriest Avvakum*, which was published in October 1924 by Harrison's friends Virginia and Leonard Woolf at The Hogarth Press.[19] Harrison then undertook the Remizov translation—four short tales, anchoring the collection *The Book of the Bear*—immediately on completion of the *Avvakum* translation. This collection of Russian animal tales continued Harrison's ongoing advocacy of what the British could learn from the Russians—the revival of a consciousness more attuned to the psyche's interior and religious capacities, qualities she found in Remizov's writing.[20] Since *Avvakum* had been placed with a Bloomsbury

---

(Cambridge, 1919), p. 33; see also M.S. Smith, 'Bergsonian Poetics and the Beast: Jane Harrison's Translations from the Russian', *Translation and Literature*, XX (2011), pp. 314-33 (p. 325).

17 Jane Harrison to Jessie Stewart, 27 April 1923 (Shestov to tea); Henri Bergson to Jane Harrison, 9 May 1923 (cannot come to meet Shestov), Harrison Papers; Lev Shestov to Hope Mirrlees, 30 July 1923 (reply to letter, continuing conversation on Pascal), Mirrlees Papers, Newnham College Archive, Cambridge University. I thank Anne Thomson for assistance in using the Mirrlees Papers. Three letters Shestov wrote to Remizov in September mentioned the promise of funds for the move. Lev Shestov to Aleksei Remizov, 3 September 1923, 12 September 1923, 13 September 1923. Remizov Papers.

18 Hope Mirrlees to Lina Mirrlees, 29 March 1924, Mirrlees Papers 2/1/3. I thank Sandeep Parmar for bringing the relevant Mirrlees correspondence to my attention.

19 *The Life of Archpriest Avvakum by Himself*, trans. Jane Harrison and Hope Mirrlees (London, 1924). For a brief discussion of the translation, see Marilyn Schwinn Smith, 'Bears in Bloomsbury: Jane Ellen Harrison and the Russians', in Maria Cândida Zamith and Luisa Flora (eds.), *Virginia Woolf: Three Centenary Celebrations* (Porto, 2007), pp. 125-9. For a discussion of the political context within which the translation was published, see Jean Mills, 'The Writer, the Prince and the Scholar: Virginia Woolf, D.S. Mirsky, and Jane Harrison's Translation from Russian of *The Life of the Archpriest Avvakum, by Himself*—a Revaluation of the Radical Politics of the Hogarth Press', in Helen Southworth (ed.), *Leonard and Virginia Woolf, the Hogarth Press and the Networks of Modernism* (Edinburgh, 2010), pp. 150-75.

20 See M.S. Smith, 'Bergsonian Poetics and the Beast'.

house, Harrison's and Mirrlees's agent successfully negotiated with a new house managed by Bloomsbury friend, David Garnett—the Nonesuch Press—for a 1926 publication timed for the Christmas market. *The Book of the Bear* was Harrison's final work engaged with Russia, but she continued her correspondence with the Remizovs until her death in 1928.

The Remizov translations produced in the 1920s reflect a small, but not insular, community. A web centered on Remizov in Paris emanated outwards, connecting his cosmopolitan translators. Brown's dedications—of *Stratilatov* to Mirskii and of *The Fifth Pestilence* to Remizov's great friend, Evgenii Anichkov—is emblematic. These few details—Brown consulting with Remizov in Paris, with Mirskii in London, with Anichkov in Belgrade—chart a topography of relations between émigré Russians and British modernists. From the beginning, the figures involved in translating Remizov were multi-lingual, of diverse nationality and national status, and operated internationally. Cournos, born in Russia, subsequently an American citizen residing in England, harnessed his knowledge of Russian to promote his own literary aspirations. An Englishman of literary ambition, Brown adopted the Slavonic literatures of Russia and Serbia, as the Russian-born Cournos had adopted English. Cournos had made Shakespeare's homeland his own base, as Brown made Serbia, both men spending considerable time in Paris. A younger generation was to continue this pattern.

After the intensity of efforts to publish English translations of Remizov during the 20s, the 30s was a barren decade, followed by the darkness of the war years. Thus, it must have been a delightful surprise when, on 16 January 1947, Remizov received a letter from Beatrice Scott in Oxford announcing the publication of her translation, *On a Field Azure,* with an introduction by George Reavey. This title was the sixth issue of Stefan Schimanski's 'Russian Literature Library', a series only established in 1945.[21] Scott also mentioned in passing, perhaps expecting that the name would impress Remizov, 'During the war, I also spoke to Herbert Read [the well known poet, art critic] and he was interested in a collected volume of

21 Both Schimanski and Reavey were Russian-born and British-educated, intensely active in European modernist circles (often in Paris), and worked assiduously to promote Russian literature in England, whether émigré or Soviet. For more about the work of Schimanski, Reavey and Read in connection with Pasternak, see Lazar Fleishman, 'Boris Pasternak i gruppa "Transformation"', in *Ot Pushkina k Pasternaku* (Moscow, 2006), pp. 715-30.

your fairy tales'. Remizov clearly made due note of this, writing next to one of his drawings on an envelope: 'Herbert Read/skazki'.[22]

Born in London of a British father and Russian mother, Scott was well-versed in, and sophisticated about, contemporary Russian literature, as evidenced by her correspondence with Read as well as by the choice and quality of her translations. In her letter to Remizov, she was not entirely forthcoming about Read's interest in publishing him. In 1943, Schimanski had directed Scott to contact Read—a partner at Routledge—about translating for the firm.[23] Scott wrote to Read on 22 May:

> I understand from Mr. Schimanski that you contemplate publishing a volume of Pasternak, and I feel very strongly that representative volumes of single authors are particularly needed. I am very keen myself to prepare and translate a selection from the work of Remizov and hope you may be interested in this. As you will know his work is of a high standard and very varied, and since he has had a great influence on younger Russian authors his work should be known in England, which it is not. The selection would of course depend partly on the length allowed for the book. The following is a possible selection:-
>
> (1) Extracts from Remizov's diary, printed in EPOPEYA, a literary magazine.
> (2) ON A FIELD AZURE.
> (3) THE TALE OF I.S. STRATILATOV.
> (4) Fairy tales.
> (5) Folk tales.
> (6) Dreams and prose lyrics.
> (7) The short novel SISTERS OF THE CROSS.
>
> Yours sincerely, Beatrice Scott.

After further discussion and personal meetings, Read concluded that Scott's projected publication was not feasible:

---

22 Aleksei Remizov, *On a Field Azure*, trans. Beatrice Scott (London 1946); Beatrice Scott to Aleksei Remizov, 12 January 1947, Remizov Papers.

23 In the early 1940s, Schimanski consulted for Herbert Read at Routledge for Russian titles and had brought Beatrice Scott into the fold, as one of his Russian translators. Scott was to translate 'The Safe Conduct' for the first significant publication of Pasternak's prose in England. It was a major undertaking, involving Pasternak's family in Oxford and orchestrated by Schimanski. Read was an enthusiastic supporter of the publication. But when the other Routledge directors were slow to give final approval, Schimanski accepted an offer to assume a position with significant discretion in terms of publication at Drummond's new publishing firm. The Pasternak title, *The Collected Prose Works*, appeared as a Lindsay Drummond imprint in 1945. It was at this time, and under these circumstances that Schimanski's 'Russian Literature Library' came into being, and Schimanski's translators went with him to the new house. For more about the work of Schimanski, Reavey and Read in connection with Pasternak, see Lazar Fleishman, 'Boris Pasternak i gruppa 'Transformation''. I am grateful to Prof. Fleishman for bringing his essay to my attention.

Dear Mrs. Scott,

Since your visit the other day we have found a copy of the translations from Remizov by Wishart & Company, published in 1927. The volume includes 'The Fifth Pestilence' and 'The Tale of I. S. Stratilatov', which you propose to translate. This volume, as I told you, was a failure, and we feel that a similar volume at the present time would not stand any better chance. Remizov's work seems to be of a type which is almost untranslateable, and even when translated does not convey the linguistic qualities upon which the virtues of the original so much depend.

In the circumstances we do not feel that we can encourage you to go ahead with a translation of the further volume of Remizov's writings. We should, however, always be pleased to consider any other proposal which you might care to make.

Yours sincerely, [*HR*][24]

Presumably, Read eventually indicated interest in publishing a volume of fairy tales, a genre of considerable popularity. What is clear is that Scott herself was the initiator and, when she moved with Schimanski to Lindsay Drummond, was able to proceed with *On a Field Azure* under more hospitable circumstances.

In her letter to Remizov of 1947, Scott also expressed hope that he was not 'displeased that one of your books should have been translated in England without your previous knowledge'. Simultaneously, she asked to become the 'sole authorized translator into English at this time' of 'the second and third volumes of 'Olia''. There is a certain irony in the fact that *On a Field Azure* was published without Remizov's knowledge. A work dear to his heart which he was eager to see published in translation, *V pole blakitnom*, published in 1922, was the first installment of Remizov's fictionalized biography of his wife. When the Russian text was finally published in 1927, it was re-titled *Olia*.[25] German, French, Croatian, Bulgarian, and Slovenian translations appeared between 1924 and 1931. Just as Remizov had not known of Scott's translation, she had not known of the manuscript translations completed in the mid-20s.

Returning to that active month of May 1924, Hope Mirrlees wrote home that 'a young man called Dixon' was helping explain the Avvakum text. Since the text was both difficult to obtain and its language difficult, Shestov had enlisted Remizov to read to the translators from his personal copy and

24 University of Reading, Special Collections: Archives of Routledge & Kegan Paul. UoR RKP 202/4. I thank Nancy Jean Fulford for assistance with the Routledge archives.

25 Aleksei Remizov, *Olia* (Paris, 1927).

assist them with its Old Russian.[26] Dixon, evidently, served as a translator between Remizov and the Englishwomen during these readings. Mirrlees continued: 'He is going to translate the Remizov book I told you about last time—we have promised to touch it up, as his English is not as good as his Russian'.[27] That book was the first two parts of *Olia*. At the end of the year, Remizov requested Brown to polish Dixon's manuscript. Brown agreed to look at the draft, but counter-proposed that he, himself, be granted translation rights.[28] Apart from an announcement appended at the end of the 1927 Russian edition of *Olia* for a forthcoming English translation titled *Olga*, Brown's translation remains un-remarked.[29] Aside from Mirrlees's and Brown's letters, Dixon's translation is totally unknown.

Even so, Remizov continued to associate Dixon with the book, inscribing the copy now held by the Amherst Center for Russian Culture: 'To Vladimir Vasil'evich Dikson, without whom this book would not have appeared. 23.7.27. Paris. Humbly dated. Aleksei Remizov'.[30] Other than the author

---

26 'Miss Harrison pishet mne, chto Vy dali-taki ei Vashego Avvakuma. Naverno po khodataistvu Shestova?', Mirskii to Remizov, 20 May 1924, in Hughes, '...S Vami Beda – ne Perevesti', p. 356. Remizov described his contribution to the translation in a short article published in 'Poslednikh novostiakh', 2 March 1939: 'V 1924 godu Avvakum zagovoril po-angliiski. Perevod sozdavalsia v Parizhe miss Kharrison Elenoi Karlovnoi, i ee uchenitsei Khop Mirrliliz Nadezhdoi Vasil'evnoi v sotrudnichestve S.P. Remizovoi-Dovgello i D. P. Sviatopolka-Mirskogo. Moe uchastie bylo v zvanii 'chtetsa': intonatsiia i ritm vshepchut i samoe zakovyristoe i neprivychnoe – ne 'literaturnoe' – zhivuiu rech', kotoruiu vsegda mozhno predstavit' 'knizhno' i perevesti na zhivuiu rech' drugogo iazyka', 'Avvakum (1620-1682)', pp. 235-7, in A.M. Remizov, 'Neizdannyi 'Merlog'' (ed. by Antonella d'Amelia), in *Minuvshee. Istoricheskii Al'manakh*, III (Moscow, 1991), pp. 199-261 (p. 236). As late as November 1924, that is, no longer related to the Avvakum project, Shestov was inviting Remizov to his flat where Harrison could hear him read. Lev Shestov to Aleksei Remizov, 11 November 1924 and 13 November 1924. Remizov Papers.

27 Hope Mirrlees to Lina Mirrlees, [29] May 1924. Newnham, Mirrlees Papers. Dixon evidently remained in contact with Harrison and Mirrlees beyond this first meeting over *Avvakum*. A copy of their *The Book of the Bear* is among the Dixon Papers (Addendum) held by the Amherst Center for Russian Culture. On 16 May 1927, Harrison wrote to Gilbert Murray, 'Also the whole of my bear-dream has been published in Russian!' Harrison Papers 1/1/38. Newnham College Archive, Cambridge University. The 'bear-dream' appeared in Jane Ellen Harrison, *Remininscences of a Student's Life* (London, 1926), pp. 77-8. The Russian translation appeared in Dixon's review. Vladimir Dixon, 'O liubvi Rossii', in *Versty*, III (1927), pp. 181-3.

28 Alec Brown to Aleksei Remizov, 5 January 1925. Remizov Papers. When publication of *Stratilatov* and *The Fifth Pestilence* was jeopardized, Brown had lobbied hard for its postponement, proposing instead that Chatto & Windus publish first his translation of *V pole blakitnom*—a text more accessible to British readers.

29 Remizov, *Olia*, n. p.

30 *Idem*. The inscription appears on the page preceding the title page, which otherwise shows only the 'Vol' logo. Volume donated to the Amherst Center for Russian Culture as part of the Dixon bequest.

of an unknown English-language translation of *Olia*, who was Vladimir Dixon?[31] He had much in common with Remizov's other translators. His mother was Russian, as was Reavey's and Scott's; like Cournos, Reavey and Schimanski, his earliest youth was spent in Russia; like Cournos, Brown and Reavey, he wrote poetry and prose; but, unlike any others in this cast, he was in business. His interest in modernist art engaged him in correspondence with Ezra Pound on the subject of music and mathematics.[32] To Remizov, however, he was, to adopt the language of *Avvakum*, like a 'ghostly' son.[33]

The Dixon translation prompts a few remarks on Remizov's position vis-à-vis that nexus of European modernism—James Joyce. As famously reported by Nabokov, Joyce seemed to think 'Remizov *mattered* as a writer!!'[34] There are various routes by which Joyce may have formed such an opinion of Remizov. Had Joyce happened to read Brown's translation of *Stratilatov*, he may have noted the following: 'It is easy, in fact, to imagine [Remizov] working as legend has made James Joyce work, with various coloured crayons for the various passages, to aid the mind in composing the preconceived pattern'.[35] Or, he may simply have heard about the Russian author in the offices of left-leaning journals, such as the *Nouvelle revue française*, *transition* and *This Quarter*. Andrew Field comments that, apart from Nabokov, Remizov was the only other writer of the emigration 'adopted and fully accepted by French avant-garde circles in Paris'.[36] He may have learned of Remizov from Reavey, whom Joyce would have known in the early 30s through their association with *transition*, or through

31 Vladimir Dixon. b. 16 March 1900, Sormovo, Russia – d. 17 December 1929, Paris, France. Educ.: Podolsk Gymnasium, June 1917; B.S. M.I.T 1921; M.S. Harvard University 1922; Auditor for the Singer Company in Europe. See John Dixon, 'Ecce Puer, Ecce Pater: A Son's Recollections of an Unremembered Father', *James Joyce Quarterly*, XXIX, no. 3 (1992), pp. 485-509.

32 See Robert Spoo, 'The Letters of Ezra Pound and Vladimir Dixon', *James Joyce Quarterly*, XXIX, no. 3 (1992), pp. 533-56.

33 Remizov undertook the preservation and publication of Dixon's literary papers after his untimely death in 1929. A manuscript English translation titled *Olia* is held in the Dixon Papers (Addendum) at the Amherst College Center for Russian Culture. On 3 November 1932, Reavey wrote to Remizov from London, saying that he had met Brown and arranged for him to transmit the manuscript of *Olia* (George Reavey to Aleksei Remizov, 3 November 1932. Remizov Papers). On 12 November 1932, Brown wrote: 'Dear Aleksei Remizov, If Reavey had not been born, and founded the European bureau, I would not have learned your new address' (Alec Brown to Aleksei Remizov, 12 Novrmber 1932. Remizov Papers). The text under discussion may have been Dixon's draft.

34 See Andrew Field, *Nabokov: His Life in Part* (New York, 1977), p. 222.

35 Alec Brown, 'Preface', in Aleksei Remizov, *The Fifth Pestilence*, p. xvii.

36 Field, *Nabokov*, p. 205.

their mutual friendships with Beckett. Reavey was a frequent visitor to Remizov's flat, beginning in 1930, just when Remizov wrote in his introduction to the 1930 posthumous edition of Dixon's verse and prose: 'Of all the contemporary foreign writers who are comparable to Dixon in perception and in their means of expressing 'life,' I would name Max Jacob and James Joyce'.[37] Reviewing this book, B. Sosinsky suggests that the prose in the volume indicates that Dixon had learned from Joyce, with whom Dixon was personally acquainted.[38] S.S. Khoruzhii notes that Joyce's familiarity with Remizov's work may have come through Paul Leon, Joyce's secretary. Or, Joyce may have known Remizov through Dixon himself, as the connecting link between Joyce and the Russian literary Paris.[39]

Joyce's esteem for Remizov may have been rooted in an awareness, whatever its origin, of the Russian author's deep regard for the word, for his subversive use of words, for the mystifications of the often pseudonymous author, for just the sort of exuberant playfulness of Remizov's mock-literary society, 'The Great Free Order of the Apes', channeled through Remizov's 'ghostly' son. I refer to the letter published in 1929, over the signature Vladimir Dixon, which opens: 'Dear Mister Germ's Choice'.[40] There is an aura of mystification to Joyce's response. He and the publisher, Sylvia Beach, fostered the notion that Joyce himself was the author of this so-Joycean bit of prose, when they knew full well the author was its signatory. Joyce clearly thought highly of the letter. Otherwise, why would he have encouraged the mis-attribution? Joyce's regard for 'Mister Germ's Choice' may be the first indication of his later esteem for one of the more fabulous prose experimenters of the Russian emigration, an author who indulged in comparable, public mystifications.

---

37 Aleksei Remizov, 'Introduction', trans. Elizabeth Meyendorff Myers, in Edward Manouelian, 'Aleksei Remizov and Vladimir Dixon', *James Joyce Quarterly*, XXIX, no. 3 (1992), pp. 559-62 (p. 561).

38 'Vozmozhno, chto etomu iskusstvu Vl. Dikson nauchilsia u Dzhoisa, s kotorym byl v lichnykh otnosheniiakh.' (Review of 'Vladimir Dikson. Stikhi i proza. S predisloviiem Alekseiia Remizova', *Chisla*, IV (1931), p. 270).

39 S.S. Khoruzhii, '"Uliss" v russkom zerkale', in James Joyce, *Sobranie sochinenii*, III (Moscow, 1994), pp. 363-605, http://www.james-joyce.ru/articles/ulysse-v-russkom-zerkale.htm [accessed 15.10.2012]. I thank Ekaterina Turta for bringing this publication to my attention.

40 Appended to a 1929 collection of essays on Joyce's *Finnegan's Wake*, *Our Exagmination Round His Factification for Incamination of Work in Progress* (Paris, 1929). The manuscript of the 'litter' is re-produced on pp. 517-20 of John Whittier-Ferguson's 'The Voice behind the Echo: Vladimir Dixon's Letters to James Joyce and Sylvia Beach', *James Joyce Quarterly*, XXIX, no. 3, pp. 511-31. See also, Thomas A. Goldwasser, 'Who Was Vladimir Dixon? Was He Vladimir Dixon?', *James Joyce Quarterly*, XVI, no. 3 (1979), pp. 219-22.

14. Chekhov and the Buried Life of Katherine Mansfield

Rachel Polonsky

'Tchekhov is dead; therefore we may now speak freely of him…'
Lev Shestov[1]

The critic John Middleton Murry marked the first anniversary of the death of his wife, Katherine Mansfield, with a notoriously bad poem, which he published in his own magazine *Adelphi* in January 1924. 'Was she not a child', the elegy asked, 'A child of other worlds, a perfect thing/ Vouchsafed to justify this world's imagining?'[2] In casting Mansfield, a short story writer who died young of tuberculosis, as a 'perfect thing', Murry recycles the terms of his own characterization of Anton Chekhov. In a review of Constance Garnett's translation of Chekhov's Letters published in the *Athenaeum* less than four years earlier, in which he called him '<u>the</u> hero of our time', Murry hailed the publication of his Letters as 'an opportunity for the examination of some of the chief constituents of his perfect art'. For Murry, the chief constituents of the art are the moral and spiritual perfections of the artist:

> We do not consider [Chekhov] under the aspect of an artist. We are inevitably fascinated by his character as a man, one who, by his efforts […] worked on the infinitely complex material of the modern mind and soul, and made it in himself a definite, positive, and most lovable thing…Somehow he achieved […] the mystery of pureness of heart, and in that though we dare

1 Leon Shestov, *Anton Tchekhov and Other Essays*, trans. S. Koteliansky and J.M. Murry (Dublin and London, 1916), p. 7.

2 J.M. Murry, 'In Memory of Katherine Mansfield', *Adelphi*, I (1924), pp. 664-5. See also Jeffrey Meyers, 'Murry's Cult of Mansfield', *Journal of Modern Literature*, VII (1979), pp. 15-38.

> not analyse it further lies the secret of his greatness as a writer [...] measured by the standards of Christian morality, Tchehov was wholly a saint.[3]

Unlike Murry, the Russian émigré critic D.S. Mirskii did not tremble before the sacred mysteries of Chekhov's greatness. 'Chekhov's English admirers think that everything is perfect in Chekhov', he complains, 'to find spots in him will seem blasphemy to them'.[4] Mirskii did dare to analyse Chekhov's art in formal terms. 'His method of constructing a story is akin to the method used in music', he writes, 'the lines along which he builds them are very complicated curves, but they have been calculated with the utmost precision'.[5] With laconic respect, Mirskii adds that 'if Chekhov has had a genuine heir to the secrets of his art, it is in England, where Katherine Mansfield did what no Russian has done—learned from Chekhov without imitating him'.[6]

When Mirskii wrote this, Murry was about to publish his two-volume edition of Mansfield's *Letters*,[7] imitating the example of Chekhov's brother, Mikhail Chekhov, who published around 2000 of his letters in a six-volume edition between 1912 and 1916, creating a new model of literary 'life and letters'.[8] Chekhov arrived in England—through the translations of Constance Garnett and others—as simultaneously a great letter-writer, with a biography 'perfected' by early death, and as a dramatist and short story writer.

Murry's publication of Mansfield's Letters was a crucial part of his attempt to create a composite image of literary perfection out of her life and work. This so disgusted Mansfield's close friend, the émigré translator, S.S. Kotelianskii, that he broke off relations with Murry, complaining that he had 'left out all the jokes' to make Mansfield into an 'English Tchekov'.[9] However, it was not just Mansfield's jokes that Murry left out when he edited the letters left by her in his trust for publication, turning her into

3 J.M. Murry, *Aspects of Literature* (London, 1920), pp. 86-7.

4 D.S. Mirsky, *A History of Russian Literature From its Beginnings to 1900* (1926), ed. Francis J. Whitfield (New York, 1958), p. 382.

5 Mirsky, p. 378.

6 *Ibid.*, p. 383.

7 Katherine Mansfield, *The Letters of Katherine Mansfield*, ed. J. Middleton Murry, 2 vols. (London, 1928). Here and elsewhere all incorrect spelling and punctuation in Mansfield's quotes are in the original.

8 See A.P. Chekhov, *Polnoe sobranie sochinenii v tridtsati tomakh* (Moscow, 1974), *Pis'ma*, I, p. 6.

9 Quoted in Beatrice Lady Glenavy, *Today We Will Only Gossip* (London, 1964), p. 69.

his (bestselling) hagiographical image of an English Chekhov.[10] In the last 5 years of her life, in a dialogue with Chekhov that runs through her letters and notebooks, of which Murry left few traces, Mansfield worked at (rather than worked *out*) her thoughts on the writer's vocation, literary form, illness, life, death, and time. Murry excised all but a few of the references to Chekhov in her letters, almost entirely erasing from the record the work she did on Kotelianskii's literal translations of Chekhov's letters for publication in the *Athenaeum*, which Murry himself edited. Murry also removed all traces of Mansfield's discomfort with his part, as an influential critic, in creating the English cult of Chekhov.

In a footnote in the preface of his 1927 edition of Mansfield's *Journal*, in which assertiveness seems to stand in inverse relation to persuasiveness, Murry protested that Chekhov had had no influence on her imaginative writing:

> There is a certain resemblance between Katherine Mansfield's stories and those of Anton Tchehov. But this resemblance is often exaggerated by critics, who seem to believe that Katherine Mansfield learned her art from Tchehov. That is a singularly superficial view of the relation, which was one of kindred temperaments. In fact, Katherine Mansfield's technique is very different from Tchehov's. She admired and understood Tchehov's works as few English writers have done; she had (as her *Journal* shows) a deep personal affection for the man, whom, of course, she never knew. But her method was wholly her own, and her development would have been precisely the same had Tchehov never existed.[11]

Introducing his two-volume edition of Mansfield's Letters, Murry expressed the hope that, 'together with her *Journal*', they would 'form an intimate and complete autobiography for the last ten years of her life'. Mansfield's 'one concern was to leave behind her some small legacy of truth', he explained: 'because I believe that not a little of her 'truth' is contained in these letters, I have tried to make the record as complete as I could'.[12] In a 'literary study' of Mansfield, Murry writes of her as a possession. He made up his mind,

10 In 'Murry's Cult of Mansfield', p. 29, Jeffrey Meyers notes, 'Murry [...] wanted to have it both ways: to affirm Katherine's spiritual affinity and greatness by association with Chekhov and, at the same time, to deny any direct influence which might compromise her absolute originality. He wrote, somewhat mystically, in 1924, 'Though Chekhov was dead, some essential communication seemed to pass between his spirit and hers. He was always living to her, always at her elbow to remind her of the necessity of that strange purity of soul which they shared'.

11 Mansfield, *Journal*, ed. J. Middleton Murry (London, 1927), pp. xiii-xiv.

12 Mansfield, *Letters*, ed. Murry, I, p. viii.

he says, that after her death, Mansfield 'no longer belonged to me but to the world'. 'It seemed to me a matter of cardinal importance that the world should know what manner of woman—or girl (for she wasn't much more when she died) —Katherine Mansfield was'.[13] Mansfield was 34 when she died: not at all a 'girl', as she herself had insisted. Someone like Murry, who claimed that he had read her letters 'many times', might have recalled this letter that she wrote to him from Paris in May 1915: 'Whose fault is it that we are so isolated—that we have no real life—that everything apart from writing and reading is 'felt' to be a waste of time', she asked, before setting out, over the course of a lengthy paragraph, all that she had seen and sensed as she sat on a bench in a flowering garden behind Notre Dame: mothers, nurses (one Chinese, in green trousers), grandfathers, and 'little staggering babies with spades and buckets':

> Why haven't I got a real 'home', a real life – why haven't I got a chinese nurse with green trousers and two babies who rush at me and clasp my knees – Im not a girl – Im a woman. I *want* things. Shall I ever have them [...]

Registering the tension between 'life' and 'writing' that was to become a preoccupation of her later letters, and in which the figure of Chekhov was to become imbricated, Mansfield ends, 'Oh, I want life – I want friends and people and a house. I want to give and to spend (the P.O. savings apart, darling.)'[14] When Murry edits this letter (without indication) for publication, he cuts everything after 'waste of time', deleting her vivid paragraph about the Parisian babies, her protest that she is 'not a girl', and her dig (laced with the endearment 'darling') about his tight-fistedness.[15] This was just one of many passages in her letters that contradicted the perfect image of the writer that Murry was trying to create out of the materials left, with ambiguous instructions from Mansfield, in his trust. For Murry, shaping her letters, journals, and short stories into a 'single whole' (following the model of Keats, and implicitly of Chekhov) involved de-professionalizing Mansfield. 'She was never what we understand by a professional writer', he wrote; 'her art was not wholly distinct from her life':

> She was distinguished by the peculiar gift of *spontaneity*' which 'means [in this critical sense] an absence of any cleavage or separation between the

---

13 John Middleton Murry, *Katherine Mansfield and Other Literary Studies* with a forward by T.S. Eliot (London, 1959), p. 71-2.

14 Katherine Mansfield, *The Collected Letters of Katherine Mansfield*, eds. Vincent O'Sullivan and Margaret Scott (Oxford, 1984-2008), I, p. 177.

15 See Mansfield, *Letters*, ed. Murry, I, p. 25.

> living self and the writing self... When the human being is confused, at a standstill, bewildered in its own living experience, then the voice of the art is silent.[16]

However, the lines that he has cut from Mansfield's letters are, precisely, 'bewildered'; they register a 'standstill', a sense of painful cleavage and separation between the living self and the writing self. The voice is not silent, rather it has been silenced by the now all-powerful editor. Murry is at pains to present her writing as something other than a 'technical achievement'[17]:

> She was not a person who constructed patterns of objective beauty; she was not a person who 'told stories'; she was essentially a person who responded through the instrument of a 'more than ordinary organic sensibility' – to her experience of Life.[18]

He writes of the 'last perfection of her work', which is achieved through a 'serene', 'completely submissive', acceptance of hopelessness.[19]

Like a Chekhov story, Mansfield's encounter with Chekhov follows a 'very complicated curve', which gathers into itself the interwoven themes of illness and short-story writing. The evidence suggests that Mansfield first encountered Chekhov's writing through her Polish lover, Floryan Sobienowski, in the German spa town where her mother had deposited her, embarrassingly pregnant, in 1909.[20] As is now well-known, Mansfield's first published story, 'The-Child-Who-Was-Tired', was an unacknowledged version of Chekhov's story, 'Spat' khochetsya'.[21] Mansfield turned to Chekhov in a new way after her own diagnosis with consumption in 1918. He became a powerful imagined presence at the very points in her illness when creative writing seemed no longer possible. In her notebook, she wrote:

> ...I'd like to put on quiet record that the physical pain is just not unbearable – only just not.
>
> At four 30 today it did conquer me and I began, like the Tchekov students, to 'pace from corner to corner', then up and down, up and down and the pain racked me like a curse and I could hardly breathe...I feel too ill to write. I could dictate I think praps – but write, no. Trop Malade.

---

16 Murry, *Katherine Mansfield*, p. 73.
17 *Ibid.*, p. 81.
18 *Ibid.*, p. 73.
19 *Ibid.*, pp. 88-93.
20 See Claire Tomalin, *Katherine Mansfield: A Secret Life* (London, 1987), pp. 71-4.
21 See Tomalin, pp. 208-11 and 261-72.

She consoled herself with thoughts of heaven, which for her, was the living presence of Chekhov:

> I must start writing again... Ach, Tchekhov! Why are you dead! Why cant I talk to you – in a big, darkish room – at late evening – where the light is green from the waving trees outside. Id like to write a series of Heavens: that would be one. [22]

She writes of what she has learned from Chekhov about the right length of a short story, and about the race against time of the writer who lives in fear of imminent death.[23] When Mansfield was overcome by the horror of her illness or the fear of death, she would invoke Chekhov almost as an Orthodox believer would invoke a beloved saint. She addresses him as 'dear Chekhov', greets him in her notebooks, and says she thinks of him every day. She wrote to Kotelianskii from the Italian Riviera in 1920:

> I am ashamed that I broke down in my last letter. That night I went to bed with pneumonia. That was why I was so depressed. Of course I am still in bed but it does not matter. *All is well* [...] I shall try and get well here. If I *do* die perhaps there will be a small private heaven for consumptives only. In that case I shall see Tchekov. He will be walking down his garden paths with fruit trees on either side and tulips in flower in the garden beds. His dog will be sitting on the path, panting and slightly smiling as dogs do who have been running about a great deal.
>
> Only to think of this makes my heart feel as though it were *dissolving* [...][24]

Chekhov's presence in her private writings remains vivid to the end. She fantasized about moving to Yalta.[25] 'Dead Tchekhov', she wrote in her notebook, was one of the 'two good men' she had known. The other she named as the physician Dr Sorapure (himself a consumptive), who had finally diagnosed the venereal infection that had destroyed her health years earlier, and which she had contracted in all probability, from Sobienowski, who had also introduced her to Chekhov. Sorapure was 'pure of heart as Tchekhov was pure of heart', Mansfield wrote, and 'helped me not only to bear pain but [...] suggested that perhaps bodily ill health is necessary, is a repairing process'. 'It is hard to make a good death!' she noted, telling herself

---

22 Katherine Mansfield, *The Katherine Mansfield Notebooks*, ed. Margaret Scott (Minneapolis, 2002), II, p. 141.

23 *Collected Letters*, V (2008), p. 318.

24 Mansfield, *Collected Letters*, IV (1996), pp. 160-1.

25 *Collected Letters*, II (1987), p. 354, and III (1992), p. 354.

to 'leave Life on this earth as Tchekhov left Life [...]'.[26] On Kotelianskii's recommendation, she moved from the Swiss Alps to Paris to be treated by a Russian doctor, Ivan Manoukhin (whom, she says, 'Tchekhov would have liked [...] very much'), who promised a 'cure' for tuberculosis using X-rays. The sound of Russian being spoken in Manoukhin's office made her think of Chekhov. She fantasized about another way of communing with Chekhov in this life rather than the next:

> ...I begin to plan what I will do when – Can it be true? What shall I do to express my thanks? I want to adopt a Russian baby, call him Anton & bring him up as mine with Kot for a godfather and Mme Tchekhov for a godmother. Such is my dream.[27]

Through Manoukhin, Mansfield met a group of Russian émigré writers in Paris, including Bunin, Dmitrii Merezhkovskii, and Zinaida Gippius (Hippius), who fascinated her with their stories of the horrors of Bolshevism, and about whom she was gaily satirical. 'Russians seem to haunt me', she told her father.[28] She repeatedly asked for Chekhov to be sent to her, by Murry, 'when you have finished with them',[29] and from Ida Baker, the school friend who became her devoted and longsuffering caregiver. By October 1922, it was clear that Manoukhin's treatment had failed. On 4 October, she wrote to Murry that Chekhov was 'much nearer to [her] than he used to be'.[30] She resolved to move to the Gurdjeff Institute for the Harmonious Development of Man at Fontainebleau outside Paris, a commune of about fifty or sixty people ('mostly Russians', as she wrote to her sisters),[31] disciples of the Caucasian guru George Gurdjeff. The last book she asked Murry to send her before she left for Fontainebleau was Garnett's translation of *Love, and Other Stories*, with Murry's review of the volume for the *Times Literary Supplement*.[32] (For several years, as editor of the *Athenaeum*, Murry had kept for himself the task of reviewing Garnett's volumes of Chekhov as they appeared, while sending Mansfield second-rate works of fiction to review for much-needed income.) [33] The day after repeating her request for his *TLS* review, she adds an exasperated postscript to a letter to Murry:

---

26 Mansfield, *Notebooks*, II, p. 202.
27 *Ibid.*, p. 316.
28 Mansfield, *Collected Letters*, V, p. 315.
29 *Ibid.*, p. 43.
30 *Ibid.*, p. 285.
31 *Ibid.*, p. 347.
32 *Ibid.*, p. 295.
33 See *Collected Letters*, III, p. viii.

> About being like Tchekhov and his letters. Don't forget that he *died* at 43. That he spent – how much? – of his life chasing about in a desperate search after health. And if one reads 'intuitively' the last letters are terrible. What is left of him. 'The braid on German women's dresses – bad taste', and all the rest is misery. Read the last! All hope is over for him. Letters are deceptive, at any rate. Its [sic] true he had occasional happy moments. But for the last 8 years he knew no *security* at all. We know he felt his stories were not half what they might be. It doesn't take much imagination to picture him on his deathbed thinking 'I have never had a real chance. Something has been all wrong [...][34]

Mansfield's last letters to Murry tend to skid between deferential requests for books, declarations of love, workings out of her spiritual longings, and exasperated semi-veiled critiques of his literary-critical essays. In emphasizing Chekhov's final sense of failure and defeat, she rejects Murry's hollow aesthetics of 'moral and spiritual victory',[35] the very aesthetics that would envelop her own writings after her death. Mansfield's exasperation with Murry's misreading of Chekhov is even more evident in the version of this insight that she recorded in her notebook on the previous day:

> Risk! Risk anything! Care no more for the opinions of others, for those voices. Do the hardest thing on earth for you. Act for yourself. Face the truth.
>
> True, Tchekhov didn't. Yes, but Tchekhov died. And let us be honest. How much do we know of Tchekhov from his letters. Was that all? Of course not. Don't you suppose he had a whole longing life of which there is hardly a word? Then read the final letters. He has given up hope. If you de-sentimentalize those final letters they are terrible. There is no more Tchekhov. Illness has swallowed him. But perhaps to people who are not ill this is nonsense. They have never travelled this road. How can they see where I am? All the more reason to go boldly forward alone. Life is not simple. In spite of all we say about the mystery of Life when we get down to it we want to treat it as though it were a child's tale [...][36]

Was it Murry, who was 'not ill' and had 'never travelled this road', who could not read Chekhov's last letters 'intuitively', without sentimentalizing? Was it Murry who treated the mystery of life like a child's tale? The next day, she wrote to Murry that she wanted no more books of any kind, that she was 'sick and tired of them'.[37] What she has discovered in being so 'near' Chekhov, is not harmony, but an intimation of the writer's sense of

34 *Collected Letters*, V, p. 299.
35 See Murry, *Katherine Mansfield*, p. 81.
36 Mansfield, *Notebooks*, II, pp. 286-7.
37 Mansfield, *Collected Letters*, V, p. 303.

failure in the face of early death. In the end, she does not want to 'leave this life' like Chekhov, who was reduced to pointing out the poor taste of the German women's dress in his final letter. Instead, she wants to stop writing, and, as she tells Kotelianskii, 'to try to live—really live'.[38] At the Gurdjeff Institute, she immersed herself in Russian company, Russian habits and food, and the Russian language. As soon as she arrived, she wrote to Kotelianskii, and a few days later to Murry, that she had 'been through a little revolution'.[39] Immediate daily life is all she now wishes to inscribe in her notebook. In the last pages she wrote are lists of words for which she needed the Russian:

> I am cold/ bring paper to light a fire... No more fire/ because there is no more fire... what is the time/ it is late/ it is still early/ good!/ I would like to speak Russian with you[40]

In her last letter to Murry, written 10 days before she died (the last day she sent letters), she was still yearning for any kind of closeness to the living Chekhov: 'I hope you will decide to come, my dearest [...] I hope Tchekhov's wife will be here [...]'.[41]

Mansfield's veiled contest with Murry over Chekhov dates back at least to the early summer of 1919, when she was working on Kotelianskii's English renditions of Chekhov's letters. 'I realize how little Jack shares with me',[42] she wrote in her notebook, and then called Dr Sorapure 'quite the right man to have at one's dying bedside'. Sorapure's 'view of medicine', which seemed to her 'just completely right', led her to think about the meaning of disease—parasites and strange viruses, dysentery, hydrophobia, and lockjaw—about art and nature, and about another consumptive doctor, Chekhov:

> I had a sense – of the larger breath – of the mysterious lives within lives, and the egyptian parasite beginning of being in a water snail affected me like a great work of Art. No, that's not what I mean: it made me feel how perfect the world is, with its worms & hooks and ova. How incredibly perfect. There is the sky & the sea & the shape of a lily & there is all this other as well. The balance how perfect. (Salut, Tchekov.) I would not have the one without the other [...] I have consumption. There is still a great deal of moisture (&pain) in my BAD lung. But I do not care [...][43]

---

38 *Ibid.*, p. 304.
39 *Ibid.*, pp. 303-4.
40 *Notebooks*, II, p. 343.
41 *Collected Letters*, V, p. 342.
42 *Notebooks*, II, p. 171.
43 *Ibid.*, p. 173.

Mansfield happened to be living in London with Murry when she wrote this in June 1919. In August of that year, Murry published a review of one of Garnett's Chekhov volumes, which included a prettified version of Mansfield's insight, washing out all its complexity:

> [Chekhov] is like a man who contemplates a perfect work of art; but the work of creation has been his, and has consisted in the gradual adjustment of his vision until he could see the frustrations of human destinies and the arbitrary infliction of pain as processes no less inevitable, natural, and beautiful than the flowering of a plant.[44]

In March 1920, Murry published his 'Thoughts on Tchekhov', his review of Garnett's edition of the *Letters*, in the *Athenaeum*. Mansfield was still working with Kotelianskii on a rival version of Chekhov's letters, which they hoped to publish as a book: 'Worked at Tchekhov all day', she recorded in her notebook on 5 January.[45] When Murry's review was republished in his book *Aspects of Literature* at the end of that year, Mansfield wrote him a devastating letter from Menton, headlined 'About your Book'. After a paragraph of fulsome praise—'Im your admirer. Accept my admiration [...] I want to make you feel what a great little fellow you are for this book!'—she launches her critique with the words, 'here goes'.[46] Mansfield senses a 'faint breath of *pride*' in his essay on Keats, detects insincerity in his praise of Edward Thomas, whom he has filled out 'to suit what you want him to be', and something similar in his 'thoughts' on Chekhov:

> Take your Tchekhov. Now you make Tchekhov 'greater' than one sees him but NOT greater than he was. This is an *important dangerous* distinction. A critic must see a man as great as his potentialities but NOT greater. Falsity creeps in immediately then. You ought to guard against this. Its another 'aspect' of your special pleading danger...[47]

She goes on to call a remark in Murry's preface 'naïve', 'silly', 'arrogant', says that if he were to send her back his wedding ring on account of the letter, she would send it anyway, and ends by asking his forgiveness—'Forgive me if I hurt you—please forgive me!'—and telling him she loves and believes in him.[48] Perhaps Murry could not forgive Mansfield for her

44 Murry, *Aspects of Literature*, p. 78.
45 Mansfield, *Notebooks*, II, p. 187.
46 Mansfield, *Collected Letters*, IV, p. 139.
47 *Ibid.*, pp. 140-1.
48 *Ibid.*, p. 141. Mansfield had written to her friend Sydney Schiff a week earlier 'about the Russians': 'though I hate to agree with so many silly voices I confess that Tchekhov does

well-judged criticism, despite all the sugaring of flattery and declarations of love. He excluded this letter from his two-volume edition, along with several other letters full of sharp literary insight and useful editorial advice about the *Athenaeum* written in the same month, leaving only 2 letters, mostly concerned with weather, scenery, and birdlife.

One cannot adduce intentions, but a kind of quiet vengeance may have been at work when Murry suppressed the traces of Mansfield's collaboration with Kotelianskii on Chekhov's letters. Her ample correspondence about Chekhov with Kotelianskii, and with others, including Ottoline Morrell, Virginia Woolf, William Gerhardie, and Sydney Schiff, consisted of repeated references to hard work, payment, deadlines, and the post—all the tiresome business of being a 'professional writer'—interwoven with fine insights into Chekhov's art and literary significance, both to her as a writer, and to the future of English prose. In April 1919, after the first 4 letters had been published in the *Athenaeum*, she wrote to Kotelianskii:

> I was as much surprised as you to find that we were nameless. No reason was given. I shall ask M[urry] on your behalf tonight; I shall also mention the question of a cheque [...] I dislike IMMENSELY not going over the letters with you [...] I feel Tchekhov would be the first to say we must go over them together.[49]

All that Murry leaves of this letter are her expressions of desire that Kotelianskii would come in and have tea, a memorable comparison of her consumptive cough to a 'big wild dog', and chat about the weather and her cat Charlie's kittens.[50] He omits altogether 2 further letters dealing with the practical business of meeting to discuss 'new letters' and make revisions, and appreciative remarks on a letter of 1888, in which Chekhov decries the idea of 'solidarity' among writers.[51] Likewise, he omits the letter in which Mansfield marvelled at Chekhov's remarks on the 'duty of the artist', a treasured discovery for Mansfield, which was of profound value in her discussions with Virginia Woolf about literary fiction:[52]

---

seem to me a marvelous writer.' (*Collected Letters*, V, p. 131). She may have had Murry in mind as one of the 'silly voices'.

49 Mansfield, *Collected Letters*, II, p. 309. Between 4 April and 31 October 1919 the *Athenaeum* ran thirteen installments of Chekhov's letters translated by Kotelianskii and revised by Mansfield, see *Collected Letters*, IV, p. 312.

50 Mansfield, *Letters*, ed. Murry, I, p. 225.

51 See Mansfield, *Collected Letters*, II, pp. 311-12.

52 See Angela Smith, *Katherine Mansfield and Virginia Woolf: A Public of Two* (Oxford, 1999), pp. 154-5.

> I do not feel that all the money should be mine. And I WISH our collaboration were closer. However, *I do my very best* always with these wonderful letters & can do no more. Wonderful they are. The last one – the letter to Souverin [sic] about the duty of the artist to *put* the 'question' – not to solve it but to put it so that one is completely satisfied seems to me one of the most valuable things I have ever read. It opens – it discovers rather, a new world. May Tchekov live for ever.[53]

Though he published excerpts from her letters to Kotelianskii in his two-volume edition, Murry left out altogether a letter in which she revealed to Kotelianskii that she was working on the translations for 'some hours of EACH day', with the hope of racing 'Mrs G' to publication as a book, and that she believed that Chekhov carried the cure for the 'English literary world'.[54] He omits a letter in which she thanks Kotelianskii for a cheque and says that she believes 'Tchekhov has said the last word that has been said… and given us a sign of the way we should go', and exclaims, 'if I am sitting on the back bench A.T. [Chekhov] is *my* master'.[55] All that Murry leaves of an August 1919 letter to Kotelianskii is the news that she is going to the Italian Riviera where she will have '*unlimited time* to work', editing out all references to payment for the Chekhov translations, and the hope she and Kotelianskii shared that the letters would soon appear as a book.[56] Murry omits the letters she wrote to him in January 1920, which give an insight into the difficult financial aspects of their relationship as writer and editor:

> I send a long Tchekov letter. If you don't care to use it will you please have it typed for my (at my charge) & send the typed copy to Kot for our book? I hope to send off another review tomorrow' […] 'I send you today […] some autobiographical notes on Tchekhov. Do you care for them? […] If you don't would you have them typed (at *my* charge) and sent to Kot […][57]

The only substantial trace that Murry's edition mercifully retains of her work on Chekhov is a paragraph of acute literary appreciation on his story

53 *Ibid.*, p. 324.
54 *Ibid.*, p. 341.
55 *Ibid.*, p. 345.
56 See *ibid.*, p. 341. Gerald L. Conroy, '"Our Perhaps Uncommon Friendship": The Relationship between S.S. Koteliansky and Katherine Mansfield', *Modern Fiction Studies*, XXIV (1978), p. 363 for a letter from Kotelianskii to Mansfield which reveals how much he valued her work: 'My ambition is to see *our* Tchekhov letters in book form […] it is not sentimentalism, but a real desire that a book bearing both our names, should see the light. Perhaps, if you should like, that will not be the only one. I want this book as a token of our perhaps uncommon friendship.'
57 Mansfield, *Collected Letters*, III, p. 171.

'The Steppe'—a story which succeeds in having 'no beginning or end'—from a letter to Kotelianskii of 21 August 1919:

> I have re-read 'The Steppe'. What can one say. It is simply one of *the* great stories of the world – a kind of Iliad or Odyssey – I think I will learn this journey by heart. One says of things: they are immortal. One feels about this story not that it *becomes* immortal – it always was. It has no beginning or end. T. just touched one point with his pen (.------.) and then another point – *enclosed* something which had, as it were, been there for ever.[58]

Murry quietly dispossessed his late wife of credit for the work she did on Chekhov's letters, and kept for himself the privilege of writing for the public about Chekhov, while he recycled her insight as his own. In doing so, he may have deprived posterity of the essays on Chekhov that Mansfield might have written, and obscured her deep and serious engagement with Chekhov's art and life-story. In 1926, he also went against her express wishes and republished her first collection of short stories, *In a German Pension*, exposing her to the charge of plagiarism for 'The Child-Who-Was-Tired'.[59]

Mirskii, who tersely dismissed the English cult of Chekhov, in which Murry's criticism had played an important role, and who respectfully noted Mansfield as a writer who had learned from Chekhov without imitating him, described the 'construction' of a Chekhov short story as 'a series of points marking out with precision the lines discerned by him in the tangled web of consciousness':

> An infinitesimal touch, which at first hardly arrests the reader's attention, gives a hint at the direction the story is going to take. It is then repeated as a leitmotiv, and at each repetition the true equation of the curve becomes more apparent, and it ends by shooting away in a direction very different from that of the original straight line.[60]

He praised Chekhov for his skill in bringing out the leitmotiv of 'mutual isolation' with 'great power'. It would take a writer of Chekhov's or Mansfield's skill to describe the 'tangled web of consciousness' and the 'mutual isolation' in the short literary marriage of Mansfield and Murry. Certainly, notwithstanding all the infantilizing endearments in their correspondence, it was 'not a child's tale'. A letter to Murry, written on

58 *Collected Letters*, II, p. 353.

59 See Meyers, 'Murry's Cult', pp. 24-6, and Tomalin, *Katherine Mansfield*, pp. 72, 80, and 261-72.

60 Mirsky, *A History of Russian Literature*, p. 378.

11 October 1922, days before she turned away from books and writing, sketches its curve:

> I think of the garden at the Isola Bella and the furry bees and the house wall so warm. But then I remember what we really felt there. The blanks, the silences, the anguish of continual misunderstanding. Were we positive, eager, real – alive? No, we were not. We were a nothingness shot through with gleams of what might be. But no more.[61]

When Mansfield's letters were finally published without Murry's cuts, the 'truth' of Chekhov's importance to her was revealed, as well as 'gleams' of what might have been if her editor-husband had given her the opportunity of writing about Chekhov, 'under the aspect of an artist', for the reading public.

In the last sentence of her sad letter to Murry about their marital 'nothingness', Mansfield 'shoots away in a very different direction', writing: '*You won't forget the Tchekhov will you?* Id *like* the Lit. Sup. with your review if it wasn't too much of a bore to send it'.[62]

61 Mansfield, *Collected Letters*, V, p. 294.
62 *Ibid.*, p. 295.

15. 'A Gaul who has chosen impeccable Russian as his medium':[1] Ivan Bunin and the British Myth of Russia in the Early 20th Century

Svetlana Klimova

When in 1915 Maurice Baring published his 'talented and illuminating'[2] *Outline of Russian Literature*, the social and intellectual atmosphere in the country made him confident enough to state that 'a new interest [...] with regard to Russian literature' was now perceptible among 'English intellectuals'.[3]

There were, it would seem, many reasons for such an interest—social and political as well as cultural. Since the Crimean War Russia had been viewed as a political rival by the British, and this political interest was only increased by social and political instability, the phenomena of nihilism, terrorism and anarchism, in the run-up to the October Revolution. In the period between 1856 and 1916 hundreds of books were published in Britain that provided authentic information about Russian history, society and politics,[4] and about three hundred novels and books of collected poems which explored the Russian theme.[5] It was an interest that was stimulated and sustained

1 Bernard G. Guernay, *A Treasury of Russian Literature* (London, 1948), p. 905.

2 Bernard Pares, 'The Objectives of Russian Study in Britain', *The Slavonic Review*, I (June 1922), p. 59.

3 Maurice Baring, *An Outline of Russian Literature* (London, 1915), p. 5.

4 Andrei N. Zashikhin, *Britanskaia Rossika vtoroi poloviny XIX–nachala XX veka* (Arkhangel'sk, 2008), p. 14.

5 Anthony G. Cross, *The Russian Theme in English Literature from the Sixteenth Century to 1980: An Introductory Survey and a Bibliography* (Oxford, 1985).

by the presence in London and elsewhere in Britain of prominent Russian intellectuals and political activists, including Herzen, Bakunin, (Stepniak) Kravchinskii and Kropotkin, whose work often appeared in English.[6]

There is little doubt that the interest in Russian culture was closely connected with political concerns. A good example of these intertwined aspirations to understanding Russia and Russians is provided by another of Baring's books, *The Mainsprings of Russia* (1914), in which he explored the national 'Russian character' through both Russian history and politics, contemporary social life and literature, and through personal insights into people's beliefs and hopes.

Yet there was another very important impetus to English interest in Russia at that time.[7] It was purely cultural and was directly connected with the general European enthusiasm for the novels of Turgenev, Tolstoi and Dostoevskii.[8] Baring's book on Russian literature is very revealing in this respect: indicating Turgenev as the one who 'led the genius of Russia on a pilgrimage throughout Europe', he refers exclusively to his noted French admirers—Flaubert, George Sand and Taine.[9] And in doing so, he reveals his spiritual debt to one of the most influential book about Russia in England and in the whole of Europe of that time—written by Eugène-Melchior de Vogüé. Vogüé was first to present the Russian novel as a cultural European phenomenon that was meaningful not only for its present, but for its future. The number of editions of his *Roman russe* speaks for itself: by 1913, when it was first translated into English, eleven French editions had come out. Vogüé and Baring were the key figures among numerous Western writers who made a way for a new, modern British myth of Russia—the myth that, the October Revolution notwithstanding, remained crucial for the

6 Monica Partridge, 'Alexander Herzen and the English Press', *The Slavonic and East European Review*, 87 (June 1958), pp. 453-70. Vladislav Ya. Grosul, *Londonskaya koloniya revolutsionnykh emigrantov i Kropotkin (70-80 gody XIX v.)*, in 'Trudy mezhdunarodnoi nauchnoi konferentsii, posveshennoi 150-letiyu so dnia rozhdeniya P.A. Kropotkina', IV (Moscow, 2002), pp. 120-32. Françoise Kunka, *Alexander Herzen and the Free Russian Press in London* (Saarbrücken, 2011).

7 Significantly Georg Brandes, writing in 1887–8, mentions 'the great interest taken at the present time in the literature of Russia and in everything which relates to that great country' (Georg Brandes, *Impressions of Russia*, trans. from the Danish by S. C. Eastman (London, 1890), p. iii).

8 See, e.g.: *Ivan Turgenev and Britain*, ed. P. Waddington (Oxford, 1995); Glyn Turton, *Turgenev and the Context of English Literature, 1850–1900* (London, 1992); *Tolstoi and Britain*, ed. W. Gareth Jones (Oxford, 1995); Peter Kaye, *Dostoevsky and English Modernism, 1900–1930* (Cambridge, 1999).

9 Baring, *Outline*, p. 162.

understanding of Russia and its culture by British intellectuals in the early 20th century.

There were several major concepts in this pastoral and spiritual myth, all of them primarily rooted in the widespread feeling of 'the end of civilization' and desire for spiritual renewal. Thus, criticizing Flaubert and the late French realism, Vogüé observes a close correspondence between contemporary analytical science and positive philosophy, on the one hand, and mechanically treated fictional characters, on the other. Hence he opposes the 'agglomeration of atoms' or of 'sensations' to the integrity of the 'soul', the 'scientific' to the 'religious', the dead 'mechanical' to the 'living'.[10] The positive pole of these oppositions can be found in the English and Russian novel, but Russia is treated by the author as the more essential, enchanting and pure mystery. In his two books mentioned above, Baring describes the 'sealed book' of Russia in similar manner, trying to grasp the idea of 'the Russian temperament' in Russia's history and literature in terms of 'naturalness', 'simplicity', 'vividness' and 'religious mysticism'.[11]

In Russian literature and Russian spirit Vogüé stresses 'compassion', 'glorified by the spirit of the Gospel';[12] he famously terms Dostoevskii's writings as 'the religion of suffering'[13] and speaks about the 'impulsiveness', 'mysticism' and 'pantheism' of Tolstoi's realism.[14] Correspondingly, Baring sees 'the divine aura of love that is in the Gospels' immanent in Dostoevskii's novels[15] and 'the truth to nature' and 'intense and vivid' reality in Tolstoi.[16] In his conclusion to *The Mainsprings of Russia* he states that 'love of man' and 'faith in God', together with impulsiveness, are the essence of the Russian character.[17]

This newly created myth clashed violently with the long European tradition of perceiving Russia as a 'colossal aggressive state, permanently expanding and [...] threatening Europe's peace and independence', a 'political Ahriman, a sort of dark power, inimical to the ideas of progress

---

10 Eugène-Melchior de Vogüé, *The Russian Novel*, trans. from the 11th French edn by Colonel H.A. Sawyer (London, 1913).

11 Baring, *Outline*, p. 162; Maurice Baring, *The Mainsprings of Russia* (London, 1914), pp. 47, 60, 160-2, 201-2.

12 de Vogüé, *The Russian Novel*, p. 18.

13 *Ibid.*, p. 204.

14 *Ibid.*, p. 324.

15 Baring, *Outline*, p. 222.

16 *Ibid.*, p. 205.

17 Baring, *Mainsprings*, p. 322.

and freedom'.[18] It was this very tradition that made Byron, Wordsworth, Tennyson and Swinburne feel 'hatred and contempt' for the (in many senses) unknown country.[19] Yet, even the purely political background, beginning from 1907—the year of establishing closer and friendlier relations between Britain and Russia—worked in favour of the new myth.[20] The old negative perception of Russia is obviously the main target of Charles Sarolea's protest in his *Europe's Debt to Russia* (1915), in which the author claims 'the Russian peril' to be a widely spread 'prejudice' in the USA and Great Britain—the prejudice far from corresponding to the reality.[21]

The tradition, however, did not (and, indeed, could not) cease to exist. It continued to play an important role in British understanding of Russia's politics and fate. The old and the new visions of Russia were in many cases attached to different spheres of human reality—that of the human soul and culture (for the new myth) and that of politics and government (for the traditional perception).

The two visions and the two spheres form an evident background to the conclusion made by Bernard Pares—the 'most influential British scholar of Russian history' at that time[22]—in his paper on the objectives of Russian study in Britain (1922): 'The Russian peasant, by his practical *instinct of brotherhood,* is capable of doing remarkable things whenever he can free himself from a superimposed dead weight of political theory, *whether autocratic or communist…*'[23] Not only the new myth, but also the old tradition, as we shall see, are key approaches in evaluating the writings of Ivan Bunin.

It comes as no surprise, however, that for many modernist British writers the new myth seemed much more appealing. Thus, pondering the essentially 'Russian point of view' in her essay under the same title (1925), Virginia Woolf writes about 'the soul that is the chief character in Russian fiction', 'the simplicity, […] the assumption that in a world bursting with misery the chief call upon us is to understand our fellow-sufferers […] with the heart'.[24] Touching on the same subject in another essay, 'Modern

18 Nikolai Ia. Danilevskii, *Rossiia i Evropa* (St Petersburg, 1895), p. 21.
19 Patrick Waddington, *From the Russian Fugitive to the Ballad of Bulgarie* (Oxford, 1994).
20 Andrei N. Zashikhin, *'Gliadia iz Londona'. Rossiia v obshchestvennoi mysli Britanii. Vtoraia polovina XIX–nachalo XX v. Ocherki* (Archangel'sk, 1994), p. 107.
21 Charles Sarolea, *Europe's Debt to Russia* (London, 1915), pp. 53-4.
22 Zashikhin, *Britanskaia Rossika*, p. 98.
23 Italics are mine. Pares, 'The Objectives', p. 72.
24 Virginia Woolf, *Collected Essays*, I (London, 1966), p. 239.

Fiction', she again stresses 'understanding of the soul and heart', 'a natural reverence for the human spirit', and 'sympathy for the suffering of others'.[25]

Similarly, though in a narrower sense, Arnold Bennett in 1928 writes about *The Brothers Karamazov* as of the most 'moral' and 'profound' novel, 'philosophical in intention and execution', and states that Dostoevskii's 'outlook upon the world was [...] kindly' and that he 'loved men'.[26] And even D.H. Lawrence, austere critic as he was, puts it in a much harsher, satirical, but still recognizable, way, speaking about the too 'obvious' character of the Russian novelists' art[27] and about a strict 'moral scheme' in 'Turgenev, and Tolstoi, and in Dostoievsky';[28] he recognizes Dostoevskii's 'urge towards the selfless ecstasy of Christianity'[29] and the 'explicitness' and 'the phenomenal coruscations of the souls of quite commonplace people' that lie at the core of Russian literature.[30]

From what has been quoted it can be seen that the English 'Russian myth', which came into being with the turn towards modernity and modernism, consisted above all of such major characteristics as 'soul', 'simplicity', 'impulsiveness', 'compassion' and 'religiousness'. It would be no exaggeration to say that the myth evolved to meet the contemporary European wish to find 'the other', and was to quench the thirst for non-civilized, pure being.

The characteristics of 'simplicity' and 'religiousness' were eagerly searched for and found in Russian history and landscape, as well as in the Russian people and the writings of the three major Russian novelists discussed here. Thus, Baring treats the legend about Rurik, Sineus and Truvor as a real historical event and, stressing the civilizing influence of 'Norsemen' on Russia in the 9th century, creates the image of a passive nation and country which needed to be formed by means of 'organized principalities'.[31] He even misinterprets the legend, for he replaces the legend's version of Rurik being invited by the people of Novgorod with his own, according to which Norsemen 'took Novgorod and Kiev'.[32]

25 Virginia Woolf, *The Common Reader* (New York, 1948), p. 217.
26 Arnold Bennett, *The Savour of Life: Essays in Gusto* (New York, 1928), pp. 131-2.
27 David H. Lawrence, *Collected Letters*, ed. Harry T. Moore , I (London, 1962), p. 488.
28 *Ibid*., p. 281.
29 John M. Murry, *Reminiscences of D.H. Lawrence* (London, 1936), p. 82.
30 David H. Lawrence, *Selected Letters*, ed. by Diana Trilling (New York, 1958), p. 276.
31 Baring, *Outline*, pp. 11-12.
32 Vasilii Kliuchevskii, recognized by British scholars at that time for his *A Course of Russian History* (the English version was entitled *A History of Russia* and came out in 5 volumes between 1911 and 1931), gives an accurate account of the legend's initial version and

A similar 'insignificant' change is to be found in his interpretation of Russia's baptism. Baring omits the story according to which Vladimir invited missionaries of different religions and listened and watched them to understand what would be the best for his country. In Baring's version it is said only that 'Vladimir, Prince of Kiev, married the sister of the Emperor of Byzantium and was baptized', and that as a result 'Russia was committed to the tradition, the Greek rivalry with the West, and was consequently excluded from the civilization of the West'. The same sub-textual meaning of passiveness is rendered by a small passage about the Russian landscape: 'Russia is a flat country, without an indented seacoast, and without sharp mountain ranges'.[33]

A similar implication occurs in a passage about the Russian landscape in Charles Sarolea's book:

> The first feature and the essential fact in the physical geography of Russia is the infinite plain, the uniform steppe and prairie [...] And this unity of the infinite plain is still rendered more striking through the unity of climate.[34]

Stephen Graham's book *The Way of Martha and the Way of Mary* (1916), the publication of which was hailed in its time by Maurice Baring, gave a vivid impression of what was to be seen in the Russian people at that time:

> The Russians are always *en route* for some place where they may find something about God. [...] The Russians have the child-soul, the peasants get to heaven where we fail. Because they are 'as little children'.[35]

It applies equally to the history of Russian literature. Thus, Baring argues firmly and directly that 'from the fourteenth century until the beginning of the nineteenth century Russian literature has nothing to show at all to the outward world'.[36] Vogüé's more precise and less categorical statement that the 'appearance' of Russians 'in the great literary sphere' of the novel 'was sudden and unexpected'[37] contributes to the same myth.

The numerous English translations of Russian realist novels that were made in this period seemed to confirm this scheme. The translations of novels by Turgenev, Goncharov, Tolstoi, Dostoevskii and Gogol that

---

provides the following prosaic explanation: 'These Princes and their following were engaged at a fixed rate of pay to defend the country from invasion' (Vasilii O. Kliuchevskii, *A Russian History*, trans. C.J. Hogarth, I (London, 1911), p. 66).

33 Baring, *Mainsprings*, p. 16.

34 Sarolea, *Europe's Debt*, p. 21.

35 Steven Graham, *The Way of Martha and the Way of Mary* (London, 1916), pp. 53-74.

36 Baring, *Outline*, p. 19.

37 de Vogüé, *The Russian Novel*, p. 16.

Constance Garnett produced between the 1890s and 1920s, 'put Russian literature on England's literary map'.[38] Yet these novels (especially those of Tolstoi and Dostoevskii) were considered not only typically Russian, but European and modern. Edward Garnett in 1903 speaks both about the contemporaneity and the nationality of Tolstoi's characters:

> Tolstoi must be finally looked on, not merely as *the conscience of the Russian world* [...] but also as the soul of the modern world seeking to replace in its love of humanity the life of those old religions which science is destroying day by day.[39]

Thus, the new British concept of Russian culture worked well for Tolstoi and Dostoevskii. But could another Russian 'major' author, who was gradually becoming known in Europe at that time—Chekhov—be perceived through this model?

In Britain Chekhov's art was established as a new Russian phenomenon in the period between the late 1900s and the early 1920s. Through Chekhov's art British critics strove to find the clue to the Russian revolution. A number of reviews (in *The Nation* and *Everyman*) written in the late 1910s seem to imply that it was a supposed connection between Chekhov's art and the Russian events of 1917 which made it possible for the British public to accept the writer's 'morbid self-analysis' and his heroes' 'inane submission to imaginary obstacles'.[40] However, with regard to supposed immaturity and implied impulsiveness and passiveness, as well as the delicate analysis of the soul's relation to goodness, Chekhov could, certainly, be perceived within the framework of the new British myth of Russia.

In the early 1920s another Russian writer—Ivan Bunin—was seen by the British public in a similar light and his writings appeared no less equivocal. Bunin was translated into English for the first time in 1917, when Peter Selver translated two of his short poems and included them in his anthology *Modern Russian Poetry: Texts and Translations*. Significantly, but ambiguously, Bunin's poetry was described in the 'Preface' as 'showing no traces of the later developments of Russian poetic style' and thus was 'more typically Slavonic than any of the modernists'.[41]

---

38 Peter Kaye, *Dostoevsky and English Modernism, 1900–1930* (Cambridge, 1999), p. 7.

39 Edward Garnett, *Criticism and Interpretations*, VI [*Tolstoi's Place in European Literature*], in Leo Tolstoy 'Anna Karenin' (New York, 1917), pp. xvii-xix (p. xviii).

40 *Chekhov: The Critical Heritage*, ed. by Victor Emeljanow (London, 1981), p. 93.

41 *Modern Russian Poetry. Texts and Translations*, selected and edited with an introduction by P. Selver (London, 1917), p. xv.

The person who really brought Bunin into the English literary world, however, was S.S. Kotelianskii. Kotelianskii enjoyed close relations with such 'apostles' of British Modernism as D.H. Lawrence, Virginia Woolf, and Katherine Mansfield, collaborating with Lawrence and Leonard Woolf to produce translations from Russian. Bunin was among the first contemporary Russian writers on his list. Leonid Andreev apart, he was the only contemporary Russian writer published by Leonard and Virginia Woolf's Hogarth Press. The first collection of Bunin's stories translated by Kotelianskii together with D.H. Lawrence (the story 'The Gentleman from San Francisco') and Leonard Woolf ('Gentle Breathing', 'Kasimir Stanislavovitch', 'Son') came out in 1922. Later, in 1933 and 1935 respectively, the Hogarth Press published Bunin's novel *The Well of Days* (translated by G. Struve and Hamish Miles) and the short story 'Grammar of Love' (translated by John Cournos).[42] In 1923 Bunin's novella *The Village* and in 1924 a volume of *Fifteen Tales*, translated by Isabel Hapgood and Bernard Guernay respectively, were published. All the publications were reviewed, or at least, mentioned, in *The Times* and in the *Times Literary Supplement*. There were also a number of American editions of Bunin's works at that time, which may have been available to the English reader. They were: *Mitya's Love*, a novella published by Henry Holt in 1926, *The Gentleman from San Francisco and Other Stories*, *The Village*, and *Dreams of Chang and Other Stories*, all published by A. Knopf (New York) in 1923; *The Well of Days* and *The Elaghin Affair and Other Stories* were published by the same publishing house in 1934 and 1935 respectively.

The intriguing history of relations between the Hogarth Press and Bunin has been vividly narrated and analysed in detail by N. Reingold [43] and A. Rogachevsky.[44] To illustrate the character of these relations, it suffices to say that it was Kotelianskii who, on his own initiative, made the first translation of Bunin's prose work into English (at least, in Britain); that the Woolfs made great efforts to find the author in Paris and received Bunin's first answer on 17 August 1922; and that it was Bunin himself who, in a letter dated 17 October 1931, suggested the Woolfs publish his new novel, *The Well of Days*, recommending Gleb Struve and Hamish Miles as translators.

---

42 J.H. Willis, *Leonard and Virginia Woolf as publishers: the Hogarth Press, 1917–41* (Charlottesville, 1992), p. 93

43 Natalia Reingol'd, 'Redingskii biuvar s pis'mami Bunina', *Voprosy literatury*, VI (2006), pp. 152-68.

44 Andrei Rogachevskii, 'I. A. Bunin i Hogarth Press', in *Ivan Bunin, Novyye materialy*, I. (Moscow, 2004), pp. 333-53.

The English public's reaction to the translations was neither simple nor consistent. On the one hand, we have Leonard Woolf's and D.H. Lawrence's high opinion of 'The Gentleman from San Francisco', and Woolf's attesting to its popularity. In his *Autobiography* Woolf writes that 'Bunin's *Gentleman from San Francisco* is one of the greatest of short stories', and adds: 'We printed, I think, 1,000 of each of the three books [*Bunin's, Tolstoi's and Dostoevskii's*] [...] Each of them sold between 500 and 700 copies in twelve months and made us a small profit'.[45] And D.H. Lawrence, having read it for the first time, praised the story in a letter to Kotelianskii: 'Have read The Gent—and in spite of its lugubriousness, grin with joy. [...] it is screamingly good of Naples and Capri: so comically like the reality: only just too earnest about it'.[46] On the other hand, we have Lawrence's very different opinion about the rest of the stories in the collection—and about many other controversial publications of Bunin's work: writing to Kotelianskii in 1922, he declared: '...the tales are not very good: *Gentleman* is much the best'.[47] A similar opinion can be found in many British reviews of Bunin's works in the 1920s and 1930s.

Reviews of Bunin's writings began to appear in 1921, with an anonymous review in the *Times Literary Supplement* on 18 August of a Russian-language collection of his tales published in Paris, *Gospodin iz San Francisco.* The reviewer felt the need to present the still unknown author to the British reader as one who 'has won distinction among contemporary Russian writers', having started his literary career 'in the first year of the present century' and 'made his way to Paris in 1920'.[48] It is the first of the three reviews in *The Times* and the *Times Literary Supplement* that were to make the title of Bunin's story 'The Gentleman from San Francisco' familiar to the British ear. As it was ironically pointed out in a much later review of Bunin's writings in *The Times* of 17 October 1957, 'Bunin burst upon the western world as the author of 'The Gentleman from San Francisco' [...] *The Times* reviewed it three times (Russian, French and English versions) in the nine months August, 1921–May, 1922'.[49] The other two reviews appeared on 20 April 1922 in the *Times Literary Supplement* (of the French

45 Leonard Woolf, *Autobiography: Downhill All The Way* (London, 1967), p. 74.

46 Lawrence, *Collected Letters,* II, p. 656.

47 On Lawrence's attitude to Rozanov, see: G.J. Zytaruk, *D.H. Lawrence's Response to Russian Literature* (The Hague and Paris, 1971).

48 Anonymous, 'Russian Short Stories' (review of 'The Gentleman from San Francisco' by I.A. Bunin), *Times Literary Supplement* (18 August 1921), p. 530.

49 Oliver Edwards, 'Some Secret Fibre?', *The Times* (17 October, 1957), p. 13.

version, published in Paris by Bossard) and 17 May 1922 in *The Times* (of the English version, published by the Hogarth Press). Both reviews argue that 'The Gentleman from San Francisco' is 'certainly one of the most impressive stories of modern times'[50] and that 'the other three stories in the book are, in comparison, slight'.[51] The *TLS* review, written by J. Middleton Murry, manifests the sort of criticism that was characteristic of the British reception of Bunin's writings both at this time and later. His three negative comments on Bunin's stories concern 'a disturbance of vision' (or 'the authentic power of revelation' which is 'not altogether under his control'), an 'obsession with the facts, and with his way of regarding them' ('instead of penetrating the reality [...] he has scoured the world') and the 'indefinite' character of his works on the whole.[52] The equivocal vigour with which the reviewer stresses Bunin's 'delicate style' is also to be seen in later British critical writings.

Planning in 1925 a series of articles on Russian writers in exile, Stephen Graham starts with Bunin as 'the only one Russian writer who has gained in prestige during the seven years of revolution'.[53] What Graham chooses to stress in Bunin's image and art is not in general unexpected: this is the 'limitedness' of 'his appeal' (he is 'a writer's writer'), the 'gentleness' of his nature and behaviour, and a stern opposition to everything Soviet. The inner message of the emphasized points becomes more conspicuous when the interview is projected against Graham's next article, on Remizov (April 1925). Unlike Bunin, Remizov is said to be 'one of the few undoubted geniuses of modern Russia' and is claimed to know Bolshevists 'more intimately' since he 'lived' with them 'until 1921' and, hence, to be able to 'correct' 'the opinions of Bunin'.[54] The date of Bunin's exit from Russia, changed by Graham (intentionally or unintentionally?) from (the accurate) 1920 to (the inaccurate) 1918 serves as a proof of Bunin's obsoleteness, or narrow-mindedness.

---

50 J. Middleton Murry, 'The Stories of Ivan Bunin', *Times Literary Supplement* (20 April 1922), p. 256.

51 Anon., 'Ivan Bunin. Review of the book 'The Gentleman from San Francisco and Other Stories' by the Hogarth Press', *The Times* (17 May 1922), p. 16.

52 J. Middleton Murry, 'The Stories of Ivan Bunin', *Times Literary Supplement* (20 April 1922), p. 256.

53 Stephen Graham, 'Russian Writers in Exile. I. – Ivan Bunin', *The Times* (3 April 1925), p. 17.

54 *Idem*, 'Russian Writers in Exile. II. – Alexey Remizof', *The Times* (28 April 1925), p. 17.

Reservations about the 'vagueness' of Bunin's themes, the 'inconclusiveness' of his composition and the lack of 'meaning' in his lyrical 'bursts' are expressed in *The Times* in March 1935.[55] John Cournos's bitter review of the Parisian Russian émigré journal *Sovremennye zapiski* in the April 1934 issue of *The Criterion* adds further to the early reception of Bunin's writings in Britain. The critic sternly places Bunin within the frame of 'émigré literature', which he says 'is willy-nilly forced to subsist on the cumulations of the past, with few stimulations from the present'.[56] Cournos's vividly disparaging and hostile attitude to everything coming from the émigré makes him doubt not only the aesthetic value of *The Life of Arsenyev* (he equivocally describes it as 'a longish novel', 'an evocation of the past', and 'simplicity itself in its theme, prose and unaffected loveliness'), but also the fairness of the Nobel Committee's decision and the value of Bunin's art on the whole (in brackets he says that Bunin, 'I hear, has snatched the laurels from Gorky at the Nobel Committee conference').[57]

In May 1957 in the *Times Literary Supplement* Georgette Donchin, following the well-trodden path, defines Bunin as 'one of its [*Russia's*] finest craftsmen', 'the best Russian stylist of the first half of the twentieth century', who 'does not ask questions' since he is 'no psychologist', whose stories about Russian peasants, 'painted in the blackest possible tones'', seem 'slightly unconvincing' and who brings forth too much 'the lyrical element' in his prose.[58] In Oliver Edwards's musings entitled 'Some Secret Fibre?' (*The Times*, 17 October 1957) the idea of Bunin's indefiniteness is pushed to absurd extremes: the author claims that 'there was little that was pathetic about Bunin', that 'he seems no more than a moderate practitioner when compared with the masters' and even that in photographs, sitting next to Gor'kii, Andreev, and Chaliapin, he looks an 'insignificant little mouse'.[59]

Much of this criticism, including that of his appearance, sounds strikingly similar to the perception of Bunin and his art by contemporary Russian writers and readers. Bunin, who confessed that 'everything' tortured him

55 Anon., 'Review of Ivan Bunin's Short Stories: *Grammar of Love,* trans. John Cournos, Hogarth Press', *The Times* (8 March 1935), p. 11.

56 John Cournos, *Review of Russian periodicals, The Criterion*, XIII/LII (April 1934), pp. 529-35.

57 *Idem*, 'Review of *Sovremennya Zapiski*, Paris, 1934', *Criterion*, XIII/LII (April 1934), p. 535.

58 Georgette Donchin, 'Ivan Bunin', *Times Literary Supplement* (10 May 1957), p. 288.

59 Edwards, 'Some Secret Fibre?', p. 13.

'with its charm',[60] who was called in his childhood 'Spasmodic',[61] and who was known for his 'passion' and 'hot temper' among his close friends and relatives,[62] was labelled by his Russian contemporaries 'a cold, icy writer',[63] 'a fierce egoist',[64] 'a guardian of traditions', 'standing apart from the general tendencies' of contemporary Russian literature.[65]

What was not taken into account by both Russian and British critics is Bunin's deliberate choice of the role, played to protest against the 'theatricality' of his epoch.[66] In this respect the photograph referred to in Edwards's review is extremely significant: the 'strong' postures and the decorative 'folk' style of Gor'kii, Andreev and Chaliapin form a sharp contrast to Bunin's sensibly classical image.

To what extent the British reception of Bunin was influenced by this Russian point of view is still to be researched. It is obvious, however, that, close to each other in many aspects, they differ, and it is mainly British critics who feel dissatisfied with the supposed lack of psychological profundity and partiality of Bunin's writings. The opinion of a more scholarly Russo-British critic, D.S. Mirskii, supports this view.

There is little evidence of scholars' interest in Bunin in this early period of his reception in Great Britain. In all 17 issues of the *Slavonic Review* that appeared in Britain between 1922 and 1927 his name is mentioned only once, and then with disapproval, in D.S. Mirskii's article on the 'revival of Russian prose-fiction'. Pointing out the 'elegant and perfect style of Bunin and Sologub', Mirskii interprets it as a sign of 'the rapid decline of Russian prose' after 'the death of Chekhov'.[67] Unlike Bunin's writings, the work of Solov'ev, Blok, Voloshin, Bal'mont, Remizov, Tsvetaeva and Averchenko was either reviewed or published in various issues of the *Slavonic Review*.

Given Mirskii's status as a Lecturer in Russian literature at the University of London (1922–32), his position as 'the leading historian of Russian literature in England and in Russian émigré circles', and his influence on the opinion not only of the general public, but of Western writers (including Virginia

60 Galina Kuznetsova, *Grassky dnevnik* (Moscow, 2001), p. 42.
61 Oleg N. Mikhailov, *Zhizn' Bunina. Lish' slovu zhizn' dana…* (Moscow, 2002), p. 20.
62 Galina Kuznetsova, 'Grasskii dnevnik', in *Ivan Bunin: pro et contra* (St Petersburg, 2001), p. 117.
63 A. Sedykh, 'Ivan Bunin', *ibid.*, p. 157.
64 Irina V. Odoevtseva, *Na beregakh Seny', ibid.*, p. 230.
65 Vladimir V. Veidle, *Na smert' Bunina, ibid.*, p. 420.
66 Ivan A. Bunin, 'Zametki', in *Sobraniye sochinenii v 9 tomakh,* IX (Moscow, 2009), p. 210.
67 Prince Dmitry S. Mirskii, 'The Revival of Russian Prose-fiction', *Slavonic Review,* II (June 1923), p. 200.

Woolf and D. H. Lawrence),[68] his attitude to Bunin's art deserves special attention. It was, certainly, expressed more than once. In 1926, for instance, reviewing the émigré journals *Sovremennye zapiski* and *Vol'ia Rossii* (1920–5), Mirskii includes a harsh paragraph about Bunin's 'profound provinciality' and 'hatred for everything new' and labels him 'a rare phenomenon of a great gift not connected with a great personality'.[69] It is, however, a chapter on Bunin in his famous *Contemporary Russian Literature*, also published in 1926, that contains Mirskii's best-known and most influential judgement. Before he actually starts writing about Bunin, he claims Gor'kii to be 'the greatest name in the realistic revival', 'the only Russian author with a really world-wide reputation' and 'the obvious champion' of contemporary Russian literature.[70] So, when he comes to Bunin and recommends him as a 'greater *artist* than either Gorky or Andreev' and, 'in the opinion of some competent judges, one of whom is Gorky, the greatest of living Russian writers', the reader senses the implied distrust. It is more explicit in his views on the obsoleteness of Bunin's poetry ('as a poet Bunin belongs to the old, pre-Symbolist school. His technique has remained that of the eighties'), the imperfections of the story 'The Village' ('it is too long and loose and contains too much definitively 'publicistic' matter'), and the author's lack of psychological profundity ('*The Gentleman from San Francisco* [...] is not a work of analysis [...] It is a "thing of beauty"') and his overuse of lyricism ('The lyrical element seems to be growing, and bursting the bonds of that strong restraint').[71]

The 'reproaches' Mirskii directs against Bunin are essentially similar to the predominant early English perception of the Russian writer's art: very much like J. Middleton Murry, he stresses Bunin's obsoleteness, 'obsession with facts', 'a disturbance of vision' and lack of psychological profundity. Two of the 'reproaches'—the most serious ones, those of impartiality and lack of psychological analysis—when compared to the early Russian reception of Bunin's writings, can be seen as especially characteristic of the British reception, to be explained by an extreme discordance between what British critics were ready to accept in a Russian author and what they saw in his writings. It occasions no surprise that the British public, prepared to see

68 Ol'ga Kaznina, 'Kniaz' D.P. Sv'iatopolk-Mirskii: talant i sud'ba', in N.V. Makarova and O.A. Morgunova (eds.), *Russkoye prisutstvie v Britanii* (Moscow, 2009), pp. 210-11.

69 Prince Dmitrii S. Mirskii, 'Retzenziia na 'Sovremennye zapiski' i 'Vol'iu Rossii' za 1920–1925 gg', *Versty*, I (1926), p. 209.

70 Prince Dmitrii S. Mirskii, *Contemporary Russian Literature* (London, 1926), pp. 104-6.

71 *Ibid.*, pp. 124-30.

'compassion', either in the form of the 'religiousness' of the author and his heroes or of inner 'socialism' and natural 'democracy' of his artistic world,[72] was puzzled by the bold and shockingly revealing portrait of peasants' life in Bunin's *Derevnia* (*The Village*), and by the unique 'unity of sense and language' in Bunin's writings:[73] his restrained and capaciously laconic style was perceived as 'indefiniteness', or 'meaningless', or deficiency in analysis.

Mirskii's chapter and Stephen Graham's article on Bunin, as well as *The Criterion*'s evidently preconceived understanding of Bunin's art within the framework of the artistic impotence of Russian émigré circles, provide another insight into the deep context of this early perception of Bunin in Britain. Mirskii's chapter is especially interesting in this respect. In its conclusion the author argues that 'since 1918 Bunin has not written anything on the same level' as 'The Gentleman from San Francisco''.[74] In the Addenda, however, he notes that 'Bunin has published (in 'Sovremennya Zapiski', 1925, books 23 and 24) a new nouvelle 'Mitya's Love', which is superior to all he has written since 1918, and shows that the writer has by no means uttered his last word'.[75] Mirskii, it would seem, was manipulating the facts he was reluctant to recognize. The reluctance implies his negative attitude to the 'obsolete', 'non-socialistic' and, thus, non-compassionate Russian émigré. The same message is more than overtly expressed in *The Criterion*—not only in the above-mentioned issue, but in the whole tendency of its reviews—which by 1937 had stopped including Russian émigré books and journals in the list of the reviewed publications, having chosen Soviet writings as the only representative of contemporary Russian literature. The deeper motive behind this choice is revealed in Graham's article in a very simple statement: '[...] we had in England before the revolution a strong propaganda against Tsarism. [...] Half England still believes that Russia was foully and hideously governed under the Tsar and that it was impossible to live happily there'.[76] At this point the new Russian myth, projected upon Bunin's writings, encounters the traditional and deep-seated negative attitude to the Russian Empire. Associated with

72 Serge Persky, writing in 1907, notes 'that which has always been called socialism, has had an irresistible attraction to the more intelligent Russians' and that 'all of Russian literature is permeated with it' (Serge Persky, *Contemporary Russian novelists*, trans. from French by Frederick Eiseman (London, 1907), p. 23).

73 Vladislav Khodasevich, 'Knigi i liudi', *Sovremennye zapiski*, LXIII (9 November 1933), p. 3.

74 Mirskii, *Contemporary Russian Literature*, p. 130.

75 *Ibid.*, p. 363.

76 Graham, *Ivan Bunin*, p. 17.

the old regime both through his political position and artistic style, Bunin was not to be easily accepted by the British reader.

It was this early perception of Bunin's writings in Britain that Gleb Struve, a Russian literary critic, translator, historian, Lecturer in Russian Literature and Language at the University of London (from the early 1930s to the mid-1940s), and Bunin's friend, opposed in his article, 'The Art of Ivan Bunin' (published January 1933). Addressing himself to the British reader and, hence, basing his review on the predominant opinion about Bunin in Britain, Struve persistently stresses and declaims against 'wrong' judgements. Here are some excerpts to illustrate Struve's tactics:

> It is wrong to regard him [Bunin] as an out-and-out realist [...] Bunin's realism is of a poetical quality, and his details [...] are always subordinated to the whole...[77]
>
> Nothing could be more wrong than to regard Bunin as a soothing, quieting author. Himself at bottom unquiet, he is capable of acting disquietingly upon us [...] in a [...] suggestive way.[78]
>
> From the purely literary point of view Bunin was blamed for the abnormal development of his outward visual capacity and the lack of psychological insight. Nowadays, after the Russian Revolution of 1917, we are inclined to view many things in Bunin's 'Village' as prophetic foresight.[79]
>
> Here we come to [...] the philosophical and psychological leitmotiv of Bunin's work, [...] which may be described as a marveling perplexity before the mysteries of the world.[80]

Whether Struve succeeded or not in his argument with British critics is hard to say. According to what we read in the already quoted reviews by Georgette Donchin and Oliver Edwards (both written in 1957), he did not. According to another scholarly paper also published in the *Slavonic and East European Review* in 1955, he did, at least in part. It is true that in his 'Ivan Bunin in Retrospect' A. Guershoon Colin still labels the Russian author a 'pessimist' and 'the foremost Russian stylist of the first half of the 20th century'. Nevertheless, the paper provides a very favourable and objective view of Bunin's works: unlike many of his predecessors, Colin argues that Bunin was a 'great psychologist', 'a man of truly outstanding intellect', whom 'richness of themes', 'bold frankness', 'penetrating judgement',

77 Gleb Struve, 'The Art of Ivan Bunin', *Slavonic and East European Review*, XI/32 (January 1933), p. 425.

78 *Ibid.*

79 *Ibid.*, p. 426.

80 *Ibid.*, p. 434.

'profound wisdom' and 'enormous vocabulary' make 'the most prominent of' all Soviet and émigré writers.[81]

This was not and is not the end of the story of the British reception of Bunin's works, which continued in the second half of the 20th century and into the 21st, but that story is beyond the scope of this paper.

81 A. Guershoon Colin, 'Ivan Bunin in Retrospect', *Slavonic and East European Review*, XXXIV/82 (December 1955), pp. 156-73.

16. Russia and Russian Culture in *The Criterion*, 1922-1939

Olga Ushakova

In 1922 T.S. Eliot founded *The Criterion* as an international literary review with the aim of introducing the literatures and cultures of different countries and to discuss cultural, social and political problems of global relevance. In 'Last Words', his farewell 'Commentary' published in *The Criterion*'s final issue in January 1939, Eliot emphasized the international mission of his periodical: 'It was the aim of *The Criterion* to maintain close relations with other literary reviews of its type, on the Continent and in America; and to provide in London a local forum of international thought'.[1] The international character of Eliot's literary review set it apart from the traditional type of British quarterly. *The Criterion* became the practical embodiment of modernist universalism and cosmopolitanism, the realization of Eliot's concept of 'the mind of Europe'. The presentation of Russia and Russian culture played an important part in the journal's international programme.

The main themes of the 'Russian items' were the country's classical and contemporary literature, its arts and philosophy, as well as the political situation in the USSR and debates on Communism and Socialism. The themes and content of the pieces published and the range of names and subjects treated reflected the historical and social changes of the period. The sixteen years of *The Criterion* reflected also global changes in intellectual and artistic output which required new images and words. The dancing of Russian ballet stars during the Diagilev seasons in the reviews of the 1920s, for example, gave way in the 1930s to beating drums and Stalin shaking

1 *The Criterion: The Collected Edition*, XVIII (London, 1967), p. 271.

hands with the Arctic heroes on the Red Square (the poem 'Chelyuskin') and to new songs about Lenin sung by folk bards, ('ashugs', 'bakhshis', 'hafizes') in the Soviet Far North, Middle Asia and the Caucasian highlands.[2] 'Russia' was present throughout the life of *The Criterion,* beginning with the first volume in October 1922 (F.M. Dostoevskii's *Plan of the Novel 'The Life of a Great Sinner',* translated by V. Woolf and S.S. Kotelianskii),[3] to the very last issue of January 1939 that offered a review of Sergei Bulgakov's *The Wisdom of God, a Brief Summary of Sophiology* by G. Curtis.[4] In general, the subjects and themes of the articles reflected the three main elements of Russian influence on Western and English modern culture: Russian Literature, Russian Ballet and the Russian Revolution.

Russia and Russian culture were presented in various genres: the short stories and letters of Russian writers, poems on Russian themes, essays of literary criticism, articles on the political situation in Russia, notes on Communism and Socialism, chronicles of cultural life in the Soviet Union ('Russian chronicles') and reviews of Russian periodicals, reviews of Russian books and monographs on Russia by Western scholars. What follows is merely a selection from a very long list of titles spanning a wide range of genres: short stories (Ivan Bunin's 'A Night at Sea', translated by N.A. Duddington, April 1926; Panteleimon Romanov's 'A Catastrophe', translated by E. Vishnevskaia, January 1931); essays (V.I. Pudovkin's, 'Acting—The Cinema v. The Theatre' (October 1933)); poems on Russian/Soviet themes (Hugh McDiarmid's 'Second Hymn to Lenin', July 1932; Michael Roberts' 'Chelyuskin', January 1936); literary criticism (C.M. Bowra's 'The Position of Alexander Blok', April 1932; D.A. Traversi's 'Dostoievsky', July 1937); reviews of books by Russian/Soviet authors (Vasilii Rozanov's *Solitaria* (February 1928); Dmitrii Merezhkovskii's *Napoleon. A Study* (April 1930); Lenin's *Materialism and Empirio-Criticism* (April 1932); Lev Shestov's *In Job's Balances* (June 1933); Nikolai Berdiaev's *The Bourgeois Mind* (April 1935); Karel Radek's *Portraits and Pamphlets* (July 1935); Dmitrii Mirskii's *The Intelligentsia of Great Britain* (July 1935); N.I. Bukharin's *Marxism and Modern Thought* (January 1936)); reviews of books on Russia and Russian culture (H. L'Anson Fausset's *Tolstoy: The Inner Drama* (January 1928); P. Istrati's *Russia Unveiled* (July 1931); C.F.A. Maitland-Macgill-Crichton's

---

2 See the essay 'Myth in the Making' by John Cournos, published in January 1934. *The Criterion: The Collected Edition,* XIII (London, 1967), pp. 225-9.

3 *The Criterion,* I (London, 1967), pp. 16-33.

4 *The Criterion,* XVIII (London, 1967), pp. 346-50.

Russian Close-up (July 1932); W. Gurian's *Bolshevism: Theory and Practice* (January 1933); M. Muggeridge's *Winter in Moscow* (July 1934); S. and B. Webb's *Soviet Communism: A New Civilisation* (April 1936); Prince P. Levin's *The Birth of Ballet-Russes* (October 1936); B. King's *Changing Man: The Soviet Education System* (January 1937)).

The articles on Russia reflect dominant preoccupations of the time, particularly the widespread interest in literary theory (cf. Boris Eikhenbaum's *Tolstoi's 'War and Peace'*, No. 42, October 1931) and cinema (cf. Pudovkin's already mentioned essay on film theory). By the time of this publication Vsevolod Pudovkin was already known in England as a director and theorist, not least for his book *Film Technique,* translated into English in 1933 by the British director Ivor Montagu. In the essay he published in *The Criterion* Pudovkin reviews his experience as a director. His piece starts by emphasizing that a film actor should not over-perform or exaggerate his gestures, as he might in the theatre:

> It was clear to me that the man before the cine-camera must behave differently from the man behind the footlights [...] In the cinema [...] the camera commands an ever-changing distance. It takes the spectator face to face with the actor, and, at will, makes the actor a mere speck on the horizon. The actor is thus freed from the necessity of overcoming distances. His slightest movement is conveyed to the spectator, not because he exaggerates it, but because it is stressed by the camera which is the eye of the audience drawing nearer.[5]

Pudovkin also discussed his theory of 'Montage', explaining that directors use this technique to reveal the character's psychology by focusing on small details and shades of expression. Thus at the editing table the director is able to highlight emotional moments and create a new psychological and aesthetic reality: 'When I am speaking of realism I mean pieces of reality, which has nothing to do with the copying of actuality'.[6] Pudovkin's essay provided an important contribution to the theory of film-making, later echoed in film reviews published in *The Criterion*.

Articles on Russian topics followed the changing features of British public interest in Russia. For instance, the 1920s issues of the journal clearly reflect the British cult of Dostoevskii between 1912 and the early 1920s.[7] It

5 *The Criterion*, XIII (London, 1967), p. 1.

6 *Ibid.*, XIII (London, 1967), p. 3.

7 The 'Dostoevskii' publications included *F. Dostoevskii: Two Unpublished Letters* (No. 3, April 1923), *L.N. Tolstoi and N.N. Strakhov: Extracts from Letter relating to F.M. Dostoevskii* (No, 10, January 1925), *Dostoevskii on 'The Brothers Karamazov'* (No. 3, June 1926), a review

is generally accepted that that Dostoevskii's fame in England swelled after the appearance of Constance Garnett's translation of *The Brothers Karamazov* in 1912. By the 1920s most Dostoevskii's works had been translated into English. The zenith of his cult coincided with the time of the First World War being the important catalyst of the tragic events and global social and psychological changes. The 1920s became the period of reconsideration and re-reading of his heritage. The Dostoevskii's publications in *The Criterion* reflected this process of more thorough and detached interpretation of his works. It was also important to present some new 'artifacts' to the readers. Thus the first volume of *The Criterion* (October 1922) introduced the English translation of Dostoevskii's *Plan of the Novel 'The Life of a Great Sinner'*. It was in this same issue that one of the most 'Dostoevskian' of Eliot's poems, *The Waste Land*, was also published. Eliot's masterpiece reveals the influence of Dostoevskii's *Weltenschauung* on the English poet's idea of the decline of Europe. Moreover modern Russia, seen through the prism of Dostoevskii's art, plays a role in the poem. In lines 368-76 Eliot describes the collapse of Western civilization:

> Who are those hooded hordes swarming
> Over endless plains, stumbling in cracked earth
> Ringed by the flat horizon only.

The reference to H. Hesse's *A Glimpse into Chaos*, specifically the passage in which the German writer analyzed Dmitrii Karamazov's song in the contemporary historical context (the Russian Revolution), demonstrates that Eliot's take on Russia and Dostoevskii shared widespread stereotypes among contemporary Western intellectuals. In particular Eliot's mystical urban visions of London in *The Waste Land* recall Dostoevskii's descriptions of Petersburg. Like Dostoevskii Eliot combined biblical imagery and mythological patterns to condemn social inequality.

This 'Hesse-Dostoevskii' influence in *The Waste Land* is testified by Eliot's thoughts and reflections on the Russian Revolution and the political situation in Russia—which he also expressed in regular editorial commentaries appearing in subsequent issues of *The Criterion*. In the fragment of *A Commentary* entitled 'Light from the East' (January 1925) Eliot mentions: 'A revolution staged on such a vast scale, amongst a picturesque, violent, and

---

of the book *Dostoevskii Portrayed by his Wife*, edited by S.S. Kotelianskii (no. 4, October 1926). On the popularity and literary influence of Dostoevsii in Great Britain see also Muireann Maguire, 'Crime and Publishing: How Dostoevskii Changed the British Murder' in this volume.

romantic people; involving such disorder, rapine, assassination, starvation, and plague should have something to show for the expense: a new culture horrible at the worst, but in any event fascinating'.[8] 'Hooded hordes' is a poetic image of the Asian threat and the downfall of Europe—the 'Asiatic Ideal' that Hesse borrowed from Dostoevskii. In his editorial commentary (August 1927) Eliot writes about a new feeling of insecurity and danger, warning Europeans to develop a new European consciousness to guard their culture against the Asian spirit of the Russian Revolution: 'For the Russian Revolution has made men of the position of Western Europe as (in Valéry's words) a small and isolated cape on the western side of the Asiatic Continent'.[9]

In the first issue of *The Criterion* Eliot was even more Dostoevskian. In his letter to Hesse of 13 March 1922 the poet wrote:

> I have now been entrusted with the founding, in London, of a new, serious review, which will, at any rate, be more important than the existing ones, and much more welcoming to the ideas from abroad. My first thought was to ask for one or two sections of *Blick ins Chaos*. Unfortunately, the 'Karamazov' section is too long for a single issue (only 80 pages in all), and since the review is to appear only once three months, we can hardly subdivide the text. And the 'Muishkine' section, I think, should not be separated from the other. But I am sure that you must have many other equally important writings, that I should very much like to be the first to present to the British public [...] I find in your *Blick ins Chaos* a seriousness the like of which has not yet occurred in England, and I am keen to spread the reputation of the book.[10]

In the same issue Eliot published Hesse's essay 'On Recent German Poetry', in which the German writer developed ideas first aired in *Blick ins Chaos*. The last paragraph in particular paraphrases the opening paragraph of 'The *Brothers Karamazov*—The Downfall of Europe':

> And the new psychology, whose harbingers were Dostoievsky and Nietzche, and whose first architect is Freud, will teach these young men that the emancipation of the personality, the canonization of the natural instincts, are only the first steps on the way, and that this personal freedom is a poor thing and of no account in comparison with the highest of all freedoms of the individual: the freedom to regard oneself consciously and joyously as a part of humanity, and to serve it with liberated powers.[11]

---

8 *The Criterion*, III (London, 1967), p. 163.

9 *Ibid.*, VI (London, 1967), p. 98.

10 *The Letters of T.S. Eliot*, I (1898-1922) (San Diego, New York and London, 1988), p. 510.

11 *The Criterion*, I (London, 1967), p. 93.

The last article on Dostoevskii to appear in *The Criterion* was a critical essay by D.A. Traversi—'Dostoievsky' (July 1937),[12]—discussing M. (*sic*) Berdiaev's book on Dostoevskii:

> It is interesting to see how this observation connects Dostoievsky with a theme essential to English literature, especially in the metaphysical tradition. Shakespeare and Donne were also occupied with the contradiction essential to human passion—the contradiction between the desire for absolute unity which prompts it, and the final independence of the separate personality upon which that desire breaks. But in the great English poets the contradiction is resolved by the intensity of emotion. The element of separation by 'devouring' time is seen as necessary to a greater intensity of living, as the condition of a new life of 'sensation' (using the word to imply a completeness of human experience, bodily, mental, and spiritual), whose value is absolute. Dostoievsky's 'metaphysical' impatience made such a conception impossible for him.[13]

In his resumé Traversi adopts traditional British stereotypes of Russian writers: 'The finding of criticism, I suggest, is that Dostoievsky was the master of all explorers of physical and spiritual disorder, and that his findings expose an erring adventure in human experience—the experiment, ultimately, of replacing the true balance of living by the despotic activity of the independent mind'.[14] His interpretation of Dostoevskii in the context of the metaphysical tradition chimes with Eliot's vision of Dostoevskii as a metaphysical author. As we know from a note by American scholar Ronald Schuchard, Eliot planned to publish a further piece on Doestoevskii based on a lecture on Chapman, Dostoevskii and Dante that he gave at Cambridge University in November of 1924 .[15]

---

12 *The Criterion*, XVI (London, 1967), p. 585-602.

13 *Ibid.*, XVI (London, 1967), p. 601.

14 *Ibid.*, p. 602.

15 'TSE gave his lecture on Chapman before the Cam Literary Club at Cambridge University on 8 November 1924 [...]. On 12 November TSE wrote to Virginia Woolf that after all the labour it had not proved worthy of publication, and on 30 November he wrote to Ottoline Morrell, pleased that she liked some poems that he had sent: 'They are part of a larger sequence which I am doing—I laid down the principles of it in a paper I read at Cambridge, on Chapman, Dostoevskii and Dante – and which is a sort of avocation to a much more revolutionary thing I am working on'. He planned to revise and publish the essay in *The Criterion*, where he announced to his readers that due to illness the editor had been 'unable to prepare his essay on 'A Neglected Aspect of George Chapman' for this number' (April 1925, p. 341). The essay is lost, but TSE may have given a summary of it in a review, 'Wanley and Chapman' (TLS, 31 December 1925, p. 907). [...].TSE did not return to the manuscript [...]'. T.S. Eliot, *The Varieties of Metaphysical Poetry*, edited and introduced by Ronald Schuchard (San Diego, New York and London, 1996), pp. 151-2.

Eliot may have planned to write further articles on Dostoevskii for *The Criterion* as we can infer from his letter to Kotelianskii dated 23 May 1927:

> Dear Koteliansky, I am sorry to have kept you waiting so long but have been exceedingly busy as I understand that you are particularly anxious to know about the 'Rozanov'. I am sending it back to you. It may be merely that I do not understand it. As for 'Dostoevsky', that is quite another matter to me and I have simply been waiting to clear up the next two numbers in order to consider how and when I should be able to use it. I am probably going away for a few days but I should very much like to see you on my return.[16]

The correspondence between Eliot and Kotelianskii in the years 1923-7 reflects some of the tensions encountered by the Russian in its dealings with *The Criterion*—for example on the occasions when Kotelianskii's pieces were rejected by the journal. However, notwithstanding the occasional disagreements, Kotelianskii and the other Russian contributors to the journal, Mirskii and Cournos, played the important role of mediators between Russian (Soviet) and British culture.

Mirskii, in particular, was the author of several articles and reviews, as well as the subject of reviews of his work.[17] *The Criterion,* in its turn, seems to have influenced Mirskii in more ways than one. For example the format of *Versty* , a magazine co-founded by Mirskii in Paris in 1926-8 while he was working at *The Criterion,*[18] seems to be modelled on the English periodical. Although the chief editors of *Versty,* Mirskii and Petr Suvchinskii, launched *Versty* as a vehicle for the dissemination of Eurasian ideas in actual fact the journal soon became a cosmopolitan forum for a wide range of political and artistic ideas.[19] The most distinctive feature of the 1927 issues of *Versty,* for instance, was the participation of a number of non-Russian critics, such as Bernard Groethuysen, Ramon Fernandez and many others. Among the most remarkable articles to appear that year was the essay by E.M. Forster, 'Contemporary English Literature' and Mirskii's review of *The Book of the Bear,* edited by Jane Harrison and Hope Mirrlees[20] in which Mirskii introduced the works of the British authors to Russian readers. Interestingly Mirskii writes about writers whose names often appeared in *The Criterion.* In the

16 British Library, Koteliansky Papers. F. 107. Add. 48974.

17 Most notably a review of Mirskii's seminal *A History of Russian Literature to 1881* was published in June 1928.

18 Mirskii's essay 'Chekhov and the English', for instance, appeared in October 1927.

19 For example, the second edition of *Versty* contained some English materials, including Mirskii's review of T.S. Eliot's *Poems, 1905-1925.*

20 *Versty,* 2, 1927, pp. 240-6; *Versty,* 3, 1928, pp. 158-160.

review mentioned above, for example, Mirskii analyzes Eliot's poem *The Waste Land*, works by James Joyce, and describes *The Golden Bough* as 'the Bible of anthropology and symbolic book of English literature'. The two writers were further mentioned in Mirskii's review of contemporary French journals (where translations of Eliot and Joyce had appeared) and in an essay marking the fifth anniversary of the publication of Joyce's *Ulysses*.

John Cournos (Johann Gregorievich Korschoon, as he introduced himself in his *Autobiography*)[21] was the most active Russian contributor to *The Criterion*, the author of numerous reviews of Russian periodicals and analytical essays. Cournos was a man of exceptional gifts, with a wide range of interests. Among his works were novels, poems, writings on literature, art, politics, and translations of Russian literature. Cournos became a regular reviewer of Russian periodicals starting from June 1926 when his first article on Russian literary journal appeared. The piece was devoted to the January-February issue of *Blagonamerennyi*, a journal published by Russian émigrés. Cournos rates this number of the journal as 'excellent' and analyses some contributions by leading Soviet critics and authors: 'an amusing article' on 'Proletarian Lyricism' by K. Mochulskii and 'a particularly terse and valuable' article, 'On the Present State of Russian Literature', by Prince D. Sviatopolk-Mirskii. Other 'interesting features' he recommends include the article 'A Theatre Without a Repertory' by E.A. Znosko-Borovskii, aphoristic thoughts 'Concerning Gratitude' by Marina Tsvetaeva, and fragments of a travel diary by Ivan Bunin.

Cournos wrote a succession of reviews on Russian literary periodicals, newspapers and 'thick journals' ('tolstie zhurnali', a term alluding to their usually 200-plus pages per issue. Many novels, short stories, poems were first published in such journals). For instance, in his review published in October 1936 Cournos introduces to British readers the leading Soviet journals *Literaturnyi kritik* and *Oktiabr'* and the newspaper *Literaturnaia gazeta*. Cournos also analyses in detail 3 articles published in *Literaturnyi kritik*: the opening commentary of the March issue, devoted to the polemics on 'formalism' and 'naturalism', a literary-historical study by G. Lukitch on 'The Intellectual Countenance of the Literary Hero', and 'an extensive consideration' by Selivanovskii of the new novel by a Soviet writer, Leonid Leonov. In his review, supported by numerous quotations translated into

21 John Cournos, *Autobiography* (New York, 1935), p. 8. See also on John Cournos as a contributor to *The Criterion*: David Ayers '*The Criterion* and Communism', in *Otobrazhenie i interpretatsiia istorii v kul'ture SShA*, ed. Larisa Mikhailova (Moscow, 2001), pp. 302-12.

English,. Cournos emphasises the excellent quality of the journal, 'perhaps indicative of the general upward trend in criticism during the past year or two, which no observer can have failed to notice'.[22]

In his essay 'Russian Chronicle: Soviet Russia and the Literature of Ideas' (January 1935) Cournos focuses on Russian literature in the early 1930s. He examines the issue of the relationship between literature and the social and political context and identifies the social message as the basis of Soviet literature. Cournos also provides a survey of the first Congress of Soviet Writers of 1934, which he considers 'an event of outstanding importance', and comments ironically about the famous characterization of a Soviet writer as 'an engineer of human souls': '[...] Stalin provided the slogan of the Congress in the phrase, 'the writer is the engineer of the spirit'. In the old days the word would have been 'priest', but Russia is 'engineer-mad'—so I am told by a returned traveller—and Stalin's word, in any case, more aptly describes the mood of the new Russia, building on materialist doctrines and attaching the greatest significance to technical achievements'.[23]

Although the critic strives to look at Soviet literature with appreciation Cournos's tone is polemical, his literary judgements often sarcastic and his appreciation is for contemporary writers belonging to the pre-Soviet tradition: 'With a free conscience one may affirm that what has been good in the literature of Soviet Russia during the past several years—and I have such names in mind as Babel, Pasternak, Sholokhov, Leonov, Ivanov, Alekseyev, etc.—is something that belongs to the old rather than to the new, to tradition rather than to Communism'.[24] He concludes his essay informing readers about the death of Andrei Bely. In Cournos's opinion 'as thinker and writer, he was infinitely greater than either Bunin or Gorky',[25] drawing comparisons between Bely's *Petersburg* (which Cournos was to translate in 1959) and Joyce's *Ulysses*. The article contains deep insights on the historic, philosophic and aesthetic aspects of the so-called 'Russian tragedy' embodied in Bely's novels *Petersburg* and *Silver Dove.*

Fascinating material can be found in Cournos's essay 'Myth in the Making', in which he attacks the creation of the Lenin myth in Soviet Russia. Cournos remarks, with a sarcastic reference to Greek mythology:

---

22 *The Criterion,* XVI (London, 1967), p. 195.
23 *Ibid.,* XIV (London, 1967), p. 289.
24 *Ibid.,* p. 290.
25 *Ibid.*

'As for the connection of the Lenin legend with literature, it is true—the critics of Soviet Russia frankly admit—that no Homer has yet arisen adequately to sing the epic of his or Russia's deeds begun in 1917'.[26] The closing paragraphs of the essay provide the English translations and an ironical commentary of two folklore songs about Lenin, 'A Kirgiz Song' and 'A Ferghana Folk Song', as examples of the new Communist mythology.

It should be noted that many passages in Cournos's articles are the result of deeply-felt experience, rather than academic debate. In 1917 Cournos joined the Anglo-Russian Commission sent by the Foreign Office to Petrograd to observe the Bolshevik Revolution and returned home with a very pessimistic view of events. The immediate outcome of his experience was a pamphlet *London under the Bolshevics: Londoner's Dream on Returning from Petrograd* (1919), where he describes 'the realities of the Bolshevist nightmare'. In *The Criterion* Cournos also published a number of book reviews on works describing life in Soviet Russia, including *New Russia* by A. De Monzie, *Youth in Soviet Russia* by K. Menhert, and *Winter in Russia* by M. Muggeridge.[27] The last review by Cournos of Russian periodicals appeared in January 1938.

The quantity, variety and intellectual and artistic quality of the articles published in *The Criterion* provide not only a record of Russian history and culture but were instrumental in shaping the perception and reception of Russian culture in Great Britain.

26 *The Criterion*, XIII (London, 1967), p. 227.

27 *Ibid.*, XII (London, 1967), p. 524; *The Criterion*, XIII (London, 1967), p. 490; *The Criterion*, XIII (London, 1967), p. 670.

17. 'Racy of the Soil': Filipp Maliavin's London Exhibition of 1935

Nicola Kozicharow

The Exhibition of Russian Art in London in the summer of 1935 was the most extensive showcase of Russian art displayed to the British public since 1917 and prompted much discussion of Russian art at the time.[1] As Herbert Zia Wernher stated in his introduction to the catalogue, '...it may confidently be claimed that the present exhibition... will, for the first time in history, present to the world outside Russia a picture of Russian art in its various branches and phases, which does something like justice to its task'.[2] The Exhibition of Russian Art, however, was not the only exhibition of Russian art in London that year as one artist—Filipp Andreevich Maliavin (1869-1940)—held his first solo show in Britain in October 1935. Maliavin was not represented at The Exhibition of Russian Art, most likely because he did not fit easily into any of the categories of display, which included Silver and 19th-century Paintings, Icons, Porcelain, and Foreign Artists in Russia. Stage Designs was the only section open to an artist of Maliavin's generation, and works by some of his contemporaries such as Leon Bakst and Ivan Bilibin were displayed, for example, but Maliavin did not participate in theatre production at any point in his career.

Maliavin's work may not have been selected for this groundbreaking exhibition, but his Pictures and Drawings of Russian Life solo exhibition at the New Burlington Galleries in London was a significant achievement

1 For a more detailed analysis of this exhibition, see Anthony Cross, 'Exhibiting Russia: The Two London Russian Exhibitions of 1917 and 1935', *Slavonica,* XXI (2010), pp. 29-39.

2 Herbert Zia Wernher, 'Introduction', *Catalogue of the Exhibition of Russian Art* (London, 1935), p. 6.

for the artist. The exhibition not only forged an important place within Maliavin's career but also represents a noteworthy moment in the British discourse on Russian art. This chapter investigates the reception of Maliavin's work by the British public with particular attention to the response of the press.

The Exhibition of Russian Art and Maliavin's solo exhibition occurred precisely at the moment when British relations with the Soviet Union took a more positive turn.[3] The upheaval caused by the Revolution, subsequent Civil War, and death of Lenin made the political situation in Russia appear unpredictable and unstable. By the mid-1930s, however, the permanence of the Soviet government seemed clear. In March 1935, Foreign Secretary Anthony Eden met with Iosef Stalin in Moscow, and this was the first time Stalin had received a Western political leader. The official communiqué of this exchange read: 'The representatives of the two Governments were happy to note as the result of a full and frank exchange of views that there is at present no conflict of interest between the two Governments on any of the main issues of international policy [...].'[4]

An interesting viewpoint from which to view this shift in relations is through examining the surge of books on the Soviet Union of both scholarly and popular interest in the Soviet Union appearing in 1930s England. In 1935 alone, 64 Russian or Soviet-related books were reviewed in *The Times Literary Supplement*, and many of these concerned daily life in the Soviet Union with titles such as *Law and Justice in Soviet Russia, Modern Moscow*, and *We Soviet Women*. One book review in *The Times Literary Supplement* of *The Russian Revolution, 1917-1920* by William Henry Chamberlain reflected upon the positive change in Anglo-Soviet relations: 'The question is no longer, "Where will the Russian Revolution end?" but "When did it end?"'[5]

Though improved, the political situation between the Soviet Union and Britain was still an obstacle when it came to the study and display of Russian art. In the introduction to the book *Russian Art*, which was published in 1935 to complement The Exhibition of Russian Art, the art historian Tancred Borenius noted this difficulty:

> [The study of Russian art] has, unfortunately, in the past, owing to a variety of circumstances, never been easy of attainment for anyone in Western

3 Cross, p. 39.

4 Quoted in Major E.W. Polson-Newman, 'Anglo-Russian Relations', *The Contemporary Review* (October 1935), p. 416.

5 'Problems of the Russian Revolution', *Times Literary Supplement*, 17 October 1935, p. 637.

> Europe taking an interest in Russian art; nor can the present—for a number of reasons which need not here be gone into—be regarded as a particularly propitious moment for studying Russian art on the spot.[6]

Indeed, none of the objects in the exhibition was lent by Soviet institutions. Instead, the exhibition was formed from an impressive set of European collections, and the selection committee consisted of Russian émigrés, British scholars, and academics. As Anthony Cross discussed in his article 'Exhibiting Russia: The Two London Russian Exhibitions of 1917 and 1935', the exhibition emphasised old Russia as opposed to Soviet Russia.[7] As an émigré, Maliavin, too, would have been firmly identified as a Russian, and not Soviet, artist.

Before emigrating to France, Maliavin had a highly successful career in Russia. He was born in the peasant village Kazanka, and between 1885 and 1891, he trained as an icon-painter at the Panteleimon Monastery in Mount Athos. Having received funding procured by the sculptor and Imperial Academy Professor Vladimir Beklemishev, Maliavin began his studies at the Academy in 1892, working under Il'ia Repin. In 1899, he earned the title of Artist and became an Academician in 1906. Maliavin also achieved success in Europe; his painting *Laughter* won a gold medal at the Paris World Fair in 1900. After the Revolution, Maliavin taught at the Free Artists Studio in Riazan' but produced few works over the next few years, and his financial situation became increasingly precarious. These circumstances most likely led to Maliavin's decision to leave Soviet Russia in 1922 and emigrate to France. Throughout the 1920s and the early 1930s, he exhibited widely across Europe at international shows such as the Salon d'Automne, the Salon des Indépendants, and the International Exhibition in Venice. He also took part in group Russian exhibitions, including those in Brussels, Wilmington, Prague and Pittsburgh. By the mid-1930s, Maliavin had earned enough recognition to hold, over a two year period, solo exhibitions in Oslo, Nice, Prague, Stockholm and Belgrade. Despite actively exhibiting across Europe and America, Maliavin, like many Russian émigrés of his generation, struggled to adapt to a new art scene.[8] Shifting from a Russian public to a European one was difficult for Maliavin, who continued to paint

6 Tancred Borenius, 'Russian Art – An Appreciation', in D. Talbot Rice (ed.), *Russian Art* (London, 1935), p. 1.

7 Cross, 36.

8 For an in-depth discussion of the emigration of Russian artists to France, see Kirill Makhrov, 'History and Modernity: Russian Artists in Paris', in Joseph Kiblitsky (ed.), *Russian Paris 1910-1960* (St Petersburg, 2003), pp. 6-16.

the colourful canvases of Russian peasants that had been popular in Russia. An active exhibitor with the World of Art in Russia, Maliavin did not participate in the group's revival in Paris and never took part in the Ballets Russes or other theatre productions. Instead of settling in Paris along with the majority of the Russian émigré community in France, Maliavin moved to Nice, where he lived an isolated life away from the capital. Although Nice became a popular destination for prominent artists such as Matisse, Picasso, and Léger, Maliavin never learnt a foreign language, so his interaction with other artists was limited. Upon his death in 1940, many paintings which he had exhibited during the 1930s remained in his studio, suggesting he struggled to sell even his most important works.

Before his solo exhibition in London in 1935, Maliavin had taken part in two British exhibitions: one in Birmingham in 1928 and one in London in 1930. The press response to these exhibitions gives an indication of how Maliavin's work had been interpreted in England prior to his solo show. In 1928, the Russian Department at Birmingham University organised an exhibition of seventy contemporary Russian paintings at the Ruskin Galleries, including a range of other Russian artists such as Konstantin Korovin, Natal'ia Goncharova, Mikhail Larionov and Isaak Levitan. A reviewer from *The Observer*, however, found the exhibition lacking in variety as it was mostly limited to painters in emigration and could not, therefore, provide a complete picture of contemporary Russian art. The review also attested to 'the spirit of renaissance animating Russian art today', of which this exhibition was a prime example.[9] The review focused its attention principally on Korovin and Maliavin from the 15 artists who participated. Maliavin, who had 8 pictures at the exhibition, was interpreted, along with Korovin, as 'an early rebel against accepted traditions in Russian painting'.[10] In 1899, the Academy did reject Maliavin's painting *Laughter*, awarding him the title Artist for his portraits instead, but this decision stemmed more from the strict traditionalism of older academicians as opposed to radicalism on Maliavin's part. It is not clear if *The Observer* reviewer would have been aware of this specific incident, but referring to Maliavin as a rebel reflects some knowledge of the artist's career, even if it was misinterpreted. The reviewer then especially praised one of Maliavin's paintings, *Peasant Girl*:

---

9 'Contemporary Russian Art', *The Observer* (21 June 1928), p. 8.
10 *Ibid.*

> [...] 'Peasant Girl' is perhaps the best example of his extreme love of colour. There is no muddiness or dinginess here. The canvas is a stirring glow of bold, refreshing colour, with the pigments richly worked in broad, firm strokes in the texture of the shawl which wraps a head of classical proportions – these bright Russian shawls are an oft-recurring subject in his studies.[11]

This description, above all, stressed the quality of Maliavin's artistic technique, and this emphasis continued in the press response to his work in 1935.

As for the Russian Art Exhibition at the Bloomsbury Gallery in London in 1930, a short review in *The Times* listed Maliavin's painting 'Two Peasant Women' among 'pictures worth noting'.[12] From these reviews, it is clear that Maliavin's work stood out among his contemporaries, particularly his paintings of peasant women. In addition, the focus on Maliavin reveals that the artist played a notable role in the dialogue on Russian art at the time. This praise in the press also set a positive precedent before his solo show.

Without a published catalogue or any related correspondence, it is difficult to construct a complete picture of Maliavin's Pictures and Drawings of Russian Life Exhibition in 1935. Newspaper reviews from the time, however, reveal several of the paintings which were exhibited and other significant information. The exact number of paintings and drawings is unknown: according to the *Observer* there were 200, but *The Times* reported there were 100. 100 is a more likely number, but given that many drawings were exhibited, 200 may indicate the combined total. In any case, both numbers show that this was no small exhibition but a substantial and diverse display of Maliavin's work. The exhibition consisted of works executed both before and after Maliavin's emigration to France. The artist had managed to bring a large number of paintings with him when he left Soviet Russia and exhibited them throughout Europe in the 1920s and 1930s. It is unknown how Maliavin organised such a large solo exhibition in London, but the success of The Exhibition of Russian Art earlier in the year and his own previous critical acclaim in Britain meant that a Maliavin exhibition would have been an appealing venture for a gallery.

There were advertisements in *The Times*, *The Daily Telegraph* and *The Illustrated London News* announcing the exhibition, and the show itself lasted for two weeks. Reviews appeared in *The Times* and *The Observer*, and both reveal significant information about the exhibition itself and Maliavin's reception

11 *Ibid.*

12 'Russian Art', *The Times*, 14 February 1931, p. 10.

by the British public. *The Times* praised the subject matter of the paintings, especially their 'rollicking humour'.[13] The best example of this comedy was to be found in one picture titled 'Country Ablutions', representing '[...] a stout damsel, nude, being drenched from a blue bucket by a peasant woman before an astonished and slightly scandalized audience of cows, a horse, two goats, and a hen'.[14]

The picture's lengthy description in *The Times* review suggests that genre scenes, as opposed to more decorative works, appealed to a British public.

The Times review also highlighted other works (which, unfortunately, are currently unidentifiable from their titles) that were considered 'both racy of the soil and interesting in their direct colour-impressionism [...]. Artistically, the work of M. Maliavin belongs to the decorative realism of the late 19th century—with affinities with our 'Glasgow School''.[15] Here Maliavin's work was described as 'racy of the soil', or nationalistic, but was not classified as specifically Russian in character. By tying him to the Glasgow School and comparing him to artists like James Guthrie who also depicted the country surroundings of their national land, the reviewer placed Maliavin within the category of late 19th century's impressionist-influenced realism. This provided the British audience with a recognisable context for his art, but one that was noticeably not in any sense a contemporary one.

This review stands in sharp contrast to the French discussion of Maliavin's paintings, which emphasised the exotic. In his book *Art Russe*, published in 1922, the art historian Louis Réau wrote of Maliavin's 'jubilant peasants with their brutish gaiety and their multicoloured accoutrements, which explode with the red of the cotton fabric the Russians call *koumatch*. This orgy of colours and wild movement created the European success of "Laughter" and "Whirlwind"'.[16] The British reception of Maliavin avoided this kind of exotic language when describing his work and instead discussed him in a more concrete art historical context.

---

13 'Russian Life', *The Times*, 26 October 1935, p. 10.

14 *Ibid.* Listed as 'Sudenyi dush' (1930) in O.A. Zhivova, *Filipp Andreevich Maliavin, 1869-1940: zhizn' i tvorchestvo* (Moscow, 1967), p. 272. The painting was not illustrated in Zhivova's book but can be identified as lot 183 at Sotheby's London, 'Russian Paintings Day Sale', 9 June 2010.

15 'Russian Life', *The Times*, 26 October 1935, p. 10.

16 'les paysannes en liesse avec leur grosse gaieté animale, leur accoutrements bariolés où éclate le rouge de cette cotonnade que les Russes appellent Koumatch. Cette orgie de couleurs, ce mouvement endiablé firent le succèss européen du "Rire" et du "Tourbillon"' (Louis Réau, *L'Art Russe de Pierre le Grand à nos jours* (Paris, 1922), p. 227).

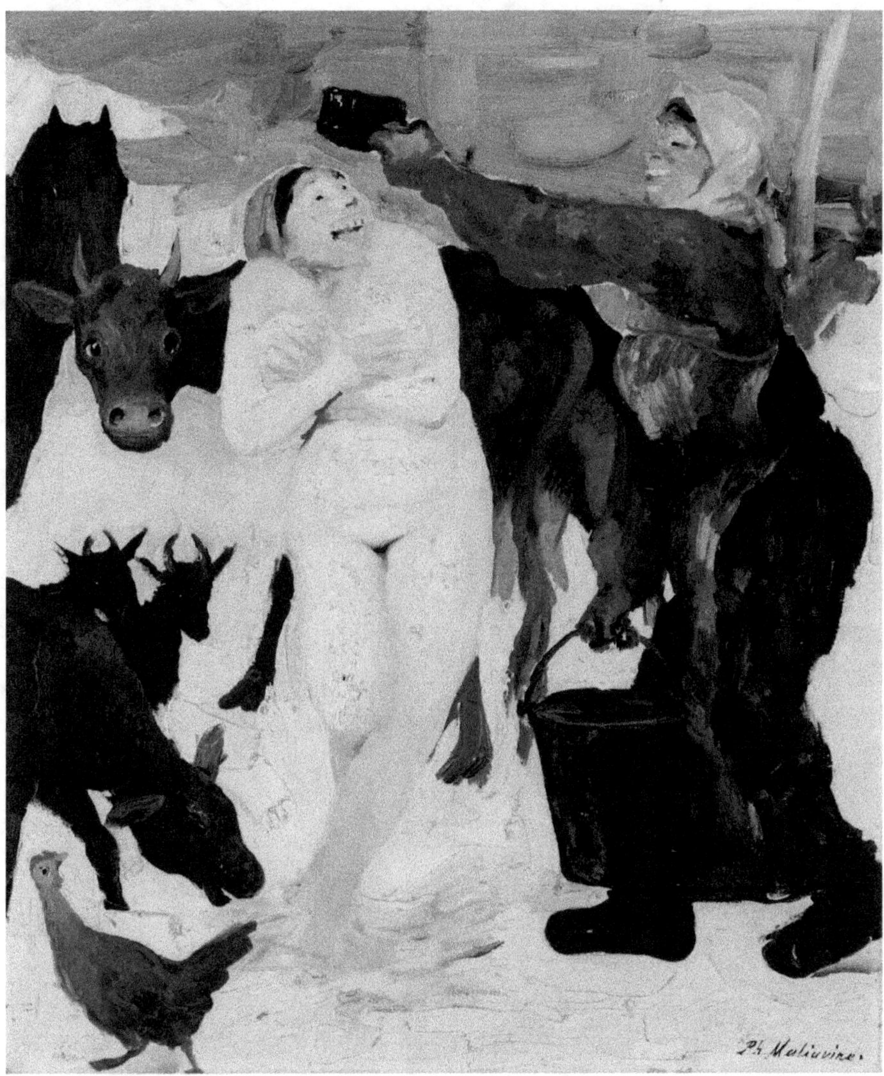

Fig. 17.1 Filipp Maliavin, *Country Ablutions* (1930). Oil on canvas, 73 x 60.5cm, Private Collection. Reproduced by permission of Sotheby's.

Unlike *The Times*, *The Observer* was more critical of Maliavin's work:

> These two hundred bold, burly transcriptions of peasants, priests, and dancers have undoubtedly been painted full... They have all the air of being tremendous *tours de force*, in which the four-inch brush has been wielded with all the gusto of undaunted improvisations. No one would attempt to deny the sheer virtuosity of such pieces as 'Country Ablutions' (23), 'Swinging Bells' (40), or of the life-sized 'Troika' (56), yet if they were four times smaller

> one might like them twice as much. That is to say, they somehow fail to justify their area by the inward complexity of their content.[17]

First of all, this review confirms that the painting *Troika* was exhibited in London;

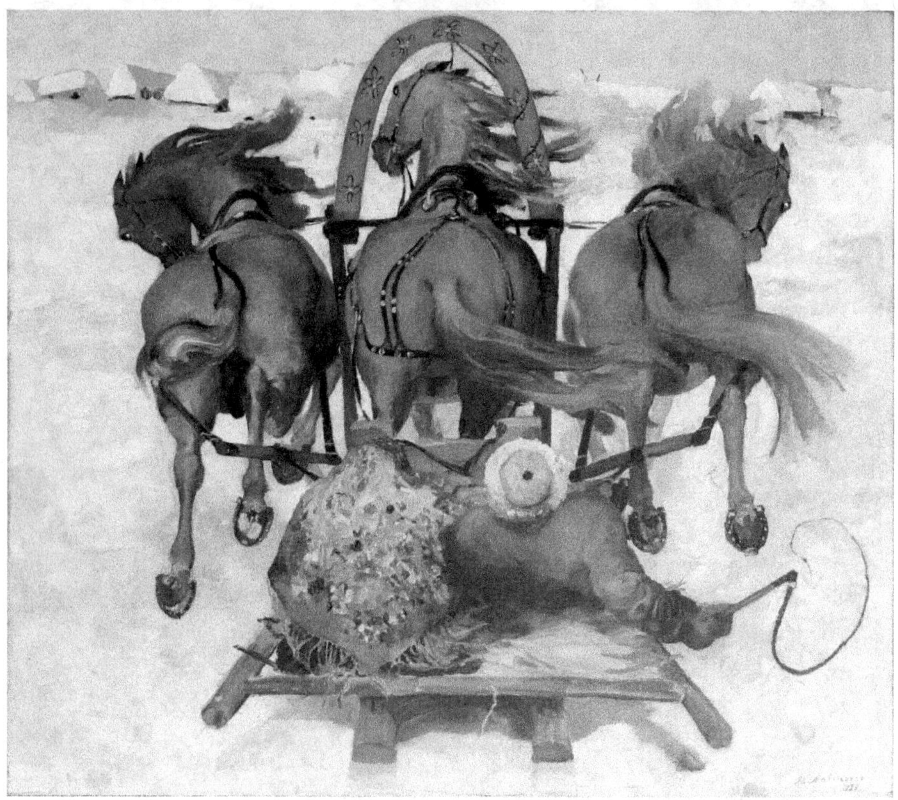

Fig. 17.2 Filipp Maliavin, *Troika* (1933). Oil on canvas, 201 x 224 cm, Private Collection. © Stockholms Auktionsverk.

Maliavin had executed this large-scale work two years earlier and subsequently showed it around Europe over the next few years, but it remained in his studio upon his death. The review's disapproval of the size of Maliavin's pictures, and *Troika* in particular, suggests a preference for restraint rather than drama, at least for one British reviewer. Overall, this analysis of Maliavin's work reflects strong admiration for the artist's technique and skill, with less regard for the paintings themselves.

17 'Phillipe Maliavine', *The Observer* (3 November 1935), p. 18.

To announce Maliavin's exhibition, *The Illustrated London News* published his *Portrait of Leon Trotskii.*

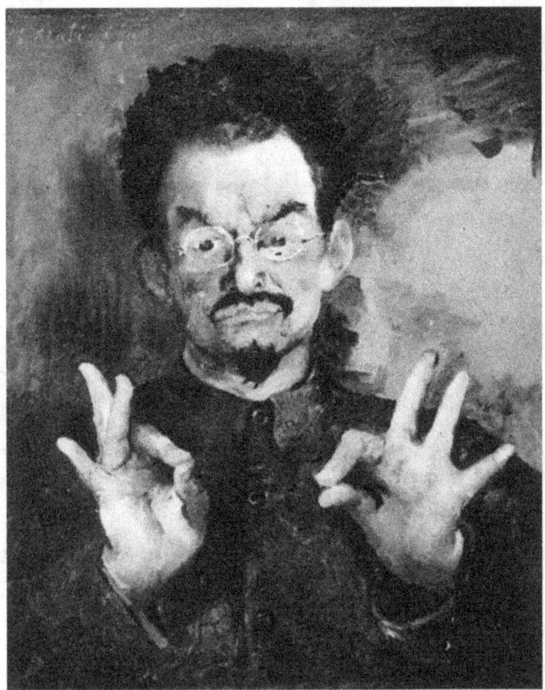

Fig. 17.3 Filipp Maliavin, *Portrait of Leon Trotskii.* Oil on canvas, whereabouts unknown © *Illustrated London News*, 26 October 1935. Ltd/Mary Evans.

Prior to leaving Soviet Russia, Maliavin had had a prestigious career under the Bolshevik government, and in 1920 was officially invited to the Kremlin to sketch portraits of members of the Soviet High Command, including Trotskii. He was allowed access to closed sessions and meetings and was one of the few artists permitted to draw Party Leader Vladimir Lenin from life. Maliavin drew Trotskii between 1920 and 1922, and several of these drawings survive, but there is no record of a finished portrait executed in Russia. Maliavin took many of his political drawings with him into emigration as life-drawn portraits of Soviet political figures would have been useful security if the artist were stopped by the authorities, and, additionally, they might have been marketable abroad. This published portrait, whose whereabouts are unknown, reveals that Maliavin finished a portrait of Trotskii. The artist may have taken the painting into emigration, and it was simply unrecorded; or, as is more likely, Maliavin may have painted it in emigration from the drawings in his possession. Regardless of when it was painted, however, this portrait has an even wider significance: with Stalin's rise to power, portraits of Trotskii were ordered to be destroyed from the late 1920s. Even this surviving black and white photograph of Maliavin's portrait is an important contribution to the body of images that remain.

In *The Illustrated London News*, the portrait was accompanied by a curious caption: 'The artist is royalist, rather than revolutionary, in his sympathies; indeed, when he has shown on the Continent, he has been frequently honoured by the patronage of the Greek royal family'.[18] A portrait of Trotskii might pique the interest of visitors to the exhibition through controversy, but by describing Maliavin as royalist, the caption purposively distanced the artist from any revolutionary or communist associations. Labelling him as loyal to the Greek royal family, however, was also not without controversy. In 1935, the Hellenic Republic was overthrown, and the royal family was reinstated to power by November, so when this caption appeared in October, the conflict between the republic and the royalists had come to a head. In reality Maliavin appeared largely apolitical, as the practical necessities of his career meant that his loyalties tended to shift towards those in power. Finding work abroad was difficult, and Maliavin depended financially on painting portraits, no matter whom they depicted.

In 1935, the British reception of a portrait of Trotskii would have been mixed. His obituary in *The Times* in 1940 stated: 'The murder of Leon Trotsky [...] will draw few tears from the vast majority of mankind'.[19] On the other hand, one might expect that this portrait would have drawn the attention of the British Left, with which Trotskii was largely popular. The fact that this portrait was overlooked in leftist circles is surprising, especially given the Left's interest in contemporary Soviet art at the time.[20] Maliavin, however, was part of a generation of Russian émigrés who fled the changes brought by the Revolution and was viewed as a Russian, not Soviet, painter. Maliavin's placement within the framework of an earlier realist tradition also most likely made him appear outdated and far from the contemporary socialist realism discussed by writers of the British Left such as Francis Klingender in the mid-1930s.

---

18 'Concerning Art Exhibitions: Notable Pictures in London Galleries', *Illustrated London News* (26 October 1935), p. 698.

19 'Trotsky', *The Times*, 23 August 1940, p. 5.

20 See, for example, the essays collected in Betty Rea (ed.), *5 on Revolutionary Art* (London, 1935).

On the whole, Maliavin's solo exhibition in London earned him positive attention from the press and individual recognition in Britain. His technique and skill were stressed above all but were done so in a way that tied the artist to a late 19th century artistic context, as opposed to contemporary developments. In reviewing an exhibition titled 'Pictures and Drawings of Russian Life', the critics markedly omitted any discussion of Maliavin's depiction of Russian life, or, indeed, Russia itself. His work may have been 'racy of the soil' and tied to Russia through its subject matter, but Maliavin was incorporated into a wider discourse on art in Britain.

18. Mrs Churchill Goes to Russia: The Wartime Gift Exchange between Britain and the Soviet Union

Claire Knight

During the years of the Anglo-Soviet Alliance (1941-45), Britain brimmed with an unprecedented enthusiasm for all things Russian. This short-lived approbation was expressed both formally—through government aid and overwhelmingly positive media coverage—and also more personally, through the gifts offered by Britons to their Soviet allies. This chapter investigates the financial gifts proffered by the British public to the USSR and the Soviet response, in order to tease out the complex political tensions that underlay the wartime gift exchange between allies.

In broad terms, scholars have interpreted gift exchange according to two paradigms. First, dating from anthropologist Marcel Mauss,[1] gift exchange has been examined as a way of establishing and reiterating social solidarity within and among different social groups. In this approach, the significance of the gift lies in its symbolic, rather than utilitarian, value. More recently, sociologists such as Jean Baudrillard[2] have analysed gift-giving instead as a form of challenge—the challenge to reciprocate. In this conceptualization, gift-giving reveals an inequality between the actors in

I would like to thank the Social Sciences and Humanities Research Council of Canada for funding this research. I am also grateful to Steve and Tracey Knowles for granting me access to the privately held papers of Grace Hamblin; the staff of the Churchill Archives Centre; and Dr Graham Knight and Robert McGee for their insightful critiques of this contribution.

1 Marcel Mauss, *The Gift: Forms and Functions of Exchange in Archaic Societies* (New York, 1967).

2 Jean Baudrillard, *Symbolic Exchange and Death*, trans. Iain Hamilton Grant (London, 1993).

the exchange: the donors exercise their material power and demonstrate their social status through their ability to sacrifice something to the benefit of the recipient, who is then indebted to the donors. I will demonstrate here how both aspects of gift-giving—solidarity and challenge—were present in the wartime gift exchange between Britain and the Soviet Union.

The Gift of Life: Mrs. Churchill's Red Cross Aid to Russia Fund

From the very outbreak of war on the Eastern Front, Britain expressed unswerving support for the USSR, with the popular press breaking news of the German invasion with headlines declaring that 'We pledge all our aid to Russia', and 'All aid for the Soviet'.[3] The press gleaned these phrases from Prime Minister Winston Churchill himself in his 22 June 1941 radio broadcast announcing the entry of the USSR into the conflict. The commitment to aid Russia was swiftly taken up by the public—as evidenced by the hundreds of letters received daily by the Soviet Embassy in London—who supplemented expressions of solidarity with financial donations to support the Soviet war effort.[4] As Churchill's daughter later recalled, '[s] pontaneously a warm wave of sympathy swept through Great Britain, as people learned with mounting horror of the sufferings of the Russian civilian population'.[5] By the end of September, the press had identified the workers of British tank factories as an object of envy throughout Britain due to their ability to support the Russian cause directly by manufacturing war *matériel* earmarked for the Red Army.[6] Other would-be contributors remained frustrated by the lack of any organised channel through which to aid the Soviet Ally.

It was into this vacuum on 7 October 1941 that Clementine Churchill launched a campaign under the auspices of the Executive Committee of the War Organisation of the Red Cross and St John, to raise funds for the supply of medical aid and clothing to the USSR. The response to Mrs Churchill's

---

3 *Daily Mirror* (23 June 1941), p. 1; *Daily Express* (23 June 1941), p. 1.

4 Mary Soames, *Clementine Churchill* (London, 1979), p. 303. The Mineworker's Federation, for instance, conveyed a cheque for £60,000 to the Soviet Ambassador, an amount equivalent to approximately £2.3 million in 2010, according to the historical currency calculator Measuring Worth, available at http://www.measuringworth.com/ukcompare/result.php [accessed 25.11. 2011].

5 Soames, p. 303.

6 *News of the World* (21 September 1941), p. 4.

Red Cross Aid to Russia Fund was immediate and enthusiastic to the extent that £370,000 was raised within its first twelve days in operation. The initial goal of £1 million was attained several weeks later, by early December 1941.[7] The donations poured in from every corner of the British Empire—Asia, North America, the Middle East, Africa, and the Caribbean[8]—and from every level of British society, 'from the King and Queen [who donated £1,000 in the first days of the Fund] to the humblest wage-earner and cottage-dweller'[9] who committed to the penny-a-week subscription. Supplementing the occasional spectacular donation, such as Lord Nuffield's £50,000 cheque, were the offerings of thousands of community groups and organisations that undertook a diversity of fundraising efforts. Cities and towns held Flag Days and festivals; schools hosted pageants; guides sold cookies, schoolboys did chores; women's groups baked, knitting groups knitted; grocers set up General Timoshenko stalls, Harrods' hosted special Aid to Russia displays; sporting tournaments, including the 1942 and 1943 Wembley Internationals, donated their proceeds; factory workers took up collections, as did hospital matrons, ministers, newspaper companies, publicans, cinemas, and soldiers; musical groups, including acclaimed pianist Benno Moisewitsch, performed recitals—all for the Aid to Russia Fund.[10]

By the end of the war, the people of the British Empire had donated more than £7 million to the cause,[11] with the accounts finally balancing at more than £7.5 million by the time the Red Cross stopped accepting donations for the appeal in January 1948.[12] As of January 1945, £4 million worth of goods had been successfully shipped to the USSR. These deliveries amounted to 11,600 tons of medical aid and clothing, with 2,000 tons of powdered medicines such as phenacetic and the 'revolutionary' new antiseptics M. and B. 693; 22,000 units of medical equipment, including 600 autoclaves for sterilising surgical equipment, 600 x-ray installations, and

---

7 *The Papers of Clementine Ogilvy Spencer-Churchill* (held at the Churchill Archives Centre: Cambridge, UK), CSCT 3/37, hereafter referenced using code only; Winston Churchill, *The Second World War, III: The Grand Alliance* (London, 1950), p. 422, hereafter referenced as Churchill, III.

8 CSCT 5/11.

9 Churchill, III, p. 422.

10 CSCT 5/11, 5/4, 5/5.

11 *The Papers of Sir Winston Churchill* (held at the Churchill Archives Centre: Cambridge, UK), CHAR 20/204A/68, hereafter referenced using code only. This £7 million would be equivalent to approximately £234 million in 2010.

12 CSCT 3/37/56.

approximately 15,000 sterilisers; over one million 'rubber goods'; countless blood-transfusion sets, emergency operating outfits, and surgical needles, several types of which were made to order, having no counterparts in Britain; and enough specialised machinery to outfit two factories for the manufacture of artificial limbs.[13] Shipments continued sporadically until late 1950.[14]

Offered as it was at considerable cost to a nation labouring under severe economic and material strain, this gift of medical aid—a veritable Gift of Life—was meaningful. It was also, according to Georg Simmel's definition, an initiatory gift: the gift that commences a gift-giving cycle, and one that is primarily identified by the spontaneity and freedom of its offering. It is apparently unwarranted, lacking explicit expression of its causality and the response it intends to elicit.[15] Letters accompanying donations to the Aid to Russia Fund frame the monetary gifts in precisely this way by refusing to provide explanations for their financial offerings. Instead, donors to the Fund implicitly identify their gifts as natural and instinctive, or to use Simmel's terms, spontaneous and free. Agnes Maiskaia, wife of the Soviet Ambassador in London Ivan Maiskii and co-worker with Clementine during the first two years of the Fund, also observed this element of spontaneity in the donations:

> When Nazi Germany treacherously attacked the Soviet Union a wave of sympathy for our country swept through Great Britain. Hundreds of letters were sent to Soviet organisations and numerous monetary contributions from individuals and organisations were made to relieve the suffering of war victims and the wounded.[16]

The gifts were also made without any apparent expectations for reciprocity. Of the several hundred donation letters that have been preserved, only three request some form of recognition: an autograph for a pensioner, a note of receipt for an event organiser, and an invitation to tea from a diplomat's wife. These requests were made of Clementine Churchill or the Aid to Russia administrative staff; none was made of Russia.[17]

Likewise, the medical supplies purchased with the monetary donations were provided freely, without accompanying demands or requests from the

13 Soames, p. 328; Churchill, III, p. 421; CSCT 3/48.
14 CSCT 3/37/56, 58.
15 Richard Titmuss, *The Gift Relationship: From Human Blood to Social Policy* (London, 1997), pp. 125-6.
16 CSCT 3/48.
17 CSCT 5/11.

Fund or the British government. At no point did Churchill attempt to use his wife's Fund as political leverage in his dealings with Stalin. Even at points when British-Soviet relations were fraying, Churchill's personal papers reveal that he sought to ensure that deliveries were made expeditiously, handling the Fund as 'a love offering' from the British people, rather than a political tool.[18] In this respect, British gift-giving may represent an attempt to overcome political self-interest, undertaking an act of self-motivated altruism. The question remains, however, as to whether others viewed it in this way as well.

The true test of this conceptualization of the Fund and its Gift of Life as an initiatory gift lies with the Soviet response. This is because an initiatory gift, though it may be offered freely, nevertheless carries a social obligation to respond. An initiatory gift must be followed by a *counter-gift* or repayment, a 'thank-you',[19] in order to rebalance relations of status and authority. Reciprocity restores equilibrium in a relationship so that both parties can continue to respect one another without a sense of indebtedness. In the case of the British Gift of Life, the Soviet 'thank you' took the form of an official invitation for Clementine Churchill to tour the USSR and view first hand what her Fund had effected across the Union.[20]

The Counter-Gift: Mrs. Churchill's Visit to Russia

Just as the initiatory Gift of Life was offered from Britain on two levels—popular offerings co-ordinated into medical aid that was delivered at the behest of the state—so too was the Soviet counter-gift, Mrs Churchill's 'Visit to Russia'. The tour served as not only the official 'thank you' from the Soviet leadership, but also as the medium through which the Soviet populace were able to demonstrate their appreciation to Mrs Churchill and through her, the British people. From the moment of her arrival at the Moscow airfield, Clementine Churchill and her two companions, Secretary of the Aid to Russia Committee Mabel Johnson and personal secretary Grace Hamblin, were overwhelmed with gifts. The first of these took the form of a 'huge bouquet of red and white roses and other flowers cut in

18 Winston Churchill, *The Second World War*, IV: *The Hinge of Fate* (London, 1951), p. 854; CHAR 20/214/91.

19 Titmuss, pp. 125-6.

20 Clementine Churchill, *My Visit to Russia* (London, 1945), p. 15.

Moscow hot houses only [that] morning',[21] from Polina Zhemchuzhina, wife of Commissar for Foreign Affairs Viacheslav Molotov. These posies were the harbinger of innumerable bouquets that were showered upon Clementine, as well as countless non-floral tributes from no doubt select representatives of the Soviet people (particularly medical staff, soldiers, and children). The gifts were so numerous that, as Grace Hamblin wrote to her family, 'at one time we wondered if the 'plane would carry them' back to Britain.[22] In this way, just as hundreds of thousands of individual donations were implicated in the British gift of the Fund, so too was the Soviet counter-gift—the 'Visit to Russia'—comprised of hundreds of gifts.

Many of the gifts followed the Soviet pattern of gifts presented to the Leader—a practice analysed at length by anthropologist Nikolai Ssorin-Chaikov. According to the findings of Ssorin-Chaikov and Olga Sosnina, the value of the 'gift-things' presented to the Soviet leader lay not in their luxuriousness, but in their uniqueness. Apropos Baudrillard, uniqueness defines the object as being beyond exchange-value. As such, it is quite literally priceless and thus implies a symbolic exchange. Gifts to the Leader were to be original and usually handmade objects, suitably reflective of whatever group within the USSR the giver(s) represented.[23] Ideally, gifts would also incorporate a portrait of the leader, thus linking the individual who made the object to the recipient and leader. For instance, portraits of Lenin were made from human hair by a barber, tobacco leaves by tobacco farmers, and stamps by postal workers; a life-sized chocolate bust of Stalin was made by the workers of a confectionery factory, while numerous ceramics factories vied to produce the largest, most intricate vase featuring Stalin.[24] The gifts functioned as a response to a perceived initiatory gift from the leader, usually identified as the Gift of Socialism or subsequent benefit (for example, 'A Happy Childhood'). It was through these counter-gifts that the impersonal, yet life-changing gift of the leader was identified. The leader himself did not enter in on the exchange.[25]

---

21 CHAR 20/204A/61 press release from Duncan Hooper, Moscow.

22 Grace Hamblin, 'Russian Diary 1945', *The Papers of Grace Hamblin, O.B.E.* (held privately), 11 May 1945.

23 Nikolai Ssorin-Chaikov and Olga Sosnina, *Dary vozhdiam/Gifts to Soviet leaders. Exhibition Catalogue* (Moscow, 2006), p. 28.

24 Nikolai Ssorin-Chaikov, 'On Heterochrony: Birthday Gifts to Stalin, 1949', *Journal of the Royal Anthropological Institute,* XII (2006), p. 358.

25 Ssorin-Chaikov and Sosnina, p. 19.

Clementine received many offerings that followed this pattern and even paralleled gifts proffered to Lenin and Stalin.[26] One of the most noteworthy of these was a handmade commemorative album presented by the young members of the Leningrad Pioneer Palace. Not only did it capture the 'type' of the leader-gift—being a unique, carefully wrought album of original artwork depicting Leningrad, the Young Pioneers, and Clementine herself—but it also skillfully implied an initiatory Gift of Life by dedicating images of happy children and recuperating soldiers to 'The Great English People'.[27] In this way, gifts from the Soviet people responded to Britain as Leader. As can be anticipated, gifts from the Soviet leadership did not conform to this pattern, but instead followed newly emerging traditions of diplomatic gift exchange.

Mrs Churchill arrived in the USSR at the precise moment when in terms of diplomatic gift exchange, the ''simplicity and modesty' of the 1920s and the 1930s gave way to a distinctly Soviet style of luxury'.[28] The 'key gift' in this case was the tour itself, with its extensive logistical requirements and demands upon hospitality including several grandly furnished train cars equipped with serving-staff; sumptuous dining and accommodation; guides, translators and a protective Red Army detachment; and endless entertainments including opera, ballet, theatre, cinema, and at least one evening of traditional song and dance, all with backstage visits and introductions to the 'leading artistes'.[29] In addition to several visits to Leningrad and Moscow, Mrs Churchill and her companions toured Kislovodsk, Essentuki, Piatigorsk, Rostov-on-Don, Crimea, Sevastopol, Yalta, Simferopol, Odessa, and Kursk. Save for the last-minute jaunt to Kursk, the tour was planned and executed entirely by the upper echelons of the state apparatus several months in advance of their arrival.[30]

Accompanying the key gift were countless incidental generosities, including several exemplary diplomatic gifts of the 'luxurious' kind: an Imperial Russian painting, a diamond ring, and several awards including the Order of the Red Banner of Labour granted to Clementine Churchill by Decree of the Presidium of the Supreme Soviet of the USSR.[31] The

26 CSCT 3/48/48, 3/48/2, 1/29/51, 3/51.

27 CSCT 3/53.

28 Ssorin-Chaikov and Sosnina, p. 29.

29 CSCT 1/29; Hamblin. 'The food is absolutely delicious', wrote Grace Hamblin of the up to twelve-course lunches on offer every other day, 'but our hosts are so kind that it is far too abundant'.

30 CHAR 20/204A/43-44.

31 Ssorin-Chaikov and Sosnina, p. 28.

sumptuousness of these gifts also indicated the capacity of the giver to give. It demonstrated that the USSR was fully capable of providing luxurious goods and experiences, which helped reaffirm an equivalence between donor and recipient. Given that British gifts were largely utilitarian (material aid), the symbolic nature of Soviet reciprocity is particularly significant—it gave of its culture rather than its financial or industrial output.

Perhaps most significant, however, was the gift that Soviet officials repeatedly charged Clementine to pass on to her husband and all Britain: Soviet friendship. This commission was ubiquitous, reaching epic proportions at the hands of one unnamed Soviet official who tendered through Mrs Churchill an invitation to every single contributor to the Aid to Russia Fund to visit the USSR and be thanked 'personally, individually'. When reminded that, including the penny-a-week subscriptions, there were over seven million donors, he replied, 'I still say [...] we should be glad to meet them all'.[32]

The excess and abundance saturating Soviet hospitality towards Mrs Churchill, and through her to the British people, demands interpretation. Is this simply another instance of the Soviet leadership striving to 'over-fulfill' and overtake the West? It was certainly in keeping with the Soviet use of diplomatic gift-giving in the post-war period to cultivate indebtedness and establish dominant-subordinate relations within its sphere of influence.[33] In fact, following the war, the Soviet state assigned a financial value to every conceivable diplomatic gift, creating a virtual checklist to guarantee the Soviet Union remained in a dominant position within the gift exchange.[34] Could it be, therefore, that the excessive generosity shown to Clementine as a representative of Britain was an attempt by a losing participant to improve its position in the hidden power struggle of gift exchange? As before, to address this question the response of the other party—this time Britain or more specifically Clementine Churchill—must be examined.

British Indebtedness and the Gift of Death

Far from perceiving Soviet excessive hospitality as an attempt to provide Britain with a counter-gift worthy of the Gift of Life, Mrs Churchill felt

32 CSCT 3/48/2.

33 During the Cold War era, Soviet-leaning developing countries were frequently referred to as 'client states'. John P. Willerton, *Patronage and Politics in the USSR* (Cambridge, 1992).

34 Ssorin-Chaikov and Sosnina, p. 29.

deeply indebted to her Soviet hosts and the Soviet people in general for the generosity she experienced. Three specific episodes serve to illustrate her overwhelming sense of appreciation and her determination to reciprocate, commencing with a telegram exchange with her husband. On 5 May 1945, with one week remaining in her twice-extended tour, Clementine received a telegram from Winston begging her to return to London no later than 8 May. He wrote of the mounting international tensions and 'poisonous politics', even authorising the British Ambassador in Moscow to show his wife the relevant secret correspondence to convince her of the severity of the situation. The Prime Minister also shared his need for her support as he struggled with worries over the serious illness of his brother Jack, and his own feelings of depression.[35] Clementine refused him with regret, holding firmly to her decision to lengthen her stay and remain in Moscow until after Victory Day. In her two messages on this theme, Clementine expressed not only a concern for propriety—how could she abandon her hosts when detailed plans were already in place? —but also a conviction that she and Britain owed this much at least to the Soviets.[36]

Upon her return to Britain, Mrs Churchill's sense of indebtedness to her Soviet hosts prompted her to commission a Russian translation of her fundraising booklet, *My Visit to Russia* (*Moia poezdka v SSSR*). Penned immediately upon her return to Britain[37] and published by Hutchinson & Co. Ltd. of London within the month, the English version of the booklet was distributed throughout Britain, North America and Australia at a price of one shilling. It was printed using cheap materials: rough heavy newsprint paper with a construction paper cover glued to a hastily sewn spine. These were the days of paper rationing, after all. In contrast, the Russian edition was printed on high quality photographic paper with a gold-embossed leather-bound hard cover and neatly sewn binding. It also included a dedication page in which Mrs Churchill wrote of her desire that her Soviet friends know of her appreciation and her hope that they would

35 CHAR 20/204B/104.

36 CSCT 1/29/63; CHAR 20/204B/103, 121, 133.

37 The booklet, a fairly detailed account of her time in Russia threaded with observations as to the nature of Russia and the Russian people, was based largely on Clementine Churchill's own telegrams to her husband throughout the journey, as well as letters home written by her personal secretary, Grace Hamblin. CSCT 3/48.

see fit to accept the gift of her small volume of reminiscences about what was for her such a significant experience.[38]

Further indicating a sense of gratitude to the Soviets, Mrs Churchill continued her Aid for Russia campaigning long after the Fund itself had ceased, and even after Winston delivered his famed 'Sinews of Peace' speech in March 1946 (better known as the 'Iron Curtain' speech), describing the deepening rift between the Soviet Union and its former Allies. She also toiled over the construction of a hefty volume entitled *From Great Britain to Russia* which combined well over a hundred typescript copies of Aid to Russia donation letters, each with a Russian translation on the facing page.[39]

Nor was Clementine the only Briton to carry a burden of gratitude to the Soviets,[40] for a similar air of indebtedness pervades the letters of donors to the Fund. This impression of gratitude is revealed in the adjectives used to describe the Russian people and the Red Army in the letters—'valiant', 'heroic', 'brave', 'amazing', 'patriotic', 'deserving'—phrases that were echoed throughout the wartime popular press and the speeches and writings of the Prime Minister.[41] In fact, the Fund itself was based on a conviction held by members of the British leadership as to the nation's indebtedness to the Soviet Union and a need to reciprocate immediately and tangibly.[42] As Winston Churchill explained after the war:

> My wife felt very deeply that our inability to give Russia any military help disturbed and distressed the nation increasingly as the months went by and the German armies surged across the steppes. I told her that a Second Front was out of the question and that all that could be done for a long time would be the sending of supplies of all kinds on a large scale. Mr. Eden and

38 Klementina Churchill, *Moia poezdka v SSSR* (London, 1945), dedication page. Two copies of this publication are held in CSCT 3/50. Published by Williams, Lea & Co., there is unfortunately no information available as to distribution or indeed the size of the publishing run.

39 CSCT 5/6/86-96. *From Great Britain to Russia* (CSCT 5/11) appears unfinished, and presumably was never presented to its intended audience.

40 Nor was Clementine simply blinded by the 'wonderful welcome' or 'the gilded hospitality' of the Soviets (Soames, p. 375). Far from it, as can be seen by her correspondence with Eleanor Rathbone (CSCT 3/37) and Kathleen Harriman (CSCT 3/43 & 46).

41 CSCT 5/11; CHAR 20/214/91.

42 The need to appease increasingly strident demands from aspects of British society (including, but by no means limited to the British Communist Party) and from the Soviet state for the opening of a second front also factored into government support for Aid to Russia campaigning (Soames, p. 304).

> I encouraged her to explore the possibility of obtaining funds by voluntary subscription for medical aid.[43]

For her part, Clementine later described the Fund as having 'provided an outlet for the feelings of sympathy and admiration, respect and gratitude which swept over our People as the noble struggle of the Russians to defend their Country grew through bitterness and agony to strength and power'.[44]

In other words, far from being the initiatory gift, the British Gift of Life was itself a response to the Soviet gift of heroism, sacrifice, and suffering. In short, the British Gift of Life was a counter-gift to the Soviet Gift of Death. As in the typical Soviet gift-to-the-leader exchange, it was the British counter-gift that identified the Gift of Death and not the Soviets, thus rendering the Soviet Union as the Leader in the gift cycle. The response of the Soviet leadership to the British counter-gift supports this interpretation. As noted by Ssorin-Chaikov, the leader generally does not acknowledge a gift from the people. If he must acknowledge the existence of the gift, he does so in such a way as to deny its function as the fulfillment of the social obligation to respond to the leader's gift. This could be done either by pointing out the insufficiency of the gift or by ignoring the *time-gap* and reacting to the gift in an untimely manner: either too quickly, implying ingratitude and the desire to be rid of the obligation to reciprocate; or too late, implying that the gift is unworthy of a timely response. Stalin was a master in maintaining the burden of indebtedness to himself as leader in his relationship with the Soviet people. A prime example involves the vast display of gifts put together for his 70th birthday by the staffs of several museums, officials from multiple ministries, and thousands of gift-makers. Although it remained in place until his death, Stalin never visited the exhibition, refusing to acknowledge the gifts.[45]

Stalin likewise denied the British people a satisfactory reception of their offering, acknowledging it neither in public—he had no involvement in Mrs Churchill's tour—nor in private. Early in their visit, Clementine and Mabel Johnson were granted an audience with Stalin during which Clementine offered the General Secretary a gold fountain pen from her husband along with his hopes that Stalin would 'write him many friendly messages with it'. Her published account concludes the incident with the assertion that

---

43 Churchill, III, p. 421.

44 CSCT 5/6/87.

45 Ssorin-Chaikov, pp. 362, 364.

'the Marshal accepted it with a genial smile';[46] however, she later confirmed to her daughter that 'although he took the pen with a genial smile, he put it on one side saying, '"But I only write with a pencil." He also added: "I will repay him".'[47] Forced to acknowledge the gift, Stalin immediately pointed out that it was an inappropriate gift, then transgressed the time-gap by declaring far too quickly that he would reciprocate to Churchill.

Similarly, beneath the overtures of appreciation and friendship that made up the rhetorical bulk of the Soviet leadership's public response to the British Gift of Life, lay undercurrents of criticism that served to deny the fulfillment of Britain's counter-gift compulsion. For instance, as they arranged for the procurement and delivery of supplies to the USSR, Agnes Maiskaia subjected Clementine to 'long lists of imperious demands or complaints'.[48] Meanwhile, the speeches delivered during the meeting of the Presidium of the Executive Committee of the Union of the Red Cross and Red Crescent Societies of the USSR (convened to thank Mrs Churchill and present her with the Gold Badge for Distinguished Medical Service), contained countless references to the shortcomings of the Fund. For example, Professor Sarkisov (Mme Maiskaia's replacement after September 1943) noted that at various points the delivery of the supplies had been 'unsatisfactory', while production rates at a British syringe factory were too low. Another speaker pointed out that although Clementine managed to locate 20kg of a scarce drug, this was only a fraction of the required amount (100kg). Yet another speaker mentioned that of four lists of supplies agreed upon during the war, only two had been fulfilled, and only just 'adequately'.[49] In this way, Soviet officials played the role of the Leader in the gift exchange with aplomb, refusing to fully accept the British counter-gift to its Gift of Death. What they refused was acknowledgement of equivalence: no end of material supplies could compensate for the loss of human life experienced by the Soviet Union.

Soviet Anxieties and the Gift of a Partisan Death

Nevertheless, the Soviet leadership harboured a persistent anxiety that Britain might not honour their Gift of Death appropriately, but might

46 Clementine Churchill, p. 17.
47 Soames, p. 369.
48 *Ibid.*, p. 326.
49 CSCT 3/48.

instead overlook its gift-ness and thereby shake free of the obligation to reciprocate. While glimpses of this anxiety are visible through numerous small details of the tour arranged for Mrs Churchill, it is most clearly revealed in the final gift presented to Clementine by VOKS (*Vsesoiuznoe obshchestvo kul'turnykh sviazei s zagranitsei* or the Society for Cultural Relations with Foreign Countries). Conferred by section head Lidiia Kislova at a formal VOKS luncheon in honour of Clementine, the gift comprised a specially-made folder containing a short biography and series of mounted photographs of Soviet partisan Zoia Kosmodem'ianskaia. Although Kislova had accompanied Mrs Churchill throughout her five-and-a-half week tour in her role as VOKS representative,[50] this was not a personal gift but rather a gift from the Soviet leadership through a loyal representative on Victory Day.[51]

It was also a gift of death. Apart from the portrait of Zoia, the eleven 5x7 photographs within the folder centered graphically on death: the empty gallows, Zoia being paraded to the gallows, her hanging body, her frozen corpse, her gravesites (she was exhumed and moved to Moscow), her posthumous award of the Hero of the Soviet Union bestowed for heroism in death. The booklet, apparently written by Zoia's mother, is the biography of a martyr: a life story defined by its ending. In the final lines, Zoia's mother quotes her daughter and defines her through her death: '"Don't see me off with tears! I'll either come back a heroine or die a heroine". And she did die the death of a heroine'.[52] As such a visceral ode to the death of a partisan-martyr, this gift was a transgression of the central tenet of the People to Leader exchange, for it spoke of the Soviet Gift of Death. It made tangible and gift-able what was supposed to be acknowledged solely through the counter-gifts of the People, not declared explicitly by the Leader. No secure Leader would need to remind the People of his gift to them, let alone hand it to them in a tidy folder.

This gift is finally, then, rendered the embodiment of Soviet anxieties with the power struggle of gift-giving in general. Even when Britain fell

---

50 Although ostensibly a public society, VOKS functioned as a branch of the state, co-ordinating with and hosting Friendship Societies from around the world (Louis Nemzer, 'The Soviet Friendship Societies', *The Public Opinion Quarterly*, XIII, no. 2 [1949], p. 271).

51 Vladimir Tolts, 'Istoriia i sovremennost': Tri dnevnika. Po marshrutu Steinbeka polveka spustia,' *Radio Svoboda*, 2004, http://www.svoboda.org/programs/cicles/Stainbeck/st_13.asp [accessed 21.6.2012] (para. 46).

52 CSCT 3/52.

in so readily with Soviet-style 'People to Leader' gift-giving conventions, responding to the Soviet Union as Leader, the Soviet leadership consciously or unconsciously presumed that Britain would fail to recognise their gift properly. To this end, they created new diplomatic gift-giving traditions and strayed from the appropriate behavior of a gift-giving Leader in the attempt to make certain that Britain did not overlook the Gift of Death. Ironically, it was these very measures that revealed the weaknesses of the Soviet position in the gift exchange and ultimately ensured that the Soviet Union would lose this power struggle.

The wartime gift exchange between Britain and the Soviet Union was initiated not by the British gift of life, but by the Soviet gift of death. While this initiatory gift was conceptual and symbolic, mirroring the initiatory gift of the Leader in Soviet society, the British counter-gift was utilitarian with a clear market value (£7.5 million). This counter-gift shifted the gift-giving cycle toward commodity exchange rather than symbolic exchange. It is also this aid gift that highlights most clearly Baudrillard's notion of the gift as a challenge: the more utilitarian the gift, the greater the sense of challenge because the gift implies that the recipient is unable to provide for themselves and is thus dependent or subordinate. In the Soviet case, the tension between the challenging nature and necessity of the British aid gift elicited an ambivalent response, mixing elements of criticism and complaint (the amounts are insufficient, delivery is untimely, Stalin uses pencils not pens) with a counter-counter gift that was lavish. What is more, this responsive gift was thoroughly non-utilitarian and was instead an elaborately crafted and luxurious experience, thus returning the gift-giving cycle to the symbolic. The Soviet experiential gift was also ephemeral because it was consumed at the moment of its production and contained no lasting presence beyond subjective memory. It could only ever be remembered by its recipients and was never a reminder in and of itself. Yet as such it could provide fuller closure to the giving cycle than could physical gifts.

In the case of these wartime Allies, gift-giving was not simply an added dimension to foreign relations, but a bridge between the realms of public sentiment and diplomatic power relations. This is because national gift-giving takes place on two levels, both privately—through the individuals who commission, craft and present the gifts—and publicly, with these individuals serving as nations during the moment of exchange. As a result of this duality, national gift exchange must balance the private political knowledge of the leadership with public opinion, weighing both when acknowledging and reciprocating the gifts. Because it takes in both the specialized diplomatic sphere and the sphere of public or mass sentiment, the power relations acted out through gift exchange do not correlate precisely with the power struggles of foreign relations. Gift-giving between actors whose political relationship is one of tension or conflict is a way of reaffirming that the underlying relationship is sound and mutually respectful, and that the tension or conflict is contingent and transitory. For this reason, the implications of the study of gift-giving in international relations are immense. Through gift exchange, we may observe both political strengths and weaknesses influencing—yet not clearly evident in—political analysis.

19. 'Unity in difference': The Representation of Life in the Soviet Union through Isotype

Emma Minns

Between 1945 and 1947 a series comprising three slim volumes, *The Soviets and Ourselves*, was published with the aim 'to promote understanding and prevent misunderstanding […] to understand is to recognize unity in difference'.[1] The first book, *Landsmen and Seafarers*, aimed to present the diverse climate, geography and natural resources of the Soviet Union and compare them to those of the British Commonwealth; the second, *Two Commonwealths*, discussed the political evolution of the USSR and the function of contemporary institutions; the final volume, *How do you do, Tovarish?* claimed to provide an accurate impression of the everyday life of ordinary Soviet men and women.[2] The series was by no means unique

1 John Macmurray, 'Preface', in Maurice Lovell, *Landsmen and Seafarers* (London, 1945), p. 5. Macmurray (1891-1976) was Grote Professor of Mind and Logic at University College London and then Chair of Moral Philosophy at the University of Edinburgh during the preparation and publication of *The Soviets* series. He was also the author of *The Philosophy of Communism* (London, 1933). The title *Landsmen and Seafarers* derives from a speech made by Winston Churchill to the House of Commons, 8 September 1942, in which he said: 'It is difficult to make the Russians comprehend all the problems of the sea and of the ocean. We are sea animals […]. The Russians are land animals.'

2 *Two Commonwealths* (London, 1945) was written by the historian Christopher Hill (1912-2003) under the pseudonym K.E. Holme. During the Second World War, Hill was a major in the Intelligence Corps, seconded to the Russian desk of the Foreign Office. R.C.S. Trahair, *Encyclopedia of Cold War Espionage, Spies and Secret Operations* (Westport, 2004), pp. 116-8. Ralph Parker, a journalist and translator based in Moscow, authored the final volume *How do you do, Tovarish?* (London, 1947). This should have been published earlier than 1947, but Otto Neurath's unexpected death in December 1945 contributed to its delay.

in presenting the Soviet Union in a favourable light to a British audience; after the USSR joined the allied forces in the Second World War numerous pamphlets appeared designed to foster pro-Russian feeling in Britain.[3] However after victory in 1945, Anglo-Soviet relations became strained, and the creators of the series felt an even greater need to overcome the 'fear, suspicion, and distrust' that 'have darkened the atmosphere'.[4] *The Soviets and Ourselves* (hereafter referred to as *The Soviets*) is a fascinating British representation of the Soviet Union, due in part to a number of the personalities involved in its creation: Peter Smollett, John Macmurray, Christopher Hill, and Otto Neurath. This chapter focuses on the role played by Neurath in the evolution of the series and the contribution made by his picture language 'Isotype' to the visual element of the books.

Otto Neurath (1882-1945) was a polymath whose occupations and interests included philosophy, political economy, sociology, education, and visual communication.[5] His time as Director of the Gesellschafts- und Wirtschaftsmuseum in Vienna (1925-34) gave him the opportunity to develop an innovative visual method that could present complex statistical data in ways that would engage the man in the street. Neurath and his team of designers and technicians produced charts on subjects such as housing, employment, health and education in order to inform the Viennese public about improvements and changes in their standard of living, as well as the economic situation overseas. The charts used a system of pictorial statistics devised by Neurath that was known as the 'Vienna Method' and from which evolved Isotype (International System Of TYpographic Picture Education).[6] The Vienna Method, and later Isotype, used a 'dictionary' of pictograms to construct charts that transformed

---

3 For a discussion of Anglo-Soviet relations in this period see Claire Knight contribution in this volume.

4 Macmurray, 'Preface', *How do you do, Tovarish?*, p. 5.

5 There have been numerous studies of Neurath's life and the different areas of his work, particularly his membership of the 'Vienna Circle'. For an overview see Elisabeth M. Nemeth and Fredrich Stadler (eds.), *Encyclopedia and Utopia: the Life and Work of Otto Neurath, 1882-1945* (Dordrecht/Boston, 1996). On Neurath and Isotype see *Graphic Communication through ISO TYPE* (Reading, 1975); Marie Neurath and Robin Kinross, *The Transformer: Principles of Making Isotype Charts* (London, 2009); Christopher Burke, 'Isotype: Representing Social Facts Pictorially', *Information Design Journal*, XVII (2009), pp. 211-23. See also Neurath's autobiography: Otto Neurath, *From Hieroglyphics to Isotype: A Visual Autobiography*, Matthew Eve and Christopher Burke (eds.) (London, 2010).

6 The term Isotype was first used in 1935 and was inspired by C.K. Ogden's term BASIC (British American Scientific International Commercial) English. The change in name was also due to the fact that Neurath and members of his Museum staff had to flee Vienna in 1934 and re-establish themselves firstly in The Hague, and then finally in Oxford, where

technical information and statistical data into a visual form that could be understood by as wide an audience as possible. Neurath's ambition was for these symbols to create an international picture language. Writing in the *Listener* in 1933, he stated: 'Here is a new method capable not only of conveying social and other information to the masses, but also of serving as a new means of cultural interaction as a whole. The pictures used are composed of symbols intelligible in all countries alike'.[7] Neurath was given an unprecedented opportunity to test the intelligibility of the Vienna Method when he was invited to help establish an institute for pictorial statistics in Moscow in 1931. Indeed, *The Soviets* was not the first time Isotype had been used to present data on aspects of the Soviet Union to an English-speaking audience.

The All-Union Institute of Pictorial Statistics of Soviet Construction and Economy (*Vsesoiuznyi institut izobrazitel'noi statistiki sovetskogo stroitel'stva i khoziaistva*) or, as it was more commonly known, the Izostat Institute, or simply Izostat, existed for almost a decade; although, Neurath and his team only worked there until 1934, employed to train Russian Izostat staff in the conventions and application of the Vienna Method.[8] Throughout the 1931-4 period Izostat produced a wide variety of materials including charts, books, window displays, and even exhibitions for Soviet holidays and celebrations. The majority of these were concerned with displaying the claimed achievements of the First Five-Year Plan (1928-32) and predicting the successful fulfilment of the Second Five-Year Plan (1933-7).

Although the charts were designed with a Russian audience in mind, some publications were also produced in English language editions. The extent to which titles such as *The Struggle for Five Years in Four* and *The Second Five-Year Plan in Construction*[9] were of interest to readers in Britain (outside members of the Communist Party or Trade Union officials) is questionable, and it is difficult to ascertain the print run of these volumes and their availability overseas. However, Neurath's time in Moscow and the development of Soviet pictorial statistics did not go completely

Neurath established the Isotype Institute in 1942. The term 'Vienna Method' no longer seemed appropriate. See Neurath & Kinross, *The Transformer*, pp. 46-7.

7 Otto Neurath, 'Pictorial statistics—An International Problem', *Listener*, 27 September 1933, p. 471.

8 For an excellent introduction to Neurath, Izostat and the 1931-4 period, see Vladimir Krichevskii,'Izostatistika i "Izostat" / Pictorial Statistics and "Izostat"', *Proekt Rossiia / Project Russia*, I (1995), pp. 63-7.

9 *The Struggle for Five Years in Four* (Moscow, 1932); *The Second Five-Year Plan in Construction* (Moscow, 1934).

unnoticed outside of Russia: the American journal *Survey Graphic* featured a number of Izostat charts that had first appeared in the newspaper *Izvestiia.*[10] The work of Izostat also influenced an early manifestation of British war-time support for the Soviet Union—*U.S.S.R: The Strength of Our Ally.*[11] This booklet credited the Izostat Institute as one of its sources and like *The Soviets* featured a combination of both pictorial statistics and official photographs. A number of the pictograms in *U.S.S.R* seem to have been inspired by those featured in Izostat publications, but this work does not use Neurath's Isotype, and the construction of many of the charts is not in harmony with Isotype principles.

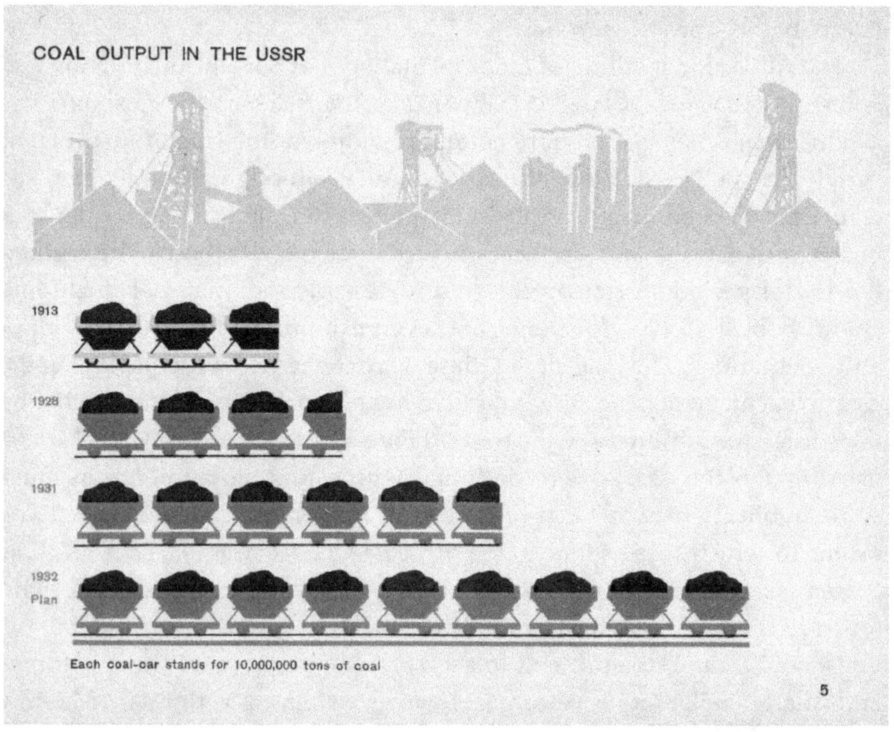

Fig. 19.1 'Coal output in the USSR', *The Struggle for Five Years in Four* (Moscow, 1932). Otto & Marie Neurath Isotype Collection, University of Reading.

The most notable English-language Izostat publication is an album produced for the 1939 New York World's Fair, the design of which was

10 'Otto Neurath visits Russia', *Survey Graphic,* XXI (1932), pp. 538-9.
11 *U.S.S.R: The Strength of Our Ally* (London, 1941).

overseen by the artist Lazar (El) Lissitskii (1890-1941).[12] *USSR: An Album Illustrating the State Organization and National Economy of the USSR*[13] could be seen as something of a precedent to *The Soviets* in its use of visual material; it intersperses Izostat charts with photographs of notable persons and events and woodcuts that present socialist realist scenes of Soviet life. Although *USSR* is never mentioned in any correspondence between Neurath and Peter Smollett, it is likely that as Director of the Russian Division of the Ministry of Information, Smollett would have, at the least, been aware of the work. Smollett had intended for woodcuts to appear in *The Soviets*, alongside photographs and Isotype charts, an idea Neurath rejected: 'I think the PHOTOGRAPH-ISOTYPE-TEXT combination has a great importance [...] I think in a "factual" argument, one should perhaps compare photograph with photograph or intentionally made simplified drawings with drawings' and Smollett conceded to Neurath's wish.[14] The use of only photographs and Isotype charts brings an air of authority and gravitas to the books, and gives the impression that these are objective works concerned with facts, rather than anecdotes or points of view. In each volume the series editor, Macmurray, emphasised to readers the importance of the photographs and the Isotype charts and was at pains to stress that 'they have been chosen and compiled with the intention, not so much to illustrate the text, as to supplement it'.[15] The photographs 'are studies in contrast and comparison, to be thought over as well as looked at'.[16] Many were supplied by the Society for Cultural Relations with the U.S.S.R, and certain photographs may seem familiar as they appeared in a number British publications from this time. For example, in *How do you do, Tovarish?* the Koshelev family is shown sitting down to dinner and according to the caption, 'they like a well-filled dish'—a wish that it is hard to believe was fulfilled in post-war Russia.[17] However this image of domestic harmony

12 Lissitzkii first met Neurath and encountered the Vienna Method at the 1928 'Pressa' exhibition in Cologne. The artist took a great interest in the work of Izostat and was in close contact with Neurath during his time in Moscow. See Sophie Lissitzky-Küppers, *El Lissitzky: Life, Letters, Texts* (London, 1980), p. 86.

13 Ivan Sautin and Ivan Ivanitskii (eds.), *USSR: An Album Illustrating the State Organization and National Economy of the USSR* (Moscow, 1939).

14 Letter from Neurath to Smollett, 19 January 1944 (Otto & Marie Neurath Isotype Collection, University of Reading, hereafter IC, 1/11). Smollett replied 'Having had time to reflect, I think you are right [...] with regard to the incompatibility of charts, photographs and woodcuts. We shall try as much as possible to conform to your wise recommendations' (Smollett to Neurath, 25 January 1944 (IC 1/11)).

15 Macmurray, 'Preface', *How do you do, Tovarish?*, p. 6.

16 Macmurray, 'Preface', *Landsmen and Seafarers*, p. 6.

17 'A Russian Family at Table', *How do you do, Tovarish?*, p. 22.

also made an appearance in 1945, in the *Legal Rights of the Soviet Family*, in which the meal is presented to readers as breakfast.[18]

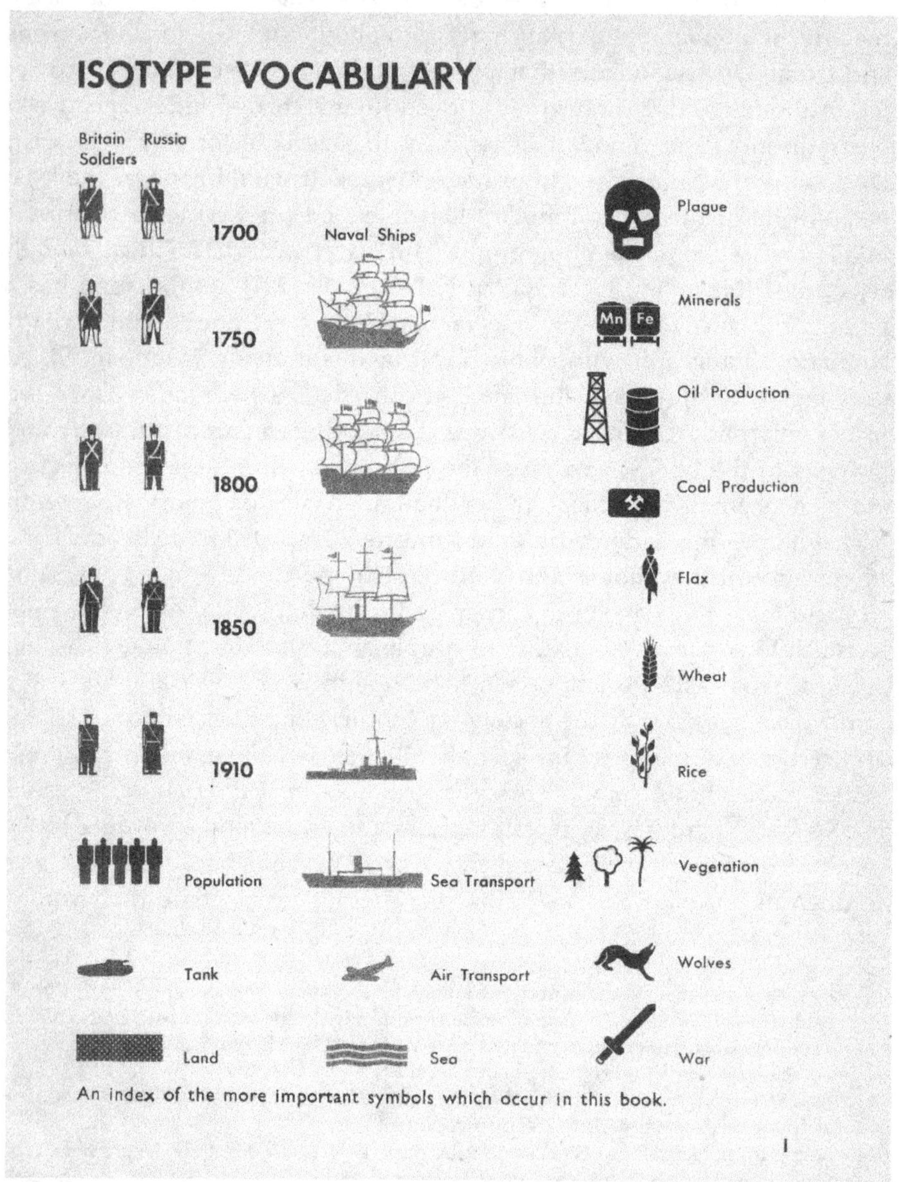

Fig. 19.2 'Isotype Vocabulary', *Landsmen and Seafarers* (London, 1945). Otto & Marie Neurath Isotype Collection, University of Reading.

18 G.M. Sverdlov, *Legal Rights of the Soviet Family* (London, 1945), p. 14.

The Isotype charts, perhaps seen by some readers for the first time, required more explanation: 'They supplement the letterpress by saying through the eye something that cannot be expressed, or something that cannot be so well expressed in words. Each diagram has one important point to make, which should be obvious at first glance; but the reader who will make the slight effort to learn the simple language of the visual symbolism which they use will find that they repay careful and repeated scrutiny'.[19] In *Landsmen and Seafarers* readers were first provided with an 'Isotype vocabulary' page of pictograms before they were presented with the charts.

One important aspect of Isotype pictograms is their neutrality; no national characteristics or stereotypes are ascribed to them. Their aim is the representation of their subject in a manner that attempts to combine accuracy with minimalism, such as the modifications made to the soldier symbol in the 'Isotype vocabulary', which reflect changes in military uniform over the course of time.

The use of colour in the Isotype charts should also be noted. When a chart compares Britain and Russia, Britain is differentiated by red and Russia by green, the traditional colour coding used on maps since the 19th century to represent the British and Russian Empires respectively. Neurath was against using red for Russia and the Soviet Union as 'red for tsarist Russia looks very strange'.[20] It seems he would have liked to have used new colours to represent the two nations so 'we may use RED for wars, revolution, killing people, etc'.[21] Izostat charts had always used red to highlight Soviet achievement (in contrast to symbols showing pre-revolutionary data which were coloured in dark or dull shades). According to Isotype conventions, red was often used to signify industrialisation, urbanisation and other aspects of society and economy associated with modernisation and development.[22] In *The Soviets* this colour association is also followed in some charts, not just for Russia but for Britain as well. Therefore in the chart 'Large-town Development in Britain and Russia', the pictogram for both British and Russian inhabitants of towns is coloured red. In the chart 'Urbanization of Great Britain' the

19 Macmurray, 'Preface', *Landsmen and Seafarers*, p. 6.

20 Letter from Neurath to Smollett, 6 November 1943 (IC 1/6).

21 *Ibid.*

22 In *International Picture Language* (London, 1936), p. 50, Otto Neurath wrote: 'If colours have to be given to the three stages of development of society—[...] Red is industry, machine, metal, warm, present, higher stage of development, worker'.

pictogram for urban dwellers is red, whereas the one representing the rural populace is green.[23]

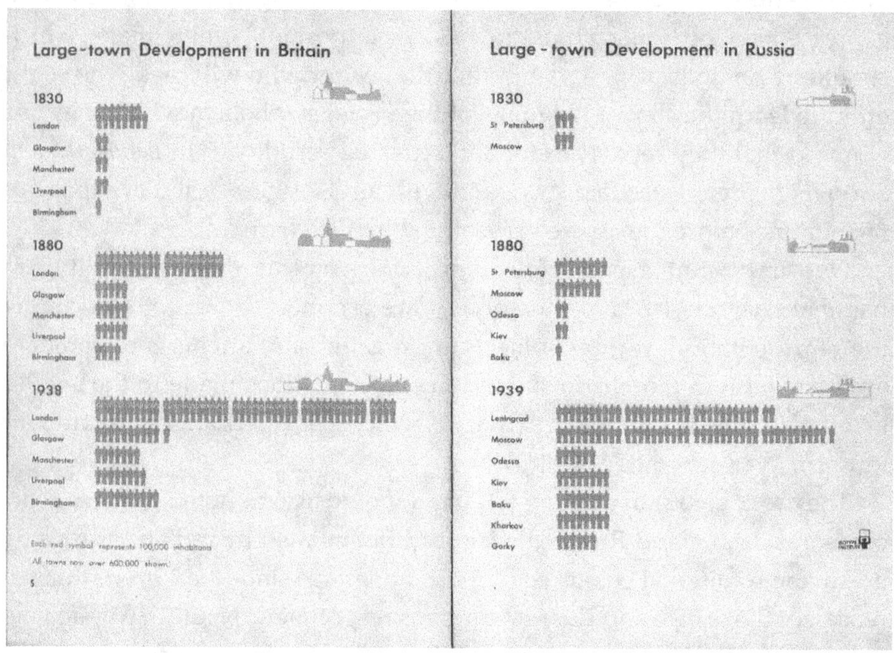

Fig. 19.3 'Large Town Development in Britain, Large Town Development in Russia', *How do you do, Tovarish?* (London, 1947). Otto & Marie Neurath Isotype Collection, University of Reading.

As regards the overall design of the books, the producers of the series, Adprint, were in the process of organising a similar series—'America and Britain'—when *The Soviets* was devised.[24] The layout, design, typeface, use of photographs and charts is exactly the same in both, and all 6 books feature a distinctive cover-design which places the Isotype pictograms for Britain, the USA or USSR over photographic images. *The Soviets* covers are somewhat striking. *Landsmen and Seafarers* is reminiscent of *USSR in*

23 'Large-town Development in Britain, Large-town Development in Russia', chart 5, *How do you do, Tovarish?*; 'Urbanization of Great Britain', chart 7, *Two Commonwealths.*

24 Adprint was a leading British producer of illustrated educational books. It was founded by Wolfgang Foges in 1937, later joined by Walter Neurath who went on to establish Thames & Hudson. See David Lambert, 'Wolfgang Foges and the New Illustrated Book in Britain: Adprint, Rathbone Books, and Aldus Books', *Typography papers,* VIII (2009), pp. 113-28. The series 'America and Britain' was edited by P. Sargent Florence: Lella Secor Florence, *Only an Ocean Between* (London, 1944); K.B. Smellie, *Our Two Democracies at Work* (London, 1944); Lella Secor Florence, *Our Private Lives* (London, 1944).

Construction, and was in fact the work of the innovative photomontage artist John Heartfield (1891-1968), who had spent time in Moscow and had worked for the journal.[25] The cover of *Two Commonwealths* appears to be the work of another distinguished designer, Alex Kroll (1916-2008), a Russian émigré who was at this time also Art director of *Vogue* magazine and who was instrumental in presenting Lee Miller's war-time photography to a British audience.[26]

Personalities

The first reference to *The Soviets* series in the correspondence of Neurath appears in late July 1943. A letter from Wolfang Foges, Managing Director of Adprint, mentions that a 'Mr Smollett [...] would like to go to Oxford to discuss with you the Russian series'.[27] This would be the first of a number of meetings Neurath would have with Peter Smollett, head of the Russian Division of the Ministry of Information and an individual who in more recent years has been exposed as an associate of Kim Philby and an agent for the NKVD.[28] Smollett, like Neurath, was an Austrian émigré to Britain (his original name was Hans Peter Smolka). He arrived in Britain in the early 1930s, and forged a career as a journalist and writer specialising in Soviet topics, publishing in 1937 a book on the Soviet Arctic.[29] By the late summer of 1941 he was in a position of some influence, directing the activities of the Russian Division and according to one source: 'The Soviet propaganda effort organised by Smollett under the guise of 'stealing the thunder of the radical left' was on a prodigious scale'.[30] As

25 See Maria Gough, 'Back in the USSR: John Heartfield, Gustav Klucis, and the Medium of Soviet Propaganda', *New German Critique*, XXXVI (2009), pp. 133-8.

26 'Alex Kroll: Magazine Art Director and Publisher' (Obituary), *The Times*, 27 June 2008, http://search.proquest.com/docview/319895858?accountid=13460 [accessed 5.9.2012].

27 Letter from Foges to Neurath, 26 July 1943 (IC 1/31). There is a considerable amount of correspondence related to *The Soviets* in the Isotype Collection. However there are no official minutes or notes of the meetings that took place between Neurath, Smollett, Macmurray and the authors.

28 Christopher Andrew and Oleg Gordievsky, *KGB: The Inside Story of its Operations from Lenin to Gorbachev* (London, 1990), pp. 265-9. Another article on Smollett focuses on his relationship with Graham Greene, and credits Smollett for providing Greene with tales of life in post-war Vienna that were featured in the screenplay of *The Third Man*. 'The Vienna Project', *Sight and Sound* (July 1999), pp. 16-9, http://gateway.proquest.com/openurl?url_ver=Z39.882004&res_dat=xri:fiaf&rft_dat=xri:fiaf:article:004/0222911 [accessed 5.9.2012].

29 H.P. Smolka, *Forty Thousand against the Arctic* (London, 1937).

30 Andrew and Gordievsky, *KGB*, p. 268.

well as Smollett's central role in the organisation and development of the series, the involvement of John Macmurray and Christopher Hill is also intriguing. Both Smollett and Macmurray were included by George Orwell in his famous 'list'[31] of 'crypto-communists, fellow-travellers or inclined that way' and the author made particular mention of Smollett: 'gives strong impression of being some kind of Russian agent. Very slimy person'.[32]

Christopher Hill, who became a member of the Communist Party in the 1930s, has also been accused of acting during his war-time service as some kind of Soviet agent.[33] This claim has caused controversy, but nevertheless it is clear from correspondence in the Isotype Collection that Smollett and Hill were in regular contact concerning *The Soviets*, and Hill's text was noted by the *Times Literary Supplement* for its 'less than impartial treatment' of Soviet political institutions.[34] Neurath's contribution to the series and his relationship with Smollett, Macmurray and Hill, raises the question of his own political allegiance and sympathies. In Vienna, Neurath's loyalty had always been to the Social Democrats, not the Communists, and his time in Moscow did nothing to alter his opinions. Moreover, Neurath, in his search for accurate information and data to transform into Isotype charts was constantly questioning sources and their reliability, and his charts did not always present the Soviet Union in the way Macmurray and Smollett wished they would. Yet the latter did do their most to make Neurath feel a valued part of the creative and editorial team: 'All concerned feel very strongly that the Isotype Institute should fulfil the function of co-author and not of illustrator [...] we suggest that you let us have counter suggestions if you feel that such are likely to improve the quality of the production'.[35]

---

31 See the *Guardian Review*, 21 June 2003.

32 Orwell quoted by Timothy Garton Ash, 'Orwell's List', *New York Review of Books* (25 September 2003), www.nybooks.com/articles/archives/2003/sep/25/orwells-list/?page=2 [accessed 28.7.2011]. Garton Ash also discusses Smollett's role as a Soviet agent and his advice to the publisher Jonathan Cape to reject Orwell's *Animal Farm*.

33 The historian Anthony Glees made this claim after interviewing Hill and studying Foreign Office files. See 'Outcry as Historian Labeled a Soviet Spy', *Guardian*, 6 March 2003, http://www.guardian.co.uk/uk/2003/mar/06/books.politics [accessed 28.7.2011]. See also Trahair, *Encyclopedia of Cold War Espionage*, pp. 116-8 for an overview of Hill's political beliefs in relation to his war-time activities.

34 'Home Life in Soviet Russia', *Times Literary Supplement*, 17 May 1947 (IC 8.2/12).

35 Letter from Smollett to Neurath, 20 October 1943 (IC 1/6).

The evolution of the series

After the series team had agreed on a topic for a chart, which in itself could be a lengthy process, Neurath and his Institute staff then required information to transform into Isotype. One might presume that in relation to the Soviet Union this would come directly from Smollett at the Ministry of Information, but the Isotype archive only holds one example of this taking place.[36] Instead, it seems that Neurath and his team gathered the material from a variety of sources; much was acquired from books available in Oxford and London libraries and from recently published pamphlets on life in the Soviet Union.[37] Some material was provided by Macmurray and the authors; Neurath was regularly seeking confirmation on figures and data from them, which they sometimes found exasperating: 'Major Hill was of the opinion that what he has already sent you through me was all that you required [...] He finds it almost impossible to answer most of your questions without the charts in front of him'.[38] In his scrutiny of contemporary publications from sources such as *Soviet News*, the Russia-To-Day Society and the Foreign Languages Publishing House, Neurath did not passively digest information. On the reverse of a Fabian Society leaflet, *How the Russians Live*, for example he has scribbled 'cosmic biliousness', though whether this is directed at the leaflet in particular, or the Fabian Society in general, is impossible to say.[39] Neurath annotated texts with vigour; some pages are full of his characteristic thickly pencilled underlining and exclamation marks. The marginalia in Neurath's copy of *Workers in the Soviet Union* by Andrew Rothstein, shows Neurath found much to take issue with. To the claim that 'scores of thousands of old-age pensioners are in paid employment' because they can receive both their

36 There is one undated note from the Soviet Relations Division, Ministry of Information, to Neurath which makes reference to sending a statistical abstract to him on the request of Smollett. However, the abstract is no longer attached, as the note states 'could you let us have it back [...] as it is our file copy and often used for reference' (Letter from A.B. Elkin to Neurath, n.d. (IC 1/40)). However, Smollett did send Neurath information privately, for example, a copy of his book on the Soviet Arctic.

37 The Isotype Collection holds a number of Isotype Institute notebooks with references to relevant books held in the Bodleian, British Museum, Royal Statistical Library, as well as various public libraries.

38 Letter from Macmurray to Neurath, 18 April 1944 (IC 1/10). Macmurray also recruited other academics to advise Neurath: 'I saw B.H. Sumner, who said he would be glad to help in any way he could' (Letter from Macmurray to Neurath, 22 May 1944) (IC 1/10).

39 Wright Miller, *How the Russians Live* (London, 1943) (IC 10/3 MILL).

pension and wages, Neurath counters 'because pensions are low'. On the final page, which praises the Soviet trade unions for their self-critical spirit and concern for socialist production, Neurath simply asks 'what about happiness?'[40] Thus, if Smollett thought he had found someone who would promote the Soviet regime without question, he was mistaken.

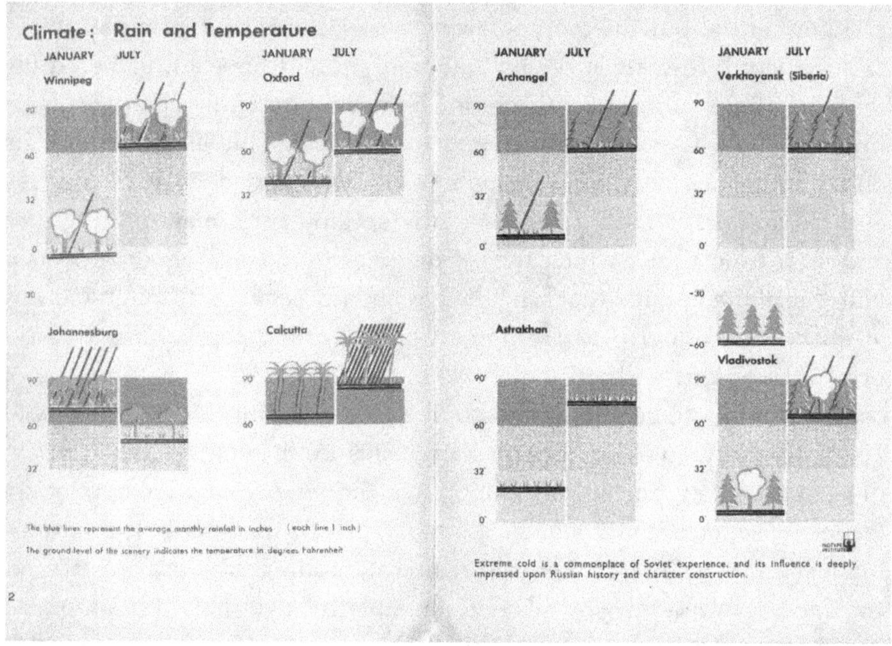

Fig. 19.4 'Climate: Rain and Temperature', *Landsmen and Seafarers* (London, 1945). Otto & Marie Neurath Isotype Collection, University of Reading.

Work on *Landsmen and Seafarers* seems to have progressed well and without much debate, perhaps because the subject matter of the Isotype charts was less controversial: climate, travelling distances, population, historical alliances and conflicts.

This book, more than the others, also stresses comparison between the various peoples and republics of the Soviet Union with British Dominions, rather than just Great Britain—one page contrasts the wheat fields of Ukraine with a sheep ranch in Australia. But even here there are statements that surprise, for example the description of Ukraine as 'Russia's own

40 Andrew Rothstein, *Workers in the Soviet Union* (London, 1942) (IC 10/3 ROT). Happiness was a great concern of Neurath's, a newspaper feature on him ran the heading 'Man with a Load of Happiness', *News Chronicle* (4 December 1945), p. 2.

surplus-producing area',[41] when the destruction by both Nazi and Red Army forces meant that in 1945 Ukraine's agricultural production was forty percent of its 1940 figure.[42]

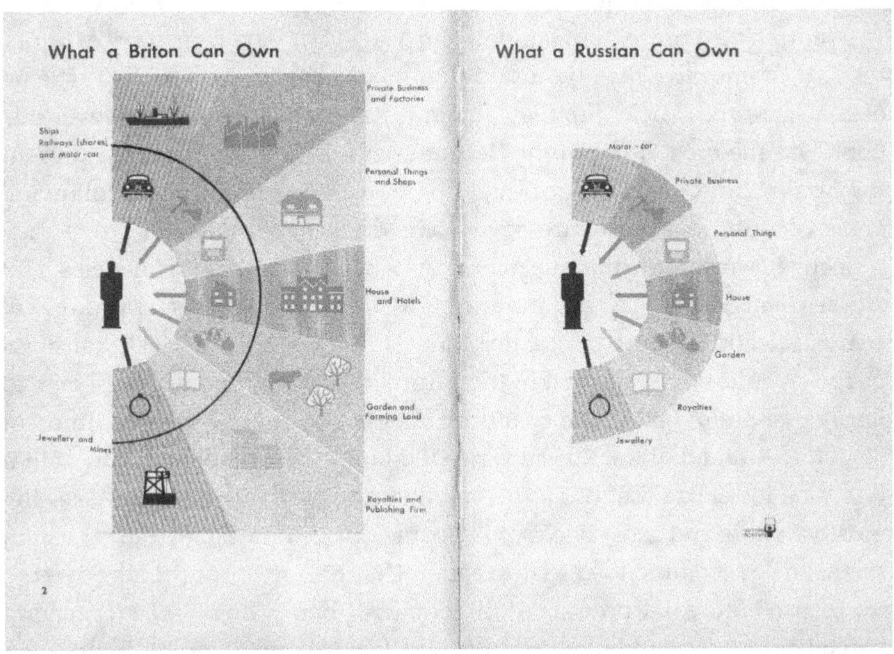

Fig. 19.5 'What a Briton Can Own, What a Russian Can Own', *How do you do, Tovarish?* (London, 1947). Otto & Marie Neurath Isotype Collection, University of Reading.

Two Commonwealths and *How do you do, Tovarish?* caused more consternation for all involved. Although Neurath died in December 1945, he had already suggested comparisons between the lives of ordinary Britons and Russians that might be shown through Isotype. Sometimes Neurath's schemes are not entirely clear in his letters: 'It should be nice, if we could tell something about TEA in the Soviet Union, that they are drinking MORE CUPS OF TEA, but less real TEA than in the UK'.[43] However, most of the ideas he initially put forward were not realised in the final book, and the Isotype charts compare marriage and divorce, births and deaths, incomes and ownership, rather than leisure pursuits, theatre trips and tea drinking.

41 Lovell, *Landsmen and Seafarers*, p. 16.

42 Paul Robert Magosci, *History of Ukraine* (Toronto, 1996), p. 644.

43 Otto Neurath, 'Isotype Russian Britain Series', III, November 1944 (IC 1/32).

One reason might be Neurath's untimely demise, the other simply lack of data concerning these everyday and seemingly trivial topics. At one stage Neurath complained to Foges at Adprint, 'we must have more genuine Russian material before we can go on'.[44]

Neurath also presented Smollett and Macmurray with an array of topics for *Two Commonwealths*—'you said you would suggest a complete scheme of charts for that book', Smollett reminds him at one stage.[45] However this book was the most difficult for Neurath, with its determination to present the Soviet Union as a democracy. The book tries to cover the following areas: constitutional structure, soviets, freedom, party systems, bureaucracy, collective farms, trade unions, planning, achievements and tendencies. Hill glosses over Stalin's purges and the show trials of the 1930s in a couple of sentences, and assures the reader that 'Stalin declared in 1939 that mass purges would not be needed in the future'.[46] On another page he seems to imply that Stalin had in the past been shocked by 'the heartless attitude of his fellows' and that the Russians needed him to 'press home the point that 'it is time to realize that of all the valuable capital the world possesses the most valuable and most decisive is people'.[47] Even the single party system seems to be recommended to the reader. Comparing the Supreme Soviet to the British House of Commons, Hill remarks: 'there is always in fact general agreement on fundamentals of policy, and consequently no desire to score debating points'.[48] The Isotype Collection contains many letters in which Neurath and Macmurray debate how democracy and freedom should be defined in reference to the Soviet Union; what Macmurray and Hill seem to have wanted was an Isotype chart that 'should not accept the British democratic tradition as standard. The chart must redefine democracy in a way that will include the Russian conception of it as well as the British. [...] I think we should drop the idea of exhibiting the consequences of democracy and concentrate on the essential—the different approaches to democracy in Britain and Russia and the contrast between sudden and

44 Letter from Neurath to Foges, 27 November 1944 (IC 1/32). After Neurath's death his wife Marie, who had worked with Otto since the late 1920s and was the senior transformer at the Isotype Institute, took over all her husband's responsibilities. There is some correspondence between Marie Neurath and Adprint concerning the third *The Soviets* book but none with Smollett or Macmurray.

45 Letter from Smollett to Neurath, 22 December 1943 (IC 1/6).

46 Hill, *Two Commonwealths*, p. 34.

47 *Ibid*, pp. 13-4.

48 *Ibid*, p. 22.

gradual achievement'.[49] In the final version of *Two Commonwealths* no chart did appear that encapsulated this, no agreement could be reached between Neurath and Macmurray; an inevitability perhaps, given a statement made by Neurath, in his own unique manner, at the most heated point in their exchange of views:

> It is one of the qualities of Isotype to give the reader an opportunity to make his conclusions himself, but not to present it full as an egg. Therefore we try to go back to the elements, which seem sufficiently accepted. Therefore we avoid, as you may see in all our charts, any GENERAL TERMS such as 'political' and 'economic'. Of course, you may use them in the book—or your collaborator—ad libitum, but not WITHIN the chart. Therefore we should present the single items, you may call together political and economic.[50]

Responses to the series

Of the three books, *How do you do, Tovarish?* received the most attention in the press. This was undoubtedly due to its focus on the lives of ordinary Soviet men and women, which from a newspaper's point of view would be of more interest to ordinary British men and women than Gosplan or pig-iron production. The reviews varied in their responses; the *Daily Worker*, unsurprisingly, declared that the book's author, the journalist Ralph Parker, gives a picture 'of a healthy and virile society of men and women who realise that a full and satisfying personal life depends on a full and satisfying communal life'.[51] Many reviews, though, were critical of what the book, and the preceding two, ignore or gloss over. Writing in the *Listener*, Isaiah Berlin conceded that Parker has 'a natural affinity with the Russian character' but felt 'it is not impartial and not convincing'.[52] This view was shared to a lesser degree by the *New Statesman*, *The Sunday Times* and the *TLS*. But what of the Isotype charts? Were they affected by criticisms of the text, or did they manage, as Neurath had hoped, to 'form a whole, which appears as an ADDITION to the text'?[53] Although

49 Letter from Macmurray to Neurath, 12 December 1944 (IC 1/10).
50 Letter from Neurath to Macmurray, 21 October 1944 (IC 1/10).
51 'The Russians at Home', *Daily Worker* (24 April 1947) (IC 8.2/12).
52 Isaiah Berlin, 'How do you do, Tovarish?' *Listener*, XXXVIII (1947), http://berlin.wolf.ox.ac.uk/lists/bibliography/index.html [accessed 5.10.2012].
53 Letter from Neurath to Macmurray, 5 August 1944 (IC 1/10).

the *Tribune* declared the charts 'near to excellence',[54] the *New Statesman* judged that 'not all of them are easy to understand'[55] and the *TLS* found them 'exasperatingly pointless'.[56] Although Neurath had hoped that the combination of 'PHOTOGRAPH-ISOTYPE-TEXT' would prove central to the success of *The Soviets,* one might argue that the books always struggled, as Neurath himself had struggled with his collaborators, to fully reconcile the objective presentation of information through Isotype with texts that frequently portrayed life in Soviet Union 'with the shadows magically lifted'.[57]

54 Fredrich Mullally, 'Landsmen and Seafarers', *Tribune* (6 April 1945), p. 14 (IC 8.2/12).
55 John Lawrence, 'Russian Lives', *New Statesman* (10 May 1947) (IC 8.2/12).
56 'Home Life in Soviet Russia', *Times Literary Supplement*, 17 May 1947 (IC 8.2/12).
57 Isaiah Berlin, 'How do you do, Tovarish?'

20. 'Sputniks and Sideboards': Exhibiting the Soviet 'Way of Life' in Cold War Britain, 1961-1979

Verity Clarkson

Approaching Earls Court exhibition centre in the summer of 1968, visitors would have been struck by the bold initials 'USSR' on the familiar façade[1] (fig. 20.1). They heralded the second of three Soviet 'Industrial Exhibitions', staged in 1961, 1968 and 1979, which brought striking Soviet cultural propaganda to London on a vast scale.[2] Whereas the reciprocal British trade fairs in Moscow of 1961 and 1966 were based on expanding Anglo-Soviet commercial contacts and eschewed blatant propaganda, the Soviet shows proudly presented eye-catching 'prestige' displays of the communist 'way of life': gleaming space satellites, welding equipment, fashions, model sanatoria, aeroplanes and handicrafts. Official publicity claimed that these exhibitions would promote 'mutual understanding between the peoples of the Soviet Union and Great Britain'.[3] But the responses of British government agencies and press indicate discrepancies between the projected socialist utopia and the image that was received.

This research was carried out as part of an AHRC funded Collaborative Doctoral Award at the University of Brighton and the Victoria and Albert Museum. I am particularly grateful to the staff at Earls Court & Olympia (EC & O) Venues for their assistance. Every effort has been made in conjunction with the archive at Earls Court to trace the copyright holder of these images. I would be grateful if anyone claiming copyright could notify the author so that corrections can be incorporated in future reprints or editions of this book.

1 On the impact of such façades, see Marla Stone, 'Staging Fascism: The Exhibition of the Fascist Revolution', *Journal of Contemporary History*, XXVIII, no. 2 (1993), pp. 215-43.

2 John Glanfield, *Earls Court and Olympia: From Buffalo Bill to the 'Brits'* (Stroud, 2003).

3 The National Archives (hereafter TNA) FCO 28/436 'Press release: The Soviet Exhibition Comes to Town: Massive Display for Earls Court 6-24 August 1968'.

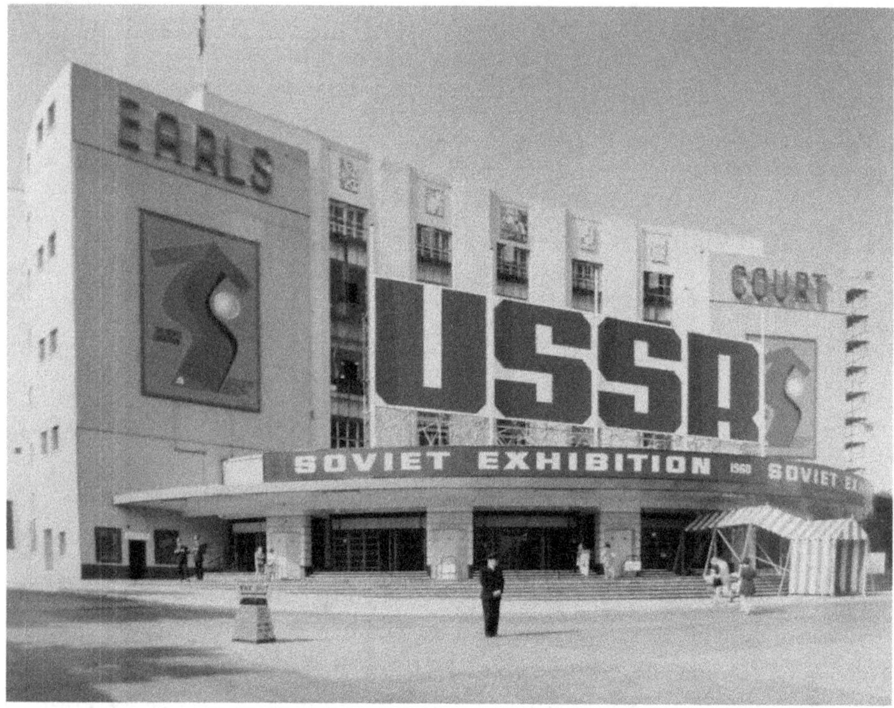

Fig. 20.1 Entrance façade of 'USSR at Earls Court' (1968). Press photo EC & O Venues Archive.

Focusing mainly on the 1961 and 1968 shows, this paper investigates changing British perceptions of Soviet culture via an analysis of the presentation and reception of these illusory visions of life on the other side of the Iron Curtain. It explores the political and cultural background of the exhibitions, examining the concept of a 'way of life' as a type of illusion or myth—a 'dreamworld'—perceived differently by Soviet organisers and filtered through the preconceptions of receiving British audiences about the quality and availability of Soviet material culture.[4] Addressing the content and press reception of the Soviet 'dreamworlds' created at Earls Court, it suggests that the reception of these exhibitions was coloured by existing British stereotypes about the Soviet Union and what types of things comprised an 'ideal' Soviet object in British eyes. Whereas in 1961 the Soviet 'dreamworld' could be separated from the political realities

4 To my knowledge, no record of audience composition or visitors' comment books survives. This paper utilises responses from published sources and The National Archives.

and tensions of the Cold War and received as a playful, amusing child-like fantasy, by 1968 this fragile illusion could no longer be maintained. In conclusion, it considers the final exhibition where the Soviet 'way of life' on show was further distanced from British observers' perceived Soviet reality.

An understanding of the phrase 'way of life' is vital to appreciate how the Cold War was fought. Unlike a conventional 'hot' war, it has been explained as a conflict between the rival political, cultural and ideological systems of East and West. In the phase of 'peaceful coexistence' which followed the Thaw of the mid 1950s, competing representations of the standard of living under each system became vital propaganda, most famously at the 1959 'kitchen debate' between Khrushchev and Nixon at the American National Exhibition in Moscow.[5] Displays of an idealised, modern 'everyday life' were presented at politically charged locations in both East and West.[6] The Soviet Union staged such displays internationally from the late 1950s. Those held in London were typical in that they aimed to present a 'promising and reassuring myth' of the USSR.[7] Consequently, the real and the represented material culture and living environments of the two blocs have become an important element of Cold War historical analysis.[8]

The British press used terms such as 'dreamland' to describe the fantastical 1968 Earls Court exhibition.[9] A similar theme has been explored in academic discussions of the Cold War.[10] Susan Buck-Morss has applied philosophy and critical theory to images from both East and West to unpick how 'dreamworlds'—two correlated visions of progress and modernity—shaped both sides' understanding.[11] The exhibitions in London can be seen as the Soviet 'dreamworld' made physical. It was not only a mass utopian

5 Walter L. Hixson, *Parting the Curtain: Propaganda, Culture and the Cold War 1945-1961* (Basingstoke, 1997), p. 179.

6 Greg Castillo, 'Domesticating the Cold War: Household Consumption as Propaganda in Marshall Plan Germany', *Journal of Contemporary History*, XLII (2005), pp. 261-88.

7 Andrej Ikonnikov, 'Architektur und Utopie', in P. Noever & MAK – Oesterreichisches Museum fur angewandte Kunst Wien (eds.), *Tyrannei des Schönen: Architektur der Stalin-Zeit* (Munich and New York, 1994), p. 35, quoted in Sonja D. Schmid, 'Celebrating Tomorrow Today: The Peaceful Atom on Display in the Soviet Union', *Social Studies of Science*, XXXVI, no. 3 (2006), p. 334.

8 e.g. Susan E. Reid and David Crowley (eds.), *Style and Socialism: Modernity and Material Culture in Post-War Eastern Europe* (Oxford and New York, 2000).

9 'Into Dreamland', *The Guardian* (22 August 1968), p. 8.

10 See also the semi-fictional 'fairytale' by Francis Spufford, *Red Plenty: Inside the Fifties Soviet Dream* (London, 2010).

11 She utilises Walter Benjamin's concept of 'dreamworlds' as an analytical tool to explain the collective mental state of a population encountering the constant shifts of modern life

illusion of how the USSR officially viewed itself, but also provided a space for British viewers to negotiate their Western dream of 'Russia': the 'dream that each side had about the other' during the Cold War.[12] In creating this vision, the London exhibitions were part of the lineage of Soviet shows such as the Exhibition of the Achievements of the People's Economy of the USSR (VDNKh), which aided the 'creation and maintenance of a Soviet identity'. In the Soviet Union, such exhibitions provided a space in which Soviet visitors could witness a new, utopian reality that was believed to be imminent.[13] In contrast, Western audiences witnessing exhibitions such as the 1959 Soviet show in New York were more conscious of the 'irreconcilability of reality with the image': it showed the USSR 'not as it is, but as it wishes to be'.[14]

British audiences at Earls Court received this 'dreamworld' by positioning it within existing discourses of what Soviet life was imagined to be like. Following World War II, there was minimal direct contact between the peoples of the UK and USSR. After the death of Stalin, contacts began to expand but remained patchy. Consequently, in the British popular imagination the Soviet Union was a mysterious, 'half known' place. The British public had pre-formed ideas of the standard and character of Soviet life gleaned from sources including news reports, literature and pre-Cold War perceptions.[15] The ambivalent attitude of one 1965 *Pathé* newsreel is typical, portraying the Soviet people as a fascinating but unknowable 'other'. Documenting a National Theatre visit to Moscow, the narrator asks: 'How do they live, these mysterious human beings, once our wartime allies but always an unknown quantity to us?'[16]

From the late 1950s, growing cultural links to the USSR prompted light-hearted travel literature on the Soviet Union. British journalists and writers who took rare trips to the country wrote of their encounters with Soviet bureaucracy, characters and culture.[17] Svetlana Boym notes that such

---

towards a hoped-for improved future. Susan Buck-Morss, *Dreamworld and Catastrophe: The Passing of Mass Utopia in East and West* (Cambridge, Massachusetts, 2000), pp. x-xi.

12 *Ibid.*, p. 238.

13 Evgeny Dobrenko, 'The Soviet Spectacle: The All-Union Agricultural Exhibition', in Valerie A. Kivelson and Joan Neuberger (eds.), *Picturing Russia: Explorations in Visual Culture* (New Haven and London, 2008), pp. 189-90.

14 Alistair Cooke, *Manchester Guardian* (1 July 1959), quoted in David Caute, *The Dancer Defects: The Struggle for Cultural Supremacy During the Cold War* (Oxford, 2003), p. 41.

15 James Morris, 'Stranger in Sputnik Russia', *The Guardian* (7 April 1960).

16 *Pathé* newsreel 'Moscow 1965', 18 November 1965 CP 569 film ID 345.04, www.britishpathe.com [accessed 7.10.2007].

17 e.g. Fred Basnett, *Travels of a Capitalist Lackey* (Watford, 1965).

accounts, 'while quite unreliable as historical documents, are exemplary texts of cross-cultural mythology'.[18] It is significant that ideas about the USSR often revolved around the perceived unavailability of modern artefacts and low quality of consumer or luxury goods. Such objects were an essential part of the Western consumerist self-image during the Cold War; thus, they were assumed to be absent in its 'mirror opposite', the Eastern Bloc.[19] At the 1959 American exhibition in Moscow, one Russian woman indignantly wrote in the visitors' book that they were being shown 'pots and kettles, frying pans and shoes, as if we were savages'.[20] These stereotypes of a 'backward' Russia were often qualified by 'real' travellers tales, which gave a more considered picture of life in the USSR, yet in the West the popular stereotype remained.[21] Soviet consumer goods were portrayed as difficult to obtain, poorly designed and faulty. Michael Frayn commented in 1959 on many Westerners' 'unreasonable surprise' that the Soviets had such modern conveniences as buses, shoes and electric razors.[22]

These stereotypes were so ingrained that never having visited Russia was no impediment to describing life there. One invented 'traveller's tale' originally from *Punch* magazine—*By Rocking Chair Across Russia* (1960)—gently mocked the inferior nature of Soviet material culture. This fabricated adventure resonated because it was grounded in a popular Western notion of an underdeveloped Soviet Union.[23] One excerpt from the satirical serialisation centred on an extensive list of useless Soviet artefacts ranging from the mundane to the military:

> [...] Sugar basins are made of some strange, soft metal, and will not bounce. Glue is not sticky enough. Men's hats are a different shape from men's heads: they make your ears stick out [...] middle C sharp sounded flat on

18 Svetlana Boym, *Common Places: Mythologies of Everyday Life in Russia* (Cambridge, Massachusetts, 1994), pp. 24-5.

19 Patrick Major and Rana Mitter, 'East Is East and West Is West? Towards a Comparative Socio-Cultural History of the Cold War', in Patrick Major and Rana Mitter (eds.), *Across the Blocs: Cold War Cultural and Social History* (London and Portland, 2004), pp. 1-22.

20 Susan E. Reid, 'Who Will Beat Whom? Soviet Popular Reception of the American National Exhibition in Moscow, 1959', *Kritika: Explorations in Russian and Eurasian History*, IX, no. 4 (2008), p. 895.

21 Reid notes how the Soviet discourse surrounding the American exhibition of 1959 'reversed this developmental hierarchy', portraying the Socialist East as advanced and civilised, and the USA as 'regressive' (Reid (2008), p. 899).

22 Michael Frayn, 'Material Progress – Victorian Taste: Russia after Two Years', *The Guardian*, 7 April 1959.

23 A complementary volume satirising the USA was also published. Alex Atkinson and Ronald Searle, *Russia for Beginners: By Rocking Chair across Russia* (London, 1960).

> most of the pianos I tried. The only inter-continental ballistic missile I saw was made partly of stiff cardboard, and would very likely blow inside out in a high wind...[24]

The list continued with ludicrous Soviet 'triumphs', strangely prescient of some of the bizarre exhibits at Earls Court the following year, including false hair, wooden ink-wells, sound-proofing, currant bread, half-inch cast-iron ball-bearings, jig-saw puzzle replacements, tortoiseshell earrings, two-way retractable flange compressors in laminated termite-proof lignite and plastic egg-separators.[25]

To a British public raised on such perceptions, the Soviet Earls Court shows were intriguing, popular spectacles. As such, they attracted large audiences and were widely covered across the press.[26] The *Daily Worker* regarded the 1961 show as the 'next best thing to a visit to the Soviet Union',[27] whilst *The Sun* newspaper described the 1968 exhibition as a 'powerful advert for the Soviet way of life'.[28] Nonetheless, these exhibitions took place at a time when the British government was committed to fighting the Cold War at home and abroad.[29] The first show was organised amidst tense incidents including the Paris Peace summit of May 1960 and the US invasion of the Bay of Pigs in April 1961. As the exhibition approached, anxiety over Berlin grew; a matter of weeks after it closed, the Berlin Wall was constructed. Against this backdrop of high-level Cold War politics, trade—the British motivation for this exchange of exhibitions—occupied an ambiguous position. On the one level it was a practical necessity; on the other, an ideological and political issue with deep Cold War significance. Both Britain and the USSR cited trade as a means to promote 'mutual understanding.[30] Unlike the USA, Britain was more willing to trade with the USSR, a valuable non-dollar market, and had a long history of commercial links with Russia. From the mid-1950s, commerce grew,[31]

---

24 *Ibid.*, p. 26.

25 *Ibid.*, p. 27.

26 The 1961 exhibition attracted over half a million visitors.

27 'Sputniks and Sideboards coming to Town', *Daily Worker*, 15 Feb 1961.

28 *The Sun* was initially a left-wing newspaper (1964-9). 'Russia Today – Tomorrow', *The Sun*, n.d. August 1968.

29 Michael F. Hopkins *et. al.*, 'Introduction', in Michael F. Hopkins, Michael D. Kandiah and Gillian Staerk (eds.), *Cold War Britain 1945-64: New Perspectives* (Basingstoke, 2003), p. 4.

30 Michael Kaser, 'Trade Relations: Patterns and Prospects', in Alex Pravda and Peter J. S. Duncan (eds.) *Soviet-British Relations since the 1970s* (Cambridge, 1990), p. 193.

31 'East West Salesmen', *The Guardian*, 22 May 1960.

culminating in the 1959 bilateral agreement to expand and diversify Anglo-Soviet trade.[32]

Resulting from this agreement, the British organisers initially believed that the Soviet show was a trade show, a reciprocal event for the British Fair held in Sokol'niki Park in May 1961.[33] Whereas dealings on the Soviet side were state-organised by the All-Union Chamber of Commerce,[34] on the British side the exhibitions were negotiated by private commercial groups: Industrial Trade Fairs Ltd (ITF) and the Association of British Chambers of Commerce.[35] However, the 'strict reciprocity' insisted upon at the signing of the contracts proved unworkable. The agreed 'trade fair' became a more ambiguously titled 'Soviet Industrial Exhibition'.[36] Earlier Soviet assurances that the exhibitions would be 'business-like affairs' and 'should not be used for political propaganda' proved hollow.[37] The Foreign Office was shocked when press reports revealed the Soviets' 'full scale national exhibition' planned in 1961.[38] But this should not have been a surprise: most government-sponsored Soviet international exhibitions of the later 1950s and early 1960s described as 'industrial' or 'trade' fairs comprised broadly similar 'way of life' exhibits. The Soviet pavilion at the Brussels Expo of 1958 had set the model for subsequent prestige shows. Its thematic divisions—beginning with science, industry, agriculture and transport before moving on to themes such as education, food, arts and fashion—were almost identical to the form of the Earls Court exhibitions in 1961 and 1968.[39] Exhibits were recycled: a visitor to bilateral Soviet exhibitions in New York (1959), Mexico (1959), Norway (1960), Japan (1961) and London (1961) could be forgiven for experiencing *déjà vu*, repeatedly encountering models of the atomic icebreaker ship 'Lenin' and ubiquitous bleeping sputniks.[40]

---

32 Curtis Keeble, 'The Historical Perspective', in Pravda and Duncan (1990), p. 37.

33 Kaser in Pravda and Duncan (1990) pp. 197-9.

34 'Britain and Russia Plan Trade Fairs: Moscow Delegation in London', *The Times*, 12 December 1959.

35 As a subsidiary of the *Financial Times*, ITF was well placed to promote issues of Anglo-Soviet trade. TNA FO371/159603 NS1861/47A Commercial Dept, British Embassy Moscow to Foreign Office (July 12 1961)'; TNA FCO28/436 no. 2054 from Foreign Office to Moscow (5 August 1968).

36 TNA FO371/159601 NS1861/11 R.H. Mason (2 March 1961).

37 TNA FO371/159601 NS1861/11 no. 1609 Sir Frank Roberts, British Embassy, Moscow to Foreign Office (17 November 1960).

38 TNA FO371/159601 NS1861/11 R.H. Mason (2 March 1961).

39 *Guide to the USSR Pavilion* (Brussels, 1958).

40 TNA FO371/159601 NS1861/17 'Organisation of Soviet Foreign Exhibition and the functions of the Soviet Chamber of Commerce'; Brigitte Schroeder-Gudehus and David Cloutier, 'Popularizing Science and Technology During the Cold War: Brussels 1958', in

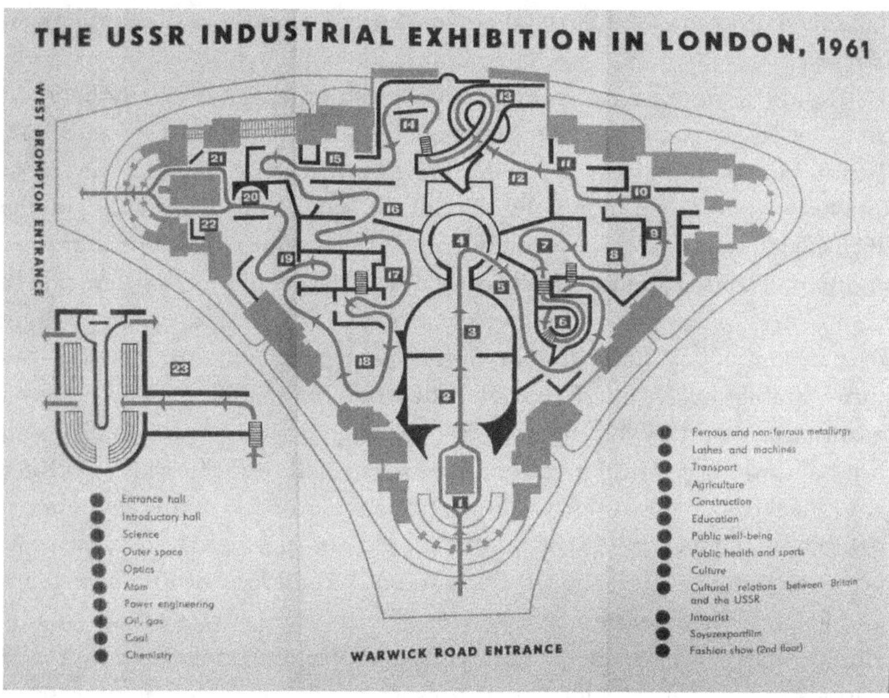

Fig. 20.2 Plan of the first Soviet Earls Court exhibition (1961). Exhibition guide. EC & O Venues Archive.

In London, responses were divided over the successfulness of these Soviet display techniques, often comparing them unfavourably with Western ones. Some were seen as clumsy, old fashioned or blatantly propagandist, undermining the effectiveness of the illusion of a Soviet 'dreamworld'. In 1961, the huge scale and proliferation of exhibits posed problems for the Soviet designers. 10,000 exhibits were arranged in a warren-like maze covering 23,000m^2—larger than the Soviet pavilion at Brussels—that didactically guided the visitor through twenty-two halls in sequence (fig. 20.2).

Unsurprisingly, this layout was overwhelming and tiring. Whilst the organisers may have intended the cumulative weight of exhibits to indicate growing Soviet material wealth, in their proliferation they became meaningless and bewildering: the critic Lawrence Alloway bemoaned the lack of a vista to survey the whole show, describing 'profusion shading into confusion [...] the halls were crowded together, leaking into each

---

Robert W. Rydell and Nancy E. Gwinn (eds.) *Fair Representations: World's Fairs and the Modern World* (Amsterdam, 1994), p. 169.

other, so there was no respite, no breathing space'.[41] A Foreign Office report condemned the aesthetic as too serious, old fashioned and lacking in taste, typified by a giant polystyrene bust of Lenin, capitalised statements of platitudes and a statistical onslaught of upward pointing graphs.[42] Alloway wryly drew attention to the illusion: triumphant graphs 'extrapolated into the future'.[43] *The Observer* thought it lacked 'the gloss of the familiar western style exhibition'.[44] But some saw progress in Soviet display techniques since the 'depressingly heavy handed' styles of Brussels.[45] Ignoring Lenin's visage, the mixture of 'eye catching' displays and 'glamour girls' at Earls Court could challenge British stereotypes of a dour, old-fashioned USSR.[46] Some techniques were quite sophisticated, utilising a variety of modern media devices. One hall contained a multi-screen display with fifteen continuous projectors;[47] another used colour closed circuit television, resulting in an 'atmosphere of discovery and movement'.[48] The darkened 'Hall of the Cosmos', a key area of the 1961 exhibition, comprised a 100-foot high cylindrical display recreating the impression of being in space via model spaceships, five simultaneous films, a revolving globe and musical accompaniment.[49] The official Foreign Office verdict—'an ambitious project somewhat spoiled by vulgar presentation and mechanical breakdowns'—suggests that this display was less successful in practice.[50] The 8000 exhibits in 1968 were similarly organised on 'a truly heroic scale'.[51] Press photographs support *Design* magazine's assertion that the design of this new show displayed 'a far lighter touch [...] in breaking the various exhibition areas up into manageable proportions'.[52] A large central space,

41 Alloway (1961), pp. 44-6.

42 TNA FO371/159603 NS1861/60 'Assessment of the impressions made by the Soviet Trade Exhibition', Northern Dept, Foreign Office to British Embassy Moscow' (8 September 1961).

43 Alloway (1961), pp. 44-6.

44 John Davy, 'From Space to Murals', *The Observer*, 9 July 1961.

45 'Soviet Display', *The Guardian*, 8 July 1961; Rene Elvin, 'Fair enough or fair too much?', *Art and Industry*, LXV, no. 387 (September 1958), pp. 74-83.

46 Michael Moynihan, 'Russia Brings Sputniks and Glamour Girls', *The Observer*, 2 July 1961.

47 'Films at the Soviet Exhibition', *British Kinematography*, XXXIX, no. 3 (September 1961), p. 80.

48 'Propaganda by Caviare, Wines and Sputniks: 10,000 exhibits in Soviet Show', *The Guardian*, 7 July 1961.

49 'Sputniks "In Orbit" At Exhibition: Soviet £1m drive in London', *The Times*, June 30 1961.

50 TNA FO371/159603 NS1861/60, 'Assessment of the impressions...'

51 'Russia on Show', *Evening Standard*, 6 August 1968.

52 'Bumper Russian display at Earls Court', *Design*, no. 236 (August 1968), p. 13.

200 feet in diameter, contained the prized space hardware, around which a series of interlinking exhibition halls were grouped.[53]

The 'dreamworlds' presented at the Earls Court exhibitions were comprised of Soviet objects. Eager British audiences wanted to extrapolate a picture of little-known Soviet lives from the displays of homes, education and culture on view at Earls Court. The *Daily Worker* summed up the content as 'sputniks and sideboards'[54]—that is, technology and consumer goods.[55] Yet their reception was often conditioned by preconceived British notions of 'ideal' Soviet objects. Whilst spaceships and satellites were almost universally celebrated in both 1961 and 1968 as Soviet objects par excellence, consumer goods received a more mixed response. Frequently, exhibits were criticised for emulating Western originals. Whilst this was sometimes with good cause—Soviet objects were often substitutes copying 'forbidden products from the west'[56] —responses at Earls Court emphasised the inferiority of these imitations. Parallel to this ran a British discourse of what an ideal Soviet object should be, drawing on notions of traditional folk and craft cultures.[57] Underlying this were constant reminders from journalists and reviewers that the 'way of life' shown at Earls Court was an illusion; such objects were unobtainable for ordinary Soviet people.[58]

Technological superiority was a 'potent symbol' for both East and West in the competitive arena of the Thaw: in 1961, over half the exhibition space was occupied by science, engineering and industry.[59] Alongside the celebrated space exhibits, visitors had to negotiate countless examples of tractors, lathes and drilling equipment to gain access to the fashion, education, and public health areas.[60] Gleaming satellites were the primary

---

53 TNA FCO28/436 'Press release: The Soviet Exhibition Comes to Town'.

54 'Sputniks and Sideboards coming to town', *Daily Worker*, 15 Feb 1961.

55 TNA FCO28/436 'Press release: The Soviet Exhibition Comes to Town'; Reuter's newsreel ref BGY504090073 (6 July 1961) www.itnsource.com [accessed 10.6. 2007].

56 Hildi Hawkins, 'Superfluous Things', *Things*, no. 4 (Summer 1996), p. 141.

57 The Soviet authorities actively promoted a civilised and refined type of folk art. Wendy Salmond, 'Reviving Folk Art in Russia: The Moscow Zemstvo and the Kustar Art Industries,' in Nicola Gordon Bowe (ed.), *Art and the National Dream: The Search for Vernacular Expression in Turn of the Century Design* (Dublin, 1993), pp. 81-98.

58 Hawkins notes the commonplace 'emptiness' of Soviet shops in the 1970s and 1980s (Hawkins, p. 141).

59 'Introduction', Reid and Crowley (eds.) (2000), p. 9.

60 The twenty-two sections were: 1. Entrance Hall, 2. Introductory Hall, 3. Science, 4. Outer Space, 5. Optics, 6. Atom, 7. Power Engineering, 8. Oil, Gas, 9. Coal, 10. Chemistry, 11. Ferrous and non-ferrous metallurgy, 12. Lathes and machines, 13. Transport, 14. Agriculture, 15. Construction, 16. Education, 17. Public well-being, 18. Public health and sports, 19. Culture, 20. Cultural Relations between Britain and the USSR, 21. Intourist,

attraction for a British public newly captivated by space exploration: Iurii Gagarin's historic space flight occurred mere weeks before the 1961 show.[61] The British press eagerly seized upon the forthcoming opportunity to see life-size replicas of sputniks and luniks. One commentator anticipated 'splendid space age fun', seemingly negating any Cold War nuclear anxieties surrounding the space race.[62] Another stated that 'The British public [...] should find it a thrilling experience'.[63] Such responses were further heightened by the extremely popular visit of Gagarin to Britain to coincide with the exhibition.[64] On his first trip to Western Europe, the cosmonaut received a hero's welcome bordering on the hysterical, boosting attendance at Earls Court.[65] Although some journalists warned that this response did not 'refute the Cold War',[66] Gagarin was an enormously valuable representative of the Soviet regime: 'never has Moscow sent a finer ambassador', commented one newsreel.[67]

Responses to other scientific exhibits were less favourable. While there was a general consensus that the displays were impressive, the lack of clear explanations of mysterious machinery caused consternation.[68] In 1968, the British press ridiculed bizarre—possibly mistranslated—Soviet gadgets like 'equipment for the reanimation of patients in a state of clinical death' and an 'electronic sleep machine'.[69] But there were also technical innovations which appealed to modern Western lives: a miniature transistor radio called the Micro, designed to be worn like a badge, aroused favourable press response.[70]

Particularly in 1961, consumer goods, architecture and transport were keenly received. Audiences were curious to see objects that supposedly offered an insight into the lives of ordinary Russians, though most British newspapers stressed that the fashions and electrical appliances were frequently prototypes and unavailable to the population at large.

---

22. Soyuzexportfilm; and, on the upper floor, a Fashion Show. *'The USSR Industrial Exhibition in London, 1961'* Guide, Private collection.

61 'New and Old From Russia', *The Times*, July 10 1961.

62 John Davy, 'From Space to Murals', *The Observer*, 9 July 1961.

63 'Propaganda by Caviare, Wines and Sputniks: 10,000 Exhibits in Soviet Show', *The Guardian*, 7 July 1961.

64 'Sputniks 'In Orbit' At Exhibition: Soviet £1m Drive in London', *The Times* (June 30 1961).

65 Gagarin was the 'prize attraction'. *The Guardian*, 8 July 1961.

66 'Cheers to the End for Gagarin', *The Guardian*, 16 July 1961.

67 Reuters newsreel REF: BP170761173205 17/07/1961, 'Hail Gagarin', www.itnsource.com.

68 'Space Highlights at Soviet Exhibition', *Daily Telegraph*, 7 August 1968.

69 TNA FCO28/436 'Press release: The Soviet Exhibition Comes to Town'.

70 'The Russians Send Dazzling Space Display', *Evening Standard*, 2 August 1968.

Preconceived notions of Soviet goods as scarce and shoddy could colour responses.[71] The general reaction to both 1960s exhibitions was that the consumer goods tended to look 'sturdy rather than elegant'.[72] As Robert Haddow's thoughts on the post-war US economic system suggest, such sturdiness was antithetical to capitalist goods which prioritised style and elegance as well as planned obsolescence.[73] A confidential Foreign Office report of 1961 condemned a vast swathe of the china, glass, textiles and carpets as being of 'inferior standard and poor taste'.[74] Similarly, *Design* magazine's overall impression was of a 'chaotic collection of poorly designed and [...] badly produced articles'. However, it praised some exhibits that fitted its modernist agenda, notably a 'delightfully clean and satisfying design' for a Moscow cinema and some 'simple' and 'restrained' children's furniture.[75]

British responses suggest a belief in a characteristic Soviet style defined in opposition to the products of the West. Many British commentators thought artefacts from the USSR should reflect this identity and not try to imitate modern Western goods. This 'typical' Soviet object was often conflated with ideas of decorative, traditional folk crafts, like those stocked at the Russian Shop in Holborn.[76] It was where the USSR was portrayed as having copied Western designs that the British press was most critical. In 1961, televisions and cars were condemned for copying dated stylistic devices from the USA and Italy.[77] Similarly, in 1968 the 12m long model of a prototype Soviet supersonic airline, the TU 144 drew adverse attention.[78] It was later nicknamed 'Concordski' amid accusations of industrial espionage. Such allegations of plagiarism were by no means confined to machines and appliances. A women's column in *The Times* criticised derivative china, glass and textiles: 'When the Russians are themselves, it seems, their designs are

71 Contrast Boym's analysis of how objects were negotiated in Russian communal apartments (Boym (1994) p. 158).

72 'Russia Today – Tomorrow', *The Sun*, n.d. August 1968.

73 I am grateful to Dr Lesley Whitworth for noting the value judgements implicit in the term 'sturdy'. Robert H. Haddow, *Pavilions of Plenty: Exhibiting American Culture Abroad in the 1950s* (Washington, 1997), p. 5.

74 TNA FO371/159603 NS1861/60 'Assessment of the impressions...'

75 Fred Ashford, 'USSR at Earls Court: Products', *Design*, no. 154 (October 1961), pp. 47-9.

76 The December 1968 edition of *Homes and Gardens* continued to carry advertising for the Russian Shop – 'Unusual gifts for Xmas from Russia'– with an illustration of Matrioshka dolls.

77 Alloway (1961), pp. 44-6.

78 TNA FCO28/436 translation of article 'At Earls Court', *Izvestiia* (2 August 1968).

excellent. But in things feminine, at least, when they too plainly copy the West, the West still does best.'[79]

Similar views extended to the daily Soviet fashion shows at Earls Court. Some took them at face value: a 1961 *Pathé* newsreel expressed surprise at the fashions, stating that 'clearly Russian women have become dress conscious to a surprising extent'.[80] The degree of shock at 'smart, attractive, up to date clothes' and 'unexpectedly frivolous hats' indicates how startling they were to British expectations.[81] This glamorous, ideologically constructed style, identified by Djurdja Bartlett as the 'official socialist dress' style of 1958-68, bore little relationship to the reality of shortages and poor quality affecting everyday clothing for the majority of Soviet women.[82] *The Times* commented that the 1961 displays should challenge western stereotypes of dowdy Soviet women 'miserably clad in out-of-date dresses and suits', but stressed that most fashions would be unobtainable.[83]

Conversely, those artefacts perceived by British observers to be typically 'Russian' were widely praised. Responses to the 1961 fashions regarded 'traditional designs' with a peasant influence, such as fringed and braided skirts, folk-inspired embroidery and furs, as 'beautiful' and 'new'.[84] Those items that reflected a Western idea of Russian traditions won the greatest approval.[85] Stereotypes of dowdy Russian women[86] continued to inform judgements: in 1968 the *Daily Mail* was surprised that the clothing was 'decidedly feminine, very much in fashion'.[87] Garments displayed a blend of the modern and the traditional, including some space age jumpsuits[88] mixed with clothing which many reporters thought mimicked Western styles: '[O]nly the modest hemlines gave the game away'.[89]

---

79 'New and Old From Russia', *The Times* (10 July 1961).

80 *Pathé* newsreel 'Russia Opens Trade Fair', 1961, Film ID: 1730.24, www.britishpathe.com [accessed 7.10.2007].

81 Katherine Whitehorn, 'The Soviet Exhibition – the Fashions', *The Observer*, 9 July 1961.

82 Djurdja Bartlett, 'Let Them Wear Beige: The Petit-Bourgeois World of Official Socialist Dress', *Fashion Theory. The Journal of Dress, Body and Culture,* VIII, no. 12, pp. 127-64 (p. 134).

83 'New and Old From Russia', *The Times*, July 10 1961.

84 *Ibid.*

85 *Ibid.*

86 Stephen Wagg, '"If You Want the Girl Next Door..." Olympic Sport and the Popular Press in Early Cold War Britain', in Stephen Wagg and David L. Andrews (eds.), *East Plays West: Sport and the Cold War* (London and New York, 2007), pp. 100-22.

87 'The Modest Revolutionaries Put Moscow on the Fashion Map', *Daily Mail*, 5 August 1968.

88 'Out of This World', *Morning Star*, 6 August 1968.

89 'Modest Revolutionaries', *Daily Mail*, 5 August 1968.

Reactions to the displays and exhibits at Earls Court indicate that the Soviet 'dreamworld' on display could be enjoyed as a mere spectacle, a 'make-believe' place distanced from the reality of Cold War politics. British commentators frequently returned to themes of dreaming, fantasy and childhood. In 1968, *The Times* stated, 'this is a child's exhibition, with its avenues of glittering, incomprehensible machines'.[90] A *Reuter's* newsreel of 1961 commented on 'a great emphasis on children throughout the exhibition [...]. A glittering fairyland of dolls and toys'.[91] *The Sun* described the 1968 Hall of the Cosmos as 'a schoolboy's paradise'.[92] In suggesting that the imagined 'way of life' on display at Earls Court was an illusion appropriate for children, British commentators deprived it of its political power. The Soviet dreamworld was not merely fantasy; it was a child's fantasy: naïve and unthreatening.

This vision of Soviet life was well received precisely because it was imaginary. Press reports encouraged visitors to disregard the 'propaganda nowadays inseparable from prestige exhibitions of national achievements'.[93] The British government asserted that no sensible Briton would take this vision at face value. Soviet pamphlets distributed in 1961 remained uncensored, the Foreign Office asserting that:

> We believe the British public are intelligent enough not to be swept off their feet by the obvious fallacies and half-truths which are contained in the literature being distributed at Earls Court.[94]

Nevertheless, the Information Research Department (IRD) of the Foreign Office felt it necessary to advise politicians and press how to counteract the Soviet propaganda inherent in the exhibitions by stressing trade motives, and emphasising the fallacy of Soviet claims to peace, freedom and high living standards.[95]

Perhaps this association with childish fantasy explains why the 1961 exhibition attracted surprisingly little controversy despite the political context.[96] However, this illusion of an unthreatening socialist utopia

---

90 Byron Rogers, 'People's Guide to Russia: Mr Wilson Toasts Peace and Trade', *The Times*, 7 August 1968.

91 Reuter's ref BGY504090073 (6 July 1961), www.itnsource.com [accessed 10.6. 2007].

92 'Russia Today – Tomorrow', *The Sun*, n.d. August 1968.

93 'New and Old From Russia', *The Times*, 10 July 1961.

94 TNA FO371/159603 NS1861/51 Foreign Office to Lloyd Jones (24 July 1961).

95 TNA FO371/159603 NS1861/48 INTEL No 81 'The Soviet Exhibition – its scope and effect – points to keep in mind' (4 July 1961).

96 TNA FO371/159602 NS1861/35 JL Bullard, 'Soviet Exhibition in London' (9 June 1961).

evaporated during the 1968 show.[97] The opening had been received cordially in Britain. Banners declaring the familiar rhetoric of 'Peace' and 'Friendship' dominated the entrance hall. But the invasion of Czechoslovakia in the final week of the exhibition prompted 'considerable' demonstrations[98] up to 1500 strong outside Earls Court and vandalism within.[99] Attendance—already half that of 1961—dropped dramatically.[100] Proclamations of peace and friendship could do little to counteract news reports of actual Soviet aggression. [101] Even British attendees from communist households saw their illusions shattered. Phil Cohen, working at the exhibition's Russian Shop outlet, recalls:

> One morning I walked the gauntlet of demonstrators protesting at the Soviet tanks rumbling into Czechoslovakia to crush the Prague Spring. Inside there was a strange atmosphere, with protestors rushing around shouting at us; one log cabin was set on fire. I suddenly felt uneasily that I was in the wrong place. I stopped going after that.[102]

Upon closure, the director of ITF described the exhibition as 'quite useless' to the Soviet Union.[103]

The 1961 Soviet exhibition had been a rare and popular 'glimpse of a contradictory and fascinating country'.[104] Life in the mysterious USSR had been brought to Britain via space technology and socialist consumer goods. Yet the dreamworld of the 1968 exhibition vanished in the face of Soviet military aggression. By the time of the final exhibition, these shows had faded from well-attended, popular spectacles which aroused playfully positive responses, to a minor diversion for a limited audience. Held in May 1979, the old, familiar themes were present: posters proclaimed 'Peace and Progress through Cooperation' and it was designed to 'strengthen trade links' and give an insight into the 'way of life' of the USSR. *The Telegraph* described a 'guarded welcome for Russia' at this 'USSR National Exhibition'.

---

97 'Into Dreamland', *The Guardian*, 22 August 1968.

98 TNA FO28/436 File NS 6/10 I. Trafford, ITF Ltd to P.T. Hayman, Foreign Office (30 August 1968).

99 Newsreel 'Russians Invade Czechoslovakia' Ref: T21086801, www.itnsource.com [accessed 5.12.2006].

100 Prior to the invasion, attendances were 11,103 per day compared to 25,688 per day in 1961. Following the invasion they averaged 6,415 per day, with a low of 4,347. TNA FO28/436 NS6/10 Trafford to Hayman (30 August 1968).

101 'Soviet Exhibition Attendance Slumps', *The Guardian*, 23 August 1968.

102 Phil Cohen, *Children of the Revolution: Communist Childhood in Cold War Britain* (London, 1997), pp. 25-6.

103 TNA FO28/436 NS6/10 Trafford to Hayman (30 August 1968).

104 John Davy, 'From Space to Murals', *The Observer*, 9 July 1961.

Less than half the size of the first show (11,000m²), it had little appeal to the public: one press headline punned that there was 'Nobody "Russian" to See the Show'.[105] The triumphant exhibitions of the 1960s seemed to have been forgotten: newspaper reports returned to clichés such as the 'lifting of the Iron Curtain'. Some even suggested that this was the first exhibition of its kind.[106] In the face of half-hearted displays of a frozen baby mammoth, Georgian folk dancers and the Saliut space station, the *Evening Standard* perceptively commented that:

> [...] all exhibitions of national triumphs are instructive in their selectivity [...] paradoxically, the constant propaganda only serves to remind visitors of the jarring disparity between the image and reality.[107]

The Soviet Earls Court exhibitions had aimed to present an idealistic vision of the 'way of life' of the USSR. This had been accepted by the British press on the proviso that it was an entertaining illusion, easily integrated with pre-existing British ideas of the mysterious Soviet Union. By 1979, this had failed: the gap between the 'reassuring myth' of socialist life and political reality was too wide to be accepted by British observers. Despite the surprisingly positive responses of 1961, the fantasy was short-lived. The Foreign Office thought that it did little to challenge British perceptions of the USSR:

> [...] we do not believe that it made any significant impression on the public attitude towards the Soviet Union in this country, which would be defined as one of rueful scepticism.[108]

In 1961, the British press and public had been prepared to overlook this 'constant propaganda' in order to marvel at the products and lifestyles of a world largely closed off to them. By 1979, the final, anachronistic show no longer offered exciting glimpses of an intriguing Soviet 'dreamworld'; instead, the once-fascinating sputniks and sideboards merely confirmed entrenched Cold War preconceptions.

---

105 Exhibitions International (June-July 1979).
106 'Fashioniski!', *Luton Evening Post*, 23 May1979.
107 [untitled], *Evening Standard*, 23 May 1979.
108 TNA FO371/159603 NS1861/60 'Assessment of the impressions...'.

21. The British Reception of Russian Film 1960-1990: The Role of *Sight and Sound*

Julian Graffy

Film is now well established in British universities as a medium for the study of Russian and Soviet culture and society—but this is a development of the last two decades. Twenty years ago, the study of Russian film in the way and on the scale in which it is practised now was unthinkable, for several reasons, not least of which was the almost total inaccessibility of the primary materials, a problem which our colleagues teaching literature (or we in our role as teachers of literature) did not encounter. The situation was no different in the USA. Here is how a leading American scholar of Russian and Soviet film, Vladimir Padunov, recently began his contribution to the eightieth anniversary edition of the Russian film journal *Iskusstvo kino*:

> Right up until the last decade of the twentieth century, Russian cinema of the Soviet period remained in fact *terra incognita* both for Western researchers and film scholars and for Slavists, whose research into Russian culture was logocentric to the same degree that that culture identified itself with the literary word. With the exception of a few directors who had become legendary figures (especially, of course, this means Sergei Eisenstein and Andrei Tarkovsky) [...] Russian Soviet cinema remained at this point for American film scholars an 'unnoticed elephant'. It was not studied in film faculties, not included in special educational programmes and monographs on questions of 'national cinemas', not mentioned in discussions or in any theoretical works. Unlike for example, French cinema, and also Italian, German, Japanese and Indian cinema, Russian cinema was a 'blank space' (*beloe piatno*) and it seemed as if there was nothing to say about it.[1]

1 Vladimir Padunov, 'Kak my otkryvali rossiiskoe kino', *Iskusstvo kino*, IV (2011), pp. 48-50 (p. 48).

Padunov does go on to make minor equivocations but he does not deviate substantially from this initial position.

In terms of the British reception and discussion of Russian film many factors came together about twenty years ago. In the first place, Russian films became purchasable for the first time as the enterprising Hendring company released about twenty classic films on video (before that they could only be hired on film from the British Film Institute (BFI) or other distributors, or seen at the occasional enterprising season at the National Film Theatre). Though the quality of these tapes now seems dire, I well remember the excitement with which they were greeted at the time. At the same time a number of key studies of Russian film appeared, books which have remained seminal texts to this day. Pre-eminent among them is *The Film Factory: Russian and Soviet Cinema in Documents 1896–1939*, edited by Richard Taylor and Ian Christie (London, 1988). And coincidentally with these technological and scholarly developments, the Soviet Union was undergoing major changes, culminating in its demise in 1991. A key role in the cultural ferment was played by the Union of Film Makers of the USSR, of which the now legendary Fifth Congress, which took place in May 1986, is considered to be the first major sign of change in the state organisation of Soviet culture.

For these reasons 1991 can be seen as a turning point, a new stage both in the functioning of the Soviet/Russian film industry and in its British reception. But how did that reception function before that? What was the situation like 'before the beginning'? In order to offer some evidence towards an answer to that question I turn to the British film journal *Sight and Sound*. First published in 1932, it has, from 1934, appeared under the auspices of the British Film Institute. As the most widely read serious film magazine for a broad, non-academic audience, it has been instrumental in informing and shaping popular taste. Coincidentally, *Sight and Sound* underwent its own *perestroika* in 1991, changing from a quarterly publication, which it had been for most of its existence, to a monthly—the last quarterly edition is that for Winter 1990-1 and the first monthly one appeared in May 1991. It also gained a new editor, Philip Dodd, to replace Penelope Houston, who had been in post since 1956. For all these reasons, technological, political and cultural-receptive, 1990 seems a useful point to end my survey, and I have chosen to look at the issues of the magazine over the previous 30 years, starting in 1960, in order to cover a period which contains historical changes from Khrushchevian Thaw to Brezhnevite Stagnation to Gorbachevian *Glasnost'*, changes which are reflected in developments in Soviet cinema. Looking at 30 years of issues of the journal I shall attempt to shed light on the following questions: How much attention did the magazine give to Soviet cinema? Was it *terra incognita*? What films, directors and other phenomena were written about? Who were the articles' authors and what was the nature of their knowledge of Soviet film? To what extent did the magazine's coverage reflect or influence the broader reception of Soviet film in the West? To what extent, from the context of the present day, did the magazine's coverage adequately reflect developments in Soviet film? Are there developments in the Soviet film industry on which it did not report at all? Are there key individuals whose careers it does not consider? Have approaches to the study of the Soviet cinema of this period changed in substantial ways?

Some Figures

I have looked at 121 issues of the journal—those from Winter 1960-1 to Winter 1990-1 inclusive. In these issues I have logged 89 items of various kinds on Russian and Soviet cinema, a high total exceeded only, in my estimation, by the coverage of British, American and French film, with Italian and German probably at a slightly lower level. Throughout the period I have observed, then, *Sight and Sound* was looking at Soviet film and reporting on it to its viewers.[2] If we look at the spread of these publications by period, we might expect to see them bunching at the beginning, to reflect the particular vivacity of Soviet cinema during the late Thaw, and at the end, to reflect a similar development under *Glasnost'*. In fact we find 21 publications in the 1960s, a further 20 in the 1970s and 43 (more than the previous two decades combined) in the slightly longer period spanning 1980 to winter 1990-1. Sustained interest in Russian and Soviet film is established slightly *before* the Soviet film industry enters its period of change, at the end of 1982, and from then on to the end of our survey period only 7 of 33 issues have no material on Russian subjects at all. The doubling of interest during this decade can be explained, I think, more by developments in the British reception of film in general and the greater ambition and reach of the serious British film press than by a prophetic anticipation of the changes in the Soviet Union. But once those changes were underway, *Sight and Sound*'s interest was acute and constant.

---

2 For further evidence of British attention to Soviet culture during the 1960s and 1970s, see Verity Clarkson's article in this collection.

Who Were the Authors?

If we look at the affiliations of the magazine's writers, then we can note that the most frequent contributors to the magazine are either film reviewers for the British broadsheets or employees of the British Film Institute. In the former category pride of place is taken by David Robinson, the author of fourteen contributions on early Russian and Soviet cinema spanning the entire period under consideration. Robinson, for many years the lead film reviewer for *The Times*, took a particular interest in Eisenstein and early Soviet film, reflected here in five reviews of books about early Soviet cinema and a comparative study of the two versions of Eisenstein's banned film *Bezhin Meadow*. But he also reported three times in the 1960s from the Moscow Film Festival and was instrumental in the showing in Britain of the films of Evgenii Bauer and other pre-revolutionary directors, a fact reflected in a pioneering article in the winter 1989–90 issue, 'Evgenii Bauer and the Cinema of Nikolai II', and an article about the leading historian and theorist of Pre-Revolutionary Russian film, Iurii Tsivian, in the following issue. Among other leading British film critics to contribute to the magazine on Russian film are Richard Roud of the *Guardian*, Nigel Andrews of the *Financial Times* and Tom Milne of the *Observer*.

Of the BFI's own employees, there are six contributions by John Gillett, whose generous curiosity about Russian and Soviet film resulted in several research trips to the Soviet Union—he reports on three Moscow Film Festivals—and in the organisation of pioneering seasons of Russian film at the National Film Theatre—he reports on the Boris Barnet season he helped organise in 1980. Beginning in 1983 there are 5 contributions by Ian Christie, who continues to write illuminatingly for the paper about Russian film to this day. At the time he was employed at the BFI, for whom he organised some wonderful seasons of Russian films, and in recent years he has been Professor of Film at Birkbeck College, University of London. His key contribution to the study of Russian film must be his editing, with Richard Taylor, of *The Film Factory. Russian and Soviet Cinema in Documents*, mentioned above, whose importance was immediately recognised in a review by David Robinson in the spring 1988 issue of the magazine.

The people mentioned above were not Russian speakers or primarily students of Russian culture. The journal did, however, also publish materials by Russians, and by people who had themselves participated in the Russian cinematic process. Ivor Montagu initiated the *Film Society* in London in 1925 and showed key films of the Soviet avant-garde there in the following years. In 1930 he visited New York and Hollywood with Eisenstein (David Robinson reviews Montagu's book, *With Eisenstein in Hollywood* in the Spring 1969 issue). Montagu himself writes three times for *Sight and Sound* between 1970 and 1975: a review of the book *Sergei Eisenstein and Upton Sinclair. The Making and Unmaking of Que Viva Mexico*; the magazine's first article about Andrei Tarkovskii (on whom more later); and 'When We Were Very Young', a piece remembering the revolutionary cinematic avant-garde. Another legendary figure for students of Russian film is Jay Leyda, who had worked with Eisenstein on the doomed *Bezhin Meadow* and who wrote *Kino: A History of the Russian and Soviet Cinema*, (London, 1960 and later editions). Leyda published a piece in the Winter 1961–2 issue, 'The Care of the Past', in which he reports on an archive exhibition at the Moscow Film Festival, and on his discoveries in TsGALI and Gosfil′mofond—this is of particular interest to those of us walking in his footsteps fifty years later. A third person with a direct connection to the history of Soviet film is Herbert Marshall, the translator and author of studies of Maiakovskii and Eisenstein. He famously took up the case of the imprisoned Georgian-Armenian director Sergei Paradzhanov in the 1970s, and he published an influential piece about him in the winter 1974–5 issue, the first time *Sight and Sound* had written about him.

Sometimes, too, the magazine turned to Russian contributors, translating Sergei Iutkevich's study of Grigorii Kozintsev's *King Lear* and publishing an extract from Kozintsev's memoirs. It turned to the 'zheleznaia zhenshchina' (iron lady) Moura Budberg, famous for her relationships with Sir Robert Hamilton Bruce Lockhart, H.G. Wells and Maksim Gor′kii, in autumn 1963 for an appreciation of a book of Eisenstein's drawings. It then turned to Soviet citizens of a new generation at the end of the 1980s, to Andrei Plakhov, now one of the leading film critics in Russia, with a worldwide reputation in film studies, in 1988 for a survey of the new Russian cinema, and to the Ukrainian director Leonid Alekseychuk for an obituary of Paradzhanov in the last issue under scrutiny here.

What Kinds of Publication?

If we divide the 89 publications by type, then we find 10 book reviews and 5 reviews of films. Of the book reviews, 8 are concerned with the work of Eisenstein, Kuleshov, Dovzhenko, Kozintsev and the avant-garde in general, while the other 2, from the end of the period under review, are about two of the earliest books on Tarkovskii, by Mark Le Fanu and Maiia Turovskaia. *Sight and Sound* does not publish many reviews of books, and 7 of the 10 reviews mentioned here had appeared by 1979. The reason for the paucity of film reviews is that the British Film Institute also published separately, until the re-organisation of 1991, the *Monthly Film Bulletin*, which reviewed all new films. *Sight and Sound* reviewed only the best of the new releases, around half a dozen films in each quarterly issue. The five films considered worthy of this accolade during this period were, in chronological order, Iosif Kheifits's *The Lady with The Little Dog* in 1962; Kozintsev's *Hamlet*, in summer 1964; Mikhail Romm's *Nine Days of One Year*, in the same issue (the most unpredictable of the films to be reviewed); Sergei Bondarchuk's *War and Peace* in spring 1969; and, the fourth of 5 literary adaptations, Kozintsev's *King Lear* in 1972. Among the films which got a British release but were disdained by *Sight and Sound* and left to the attention of the *Monthly Film Bulletin* is Vladimir Men′shov's *Moscow Does not Believe in Tears*, an omission which is revealing about the journal's understanding of film culture and its failure to see outstanding merit in popular melodrama.[3]

Studies of Individual Directors

This auteurist bent, shared with such other leading journals of the period as *Cahiers du Cinéma* (where it formally originated), and still adhered to in some measure in the journal to this day, is also strikingly evident in the number of publications devoted to individual directors. It is also consistent with the magazine's sustained attention to other giants of European cinema of the period, Antonioni and Fellini, Pasolini and Bertolucci, Godard and Truffaut, Fassbinder and Wajda. A total of 48 publications fall into this rubric, of which 10 are devoted to Eisenstein and no fewer than 16 to Tarkovskii, making these two directors the journal's absolute favourites, which is consistent with the remarks of Vladimir Padunov quoted at the start of this piece.

3 J. Imeson, 'Moskva slezam ne verit', *Monthly Film Bulletin*, no. 572 (September 1981), pp. 180-1. *Moscow Does not Believe in Tears* was seen by 84 and a half million viewers during its first release in 1980, making it the second biggest box-office hit of the entire Soviet era. See 'Fil′my, kotorye posmotreli v SSSR za pervyi god prokata svyshe 40 mln. zritelei', *Kinoprotsess*, III (2007), pp. 78-87 (p. 78).

The Eisenstein pieces include 5 book reviews, an autobiographical fragment about colour in film, the publication of 2 letters from Upton Sinclair and the study of *Bezhin Meadow* mentioned earlier. But 8 of them had been been published by the winter 1973/74 issue. The magazine's interest in the Russian cinematic avant-garde in the first half of the period under study is also evident in publications on Dovzhenko (1), Kozintsev (5, though three of them are connected with his 1970 *King Lear*), Kuleshov (1) and Vertov (1), of which the most substantial is Roland Levaco's lengthy 1971 study of Kuleshov and his theory. More inventive and original, since there was far less discussion of these directors available in English elsewhere, are studies of the 'second rank': Grigorii Aleksandrov and his musicals, in 1979; the comedies of Boris Barnet, in 1980; Chris Marker's engagement with Aleksandr Medvedkin through the Parisian *Slon* collective, in 1973, and a 1989 obituary of Medvedkin; a survey of the films of Iulii Raizman in 1985 (like the Barnet piece connected to a season of his films at the National Film Theatre) and a brief interview with him in 1983; and a report by an American scholar, with illuminating illustrations, of his belated discovery that there were now two versions of Mikhail Romm's *Lenin in October*, the original, made in 1937, and the de-Stalinised version, re-edited in 1964.

All of these publications concerned what was then considered the canon of Russian and Soviet film, upon which Ian Christie has written cogently.[4] An equally important group of publications, from the mid-1970s onwards, was devoted to contemporary directors, to those who came to prominence in the Thaw and after. There are useful introductions to the work of Vasilii Shukshin and Larisa Shepit′ko, brief interviews with Vadim Abdrashitov and Gleb Panfilov, and two brief pieces about Elem Klimov, who became Chairman of the Union of Film Makers of the USSR with its *Perestroika* in 1986. The title of one of these pieces, 'Perestroika in Person', is indicative of the magazine's usual approach. There are three studies of Paradzhanov, from Herbert Marshall's lengthy placing of him in context in Winter 1974-5, to coverage of his return to film-making after his release from prison, with *The Legend of the Suram Fortress*, in 1986, to the obituary mentioned earlier.

But it is Andrei Tarkovskii who attracts the magazine's sustained attention. The first piece devoted specifically to Tarkovskii's work appeared in the spring of 1973, which should be considered a tardy response to a

---

4 Ian Christie, 'Canons and Careers. The Director in Soviet Cinema', in Richard Taylor and Derek Spring (eds.), *Stalinism and Soviet Cinema* (London and New York, 1993), pp. 142-70, 250-6.

director whose first feature film, *Ivan's Childhood*, was released in May 1962. But that film had nothing like the resonance of Tarkovskii's second and third films, *Andrei Rublev* and *Solaris*, both of which are considered in this first, substantial article. From then on *Sight and Sound* followed Tarkovskii's every move, with lengthy and repeated engagements with all four of his subsequent films, the report of an interview he gave in London in 1981, a piece about this London operatic production of *Boris Godunov*, reviews of the first two books about him, a memoir by Michal Leszczylowski, who shot one of the first documentary films about the director while he was making *The Sacrifice* and an obituary by Peter Green. Green also published a lengthy study of *The Sacrifice* which included several stills from the film in *Sight and Sound*'s first colour section.

That Tarkovskii and Paradzhanov were the two living Soviet directors who attracted the magazine's greatest attention in the late Soviet period both reflected and influenced the taste of the time. Of course it was itself influenced by the choice of Soviet films for British distribution and that in itself had a political dimension to it, in that both directors were (rightly) seen as victims of the regime. But it is also consistent with critical opinion thirty years later, when both directors have retained their 'classic' status, when both remain the subject of numerous books and articles, when the films of both continue to be released on DVDs and Blu-ray discs of ever higher quality and ambition. If we look at the other directors whose work of this period has attracted most attention over the ensuing twenty years, then the magazine's inattention to the work of Kira Muratova, Aleksei German and Aleksandr Sokurov is entirely explainable by the fact that this trio were the most prominent victims of the system of cinematic 'shelving'—Sokurov, the only one of the three to get sustained release of his work abroad in the last two decades, is now a firm favourite of the magazine. Their inattention to Nikita Mikhalkov, who produced 10 highly successful feature films in the years under discussion, several of which were released in Britain, seems less surprising from the perspective of the second decade of the 21st century from the present day since after the worldwide success (and Oscar) of *Burnt by the Sun* in the mid-1990s Mikhalkov's career has suffered catastrophic critical and popular decline.

Other Rubrics

The 'In the Picture' section, consisting of a number of short news-based items, made it possible for the magazine to broaden its coverage and there are 17 brief reports on Russian cinema under this rubric. The first such feature in the issues under discussion offers staggering evidence about the British reception of Russian culture—and, alas, on changes in British cultural practice. Entitled 'Viewing figures' it reports on an experiment by the BBC towards the end of 1961 in showing *Aleksandr Nevskii* and the two parts of *Ivan the Terrible* on successive Friday nights, each of them attracting audiences of five million.[5] Eleven of the seventeen pieces under this rubric appeared in the last ten years under discussion, including a report on a Party Resolution on film, in 1984, and a sustained engagement with the changes in production and distribution practice following the 1986 Fifth Congress of the Union of Film Makers of the USSR.

There were also reports from nine Moscow Film Festivals, in 1961, 1963, 1965, 1967, 1969, 1973, 1975, 1983 and 1987. (The first festival took place in 1935 but there were no others until 1959, when it was allowed to begin again, as a sign of cultural openness. During the late Soviet period it took place every 2 years.) The Moscow Film Festival organisers were always torn between the desire to compete with A List festivals such as Cannes, Berlin and Venice and the need for the selected films, and especially those that won prizes, to be politically acceptable, and for this reason the Festival provided a reliable barometer of the relationship between the Soviet state and the film industry.[6] The consistency of the rubric makes it possible for us to trace changes both in the political face of that industry and in the magazine's attitude to Soviet cinematic officialdom, while the fact that on each occasion *Sight and Sound*'s journalists also manage to sample Moscow's cinematic menu beyond what was on show at the Festival means that these reports give a relatively broad picture of the state of Russian film more generally.

This is how David Robinson opens his report in 1961:

> No film festival is more whole-hearted than Moscow. For two weeks the entire city is given over to it. Mr Kruschev [*sic*] graces the opening; Mrs

5 'Viewing figures', *Sight and Sound*, XXXI, no. 2, 1962, p. 65. The anonymous *Sight and Sound* reporter describes the decision to show the films as a highly successful experiment, which attracted higher audiences than the BBC's regular film programmes. He points out that the National Film Theatre would have had to show the film to full houses for twelve years to reach such an audience figure. Now that anyone who wants to watch Eisenstein's films can buy them on DVD (or watch them online) it is unlikely that such figures could be emulated.

6 For a comparative analysis of the Moscow Film Festival with those in Western countries during these years see Aleksei Vasil′ev, 'Flagi nashikh otsov', *Seans blog*, 24 June 2011, http://seance.ru/blog/33-mmkf/ [accessed 5.9.2012].

> Furtseva, the energetic and attractive Minister of Culture, is constantly on hand. [...] Not everything goes right, of course. Before the Festival, people were laying odds against the new Rossiya Cinema (which has a restraint and elegance rare in Soviet architecture; but perhaps it is not finished) being ready in time.[7]

In the same report he tells us of the reaction to the British film *Saturday Night and Sunday Morning*: 'Mrs Furtseva was full of admiration for the film, but rather shocked. [...] she felt that it was not the sort of work that should be shown to a wider public'. Another British film shown that year was *The Trials of Oscar Wilde,* of which a leading critic opined that 'other, socially more important aspects of the famous writer's life could have been taken up to provide a fuller and pithier picture of his moral make-up'.[8]

In his survey of the 1963 festival, John Gillett reports on the sensational award of the Grand Prix to Fellini's *Eight and a Half.* This event has become legendary in Soviet cinematic history, with the brave resistance of the jury chairman, Grigorii Chukhrai, to official pressure seen as a key victory in the cultural Thaw, but it is represented here as a hard-won victory of the Western jurors over their Eastern counterparts. We are also reminded that these are matters of artistic taste as well as politics: when some young Soviet film-makers excitedly tell Gillett that Fellini's victory will help them to break away from tired old formulas in their own work, he replies that he considers *Eight and a Half* to be 'tired and vulgar' and that the best of Fellini is in his earlier films—which of course they have never seen.[9] But then, Gillett is clearly a man with ascetic tastes. He complains in the same piece that 'so much contemporary Soviet cinema [...] knocks your eye out with dollops of 'style' which are either derivative or put in because they are considered fashionable', and continues (in *Sight and Sound*'s first engagement with the work of Andrei Tarkovskii):

> This lack of a general perspective and a really lively critical climate unclouded by dogmas and persistent theorising may also explain why a film like Tarkovsky's *Childhood of Ivan,* with its defiantly humanist message and ugly bravura fireworks, is thought more worthy of discussion than, say, Heifits's *Lady with the Little Dog*...[10]

7 David Robinson, 'Moscow', *Sight and Sound,* XXX, no. 4 (1961), pp. 171-2 (p. 171).
8 *Ibid.,* p. 172.
9 John Gillett, 'Moscow Roundabout', *Sight and Sound,* XXXII, no. 4 (1963), pp. 187-9 (p. 188).
10 *Ibid.,* p. 189.

Four years later, in his article from the 1967 festival, David Robinson reports of the long delayed *Andrei Rublev*, which he has not been able to see, that 'the general impression is that it is long and dull, with occasional brilliant passages'.[11] It would be some time yet before Tarkovskii would assume his mantle as the magazine's favourite Russian.

Broader Engagements with Industry Developments

Of particular interest to twenty-first century readers may be the small number of articles published in the magazine covering developments in the Soviet film industry more broadly. Some of these were devoted to historical subjects, including David Robinson's 1989–90 study of pre-revolutionary cinema and Ivor Montagu's piece on the first years of Soviet cinema, mentioned above, to which we should add William F. Van Wert's 1980 study of the use of intertitles in the silent films of several countries, in which the Russian examples are taken from Pudovkin's *Mother* and Eisenstein's *The Battleship Potemkin*; and Herman G. Weinberg's 1962 piece on 'The legion of lost films'. Half a century later Dovzhenko's *Earth* and Kalatozov's *Salt for Svanetia* have been restored to us in their entirety, but Weinberg's remarks about the butchering of a number of Eisenstein projects and the loss of Meierkhol′d's 1915 version of *The Picture of Dorian Gray* alas remain true.

Moving forward, it is particularly interesting to read the two pieces of 1961 and 1962 by the Hungarian documentary film maker Robert Vas. 'Sunflowers and Commissars' looks at the 1930s canon, which, he admits, is at the time known 'mainly from unrevised editions of old textbooks'. Having the rare chance to re-view several of these films, he pronounces many of them over-praised, while finding his own favourites in Mikhail Romm's version of *Boule de Suif* and Kozintsev and Trauberg's *Maksim* trilogy. As he admits: 'there is only one thing more exciting than evaluating films: *re*-evaluating them'.[12] Moving on to the films of the present in 'Humanist Sputniks', he finds the new Soviet Thaw films to be determined to confront the individual but 'uneasy and tentative' in their use of contemporary screen language. He is bracingly trenchant about the work of Chukhrai and Kalatozov, now seen as key figures in the early Thaw. *Ballad of a Soldier* is 'a Primary School lesson in Humanism'.[13]

11 David Robinson, 'Moscow', *Sight and Sound*, XXXVI, no. 4 (1967), pp. 168-70 (p. 169).

12 Robert Vas, 'Sunflowers and Commissars', *Sight and Sound*, XXXI, no. 3 (1962), pp. 148-51 (p. 149).

13 Robert Vas, 'Humanist Sputniks', *Sight and Sound*, XXX, no. 3 (1961), pp. 151-2 (p. 152).

The final and most important period of change is, of course, *Perestroika*. It was at this point that the magazine first paid attention to Soviet television, reflecting an awareness of its new centrality in the lives of Soviet citizens and its fundamental role as a bringer of change. An article published in 1984 provides detailed information about the way television functioned in the Soviet Union and describes the most popular programmes before concluding with an alarming quotation from the author's Estonian guide: 'There's not enough laughter on our TV. People need to laugh. That's why they watch Benny Hill'.[14] Two more articles, both published in 1988, scoured the Soviet schedules for signs of the new openness, tracked the increasing visibility of the videocassette and reported on exchanges of experience between Soviet and British television professionals.

In terms of its specific coverage of Russian and Soviet cinema, Andrei Plakhov's 1989 study, mentioned above, is of fundamental importance. In retrospect its title 'Soviet Cinema—into the 90s' may cause a knowing smile, but Plakhov's article has turned out to be remarkably acute and prophetic. He gives a concise overview of new developments resulting from the Fifth Congress: the setting up of the Conflict Commission; unshelving; the work of a new generation of documentarists; the interest in exposing the 'blank spaces' of the Stalin period; films about young people, among which he singles out *Little Vera*; the inability of the older generation of directors to adapt to new conditions; the vogue for international co-productions. He pays particular attention to the work of Sokurov and Muratova, introducing to the readers of *Sight and Sound* the two directors who will (along with Aleksei Balabanov, whose first feature film had not yet appeared) make the most important Russian-language films of the next two decades.

Sight and Sound's Achievement

There were indeed important figures in Russian and Soviet cinema to whom *Sight and Sound* paid no attention during this period—there are no pieces on individual actors, scriptwriters or cinematographers, for example, in contrast to the coverage of the cinema of the USA and Western Europe. This is largely explicable by the paucity of accessible material—either the films themselves or English-language studies. Current scholarship pays greater attention to the formal qualities of films, on the one hand, and to the

14 Terry Doyle, 'Truth at Ten? Some Questions of Soviet Television', *Sight and Sound*, LIII, no. 2 (1984), pp. 106-10 (p. 110).

social, ideological and financial contexts on the other. But looking back from 2012, and remembering the constraints under which they were operating, one can only admire the commitment and enthusiasm, the scholarship and intellectual curiosity of the magazine's writers, as well their very real achievements in bringing knowledge of Russian and Soviet film to a broad British and international audience.

Index

This book does not end here...

At Open Book Publishers, we are changing the nature of the traditional academic book. The title you have just read will not be left on a library shelf, but will be accessed online by hundreds of readers each month across the globe. We make all our books free to read online so that students, researchers and members of the public who can't afford a printed edition can still have access to the same ideas as you.

Our digital publishing model also allows us to produce online supplementary material, including extra chapters, reviews, links and other digital resources. Find *People Passing Rude* on our website to access its online extras. Please check this page regularly for ongoing updates, and join the conversation by leaving your own comments:

http://www.openbookpublishers.com/product/160

If you enjoyed this book, and feel that research like this should be available to all readers, regardless of their income, please think about donating to us. Our company is run entirely by academics, and our publishing decisions are based on intellectual merit and public value rather than on commercial viability. We do not operate for profit and all donations, as with all other revenue we generate, will be used to finance new Open Access publications.

For further information about what we do, how to donate to OBP, additional digital material related to our titles or to order our books, please visit our website.

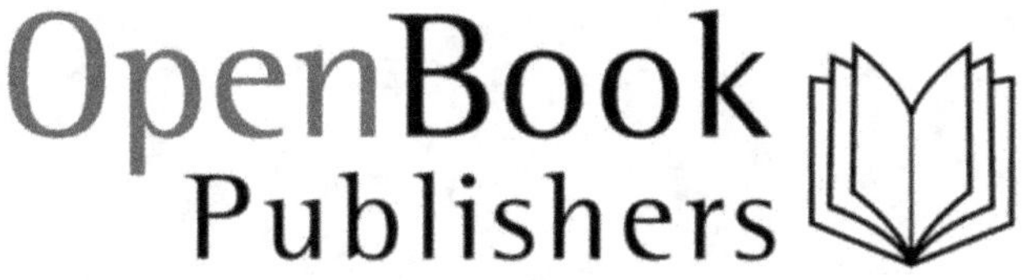

Knowledge is for sharing

www.ingramcontent.com/pod-product-compliance
Lightning Source LLC
LaVergne TN
LVHW020050110826
845155LV00021B/58

* 9 7 8 1 9 0 9 2 5 4 1 0 7 *